An Encyclopaedia of

NAPOLEON'S EUROPE

Antonio Canova Sculpt.   Engraved by Scott Wass

NAPOLEON.

Published by Septimus Prowett, 265 Strand.

An Encyclopaedia of

NAPOLEON'S EUROPE

Alan Palmer

St. Martin's Press
New York

FRONTISPIECE *An Engraving after Canova's statue of Napoleon*

Library of Congress Catalog Number: 84-51774
First Published in Great Britain by George
Weidenfeld & Nicolson Limited

First U.S. Edition

10 9 8 7 6 5 4 3 2 1

Contents

Preface

'One could forgive the fiend for becoming a torrent, but to become an earthquake was really too much', commented the Prince de Ligne as he looked back on Napoleon's career from the deceptive calm of the Vienna Congress. Goethe, once flattered by the fallen Emperor at Weimar, was more generous: 'His life was the stride of a demigod', he remarked seven years after Napoleon's death. Like most of their contemporaries, the prince and the great dramatist were awed by the phenomenon from Corsica who elevated a regicide republic into the grandeur of empire. Over the eighteen and a half years which separate Rivoli from Waterloo Napoleon branded an era of Europe's history with his name. He was military conqueror and legislator, dynastic iconoclast and kingmaker, emancipator and tyrant. It was many centuries since there had been so natural a 'sovereign among soldiers'. Ultimately his fall was as rapid as his rise to army command. 'From the sublime to the ridiculous is but a single step', he confided to Caulaincourt in a moment of truth as the two men hurried back to Paris from disaster in the Russian snows. Yet he had every confidence that History would give him the benefit of the doubt; on St Helena he could still boast, 'The memory I leave behind is of facts which mere words can never destroy.'

The Napoleonic Age has, however, a historic appeal far greater than the changing fortunes of its central figure. The long struggle of the armies transformed Europe as a whole, forcing even those governments which survived the onslaught to meet the challenge of national sentiment and at least refurbish the fabric of their administration. These were years of high expectation; for under the impact of the Revolution, men and women began to look for startling changes in their traditional ordering of life. Liberty challenged authority and convention in music and the other arts; writers, composers and painters obeyed an impulse for free and unshackled self-expression, seeking not to describe or to represent, and not to shock for the sake of a sensation, but to convey individuality from within the soul. A neoclassicism which was Roman rather than Greek in inspiration moved easily enough into Romanticism, although the transition came later in France and the Latin countries than in the predominantly Anglo-Saxon. For this sense of a reality which sprang from instinct and imagination was not an experience limited to the European mainland. Britain's cultural life at the end of the Napoleonic Wars may well have stood as high as at any period since the Jacobeans. No composers or dramatists of note but, as poets, Wordsworth,

Coleridge, Southey, Crabbe, Blake, Byron, Shelley and Keats, as novelists Walter Scott and Jane Austen. Among the painters were Constable, Lawrence and Turner, while John Nash brought an awareness of urban landscape to the gaiety of Regency architecture. Culturally and socially Britain was part of Europe, despite the artificial barriers created by war and an often ineffectual blockade.

There is thus far more to the Napoleonic era than the march of armies, the enterprise of military commanders or the privations of the seamen who patrolled the gale-tossed waters of Biscay or pursued elusive squadrons to the Caribbean. *Napoleon's Europe* is a concise encyclopaedia intended for people who are interested in the years 1797 to 1815 as a whole. The reader will find plenty in these pages about Napoleon, his campaigns and battles, his family and his marshals, but there are also entries on his ministers and principal officials as well as on the institutions of the Consulate and Empire, and on Paris, its palaces and social life. Leading political, military and naval figures – as well as writers, philosophers, artists and composers – in France, Britain, Russia, the German states, Austria, Spain, the Balkans and the Italian peninsula have separate biographical entries. There are general headings for individual countries, on social, religious and economic themes, and on developments in communications. Other entries seek to explain contentious problems of the time (the Eastern Question, Catholic Emancipation, serfdom, slavery, and so on). A dagger has been inserted beside names or words as a means of cross-reference, indicating that a fuller entry on this topic will be found somewhere else in the book.

It is a pleasure to record the help and encouragement I have received from my wife, Veronica, especially in preparing the classification system and checking the cross references. I am also grateful to Miss Elizabeth Burke and Miss Araminta Morris of Weidenfeld and Nicolson for the interest they have taken in preparing the book for publication and in finding illustrations.

A.W.P.
Woodstock: February 1984.

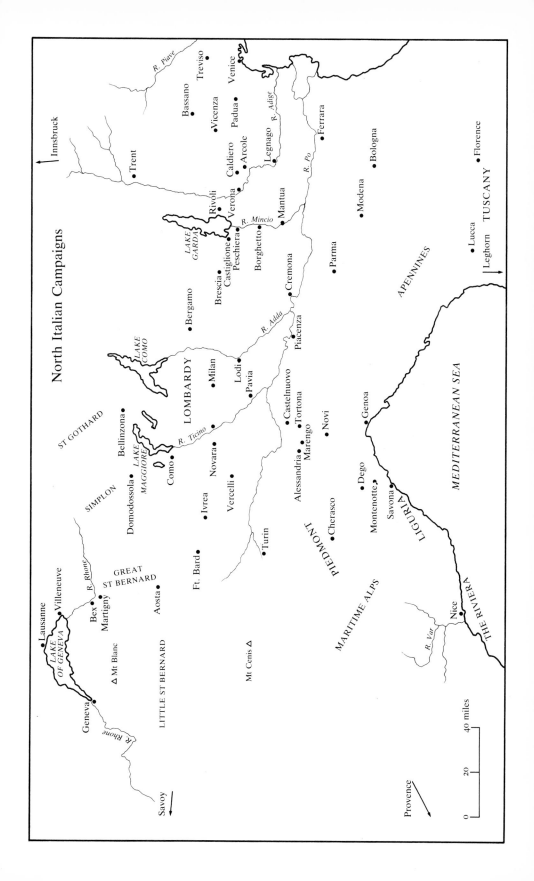

North Italian Campaigns

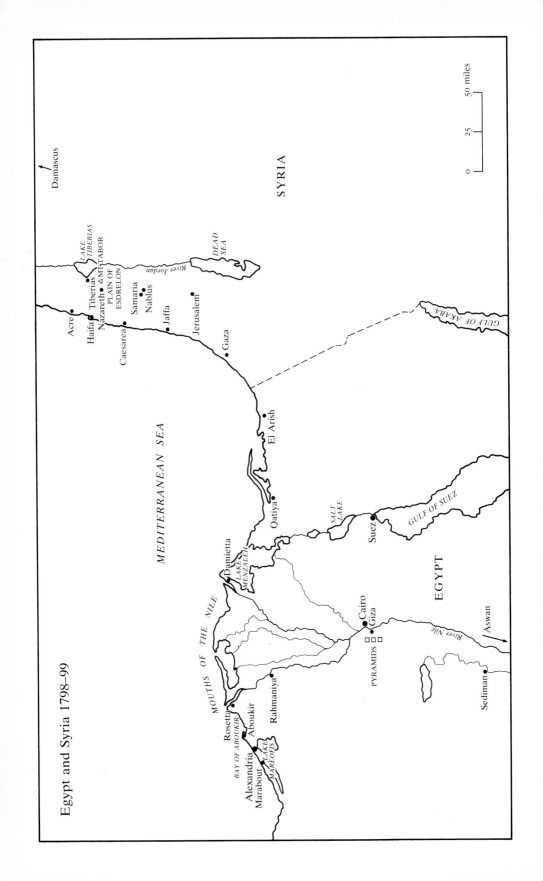

Egypt and Syria 1798–99

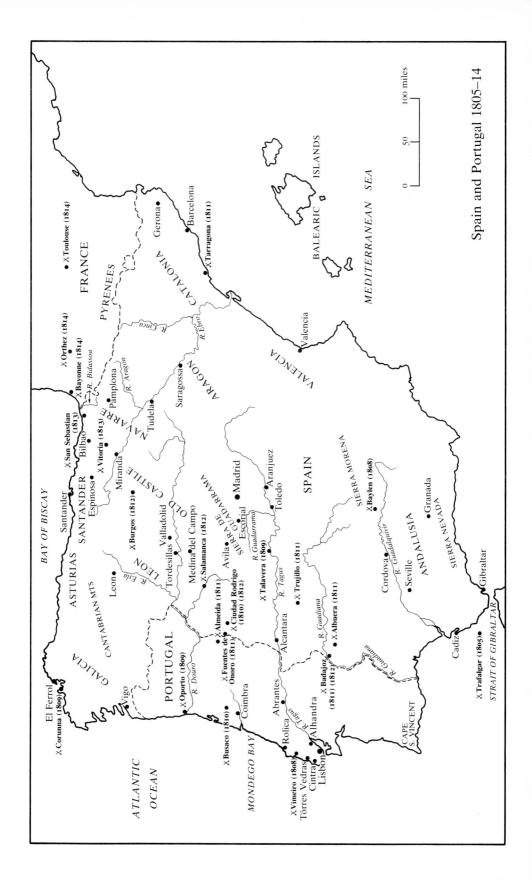

Spain and Portugal 1805–14

0   50   100 miles

MEDITERRANEAN SEA

BALEARIC ISLANDS

Barcelona
Gerona
X Tarragona (1811)

FRANCE
X Toulouse (1814)
X Orthez (1814)
X Bayonne (1814)
R. Bidassoa
X San Sebastian (1813)
PYRENEES
CATALONIA
R. Cinca
R. Ebro
R. Aragon
Pamplona
NAVARRE
Valencia
VALENCIA
Tudela
Saragossa
ARAGON

Bilbao
Espinosa
X Vitoria (1813)
Miranda
Santander
SANTANDER
BAY OF BISCAY

ASTURIAS
Leon
LEON
CANTABRIAN MTS
R. Esla
X Burgos (1812)
Valladolid
OLD CASTILE
Tordesillas
Medina del Campo
X Salamanca (1812)
Avila
SIERRA DE GUADARRAMA
Madrid
Escorial
R. Guadarrama
Aranjuez
Toledo
SPAIN

SIERRA MORENA
X Baylen (1808)
Granada
ANDALUSIA
SIERRA NEVADA
Cordova
R. Guadalquivir
Seville

GALICIA
El Ferrol (1809)
X Corunna (1809)
Vigo

PORTUGAL
X Oporto (1809)
R. Douro
X Almeida (1811)
X Ciudad Rodrigo (1810) (1812)
X Fuentes de Onoro (1811)
Coimbra
Abrantes
Alcantara
R. Tagus
X Talavera (1809)
X Trujillo (1811)
R. Guadiana
X Albuera (1811)
X Badajoz (1811) (1812)
R. Guadiana
Gibraltar
STRAIT OF GIBRALTAR
Cadiz
X Trafalgar (1805)
CAPE S. VINCENT

X Busaco (1810)
MONDEGO BAY
Rolica
X Vimeiro (1808)
Torres Vedras
Cintra
Alhandra
Lisbon
R. Tagus

ATLANTIC OCEAN

Napoleon's Europe 1811

SCOTLAND
Edinburgh

GREAT BRITAIN

ENGLAND

London
Plymouth   Brighton Dover
                            Boulo

ENGLISH CHANNEL

CHANNEL IS.   Cherbourg
                          Amiens
          Caen   R. Seine
Brest   I
                      Versailles
Nantes   Fontaineble
          Orléans

R. Loire

FRENCH EMPIRE
Rochefort

Bordeaux
          R. Garonne

CAPE FINISTERRE   Corunna
          GALICIA   Bayonne
                              Toulouse

ATLANTIC OCEAN
          Oporto   Burgos
          R. Douro
Almeida   Ciudad Rodrigo
                      Saragossa
PORTUGAL   Madrid   Barcelona
                      R. Ebro
Lisbon
          R. Tagus
                  SPAIN
          Albuera   MINOR
                  Valencia   MAJORCA
                              BALEARIC
                  Baylen
          Seville
          ANDALUSIA
Key   Cadiz

French Empire ▓   Trafalgar GIBRALTAR

French Dependencies ▒

Allied with Napoleon ☐   Algiers

          MOROCCO   ALGERIA

0   100   200 miles

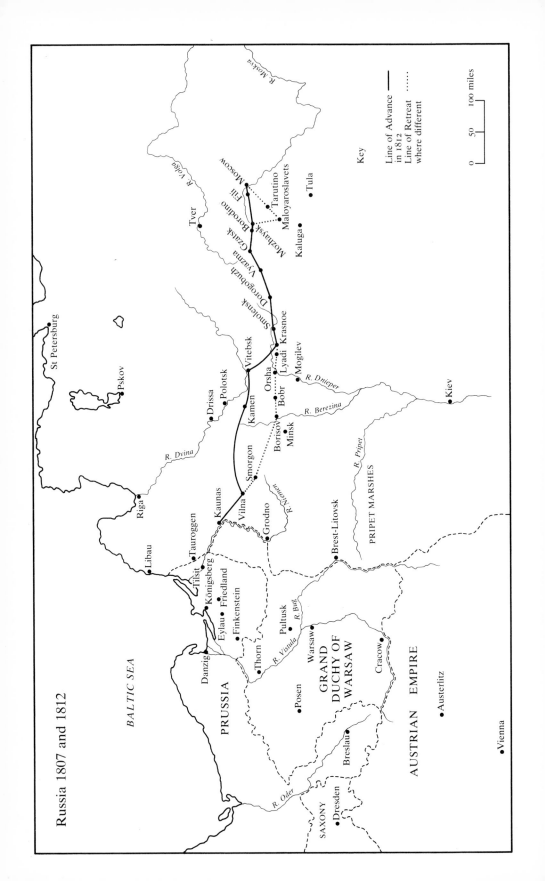

Russia 1807 and 1812

Key

Line of Advance
in 1812

Line of Retreat
where different

0   50   100 miles

R. Moskva

Tver

R. Volga

St Petersburg

Pskov

Moscow
Fili
Borodino
Mozhaysk
Gzatsk
Vyazma
Dorogobuzh

Tarutino
Maloyaroslavets
Kaluga

Tula

Smolensk
Krasnoe
Lyadi
Vitebsk
Orsha
Bobr
Mogilev
R. Dnieper

Kamen
Borisov
Minsk

R. Dvina

Drissa
Polotsk

R. Berezina

Kiev

Smorgon

R. Pripet

PRIPET MARSHES

Riga

Libau

Tauroggen

Tilsit

Kaunas
Vilna
Grodno

R. Niemen

Brest-Litovsk

BALTIC SEA

Königsberg
Eylau   Friedland
Finkenstein

Danzig

Thorn

R. Vistula

Pultusk

R. Bug

Warsaw

PRUSSIA

GRAND
DUCHY OF
WARSAW

Cracow

AUSTRIAN EMPIRE

Austerlitz

Posen

Breslau

SAXONY

Dresden

R. Oder

Vienna

Select Chronology, 1797–1815

1797

January	Battle of Rivoli.
September	*Fructidor* coup, Paris.
October	Treaty of Campo Formio.

1798

January	Rebellion in Ireland.
June	French capture Malta.
July	Battle of the Pyramids.
August	Naval battle of the Nile.

1799

March-May	Siege of Acre.
April-	
August	Successes of Suvorov in Italy and Switzerland.
October	Bonaparte arrives at Fréjus from Egypt.
November	*Brumaire* coup, Paris; Bonaparte becomes First Consul.

1800

May-June	Bonaparte crosses St Bernard Pass, victorious at Marengo.
December	Battle of Hohenlinden; Rue St Nicaise Plot.
LITERATURE	Wordsworth's Preface to *Lyrical Ballads*, on romanticism.

1801

January	Peace of Lunéville.
March	Murder of Tsar Paul; accession of Alexander I.
July	Signature of Concordat.

1802

January-	
April	French overthrow Toussaint L'Ouverture.
March	Treaty of Amiens; interlude in Anglo-French hostilities.
August	Bonaparte becomes life Consul.
LITERATURE	*April*. Chateaubriand publishes *The Genius of Christianity*.

1803

April	Sale of Louisiana to the United States.
May	Resumption of war between Britain and France.
June	Invasion camp at Boulogne (until September 1805).

1804

March	Execution of Enghien.
	Proclamation of the Civil Code.
May	Napoleon proclaimed Emperor of the French.
December	Coronation in Notre Dame, Paris.
MUSIC	Beethoven's Third Symphony ('Eroica').

1805

May	Coronation of Napoleon as King of Italy (Milan).
October	Capitulation of Ulm.
	Battle of Trafalgar.
December	Battle of Austerlitz, followed by Peace of Pressburg.

1806

July	Confederation of the Rhine established.
October	Battles of Jena and Auerstädt.
November	Berlin Decree establishes the Continental System.

1807

February	Battle of Eylau.
June	Battle of Friedland.
July	Tilsit meetings and treaties.
July-September	British attack on Danish fleet, Copenhagen.
November	French seize Lisbon.

1808

April-May	Bayonne Conference.
May	Spanish insurrection.
July	Capitulation of Baylen.
August	British expeditionary force lands in Portugal.
September-October	Erfurt Congress.
October-January (1809)	Napoleon in Spain.
MUSIC	Beethoven's Fifth and Sixth ('Pastoral') Symphonies.
ART	Goya, *Execution of Citizens of Madrid*.
LITERATURE	Goethe, *Faust*, part 1.

1809

July	Battle of Wagram.
October	Peace of Schönbrunn.
December	Divorce of Napoleon and Josephine.

1810

April	Marriage of Napoleon and Marie Louise.
August	Bernadotte becomes Prince Royal of Sweden.
October	British in Portugal retire to Torres Vedras lines.
December	Russia leaves Continental System.

1811

March	Birth of son to Marie Louise.
May	Battle of Fuentes de Oñoro.

1812

April	Wellington captures Badajoz.
June	Napoleon invades Russia; USA declares war on Britain.
September	Battle of Borodino.
November	Crossing of the Berezina.
December	Convention of Tauroggen.
LITERATURE	March, First cantos of Byron's *Childe Harold's Pilgrimage*.

1813

May	Battles of Lützen and Bautzen.
June	Battle of Vitoria.
August	Battle of Dresden.
October	Battle of Leipzig.
LITERATURE	Jane Austen, *Pride and Prejudice*; Ernst Arndt, *Was ist das deutsche Vaterland?*

1814

February	Battles of Champaubert, Montmirail, Vauchamps.
March	Treaty of Chaumont.
April	Abdication of Napoleon.
May-February (1815)	Napoleon on Elba.
September-June (1815)	Congress of Vienna.

1815

March	Napoleon returns to Paris.
June	Battle of Waterloo.
July	Napoleon surrenders, aboard *HMS Bellerophon*.
October	Napoleon arrives at St Helena (where he died, May 1821).

Classified List of Entries

Divisions of Classification System

The Arts
*General; Architecture; Literature; Music; Painting, Caricature, Sculpture;
Philosophy and Theology; Theatre, Opera, Ballet.*

Diplomacy
*General; Conferences, Congresses; Diplomats and Foreign Ministers; Treaties
etc.*

Economics and Trade

Internal Affairs
France; Great Britain; Prussia; Russia; Other States.

Napoleon Bonaparte
Self; Family; Imperial Residences; Mistresses; Personal Entourage.

Places *(other than battlefields)*
Countries; Islands; Provinces; Towns; Others.

Religion

Royalty

Science and Invention

Warfare
Land: *General; Battles; Soldiers.*
Sea: *General; Battles; Seamen.*

Classified Entries

The Arts
General
Art Treasures, Napoleonic Migration of; Censorship; Coppett; *Idéologues*;
Romanticism; Rosetta Stone; Salons; *Style Empire*.
Architecture
Arc de Triomphe; Paris; Regency.
Literature
Arnault, Antoine v; Arndt, Ernst; Austen, Jane; Béranger, P. de; Bignon,
Louis; Blake, William; Byron, Lord; Cesarotti, Melchiorre; Chateaubriand,
Vicomte de; Coleridge, Samuel T.; Constant, Benjamin; Crabbe, George;
Desorgues, Joseph; Goethe, Johann; Grimm, Jakob and Wilhelm; Hunt,
Leigh; Keats, John; Lake Poets; Romanticism; Schiller, Friedrich; Schlegel,
August von; Schlegel, Friedrich von; Scott, Walter; Shelley, Percy B.;
Southey, Robert; Staël, Mme de; Stendhal, *see Beyle*; Wordsworth, William.
Music
Beethoven, Ludwig van; Haydn, Joseph; Méhul, Etienne; Paisiello, Giovanni.
Painting, Caricature and Sculpture
Constable, John; David, Jacques-Louis; Gérard, François; Gillray, James;
Goya, Françisco de; Isabey, Jean Baptiste; Lawrence, Thomas; Turner,
William.
Philosophy and Theology
Baader, Franz; Bentham, Jeremy; Fichte, Johann; Hegel, Georg; Kant,
Immanuel; Krüdener, Julie von; Maistre, Joseph de; Schelling, Friedrich von.
Theatre, Opera, Ballet
Ballet; Bigottini, Emilie; *Comédie Française*; George, Mlle; Kleist, Heinrich
von; Opera; Talma, François.

Diplomacy
General
Coalitions; Eastern Question; Grand Design; Holy Alliance.
Conferences, Congresses
Chatillon; Erfurt; Prague; Rastatt; Teplitz; Tilsit; Vienna.
Diplomats and Foreign Ministers
Aberdeen, Lord (GB); Adams, John Q. (US); Andréossy, Antoine F. (F);
Bentinck, Lord William (GB); Bignon, Baron (F); Budberg, Baron (R);
Canning, George (GB); Canning, Stratford (GB); Caprara, Cardinal

(Papacy); Castlereagh, Lord (GB): Caulaincourt, Marquis de (F); Champagny, Jean-Baptiste de (F); Chateaubriand, Vicomte de (F); Cobenzl, Ludwig von (A); Consalvi, Cardinal (Papacy); Czartoryski, Prince (R); Dolgoruky, Peter (R); Flahaut, Charles de (F); Fox, C. J. (GB); Gentz, Friedrich von (A); Godoy, Manuel de (Sp); Grenville, Lord (GB); Grey, Charles (GB); Hardenberg, Karl von (Pr); Harrowby, Lord (GB); Haugwitz, Christian (Pr); Hauterive, Count (F): Hawkesbury, Lord (GB); Humboldt, Wilhelm (Pr); Kochubey, Victor (R); Kurakin, Prince (R); Labouchère, Peter (F); Maret, Hugues (F); Metternich, Clement von (A); Narbonne, Count Louis de (F); Nesselrode, Karl (R); Pozzo di Borgo, Count (R); Razumovsky, Count (R); Rumyantsev, Nicholas (R); Schwarzenberg, Prince von (A); Sébastiani, Horace (F); Stadion, Count (A); Talleyrand, Charles Maurice de (F); Thugut, Baron von (A); Vorontsov, Alexander (R).
Treaties, etc.
Alessandria; Amiens; Bartenstein; Basle; Bucharest; Campo Formio; Chaumont; Cintra; Concordat; Fontainebleau; Kalisch; Lunéville; Paris; Plaeswitz; Potsdam Oath; Pressburg; Reichenbach; Schönbrunn; Tauroggen; Teplitz; Valençay.

Economics and Trade
Bank of France; Barbé de Marbois, François; Bread; Canals; Commercial Code; Corn Laws; Crisis of 1811; Currency; *Domaine Extraordinaire*; Mercantilism; Ouvrard, Gabriel; Owen, Robert; Rothschild Family; Slave Trade.

Internal Affairs
France
Abdication; *Acte Additionel*; Aréna Conspiracy; Arrondissement; Autun, Bishop of; Bank of France; Barbé de Marbois, François; Barras, Paul; Bourrienne, Louis-Antoine; Brumaire; *Cabinet Noir*; Cadoudal Conspiracy; Caen Food Riots; Cambacérès, Jean-Jacques de; Censorship; Champ de Mai; Chaptal, Jean; Chauvinism; Civil Code; Codes; Concordat; Constant, Benjamin; Constitutions of France; Consulate; Council of Ancients; Council of Five Hundred; Council of State; Daru, Count; Daunou, Pierre; Directory; Divorce; Ducos, Pierre; Educational Reforms; Émigrés; Empire of the French; Enghien, Execution of the Duc de; Fontanès, Louis de; Fouché, Joseph; Fourcroy, Count; Freemasonry; Fructidor; Gaudin, Martin; Grand Dignitaries; Hundred Days; Imperial Catechism; *Institut de France*; Jews; Junot, Laure; Law of 28 Pluviôse; Law of 27 Ventôse; Law of 18 Pluviôse; Lebrun, Charles; Legion of Honour; Legislative Assembly; *Livret Ouvrier*; Malet Conspiracy; *Moniteur*; National Guard; Organic Articles; Pichegru Conspiracy; Plebiscites; Prefects; Récamier, Mme; Rémusat, Mme; Revolutionary Calendar; Richelieu, Duke of; Roads; Roederer, Count; Rue

Saint Nicaise Plot; Saint-Cyr; Savary, General Anne Jean; Senate; *Sénatus-Consulte*; Serfdom; Sérurier, Jean Mathieu; Sieyès, Emmanuel; Slavery; Staël, Mme de; Tallien, Mme de; Thibaudeau, Antoine; Tribunate; Vendée; Vendemiaire.

Great Britain

Aberdeen, Lord; Addington, Henry; Bathurst, Henry; Brougham, Henry; Catholic Emancipation; Censorship; Cobbett, William; Combination Acts; Divorce; Eldon, Lord; Enclosure Act; Fox, Charles James; Grattan, Henry; Hamilton, Lady Emma; Holland House; Liverpool, Lord; Luddites; 'Ministry of All the Talents': Perceval, Spencer; Pitt, William; Portland, Duke of; Regency; Slavery; Tories; Whigs; Wilberforce, William; Windham, William.

Prussia

Emancipation Edict; Roads; Serfdom; Stein, Baron; *Tugendbund*

Russia

Arakcheev, Alexei; Censorship; Council of State; La Harpe, Frederic; Novosiltsov, Nikolai; Roads; Rostopchin, Theodore; Secret Committee; Serfdom; Speransky, Michael; Stroganov, Paul.

Other States

Ali Pasha (Tur); Bolivar, Simon; Cadiz, Constitution of; Censorship; Colloredo, Franz von (A); Council of State; Divorce; Freemasonry; Hamilton, Alexander (US); Höfer, Andreas, (A); Imperial Recess (German lands); Janissaries (Tur); Jefferson, Thomas (US); Jews; Karadjorjordje (Serbia); Kosciuszko, Tadeusz; Madison, James (US); Mamelukes (Tur); Mediatization (German lands); Melzi d'Eril (It); Miranda, Francisco de; Palm, Johann (German lands); Paoli, Pasquale (Corsica); Roads; Schimmelpenninck, R. J. (Neth); Serbian Revolts; Serfdom; Slavery; Toussaint L'Ouverture (Haiti); Tyrolean Risings.
(And see under Royalty, below)

Napoleon Bonaparte

Self

Abdication; *Bellerophon*, HMS; Bernadotte, Désirée; Brienne; Campaigns; Coronations; Corsica; Elba; Hundred Days; Imperial Bees; Lowe, Sir Hudson; Napoleon I; St Helena; Smorgon.

Family

Ajaccio; Bacciochi, Félix; Beauharnais, Eugène de; Beauharnais, Hortense de; Beauharnais, Stéphanie de; Bonaparte family (Caroline, Charles Marie, Elisa, Jerome, Joseph, Letitia, Louis, Louis Napoleon, Lucien, Pauline); Borghese, Prince; Clary family; Fesch, Cardinal; Josephine; Marie Louise; Napoleon II.

Imperial Residences

Élysée Palace; Finkenstein; Fontainebleau; Malmaison; St Cloud; Schönbrunn; Trianon; Tuileries.

Mistresses
Dénuelle, Eleonore; George, Mlle; Walewska, Marie.
Personal Entourage
Bausset, Baron de; Bertrand, General; Duroc, Géraud; Fain, Baron;
Gourgaud, Gaspard; Las Cases, Comte de; *Maison*; Méneval, Claude de;
Montholon, Comte de; O'Meara, Dr; Roustam, Raza; Wairy, L. Constant.

Places *(other than battlefields)*
Countries, etc.
Austria; Bavaria; Belgium; Cisalpine Republic; Egypt; Finland; Great Britain;
Greece; Haiti; Hanover; Helvetic Confederation; Holland; Holy Roman
Empire; India; Ireland; Italian Republic; Italy; Ligurian Republic; Naples,
Kingdom of; Oldenburg; Ottoman Empire; Papal States; Parthenopean
Republic; Poland; Portugal; Prussia; Rhine, Confederation of the; Russia;
Sardinia-Piedmont; Saxony; Spain; Sweden; Switzerland; Syria; Westphalia;
Württemberg.
Islands
Corfu; Corsica; Elba; Ionian Islands; Malta; Martinique; St Helena; Santo
Domingo; Sicily.
Provinces
Galicia; Illyrian Provinces; Lombardy; Pomerania; Tuscany.
Towns
Äbo; Abrantès; Ajaccio; Basle; Bayonne; Berlin; Bordeaux; Brest; Brienne;
Cadiz; Cairo; Cintra; Cracow; Danzig; Dresden; Frankfurt-am-Main; Genoa;
Milan; Moscow; Odessa; Paris; Parma; Ratisbon; Rome; Salzburg; Savona;
Venice; Vienna; Warsaw; Weimar.
Other Places
Cape of Good Hope; Great St Bernard Pass; Louisiana; Spanish America;
Vincennes.

Religion
Caprara, Cardinal Giovanni; Catholic Emancipation; Concordat; Consalvi,
Cardinal Ercole; Fontainebleau; Holy Alliance; Imperial Catechism;
Krüdener, Julie von; Organic Articles; Pius VI, Pope; Pius VII, Pope; Russia;
Savona.

Royalty
Alexander I, Tsar; Angoulême, Duke of; Anna Pavlovna, Grand Duchess;
Bernadotte, Marshal (King Charles XIV John of Sweden); Bernadotte, Desirée
(Queen of Sweden); Bourbon Dynasty; Caroline of Brunswick, Pcess of
Wales; Catherine Pavlovna, Grand Duchess; Charles IV, King of Spain;
Charles XIII, King of Sweden; Charles, Archduke of Austria; Ferdinand IV,
King of Naples; Ferdinand VII, King of Spain; Ferdinand, Archduke of Austria;
Francis II, Emperor of Austria; Frederick Augustus, King of Saxony; Frederick

William III, King of Prussia; George III, King of Great Britain; Habsburg
Dynasty; John, Archduke of Austria; Joseph, Archduke of Austria; Louis
XVIII, King of France; Louise, Queen of Prussia; Mahmud II, Sultan of Turkey;
Maximilian I, King of Bavaria; Paul I, Tsar; Prince Regent (George, Pr. of
Wales); York, Frederick, Duke of.

Science and Invention
Balloons; Chappe, Claude; Chaptal, Jean; Davy, Humphry; Fulton, Robert;
Gay-Lussac. Joseph; Lamarck, Jean-Baptiste; Metric System; Semaphore.

Warfare: Land
General
Armies; Balloons; Bulletins of the Army; Campaigns of Napoleon Bonaparte;
Coalitions; Conscription; Fontainebleau Decree; *Grande Armée*; Guerrillas;
Imperial Guard; Marshals; Moscow, Retreat from; Niemen, River; Old
Guard; Peninsular War; Torres Vedras, Lines of; War of 1812; War of
Liberation; Warfare.
Battles
Aboukir Bay; Acre; Albuera; Alexandria; Almeida; Arcis-sur-Aube; Arcole;
Aspern; Auerstädt; Austerlitz; Badajoz; Bassano; Bautzen; Baylen; Bayonne;
Berezina; Bidassoa; Borghetto; Borisov; Borodino; Burgos; Caldiero;
Castiglione; Champaubert; Ciudad Rodrigo; Corunna; Dego; Dresden;
Eckmühl; Eylau; Friedland; Fuentes de Oñoro; Hohenlinden; Jena; Katzbach;
Krasnoe; Kulm; Laon; La Rothière; Leipzig; Ligny; Lodi; Lützen;
Maloyaroslavets; Mantua; Marengo; Montmirail; Oporto; Orthèz; Polotsk;
Pultusk; Pyramids; Quatre Bras; Salamanca; San Sebastian; Saragossa;
Smolensk; Talavera; Toulouse; Ulm; Vauchamps; Vilna; Vimiero; Vitebsk;
Vitoria; Wagram; Waterloo; Wavre; Zurich.
Soldiers
Abercromby, Sir Ralph; Andréossy, Antoine; Angoulême, Duke of;
Augereau, Marshal; Bagration, Prince; Balashov, Alexander; Barclay de
Tolly, Marshal; Beauharnais, Eugène de; Bennigsen, General; Bentinck, Lord
William; Beresford, Lord; Bernadotte, Marshal; Berthier, Marshal; Bertrand,
General; Bessières, Marshal; Blücher, Prince; Bourgogne, Sergeant; Brune,
Marshal; Brunswick, Duke of; Carnot, General; Castaños, General;
Caulaincourt, General; Charles, Archduke; Chauvin, Nicholas; Chichagov,
Pavel; Clarke, Marshal; Clausewitz, Karl; Davout, Marshal; Desaix, General;
Dombrowski, General; Druot, General; Eblé, General; Exelmans, General;
Ferdinand, Archduke; Flahaut, Charles de; Gneisenau, Field Marshal;
Gouvion Saint-Cyr, Marshal; John, Archduke; Jomini, General; Junot,
General; Kellermann, Marshal; Kellermann (younger), General; Kléber,
General; Kutuzov, Marshal; Lannes, Marshal; Lauriston, General; Lefebvre,
Marshal; Liechtenstein, Prince; Ligne, Prince de; Macdonald, Marshal; Mack,
General; Marmont, Marshal; Masséna, Marshal; Menou, General;

NAPOLEON'S EUROPE

A

ABDICATION

Napoleon twice renounced his imperial and royal titles, at Fontainebleau† in April 1814 and at the Élysée†, fifteen months later. The first abdication followed the entry of the Allies into Paris and the formal deposition of the Emperor by a rump of the Senate on 3 April 1814. Napoleon drafted a conditional abdication on 4 April in which he sought recognition of his son's succession, but this was rejected by the Allies. On 6 April he abdicated the crowns of France and Italy for himself and his heirs. He resumed the imperial title on 12 March 1815, after his return from Elba, only to abdicate again on 22 June, following Waterloo. On this second occasion the instrument of abdication declared, 'My political life is at an end and I proclaim my son Napoleon II†, Emperor of the French'; but the four-year-old boy was in Austrian hands and never exercised sovereign power, even through a regency.

ABERCROMBY, Sir Ralph (1734–1801)

Scottish general: born in Clackmannan-shire and served with the Dragoons in the Seven Years' War. He was MP for his native shire in 1774–5 but soon resumed his military career and fought with distinction in the Netherlands in 1793. Two years later he was given command of the expedition to the West Indies; the French colonies of St Lucia and Demerara were seized in 1796 and the richer prize of Trinidad in February 1797. After supervising the defence of Ireland against invasion he was sent to the Mediterranean with an expeditionary force intended to eject the French from Egypt†. Abercromby's army, 18,000 strong, landed at Aboukir Bay† and defeated the French, under General Ménou†, in a night battle between Aboukir and Alexandria on 21 March 1801. During the battle Abercromby was wounded in the thigh; he died a week later. His victory gave the British a firm foothold in Egypt. Sir Ralph's son, Sir John Abercromby (1772–1817), had the misfortune to be travelling in France when the Peace of Amiens† broke down. He was arrested at Calais and interned for six years. Sir John commanded the expedition which captured the French island of Mauritius, in the Indian Ocean, in July 1810.

ABERDEEN, George Hamilton Gordon, 4th Earl of (1784–1860)

British diplomat and statesman: born in Edinburgh and educated at Harrow and St John's College, Cambridge, succeeding to the earldom at the age of seventeen. Pitt was a guardian of the orphaned Aberdeen, who spent many months each summer with the Prime Minister's family. Aberdeen travelled to France in the late summer of 1802 and was received by Bonaparte at Malmaison†, the First Consul making a favourable impression on the young man. Aberdeen's interest in classical archaeology prompted him to excavate the Pnyx at Athens; he journeyed through much of Epirus and Euboea. In September 1813 Castlereagh† appointed him ambassador to Francis I of Austria. A month later Aberdeen saw the carnage of battle at Leipzig†, an experience which shocked him deeply. He was not a good ambassador, for he was over-confident and easily flattered by Metternich†, who in private referred to him contemptuously as 'that dear simpleton of diplomacy'. Aberdeen was a signatory of the first Treaty of Paris† in 1814 but then retired into private life. His public career resumed in June 1828 when he became Foreign Secretary, an office he held until November 1830 and again from September 1841 to July 1846. As Prime Minister of a Coalition Government, formed in December 1852, he was confronted by the crisis which culminated in the Crimean War. He finally resigned office in January 1855.

ÅBO

The Swedish name for the Finnish city of Turku, on the Gulf of Bothnia, capital of Finland† when Russia acquired the Grand Duchy in 1809. Tsar Alexander I† received the Swedish Prince Royal (formerly Marshal Bernadotte†) at Åbo in the last week of August 1812 and reached a political understanding with him. Sweden agreed not to assist Napoleon in his Russian campaign; the Prince Royal offered to bring Sweden into the war as Russia's ally against France, provided that the Tsar would support a Swedish expeditionary force south of the Baltic and back Swedish claims for the acquisition of Norway in the eventual peace settlement, as compensation for the loss of Finland. The Prince Royal was, however, in no hurry to intervene; it was not until the spring of 1813 that a Swedish expeditionary force entered the war. The Åbo meeting was nevertheless of great value to Alexander for it ruled out the threat of renewed hostilities in Finland during the critical weeks after Borodino†.

ABOUKIR BAY

An anchorage some fourteen miles northeast of Alexandria†. On 31 July 1798, soon after the start of Bonaparte's Egyp-

tian campaign, Nelson† found a squadron of seventeen French warships in the bay and gained there the victory generally known as the Battle of the Nile†. Almost a year later – on 15 July 1799 – a Turkish expeditionary force, supported by British and Russian warships, landed at the village of Aboukir (now Abu Qir) on the northern tip of the bay and threatened the French base of Alexandria. After initial successes the Turks were overwhelmed by Bonaparte in a counter-attack on 25 July. Murat's† cavalry charge carried the French to the approaches to the outlying fort where the Turkish commander, Mustapha Pasha, was captured, but the Turks held out in Aboukir castle until 2 August, their surrender seeming to consolidate the French position in Egypt. News of Bonaparte's victory on 25 July reached Paris only four days before the return of the general himself, thus enabling him to be welcomed as a triumphant commander rather than as one who had deserted the troops in Egypt. This reception eased Bonaparte's quest for political support on the eve of the *coup d'état* of Brumaire†.

There was a third engagement fought at Aboukir Bay in the spring of 1801. The expeditionary force commanded by Sir Ralph Abercromby† made a successful landing there on 8 March and advanced on Alexandria. Early on 21 March a four-hour night battle was fought against the main French army, under General Menou†, in which Sir John Moore†, whose troops held the ruins of a Roman villa close to the seashore, successfully resisted an enveloping movement by the French cavalry. Menou was forced back on the defences of Alexandria; he surrendered to the British five months later.

ABRANTÈS, Duke of

Title accorded to General Andoche Junot† by Napoleon in December 1808. The title commemorated Junot's successful invasion of Portugal† in 1807, the town of Abrantès being the farthest point upstream on the River Tagus navigable to small vessels.

ACRE

An ancient seaport, now in Israel and lying nine miles north-east of Haifa (which has superseded Acre as a port). The Crusader fortress of St John stood on a peninsula so that the sea protected most of Acre, while imposing ramparts dominated the town's 350 yard landward boundary. From 18 March to 20 May 1799 Acre was besieged by Bonaparte, his failure to take the port proving the turning-point of the French campaign in Syria†. The Turkish commander at Acre, Djezzar Pasha, the septuagenarian Governor of Syria for Sultan Selim III, reckoned his fortress 'the key to Palestine' and threw back eight direct assaults by Bonaparte's troops. There were three military reasons for Acre's successful defiance of the French: the support given to Djezzar by a naval flotilla commanded by Commodore Sidney Smith† which captured the French siege train at sea off Mount Carmel on 18 March; the strengthening of Acre's defences by Colonel Antoine de Phélippeaux, a French royalist engineer officer who had once been Bonaparte's classmate at the military academy and who died from sunstroke in the early days of the siege; and the need for Bonaparte to withdraw 4,000 men from Acre so as to help Kléber† to defeat the main Turkish army at Mount Tabor on 16 April. But the principal cause of Bonaparte's withdrawal from Acre – and from Syria as a whole – was the spread of bubonic plague among his troops.

Acte Additionnel (22 April 1815)

An amendment to the constitutions of the Empire introduced during the Hundred Days so as to implement Napoleon's assertion that he believed in ordered representative government. The Acte provided for a hereditary House of Peers and for a Chamber of Deputies, returned through electoral colleges on a basis of universal suffrage. The proposals were largely devised by Benjamin Constant†, and its many critics derisively called the Acte the 'Benjamine'. Although the constitutional amendment was promulgated with much pomp at the Champ de Mai† on 1 June, Napoleon resented having to make concessions to a fashionable liberalism and had every intention of rescinding them as soon as he was militarily victorious. The Chambers met on 11 June but their only achievement was the call for Napoleon's second abdication†. By the end of June military events had made the Acte a mere constitutional curiosity.

ADAMS, John Quincy (1767–1848)

American statesman: born in Braintree, Massachusetts. He was the son of John Adams, who from 1797 to 1801 was second President of the United States. After studying at Leyden and Harvard, John Q. Adams was appointed American Minister at The Hague in 1794, being transferred to Berlin three years later. He resigned from the diplomatic service in 1801, represented Massachusetts in the Senate from 1804 to 1808, and was posted to St Petersburg as American Minister in October 1809, remaining in Russia until April 1813. His printed journal is a valuable record of life at the Tsar's court during these dramatic years. Adams headed the peace commission which negotiated the Anglo-American Treaty of Ghent in December 1814. After two years as Minister in London he served as Secretary of State from 1817 to 1824 and then became the sixth President of the United States. Adams's presidency, 1825–9, was undistinguished. It could be argued that his most enduring achievements were accomplished in the final phase of his life when, as a member of the House of Representatives from 1832 to 1848 he showed much parliamentary skill in exposing the evils of slavery.

ADDINGTON, Henry (1757–1844)

British Prime Minister from March 1801 to April 1804. He was the son of a physician at George II's court and spent much of his boyhood in the company of the younger Pitt‡. Addington was elected to parliament in 1783 and, largely through Pitt's management, became Speaker of the Commons in 1789, holding office until March 1801. George III then appointed Addington to succeed Pitt as Prime Minister, mainly because the King thought his views sound on the 'iniquity' of Catholic Emancipation‡. Addington, a politician with no cabinet experience, lacked the personality or the administrative competence to lead a nation at war; he has, indeed, some claim to be reckoned the dullest head of any British government in the nineteenth century. His administration negotiated the Peace of Amiens‡ but also saw a muddled drift back to renewed war fourteen months later. He fell from office over an Irish Militia Bill, which was opposed by Pitt, who formed the new government. Addington was created Viscount Sidmouth in 1805 and held only minor office intermittently over the following seven years. He was Home Secretary from 1812 until 1822, acquiring much unpopularity by his repressive measures during the years of post-war unrest in England. His old Tory mistrust of reform continued undiminished into the 1830s.

AJACCIO

Seaport in Corsica‡, on the west coast of the island. Napoleon was born in the Bonaparte home, a four-storeyed building in Ajaccio's Via Malerba, on 15 August 1769, and he lived there until April 1779. He returned to Ajaccio in late September 1789, furthering the Revolution in Corsica as a whole, and he remained in his native town until January 1791. His only other visit to Ajaccio took place in the first week of October 1799, a five-day windbound interlude in his secret journey back from Egypt‡ to France before Brumaire‡.

Ajaccio: Napoleon's birthplace

ALBUERA, Battle of (16 May 1811)
Albuera is a village in southern Spain near the Portuguese frontier and sixteen miles south-east of Badajoz†. An Anglo-Portuguese army, under General Lord Beresford, broke off the siege of Badajoz to engage a French relief column commanded by Marshal Soult† at the crossing in the village of a small river, also named Albuera. Beresford narrowly escaped encirclement by French cavalry which forded the river further to the south. The fighting was extremely bloody, with heavy casualties on both sides and conditions worsened by heavy rain and a hailstorm. Some two-thirds of the Light Brigade were destroyed by Soult's Polish Lancers. After four hours of combat, the French retired and it was for this reason that Wellington subsequently claimed Albuera as a victory. Nevertheless it was realized in England that Albuera was, in Byron's phrase, a 'glorious field of grief'; the battle remained a contentious topic for military commentators over the following forty years, not least because in the heat of the engagement Beresford seemed momentarily to lose his nerve.

ALESSANDRIA
Piedmontese town on the River Tanaro, forty-eight miles east of Turin. During Bonaparte's north Italian counter-offensive in the War of the Second Coalition, the Austrian general, Friedrich von Melas, concentrated his army at Alessandria, emerging from the citadel on 14 June 1800 to give battle at Marengo†, a village some two and a half miles to the south-east. Bonaparte's subsequent victory forced Melas to retire on Alessandria with less than half his troops still in battle order and no prospect of breaking through the enveloping French army. An armistice – generally called the Convention of Alessandria – was concluded on 15 June: Melas surrendered all his remaining fortified positions in Piedmont and Lombardy in return for the right to withdraw east of the

River Ticino while terms for a general peace were discussed with the government in Vienna. These peace talks continued intermittently until November, but they were then broken off by Bonaparte when the French Army of the Rhine embarked on the Hohenlinden† campaign.

ALEXANDER I, Tsar of Russia (1777–1825, reigned from 24 March 1801 to 1 December 1825): born in St Petersburg in the sixteenth year of the reign of his grandmother, Catherine the Great, who supervised every detail of his upbringing until the accession of his father, Paul I†, in November 1796. The contrast between the 'enlightened' education prescribed by Catherine and the narrowly militaristic restraints imposed by Paul emphasized a natural deviousness in Alexander's character which made him consistently inconsistent. His participation in a plot to depose his father (in which, against Alexander's expectations, Paul was assassinated) troubled his conscience in later years. Over internal affairs Alexander alternated between support for the liberal reforms advocated by his friends on the 'Secret Committee'† (and, later, by Speransky†) and the autocratic principles favoured by General Arakcheev†. Alexander took Russia into the War of the Third Coalition in 1805, partly from mistrust of Napoleon after the execution of Enghien† and partly to fulfil the 'Grand Design'† for a new European order proposed by Czartoryski† and Novosiltsov†. The Tsar's influence on Russian strategy and tactics in the Austerlitz† campaign was disastrous. After Russia's defeat at Friedland†, Alexander sued for peace, met Napoleon at Tilsit† in July 1807 and, with a remarkable reversal of policy, began three and a half years of Russo-French collaboration. Alexander participated in the Continental System† and was encouraged by Napoleon to go to war with Sweden and acquire the Grand Duchy of Finland† in May 1808. The two Emperors

Tsar Alexander I

August. The Tsar rejoined his army at Christmas 1812 and accompanied his troops as they advanced across Germany to Paris, being present at the battles of Dresden† and Leipzig†. He entered the French capital in triumph on 31 March 1814, collaborating closely with Talleyrand† to secure Napoleon's first abdication†. The Tsar was given an enthusiastic reception in London in June 1814 where he was popularly regarded as Europe's enlightened liberator, but his admirers were soon disillusioned. At the Congress of Vienna† the Tsar was outmanoeuvred in negotiation by Metternich†, Castlereagh† and Talleyrand. He became increasingly concerned with spiritual affairs, influenced by Baroness Julie von Krüdener† who inspired him with the ideals of the Holy Alliance†. His last years were politically stagnant, the promise of self-government in Poland only partially realized. Alexander died unexpectedly at Taganrog from a fever contracted on a visit to the Crimea; he was succeeded by his brother, Nicholas I.

met again at Erfurt† in October 1808. Thereafter their partnership fell apart: Alexander was suspicious of Napoleon's Polish policy, failed to give France practical aid in the Austrian campaign† of 1809, resented Napoleon's subsequent choice of an Austrian rather than a Russian bride and was alarmed by French interference in the Duchy of Oldenburg†; Napoleon mistrusted Alexander's intrigues in the Grand Duchy of Warsaw† and his ambitions in south-eastern Europe. When Alexander took Russia out of the Continental System on 31 December 1810, Napoleon began to prepare for another campaign in the east, believing he could gain a rapid victory.

When Napoleon invaded Russia in 1812, Alexander was at Vilna† and remained supreme commander of Russia's armies in the field for the first month of the campaign, returning to St Petersburg before Borodino† and meeting the Swedish Prince Royal at Åbo† in the last week of

ALEXANDRIA

The principal seaport of Egypt†, was captured by Bonaparte's Army of the Orient on 2 July 1798 within hours of the first French landing, at Marabout, some eight miles west of the city. Alexandria served as the main French base until the surrender there of General Menou† to the British on 2 September 1801, more than five months after the night battle for the port on the shores of Aboukir Bay†.

ALI PASHA, (*c.* 1741–1822)

Albanian warlord: born at Tepelenë on the Vijosë River in southern Albania, and occupied himself with brigandage until given provincial authority as Pasha of Trikkala (Thessaly) by Sultan Abdul Hamid I in 1787. A year later he was made Pasha of Janina (Ioannina) in Epirus, on the mountainous borders of Albania. In this fastness the 'Lion of Janina' established a virtually autonomous despotate which made him throughout the Napoleonic period the most powerful ruler in the western Balkans. Ali showed great cunning in successfully playing off French, British, Russian and Turkish emissaries against one another. During the Consulate it was reported to Paris that he habitually wore a tricolour cummerbund although he kept a secret agent in Vienna and was in contact with London. By 1815 Ali was master of central Greece, western Macedonia and much of the Peloponnese as well as of Thessaly and Epirus; it was generally recognized that he possessed cruelly efficient administrative skills. Sultan Mahmud ii† became exasperated by his intrigues in Constantinople in 1820 and ordered the Ottoman armies to occupy his fortresses in Greece. Eventually, on 5 February 1822, he was murdered by one of the Sultan's lieutenants in the monastery of Panteleimon on an island in Lake Ioannina; his sons were butchered soon afterwards so as to prevent the establishment of a Graeco-Albanian dynasty. At the height of his powers Ali Pasha received Lord Aberdeen† at his palace beside Lake Ioannina and in October 1809 he entertained Byron† and his friend, John Cam Hobhouse, at Tepelenë. This visit is commemorated in Canto ii of Byron's *Childe Harold*.

ALLEMAND, Zacharie Jacques Théodore (1762–1826)
French naval commander: born at Port Louis in the Morbihan region of Brittany, joined the French navy at the age of twelve and held the rank of lieutenant when the monarchy fell. After some years of commerce raiding in the Atlantic, Allemand was promoted rear-admiral and given command of the Rochefort squadron in January 1805. Napoleon hoped his admirals (Villeneuve†, Allemand and Ganteaume†) would sail up Channel and cover an invasion of England from the

camp at Boulogne†. This strategic design was thwarted, but Allemand showed himself the most enterprising of Napoleon's naval commanders, posing a constant threat to British communications in the western approaches, from Portugal to his native peninsula. He was promoted vice-admiral in 1809 and given command of the French fleet in the Mediterranean. His acerbic tongue made him many personal enemies but he was respected in Paris as a dedicated professional. Napoleon created him a Count of the Empire in 1810. When Allemand died at Toulon in March 1826, it was calculated that he had spent 445 months of his life in naval service, 318 of them at sea, but he was so elusive a commander that never once were his vessels brought to battle in a major engagement.

ALMEIDA
Fortress in north-eastern Portugal commanding the principal corridor through the Serra da Estrêla range to Ciudad Rodrigo† and Salamanca† in Spain. Almeida was successfully besieged by Ney† in late August 1810 and by Wellington† from 4 April to 10 May 1811. Marshal Masséna's attempt to relieve Almeida in 1811 was frustrated by Wellington at Fuentes de Oñoro†, some eight miles to the south. However, to Wellington's chagrin, the French garrison at Almeida made a surprise sortie and broke through the British line, escaping relatively unscathed on the night of 10 May – 'the most disgraceful military event that has yet occurred to us', Wellington declared two days later.

AMIENS, Peace of (1802)
The name generally given to the fourteen months of non-belligerency in Europe which followed the conclusion of an Anglo-French treaty of peace at the Hôtel de Ville in Amiens on 25 March 1802. When the Treaty of Lunéville† (February

7

1801) took Austria out of the War of the Second Coalition†, a growing peace movement spread through business circles in London. The replacement of Pitt† by Addington†, the strains imposed on British commerce by the Armed Neutrality† of the North and the economic uncertainty caused by two bad harvests emphasized the need for a respite from the war. Peace talks began in September 1801 and the formal Preliminaries were signed on 1 October. The British hoped France would make further concessions at Amiens before the final treaty was signed, but Talleyrand† (the Foreign Minister) would give away nothing of value. Britain retained Trinidad and Ceylon but agreed to restore Cape Colony to Holland, Egypt† to Turkey and Malta† to the Knights of St John as well as surrendering all other colonial conquests. The French undertook to restore the Kingdom of the Two Sicilies (Naples) and to evacuate the Papal States. Both Powers recognized the integrity of Portugal and the independence of the Ionian Islands†; the title 'King of France', defiantly borne by England's kings since 1337, was renounced by George III for himself and his successors.

During the Peace of Amiens British visitors flocked to Paris in their thousands, joining in celebrations to mark the assumption by Bonaparte of the life consulship, on the eve of his thirty-third birthday (August 1802). But by the autumn the British government had begun to fear France was fitting out new military expeditions. Relations deteriorated during the winter: Bonaparte seemed to tighten his grip on Germany, Italy, Holland and Switzerland; the British declined to evacuate Malta until peace on the Continent was assured. By the end of January 1803 there were reports of a new French enterprise in the Levant, perhaps even an expedition to India, and English public opinion was excited by comments made by a French envoy to the Levant, Colonel Sébastiani†, published in the official *Moniteur*. Addington, anticipating a

French initiative sent a virtual ultimatum to Paris early in April 1803, following it up by an embargo on all French vessels in British ports a month later. On 17 May Britain declared war on France. The two nations remained in conflict for another eleven years.

ANCIENTS, Council of (*Anciens, Conseil des*): see *Council of Ancients*.

ANDRÉOSSY, Antoine François (1761–1828)

French soldier and diplomat: born at Castelnaudary, near Carcassonne, into an aristocratic family, originally from Lucca. He entered the royal army as an artillery officer, but he later distinguished himself as an engineer. The pontoon bridge which Andréossy threw across the Adige at Ronco on 15 November 1796 enabled the French to threaten the Austrian rear at Arcole†, and marked off Andréossy for promotion. He served as a brigadier on the Nile and in Syria, sailing from Egypt† for France with Bonaparte aboard the frigate *Muiron* and subsequently assisting him in the *coup d'état* of Brumaire†. In 1800 Andréossy was promoted major-general and given the inspectorate of artillery. From November 1802 to May 1803 Andréossy served Bonaparte as ambassador in London, where he was well received but remained sufficiently astute to give good warning to Paris of the hardening of opposition to the Peace of Amiens†. Thereafter Andréossy's career alternated between war and diplomacy: thus he fought against Austria in 1805, served as ambassador in Vienna from 1806 to 1808 (sending Napoleon clear indications of Austria's military preparations), participated in the Wagram† campaign and was Military Governor of occupied Vienna in 1809. From May 1812 until August 1814 he was ambassador at Constantinople, showing much skill in handling the Sultan's ministers and almost persuading them to resume the war against Russia. Andréossy supported Napoleon during the Hundred Days but was a member of the deputation from the Chambers which attended Wellington when he arrived at Paris after Waterloo. Louis XVIII readily gave him his confidence and welcomed his advice.

ANGOULÊME, Louis Antoine Duke of (1775-1844)
Eldest son of the Count of Artois† (Charles x) and nephew of both Louis XVI and Louis XVIII. He was born at Versailles, fled with his father to Edinburgh in 1792 and married his first cousin Princess Marie Thérèse (the only child of Louis XVI and Marie Antoinette to survive imprisonment in the Temple in Paris) at Mittau in Russian Courland in June 1799. Angoulême was attached to Wellington's staff when the Allies crossed the Pyrenees and, from Saint-Jean-de-Luz on 2 February 1814, published the first proclamation of the Bourbons calling on the French people to return to their old allegiance. Although Angoulême was welcomed in Bordeaux with white lilies and royalist cockades on 12 March, he failed to kindle enthusiasm for the Bourbon cause either in 1814 or when he re-entered France from Belgium after Waterloo. He was appointed nominal commander-in-chief of the Army of the Pyrenees, the 'hundred thousand sons of St Louis' as they were called, who invaded Spain in April 1823 to restore the absolutist rule of Ferdinand VII†. On the abdication of his father at Rambouillet on 2 August 1830, the Duke renounced the succession and went into exile at Gorizia, where he died fourteen years later. His widow survived a second wave of revolution in Europe, dying at Frohsdorf in Austria on 19 October 1851.

ANNA PAVLOVNA, Grand Duchess of Russia (1795-1865)
Sixth daughter of Tsar Paul I†. She was born at St Petersburg and was only five years old when her father was murdered. At the Erfurt Congress† in 1808 Napoleon indicated to Anna's brother, Tsar Alexander I†, that she was one of sixteen princesses whom he had short-listed as possible consorts in succession to Josephine†. In January 1810 Napoleon asked if Alexander would sanction such a marriage. Anna's mother, the Dowager Empress Marie Feodorovna, declined to 'sacrifice a daughter to a man of vile character for whom nothing is sacred'. Alexander informed Napoleon that his sister was too young for marriage and suggested that he might wait for two more years, but Napoleon had meanwhile decided on an Austrian bride, Archduchess Marie Louise†. Anna married the Prince of Orange in 1816 and was Queen Consort of the Netherlands from October 1840 to March 1849. She was the grandmother of Queen Wilhelmina (reigned 1890–1948), herself the grandmother of Queen Beatrix.

ARAKCHEEV, Alexey Andreevich (1769-1834)
Russian soldier and administrator: born on the small family estate at Garusovo, north of Moscow, became an artillery cadet at the age of thirteen and proved so competent that he was attached to the highly disciplined 'Gatchina Corps' of the future Tsar Paul†. After his accession Paul made Arakcheev commandant of St Petersburg, promoting him major-general before his twenty-ninth birthday and bestowing on him the valuable imperial estate of Gruzino. A minor incident in October 1799 lost Arakcheev Paul's favour, but his authority was restored by Alexander I† in May 1803. Arakcheev remained a close adviser of Alexander throughout his reign. His administrative energy and ruthless bullying were first employed to secure for Russia the modernized artillery vital for any war against Napoleon. Arakcheev was inspector general of artillery from 1803 to 1807 and Minister of War from

9

1807 until the closing weeks of 1809, supervising the planning and organization of the campaign which acquired Finland†. He never commanded in the field and was as unpopular with the generals as with the Tsar's civilian ministers. To most Russians he was, in Pushkin's words, 'the genius of evil', a tyrant imposing iron discipline through fear of the whip. Alexander respected him for his skill in remedying administrative abuses and getting tasks accomplished in an empire naturally inclined to embezzlement and bureaucratic knavery. Arakcheev took charge of difficult post-war reconstruction, notably the speedy rebuilding of Smolensk†. He was also responsible for the pioneer settlements known as 'military colonies', where battalions of troops lived with their families under army discipline in order to reclaim wasteland and cultivate neglected areas. So long as Arakcheev could supervise these colonies they were economically productive, but the harsh conditions were open to abuse and there were serious mutinies, brutally repressed. Alexander's successor, Nicholas I, never gave Arakcheev his confidence and the General's last nine years of life were spent at Gruzino, isolated from public events.

ARC DE TRIOMPHE

The Arc de Triomphe de l'Étoile in Paris is the most famous of several triumphal arches erected on Napoleon's orders after ancient Roman models, a reflection of the prevailing mood of classicism in the Empire. The arch was begun in 1806, on a site chosen by Napoleon, to celebrate the victories of France's armies; it was not completed until July 1836, in the reign of Louis Philippe. It was designed by Jean Chalgrin (1739–1811), decorated with sculpted *hauts-reliefs*, and inscribed with the principal military engagements of the revolutionary and Napoleonic era, together with the names of the most distinguished marshals, generals and admirals of the time. The smaller Arc de Triomphe du Carrousel, designed by Charles Percier (1764–1838) and Pierre Fontaine (1762–1853), was erected in 1808 to celebrate the victories of 1805 and 1806; it was especially admired by Napoleon who commended the graceful dignity which it brought to the approach to the Tuileries Palace.

ARCIS-SUR-AUBE

Town in Champagne, sixteen miles north of Troyes and eighty-four miles east of Paris. At Arcis, on 20–21 March 1814, Napoleon fought the last battle before his first abdication†. He launched a surprise attack on the army of Schwarzenberg†, hoping to drive a wedge between the Austrians and Russians and raid the Prussian line of communications on the upper Marne. Technically the bitter struggle for the bridge over the river Aube ended in a tactical victory for Napoleon, but he could not exploit his success; the Allied advance rolled inexorably towards Paris, which fell ten days later.

ARCOLE

A small town eleven miles south-east of Verona, standing above the marshes which mark the confluence of the rivers Alpone and Adige. It was the site of a three-day battle (15–17 November 1796) crucial to Bonaparte's first Italian campaign† and the War of the First Coalition†. Bonaparte, conscious of the growing power of two Austrian armies which were advancing to relieve Mantua, feared he was 'on the eve of losing Italy' unless he could bring their commanders, Josef Alvintzi and Paul von Davidovich, to battle separately. He therefore launched a surprise attack over pontoon bridges across the Adige against Alvintzi's troops, hoping to cut their communications in front of Verona. However, a Croatian outpost gave warning of the attack and, despite the personal encouragement of Bonaparte, the French could not seize the

Arcole: a romanticized treatment of Bonaparte's bravery on the bridge

bridge over the Alpone at Arcole. Alvintzi beat off the assault for two days until, on 17 November Masséna† and Augereau† caught the defenders of Arcole in a two-pronged thrust which forced them to retire overnight so as to avoid encirclement. Casualties were heavy: 4,500 French; 7,000 Austrians. The French victory effectively prevented any union of the two armies although the campaign was not decided until Alvintzi had been defeated again, further up the Adige, at Rivoli. Bonaparte's bravery at Arcole fired the imagination of official painters intent on romanticizing a battle of attrition.

ARÉNA CONSPIRACY (October 1800)
On 10 October 1800 Joseph-Antoine Aréna, a twenty-nine-year-old Corsican, was arrested and charged with planning to assassinate First Consul Bonaparte on his way to the Opéra in Paris. Aréna was a

Jacobin and former deputy on the Council of Five Hundred†; his elder brother, Barthélemy Aréna (1753–1832), had protested vigorously against Brumaire†, and the Aréna family – five brothers in all – were known to have little love for their ambitious fellow Corsicans from Ajaccio. Arrested with Aréna were the painter François Topino-Lebrun, the sculptor Ceracchi and several other conspirators. Fouché† treated the affair as a Jacobin plot, but there is no evidence that any attempt was planned on Bonaparte's life; the episode was magnified for propaganda purposes. A genuine *attentat*, in the Rue Saint-Nicaise† in late December, provided the authorities with an excuse for action against Aréna and his accomplices, who were executed on 30 January 1801. Bonaparte convinced himself that Jacobin regicides had resolved to kill him; in fact, the Rue Saint-Nicaise incident was primarily a royalist deed.

ARMED NEUTRALITY of the North

A confederacy of the three northern Powers (Russia, Denmark and Sweden) was formed in 1780 to protect neutral shipping from British interference during the War of American Independence. In December 1800 a second league of Armed Neutrality was created, largely on the initiative of Tsar Paul†. Once again the chief reason for armed neutrality was Britain's insistence on searching neutral shipping for contraband cargoes. On this occasion Prussia joined the original three confederates in defying the Royal Navy's attempt to blockade France. The effect of armed neutrality on Britain was twofold: it halted shipments of grain from the Baltic lands to the British Isles at a time of poor harvests, thus contributing to the trebling in the price of corn between 1798 and 1801; and it cut off supplies of timber and hemp from the Baltic for British shipyards. The Danes occupied Hamburg, thus preventing English trade with northern Germany. This move prompted the despatch of a naval squadron to Copenhagen in March 1801 so as to give material support to diplomatic efforts to dissolve the league. When these efforts failed Nelson destroyed the Danish fleet at anchor (2 April 1801). An Anglo-Danish armistice provided for the dissolving of the Armed Neutrality league and the withdrawal of Danish troops from Hamburg. Probably the league would have survived longer had not Tsar Paul been assassinated in the palace revolution that took place three days after the British warships reached Copenhagen, the change of ruler in St Petersburg throwing Baltic affairs into great uncertainty.

ARMIES (of Bonaparte)

Napoleon inherited the tradition, followed in the earliest campaigns of the revolutionary wars, of organizing France's military forces under specifically geographical denominations. Thus, when General Bonaparte was appointed to command in Italy in the spring of 1796, the French forces were divided into six armies: Moreau's *Armée du Rhin-et-Moselle;* Jourdan's *Armée du Sambre-et-Meuse;* Hoche's *Armée de l'Ouest,* from Brittany to Flanders; Kellermann's *Armée des Alpes;* the *Armée de l'Italie,* lately under General Schérer†; and an *Armée de l'Intérieur,* primarily concerned with policing duties and the maintenance of communications. This system was continued throughout the Directory, a separate Army of Egypt being created in 1798. As First Consul, Bonaparte believed strongly in centralization of command; he sought a single French army which would concentrate on the main front while smaller units would be assigned to other regions of battle. This development was foreshadowed in the Marengo campaign† when, although there was a separate *Armée du Rhin* under Moreau and an *Armée de l'Italie* under Masséna, the principal role in the Italian offensive was assigned to a newly raised Reserve Army, of which Bonaparte personally assumed command at Lausanne on 13 May 1800. In May 1803 Bonaparte ordered the formation of an *Armée de l'Angleterre,* 160,000 strong, which was concentrated near Boulogne†, but the establishment of this force was to some extent a propaganda move, running contrary to his general policy. Between 1802 and 1805 he created the *Grande Armée†,* a single unit of some 350,000 men which doubled in size over the following seven years. Separate armies were retained for Holland, Naples, Italy and Dalmatia in the 1806 campaign and for Portugal (under Junot†) in the Peninsular campaign of 1808–9 but overall command remained with Napoleon at Imperial Headquarters (*Grand-Quartier-Général*). During the Hundred Days Napoleon had to revert to the older concept of 'front' armies; thus, while he concentrated 128,000 men in the *Armée du Nord,* there were another 54,000 men in the Armies of the Rhine (Rapp†), of the West and of the Alps. Failure to centralize command in 1815 fatally weakened Napoleon's effectiveness in the field during the days immediately after Waterloo.

ARNAULT, Antoine Vincent (1766–1834)
French dramatist, poet and biographer: born in Paris, served on Bonaparte's staff during the first Italian campaign. Subsequently he was political adviser to the French general in the Ionian Islands†. Arnault's play *Oscar* (1796) was especially popular with Bonaparte who was more critical of his classical tragedies, notably *Blanche et Montcassin, ou Les Vénitiens* (1798), a play whose last act Bonaparte advised him to rewrite, saying, 'A hero must die at the end.' Four volumes of *Fables et Poésies* reveal Arnault's skill as a satirical versifier. In the year of the Emperor's death Arnault published a *Vie politique et militaire de Napoléon*, but more interesting are the recollections of the Italian campaign and of Corfu in his *Souvenirs d'un sexagénaire* (four volumes, 1833). Loyalty to Napoleon led to Arnault's imprisonment from 1815 to 1819. He was suspended from the Académie Française, but he was fully restored to favour under the July Monarchy and was secretary of the Académie when he died, at Le Havre.

ARNDT, Ernst Moritz (1769–1860)
German patriotic writer: born the son of a farmer on the island of Rügen, then a Swedish possession. He was educated at Stralsund, Griefswald and Jena. His earliest published works were vividly written accounts of travel on foot through Germany, Italy and France in 1798–9 and through Sweden in 1804. In 1806 he returned to Griefswald as Professor of History, publishing a historical study of serfdom in Pomerania which contributed to its abolition and eventually to the Emancipation Edict† in Prussia. Arndt's reputation was made by his devastating attacks, in prose and in verse, on Napoleon personally and on French hegemony over central Europe. His call for a patriotic crusade, *Der Geist der Zeit,* appeared in three volumes, published at moments of German resistance to France, in 1806, 1809 and 1813 respectively. When Prussia was overrun in the autumn of 1806, he escaped to Stockholm, later travelling to Russia where he served as secretary to the 'German Committee' set up by Stein† in St Petersburg in August 1812. Arndt accompanied Stein and the Russian liberators of his homeland, encouraging resistance to French rule by a series of trenchant pamphlets and by such popular patriotic songs as *Was ist des Deutschen Vaterland?* and *Der Rhein, Deutschlands Strom.* He became Professor of History in the University of Bonn at its inception in 1818. Although his liberal-national sentiments were frowned upon by the Prussian authorities in the 1820s and 1830s, 'Papa Arndt' was revered as a legendary inspirer of German patriotism throughout the Metternich era and beyond.

ARRONDISSEMENT
A new administrative unit in France created by Bonaparte in the Law of 28 Pluviôse† (17 February 1800) as part of the general reform of provincial government. The arrondissement was (and remains) a district comprising some one hundred communes (the basic unit of local administration). Each département would have three or four *arrondissements*. A subprefect, appointed by the central government, served as magistrate and administrative executant in each arrondissement. Within Paris the system was different: the twelve districts became arrondissements but almost all administrative authority was reserved for the Prefecture of the Seine.

ART TREASURES, Napoleonic migration of
Napoleon's armies observed the practice, followed by other victorious invaders, of

removing by force the art treasures of conquered cities as spoils of war. The Louvre in Paris thus acquired some of the Medici collection from Florence, paintings and sculpture from papal Rome, Dutch and Flemish masterpieces, swords and other relics of Frederick the Great, Murillos from the Prado, Titians and Tintorettos from Venice, prized possessions from every city in central Europe. As early as 1796 a 'Commission for the Discovery of Artistic and Scientific Objects in Conquered Countries' was established to supervise the removal to France of cultural treasures from Italy; and this systematic enrichment of the Louvre continued until the tide of war set against France.

The most famous artistic migration was Napoleon's removal of the four bronze horses of St Mark's in Venice; they were eventually placed over the Arc de Triomphe du Carrousel at the entrance to the palace of the Tuileries. This was by no means the first journey made by the horses; they had been removed from Constantinople to Venice in 1204 after the Crusaders captured the capital of the Eastern Empire; but they seem even earlier to have been spoils of conquest, for the horses probably came from Corinth in the fourth century BC by way of Nero's accumulated loot from Greek sanctuaries.

Rather surprisingly the First Treaty of Paris† in 1814 allowed France to retain the art treasures acquired over the past twenty years, but the Second Treaty of Paris† a year later provided for the restoration to their owners of all such gains. This stipulation aroused widespread resentment in Paris. Particular hostility was shown towards the Duke of Wellington who had ordered British soldiers to protect the Dutch and Flemish pictures placed at the disposal of the King of the Netherlands. The bronze horses were taken down from the Carrousel Arch on 30 September 1815, seven weeks before the treaty was finally signed. Since the horses had been Venetian loot for 600 years, the Parisians maintained that they might as justifiably remain in Paris as return to St Mark's basilica; and the Place du Carrousel was sealed off by Austrian troops while a British officer, Major Todd, supervised the lowering of the horses by the Royal Engineers and a frightened band of civilians who were deeply conscious of the abuse being shouted by a French mob from outside the square.

Artois, Count of (1757–1836)

Later King Charles X of France: born at Versailles, the fifth grandson of the reigning sovereign (Louis XV) and a younger brother of the future kings Louis XVI and Louis XVIII†. His extravagance and resolute hostility to all reform made him unpopular in France on the eve of the great revolution and, fearing for his life, he left his homeland for Italy on 16 July 1789 accompanied by his two young sons, the Dukes of Angoulême† and Berry. Artois spent several years of his exile in England and in Scotland before returning to Paris on 12 April 1814. He acted as Regent of France from 16 April until the arrival of Louis XVIII in his capital on 3 May. Over the following ten years Artois was the recognized leader of the ultra-royalists. He was crowned, with traditional ritual, at Rheims on 29 May 1825. Charles X's attachment to the clerical party and his refusal to countenance political reform led to his downfall in July 1830. He resided in Holyroodhouse, Edinburgh, until 1832 when he settled in Bohemia; he died of cholera at Schloss Graffenberg, Gorizia (now on the Italo-Yugoslav border).

Aspern, Battle of (21–2 May 1809)

Aspern was in 1809 a village on the north bank of the Danube four miles east of Vienna, which had been captured by the French on 13 May. Napoleon was eager to bring the main Austrian army to battle in the Marchfeld, the plain north-east of the city. The Danube was successfully bridged at Lobau Island but the Austrian commander-in-chief, Archduke Charles†, launched a series of attacks against the French as they sought to establish themselves on the north bank at Aspern and the neighbouring village of Essling. On the night of 22–3 May Napoleon was forced to withdraw from the villages. He ordered the construction of defensive works on Lobau Island (which survive) and his troops did not cross the Danube again for another seven weeks. The Aspern-Essling battle was the only rebuff suffered by Napoleon's army during the Wagram campaign†; careful planning and cautious reconnaissance could have delayed an action until the bridgehead was soundly established.

AUERSTÄDT, Battle of (14 October 1806) Auerstädt lies seventeen miles north-east of Weimar and fifteen miles north of Jena†; the town is on a small tributary of the River Ilm, itself a tributary of the Saale. As Napoleon pressed northwards from the River Main towards Leipzig in the Prussian campaign† of 1806, he ordered Davout's Third Corps to converge upon the main Prussian positions from the east, so as to cut off any line of retreat. On the same day that Napoleon engaged 35,000 Prussians under Prince Hohenlohe at Jena, Davout† by chance, in a fog, encountered the centre of the Prussian army near Auerstädt. Although outnumbered (50,000 Prussians: 27,000 French) Davout gave battle once the fog lifted, his troops forming defensive squares around the village of Hassenhausen. Despite sustained attacks on their right flank from Blücher's cavalry, the French took advantage of poor coordination between the senior Prussian commanders. Mortal wounds to the Prussian commander-in-chief (the septuagenarian Duke of Brunswick†) and to another Frederican veteran, the octogenarian Field Marshal von Mollendorf, led King Frederick William III† to order a retreat towards Weimar. Davout's remarkable victory was costly, with two in five of his Third Corps killed or seriously wounded, but the joint battles of Jena-Auerstädt virtually destroyed the military might of Prussia and made certain that Napoleon would control Europe west of the River Oder. Davout was created Duke of Auerstädt in recognition of his achievement; Bernadotte†, whose corps failed to reach Auerstädt until after the battle was over, was singled out for severe censure by Napoleon.

AUGEREAU, Pierre François Charles (1757–1816)
Created Marshal of France in 1804 and Duke of Castiglione in 1808. Augereau was born of poor parents in Paris. He enlisted as a private soldier in 1774, served briefly in the ranks of the Prussian army, joined the National Guard of Paris in 1789 and was a Hussar captain by midsummer in 1793. Rapid promotion won him command of a brigade by the autumn and a division before the end of the year. He distinguished himself in Bonaparte's first Italian campaign, effectively luring the Austrian vanguard into a trap at Castiglione (5 August 1796) and leading the decisive attack at Arcole†. He was Bonaparte's principal emissary in carrying out the *coup d'état* of Fructidor† (September 1797) by which the political assemblies were purged of Bonaparte's personal enemies. Thereafter Augereau showed some political ambition himself, declining to attend the banquet which celebrated Bonaparte's precipitate return from Egypt in 1799. He remained prudently non-committal in Brumaire†. During the Consulate Augereau received no high commands but he fought with distinction in the Ulm-Austerlitz campaign† and at Jena†. His corps suffered heavily at Eylau†, where he was wounded in the arm. Failing health – rheumatism, in particular – hampered him in his fifties. He

was commandant of occupation forces in Spain and Prussia but returned as a corps commander in the field in 1813–14, fighting at Leipzig† and ending his military career with the loss of Lyons on 23 March 1814. Augereau declined to support Napoleon during the Hundred Days but subsequently displeased the restored Bourbons by refusing to condemn Ney†. In contemporary memoirs Augereau appears as a foul-mouthed braggart and stern disciplinarian but he was loyal to his men, who respected his courage and his somewhat heavy-handed camaraderie.

AUSTEN, Jane (1775–1817)
English novelist: born at Steventon in Hampshire, the sixth child of the Rector (who, for a time, had been a Fellow of St John's College, Oxford). Most of Jane Austen's education was imparted by her father, although, at the age of eight, she was sent to a school at Reading. The family lived for several years at Bath, and Jane paid visits to London, South Devon, Dorset, Warwickshire and Kent. After her father's death she settled again in Hampshire, first at Southampton and, from July 1809 to May 1817, at Chawton, a village near Alton. She died, from cancer, at Winchester and is buried in the cathedral there. Although Jane Austen began *Pride and Prejudice* as early as 1796 and both *Sense and Sensibility* and *Northanger Abbey* a year later, the final versions of all her novels were written at Chawton. *Sense and Sensibility* was published in 1811, *Pride and Prejudice* in 1813, *Mansfield Park* in 1814, *Emma* in 1816, and *Persuasion* and *Northanger Abbey* after her death. The novels mirror the ways of English country families during the Napoleonic Wars, a natural creative irony lightly satirizing the sentiments and prejudices of the society in which the Austens

"Walked back with them"

Officers of a militia regiment escort the ladies of Hertfordshire; Jane Austen's Pride and Prejudice *(Illustration by Hugh Thompson for the 1894 edition)*

lived. There are no direct references to the wars, which rarely disturbed the domesticity of rural England. Nevertheless *Persuasion* faithfully conveys some of the anxiety which her family must often have felt for two of her brothers, serving afloat as officers in the Royal Navy. Her published letters suggest a repugnance towards everything French; this antipathy may have sprung from horror at the fate of her cousin's husband, the Comte de Feuillide, who was guillotined in 1794, for as a child Jane Austen had much admired her cousin. The Prince Regent reputedly enjoyed Jane Austen's novels and gave permission for *Emma* to be dedicated to him. Unfortunately author and dedicatee never met.

AUSTERLITZ, Battle of (2 December 1805) Austerlitz is a town in Moravia, fifteen miles east of Brno and now known by its Czech name, Slavkov. The town developed as a dependency of the estate of Count Kaunitz and is famous for the 'Battle of the Three Emperors' (Napoleon, Alexander, Francis) fought on the first anniversary of Napoleon's coronation. The main battlefield stretched along five miles of the Pratzen plateau, high land three miles west of Austerlitz itself and above a valley whose ponds and marshes were covered with a deceptively thin layer of ice. Tsar Alexander, as nominal commander-in-chief of the allied armies, turned for advice mainly to the Austrian chief-of-staff, Weyrother‡, rather than to the more experienced and cautious Russian, Kutuzov‡. The Allies outnumbered the French (85,000 Allies, with 280 guns: 73,000 French, with 140 guns), but Napoleon was prepared to await an attack, confident that a moment would come when his cavalry could strike decisively at the weakened enemy centre.

Austerlitz; the Pratzen plateau

Weyrother played into Napoleon's hands. His plan committed a joint Austro-Russian force to an outflanking assault on the French line of communication at half past six in the morning. A heavy mist shrouded the battlefield until the sun broke through some two hours later. Shortly before nine o'clock Napoleon ordered Soult's cavalry to strike at the Allied centre, forcing the Tsar and his staff officers to fall back through the woods and pheasantries of the Kaunitz estate while leaving the Allied vanguard isolated above the ponds south of the Pratzen Heights. Many Russians were drowned when they were forced back on to the ice. A counter-attack by the Russian Imperial Guard, led by Grand Duke Constantine†, was a brave gesture costly in lives and causing confusion to the Austrians, as it cut across their northward line of retreat. When, soon after midday, snow began to fall, the chaos in the Allied armies increased, only Bagration† on the northern sector withdrawing his cavalry in good order.

Napoleon's victory was decisive. A third of the Allied force was killed, wounded or taken prisoner and 180 cannon captured; the French lost some 1,800 killed and 6,500 wounded. Austria sued for peace, which was signed at Pressburg† three weeks later. Tsar Alexander withdrew his shattered army behind the frontiers of his empire.

AUSTRIA

By 1792 'Austria', once an eastern dependency of Charlemagne's Empire, was the heart of the dynastic realm acquired over five centuries by the House of Habsburg, whose members had reigned in Vienna since 1278. The Habsburg lands comprised present-day Austria, Hungary, Czechoslovakia, southern Poland, western Romania, the Croat and Slovene regions of Yugoslavia, north-eastern Italy, south-western Ukraine, and a number of small isolated fiefs in Germany. Technically Belgium†, too, was still a Habsburg possession, known since 1714 as 'the Austrian Netherlands', but the French Revolution overspilled into Flanders as early as November 1789 and, although from March 1793 to June 1794 the Austrians were again masters of Belgium, Emperor Francis II† accepted exclusion from the Netherlands in the Treaty of Campo Formio† (1797). As well as these hereditary possessions, sovereignty over the 'Holy Roman Empire'† gave the ruler in Vienna paramount influence over Germany and much of Italy. It was inevitable that Austria should oppose the attempts of revolutionary France to dominate the Continent. Moreover, the fact that Queen Marie Antoinette was a sister of the emperors Joseph II (reigned 1765–90) and Leopold II (reigned 1790–2) and an aunt of Francis II (reigned 1792–1835) emphasized dynastic concern with events in Paris.

Austria was at war with France on six occasions between 1792 and 1815. Participation in the First Coalition was ended by Bonaparte's victories at Arcole† and Rivoli, culminating in the Treaty of Campo Formio†. Initial success in the War of the Second Coalition† was followed by defeat at Marengo† and Hohenlinden† (1800) and the Peace of Lunéville†. In order to bolster up the central European sovereignty of the dynasty, Francis assumed the new hereditary title, *Kaiser von Österreich* (Emperor of Austria) on 11 April 1804. Fifteen months later Austria entered the War of the Third Coalition†, seeking peace at Pressburg† after the loss of Vienna to the French on 13 November 1805 and the disastrous defeat at Austerlitz†. At Napoleon's request Francis finally renounced his title of Holy Roman Emperor on 6 August 1806. Against his better judgement Francis was induced to declare war on France in April 1809, seeking revenge for earlier humiliations. Despite army reforms under the Archduke Charles† and the famous anti-French Tyrolean rising of Hofer†, the

Austrians were defeated at Wagram† and Francis was forced to accept a harsh peace signed in his own palace of Schönbrunn†. On the advice of his new Foreign Minister, Metternich†, Francis thereafter became a nominal ally of France, with a Habsburg-Bonaparte dynastic link concluded when his daughter Marie Louise† became Napoleon's second wife in April 1810. Austria sent an auxiliary corps of 34,000 men under Schwarzenberg† to protect the right flank of the *Grande Armée* in 1812 but concluded a separate armistice with the Russians at the end of the year and again declared war against France on 12 August 1813. Austrian troops participated in the battles of Dresden† and Leipzig† and in the final invasion of France. Metternich's skilful diplomacy ensured that Francis was host to the Peace Congress at Vienna†. In the 1815 campaign an Austrian army crossed into Alsace from Baden five days after Waterloo and participated in the second occupation of Paris.

All the lands lost during the revolutionary and Napoleonic wars were restored to Austria except for Belgium, some small enclaves in southern Germany and part of Galicia. The peace settlement gave Austria in addition direct rule over Lombardy-Venetia, Istria and Dalmatia and considerable influence in the new German Confederation and in the remaining states of Italy. The Austrian Empire in 1815 was half as large again as in 1810 and second in population only to Russia among the states of Europe. A new Penal Code, a General Civil Code, imperial patronage for elementary education, and a slight relaxation of censorship held out some promise of reform in the institutions of the monarchy and there was some cultural and artistic life in the greater cities: Beethoven† and Schubert maintained Austria's musical traditions. Against these assets of the newly-shaped empire must be set the chronic financial chaos, the maintenance of an army of police and a latent problem of nationalities seeking recognition and liberal assemblies. Already Magyars, Czechs, Italians, Poles, Romanians and South Slavs were beginning to challenge the mastery of a German-Austrian aristocracy whose claims to feudal authority had been questioned during the years of Napoleonic upheaval.

Autun, Bishop of
Charles Maurice de Talleyrand-Périgord, a nephew of the Archbishop of Rheims, was ordained a priest in December 1779 and consecrated Bishop of Autun on 16 January 1789, shortly before his thirty-fifth birthday. He spent only four weeks in his Burgundian diocese, thereafter concentrating on revolutionary politics in Paris, but he continued occasionally to officiate as a bishop until he was excommunicated by Pope Pius VI in March 1801. During the years in which Talleyrand† was Napoleon's Foreign Minister and Grand Chamberlain he remained secularized, his personal enemies sometimes referring to him as the 'ex-Bishop of Autun' from malice. He was reconciled with the Church on his deathbed in 1838, insisting on receiving extreme unction with the rite prescribed for a dying bishop.

B

BAADER, Franz Xaver Benedikt von (1765-1841)

Bavarian theologian: born at Munich where he spent most of his life and where he died. He qualified as a mining engineer in Saxony but developed an intellectual curiosity over questions of religion and philosophy. A tract published in 1815 emphasized the extent to which he believed that the ideas of the French Revolution had shown Christian Europe the interdependence of religion and politics. Baader urged acceptance of the need for organic unity within a society subordinate to religious authority so as to counter the natural anarchy in man's temperament. His principal work, *Fermenta Cognitionis*, was published between 1822 and 1825 and he did not become a professor at Munich University until 1826, but his views had won him a wide following in the closing months of Napoleon's reign. Although he was technically a Catholic theologian, his theosophy satisfied the intellectual demands of Protestant philosophical Romantics while his mysticism appealed to some Orthodox Christians, notably Tsar Alexander I†. Some of Baader's ideas are reflected in the Tsar's project for a Holy Alliance†, first made public in 1815. He also influenced the pantheist poet and philosopher Schelling†, whom he first met in 1806 in Munich.

BACCIOCHI, Félix Pascal (1772–1841)

Brother-in-law of Napoleon: born at Ajaccio and served in the army in northern Italy without distinction. He was a handsome small landowner achieving nothing in life except the hand of Napoleon's eldest sister, the formidable Elisa Bonaparte†, whom he married at Marseilles on 1 May 1797. Captain Bacciochi served as commandant of the Ajaccio citadel immediately after his marriage, taking command of one of the Marseilles forts a year later and receiving the rank of colonel in an infantry regiment in 1802. He was appointed a life Senator in 1804, a dignity which, to Napoleon's relief, effectively put an end to Bacciochi's military service. He was an amateur musician who enjoyed playing the violin. From 1805 to 1814 he basked in the social advancement of his wife, willingly accepting the titles (if not the political obligations) of Duke of Lucca and Prince of Piombino, and lived in some state at Florence. After Elisa's death in 1820 Bacciochi resided, comfortably and obscurely, in Bologna. His daughter Napoleone (1806–69) married Count Camerata but had no descendants.

BADAJOZ

Spanish provincial capital and fortress on the left bank of the Guadiana River, controlling the principal southern corridor from Lisbon into central Spain. Soult† besieged a Spanish garrison in Badajoz at the end of January 1811 and secured control of the fortress for Napoleon on 9 March. An attempt by Beresford† to recapture the town early in May was abandoned within a week. Wellington† then besieged the place for a month (24 May to 19 June 1811) but he broke off operations because he lacked the sappers and heavy artillery essential for the investment of so formidable a fortress. Not until 16 March 1812 did he feel able to reimpose the siege. At last, on the night of 6–7 April, he ordered the Anglo-Portuguese army to storm the defences of Badajoz. Some forty attacks were repulsed by the French before their citadel was taken and they were forced to withdraw across the river. One in eight of the Anglo-Portuguese attackers was killed or wounded; and when Badajoz fell, the British soldiery sacked the town in three days of drunken rampage which not even the might of Wellington's authority could restrain. With the capture of Badajoz the Portuguese frontier became so secure that Wellington was able to mount his great offensive and carry the war of liberation into the heart of Spain ten weeks later.

BAGRATION, Prince Pyotr Ivanovich
(1765–1812)

Russian general: born at Kislyar in Georgia, a member of the native Caucasian nobility. He entered the Russian army in 1772 and fought against the Turks and in Poland before making his reputation for daring initiative while serving under Suvorov† in the Alps in 1799: 'My Bagration possesses a spirited presence, skill, courage and good fortune', Suvorov declared. In 1805 Bagration was commanding general of Kutuzov's cavalry, skilfully retreating along the Danube valley before Austerlitz† and parrying Murat's sustained attacks during the great battle until cut off from the main Russian army by the collapse of the centre of the line. Even so he extricated his division and was subsequently fêted in Moscow as the outstanding, heroic commander of the campaign. He distinguished himself again at both Eylau† and Friedland† as well as in the occupation of Finland† in 1808. On the eve of the 1812 campaign† Napoleon remarked that Bagration was the best of the Tsar's generals, but Alexander† distrusted his impetuosity, preferring the caution of Barclay de Tolly†. Some of Alexander's mistrust seems to have originated with an episode in 1807 when the

Bagration: the Georgian Prince idolized by Russia's soldiery

Tsar's favourite younger sister, Catherine†, became the Prince's mistress.

In the 1812 campaign Bagration commanded Russia's Second Army of the West. He evaded a trap set by Davout† at Mogilev and joined Barclay's First Army in front of Smolensk† on 16–17 August. There was much friction between the two Russian generals, Barclay rather curiously ordering the Prince back down the Dnieper so as to safeguard the road to Moscow whatever happened at Smolensk. This retreat by Bagration, together with mischievous reports of his alleged intrigues against Barclay, induced the Tsar to appoint Kutuzov† rather than either of the rivals in the field as commander-in-chief once Smolensk had fallen. At Borodino† Bagration commanded the somewhat over-extended left wing of the Russian army, under Kutuzov. Characteristically Bagration was seen on more than one occasion to applaud and exclaim 'Bravo, Bravo' at the bravery of French troops attacking the three V-shaped defensive positions known as the 'Bagration flèches'. After about four hours of fierce fighting Bagration was wounded by a bullet in the leg. At first he remained in the saddle but he soon collapsed. Rumours of his death demoralized the troops around him, for he was idolized by the soldiery who referred to him as *Bog-Rati-On* ('He is God of the Army'). The Prince survived for seventeen days after the battle, his droshky bearing him back through Moscow as the army retired eastwards. News of his death reached St Petersburg five days after the confirmation of Napoleon's entry into Moscow and intensified the capital's gloom during that last week of September.

BAILÉN
Modern Spanish name for the Andalusian town more generally known as Baylen†, where a French army capitulated on 21 July 1808.

BALASHOV, Alexander Dmitrievich
(1770–1837)
Russian general: born in Moscow and pursued a worthy, if undistinguished, military career which won him the trust of Tsar Alexander I†, particularly in the Austerlitz campaign. Nominally Balashov was Russia's first Minister of Police, appointed in August 1810 and holding the office until it was again merged in the Ministry of the Interior in 1818, but from 1812 onwards his duties were undertaken by the military commander of St Petersburg. The Tsar attached Balashov to his personal suite when war threatened in 1812, and he it was who brought Alexander the news that Napoleon had crossed the Niemen. Next day the Tsar entrusted his Minister of Police with a special mission: he was to convey a letter to Napoleon promising peace negotiations if French troops at once withdrew from Russia. Balashov was detained by Davout's† troops and, when at last he was brought into Napoleon's presence, the Emperor received him in the same room at Vilna from which Alexander had de-

spatched him five days previously. That evening Napoleon entertained Balashov to dinner; he is alleged to have asked him, 'What is the road to Moscow?' Balashov returned to Russian headquarters with a long and evasive reply to the Tsar's letter. He was one of the ministers responsible for inducing Alexander to return from the army to St Petersburg, and he subsequently had some influence on the decision to appoint Kutuzov† as commander-in-chief. From 1819 to 1824 Balashov was Governor-General of Central Russia, with his headquarters at Ryazan.

BALLET
At the end of the eighteenth century ballet, especially in France, was being transformed from the traditional court spectacle of an absolute monarchy into an independent art which combined music, movement and the dramatic unities of the theatre. Much of this revolution in entertainment had been stimulated by the teachings of the great ballet master Jean-Georges Noverre (1727–1810) who, after fleeing to England during the Terror, spent the last years of his life at Saint Germain-en-Laye. The changes were facilitated by innovations in technique, by the adoption of more natural costume in place of classical robes and masks, and by the genius of individual dancers, such as the Vestris family and Émilie Bigottini†. Although ballet was already established at court in Milan, Stockholm, St Petersburg and Stuttgart, the political emigration from France encouraged acceptance of the art form in other lands. The Swedish-born French dancer, choreographer and teacher Charles-Louis Didelot (1767–1837) influenced the growth of ballet in London and St Petersburg as well as in Paris; he made effective use of stage machinery to heighten the drama of his 'action ballet'. In Russia there was, too, a strong native element. Ivan Valberkh (1766–1819) pioneered ballets on topical themes from 1799 onwards, with strong

patriotic sentiment predominant between 1812 and 1816. The Imperial School at St Petersburg turned out dancers of asto- nishing virtuosity, notably Eugeniya Kolosova (1780–1869, in her prime 1801–11) and Avdotia Istomina (1799–1848, graduated 1815) who was immortalized by the poetic grace of Pushkin. From 1811 onwards Adam Glushkovsky (1793–1870) built up the Moscow Bolshoi Ballet. In Vienna Beethoven† composed the music for *The Creatures of Prometheus*, which was first produced at the Burgtheater on 28 March 1801, with choreography by Salvatore Vigano, a heroic-allegorical ballet dedicated to Emperor Francis's second wife and intended to boost dynastic morale after defeat in the War of the Second Coalition†. Although 'ballet pantomimes' were tolerated in Paris at the Théâtre de la Porte Saint-Martin, the Opéra was expected to offer more earnest entertainment. Pierre Gardel (1758–1840), chief ballet master at the Opéra from 1787 to 1828, was at heart a traditionalist. Moreover Napoleon held strong personal views on what Gardel should mount: 'Mythological and historical ballets may be given, but never allegorical ones', the Emperor wrote a few weeks before his marriage to Marie Louise† in 1810. *Vertumnus et Pomona* was, he complained, 'cold and tasteless'; '*The Rape of the Sabine Women . . .* is more what we want', and he added that he wished to see 'four ballets produced this year'. Gardel dutifully obliged: how otherwise could he have kept his post through forty-one years of political upheaval?

BALLOONS

In the autumn of 1783 the brothers Joseph and Étienne de Montgolfier made the first hot air balloon flights over Versailles and Paris while François Pilâtre de Rozier and the Marquis d'Arlandes ascended in a hydrogen balloon over the Tuileries on 1 December of the same year. These achievements marked the beginning of a balloon craze which fascinated the public in several European countries over the next three decades. On 7 January 1785 Jean Blanchard and John Jeffries made the first aerial crossing of the English Channel, in a Montgolfier balloon from Dover to Calais. Bonaparte's fellow cadet at the École Militaire in Paris, Alexandre de Mazis, related that two months later he accompanied his friend to the neighbouring Champ de Mars where Blanchard was planning an ascent which was repeatedly postponed. The sixteen-year-old Napoleon, who was depressed at the news of his father's death, grew impatient and cut the retaining ropes of the balloon with a knife so that it soared away, unmanned, over the rooftops of Paris. In later years Napoleon certainly shared none of the popular enthusiasm for balloons. Carnot† encouraged the use of captive balloons for military reconnaissance as early as 1794, at Maubeuge, and he subsequently attached an experimental balloon corps to the army in the field; but Bonaparte ordered the corps to be disbanded in 1800. When, in 1808, an engineer officer, L'Homond, outlined to the minister of war a project for a fleet of a hundred balloons capable of mounting an aerial invasion of Kent, carrying supplies and cavalry horses as well as soldiers, the Emperor dismissed the scheme with contempt. In 1811 a thirty-six-year-old Rhinelander, Leppich, came to Paris with plans for bombarding the enemy with explosive balloons; he was hurried out of the country as a dangerous crank. In Germany he was well treated by Count Ferdinand Zeppelin (grandfather of the eponymous airship builder) who gave Leppich an introduction to some influential compatriots at Russian headquarters. Leppich was received by Tsar Alexander at Vilna on 6 June 1812 and sent to Moscow, where Rostopchin† provided him with labourers and a workshop in which to design a dirigible balloon capable of carrying fifty men or enough explosive to destroy an army corps. Leppich failed to construct the balloon before

Balloons over the Tuileries Garden in Paris, winter of 1783–4; the beginning of the balloon craze

the French invaders reached Moscow. Although he continued research at Nizhni-Novgorod and St Petersburg, the aerial weapon never materialized.

Balloons remained interesting novelties: the English aeronaut, James Sadler, delighted thousands in London by a spectacular flight over the capital as part of the centenary celebrations of the House of Hanover on 1 August 1814. Later that year the Austrian aeronaut, Kraskowitz, ascended from the Augarten in Vienna in a balloon decorated with the national flags of all the delegates to the great Congress of peacemakers. Not until 1849 were explosive balloons used in war – by the Austrians against insurgent Italian patriots in Venice.

BANK OF FRANCE

When the Consulate was established at Christmas 1799 the French financial sys-

tem was still burdened by the legacy of the *assignats*. These bonds, based on the expected sale of confiscated lands, had been legal tender from April 1790 until May 1797, when they had sunk to less than one per cent of their face value. Bankers were thereafter reluctant to advance money to the Directory, and in the first year of the Consulate over half the national revenue was absorbed by interest charges and the liquidation of arrears. The soundest banking institution in France in 1799 was the Caisse des comptes courants, established in 1796. In order to improve the prestige of the Caisse, expand its business, and give an outward impression of financial stability, Bonaparte transformed the Caisse into the Bank of France, a private corporation founded in February 1800 with a capital of 30 million francs. The Bank handled the deposits made by the tax collectors and, by controlling the money market, reduced the interest on loans. From 1803 onwards the Bank of France had the monopoly of issuing notes. An abortive project by the banker Gabriel Ouvrard†, intended to channel the flow of Spanish American silver through France, brought the Bank into grave difficulties in the closing months of 1805. The Bank survived, but only under strict government control. Within three years it was able to cover a third of the deficit in the annual budget and it became strong enough to avoid suspending payments in the crisis years, even when the Empire fell in 1814. But the Bank of France never became so successful a wartime expedient as the Bank of England, founded a century earlier. Napoleon remained suspicious of his creation, virtually limiting the circulation of banknotes to Paris; only a small issue of notes was made at Lyons, and fewer still at Lille. Like all orthodox supporters of mercantilism, Napoleon preferred a metallic monetary system based upon cash transactions rather than a complex structure of negotiated loans and credit.

BARBÉ DE MARBOIS, François
(1745–1837)

French Minister of the Public Treasury: born at Metz, a son of the director of the royal mint in that city. He entered the foreign service in 1768 and, after serving in the German states, organized the first consular posts in America. From 1786 to 1790 he was Intendant-General of the Windward Islands, residing in Santo Domingo. He returned to Paris and survived political changes by again serving in the diplomatic service in Germany until falling foul of the Directory as an alleged crypto-royalist. In 1797 he was transported, in conditions of harsh degradation, to the penal colony of Guiana. Three years later he was allowed to return to France, but found that his wife had lost her sanity in efforts to clear his name. Fortunately he was well-connected: Barbé's sister was married to Kellermann†

and his daughter to the son of the Third Consul, Lebrun†; moreover, Barbé had known Josephine† Beauharnais during the two years she revisited her native Martinique. Rapid advancement followed his return to Paris: a post in the Ministry of Finance prepared the way for Barbé's appointment as Minister of the Public Treasury as soon as the office was created in 1801. He played a leading part in the Louisiana Purchase† negotiations, signing with James Monroe the treaty which concluded the biggest land sale in history, but he was less successful in keeping the coffers of the Bank of France† filled, his dealings with Ouvrard† threatening insolvency in the winter of 1805–6. Napoleon removed him from office (January 1806) but he survived the disgrace. In 1808 he became the first President of the Court of Accounts and in 1813 he was made a senator. A year later he was one of the imperial officials who eased the problems of a Bourbon restoration; he served Louis XVIII briefly as Minister of Justice and sat in the newly created House of Peers as a marquis. He also held office under Louis Philippe from 1830 to 1834, the year in which his unfortunate wife at last died. His span of sixty-six years' public service exceeded even that of Lafayette.

BARCLAY DE TOLLY, Mikhail (1761–1818)

Russian field marshal: born on a family estate in Livonia (Latvia), his ancestors having emigrated from Banffshire in Scotland in the seventeenth century. Barclay joined the Russian army as a boy soldier at the age of fourteen and by 1790, when he was serving against the Turks, he was recognized as a competent executive officer, a natural adjutant rather than a daring commander. In the winter of 1806–7 he attracted the attention of Tsar Alexander by his stubborn opposition to the French at Pultusk† as they advanced north of Warsaw and six weeks later he fought courageously at Eylau†. He was promoted lieutenant-general and, during the Finnish campaign of 1808, he commanded the troops who crossed the frozen Gulf of Bothnia to seize the Åland Islands from Sweden. The Tsar thought highly of Barclay's administrative skill and appointed him the first Governor-General of conquered Finland†, but in January 1810 he was brought back to St Petersburg to succeed Arakcheev† as Minister of War. Barclay sought to modernize Russia's army, building up the cavalry, raising new depot battalions of infantry and redeploying the regiments in the west so as to replace the unwieldy formations of earlier campaigns with an army corps system. When Napoleon invaded Russia in 1812 Barclay combined his ministerial duties with command of the First Army in the field, an unfortunate arrangement since he habitually delegated responsibility with only the greatest reluctance. He retreated deeper and deeper down the traditional route from Vilna to Moscow, evading a major battle until forced to fight in defence of Smolensk†. Friction with the Second Army's commander, Prince Bagration†, undermined the confidence of his fellow officers in Barclay. He handed over supreme command to Kutuzov† on 29 August but remained with the army, commanding the right flank of the defensive position at Borodino† nine days later. When Moscow was abandoned, Kutuzov sent Barclay to Kaluga on sick leave and he took no part in the winter campaign of 1812–13.

After Kutuzov's death Barclay was recalled to serve under Wittgenstein† at Bautzen† in May 1813. Soon afterwards the Tsar appointed him to succeed Wittgenstein as commander-in-chief and Barclay remained in command at the battles of Dresden†, Kulm† and Leipzig† as well as in the final campaign of 1814 in France. Alexander showed more trust in Barclay than in any other field commander; he created him a prince and awarded him his marshal's baton after the Allies entered Paris. In June 1815 Barclay concentrated an army of 168,000 men at Dresden. He began to march towards the theatre of war but had only reached the left bank of the Rhine when Waterloo decided the fate of the campaign. Barclay died at Insterburg (now Chernyakhovsk) in East Prussia in May 1818, still on active service. Barclay was not a great strategist or a brilliant tactician; he was treated with some contempt by the soldiery, who punningly nicknamed him *Boltai-da-i-tolko* ('Bark and no Bite'); but he was a methodical organizer, with qualities which were in short supply in Russian service.

BARRAS, Paul François Nicolas
(1755–1829)

French politician: born into an aristocratic family at Fox-Amphoux in Provence. He served in the colonies before the Revolution, as an officer in the Languedoc Regiment and was stationed in Pondicherry. Although a viscount in his own right, he sided with the Revolution and was elected to the Convention in 1792, voting in favour of the King's execution. He became a 'deputy on mission', an agent of the central government sent to the provinces to enforce political conformity. While 'on mission' in his native département of the Var in December 1793 Barras was impressed by the skill and courage of Major Napoleon Bonaparte at the siege of Toulon†. Subsequently Barras turned against the fanatical Jacobinism of Robespierre. He was authorized by the Convention to command the troops who arrested the Robespierrists at the Hôtel de Ville in Paris on 28 July 1794. Fifteen months later Barras was in charge of the troops assigned to put down the Vendémiaire Rising† in Paris, a task effectively accomplished by General Bonaparte with his 'whiff of grapeshot'. Thereafter Barras appeared for the next five years to be the strong man of the Revolution; he was the only member of the Directory† to hold office continuously from October 1795 until November 1799. He lived in great state in the Luxembourg Palace, maintaining a dissolute 'court' there, where

Barras, in the official uniform of the Directory

'the most infamous debauchery was openly practised'. Josephine† Beauharnais was his mistress although he encouraged Bonaparte to marry her in March 1796. As one of the ruling Directors Barras became immensely rich. When the Directory became unpopular he tried to safeguard his influence by offering support to Bonaparte on the eve of Brumaire†, but the General distrusted him. Barras was induced to resign office in return for a guarantee of his life and property; on the morning of 10 November 1799 a cavalry detachment escorted Barras from the Luxembourg to his country estate of Grosbois. For the last thirty years of his life Barras remained a spectator of events, enjoying the wealth he had accumulated during his years of power. Contemporary memoirists handled him harshly: Marmont† complained that he combined the vices of the old order with the corruption

of the new; and Carnot† said that he 'masked Caligula's ferocity behind a carefully assumed casualness of manner'. Barras himself wrote Memoirs in his last years, belittling Bonaparte, but they were not published until 1895–6 and by that date advances in historical criticism, and the opening of the archives, exposed his fabrications.

BARTENSTEIN, Convention of
(26 April 1807)
A Russo-Prussian treaty concluded by Tsar Alexander I and King Frederick William III in East Prussia so as to associate their two realms in alliance against Napoleon following the indecisive battle of Eylau†. Alexander pledged himself to insist that, in any peace treaty with France, Prussia should receive back her 1805 boundaries or equivalent compensation elsewhere in Germany. The two monarchs undertook to work for the establishment of a German federation with a military frontier along the Rhine and under joint Austro-Prussian protection. The Convention was soon outdated by Napoleon's victory at Friedland† and the Peace of Tilsit†; but Bartenstein has a double historical significance: it emphasized a special relationship between the Romanov and Hohenzollern dynasties which was to endure far longer than Napoleon's Europe; and it outlined for the first time a different political structure for the future of the German lands.

BASLE
Swiss city known in German as Basel and in French as Bâle. The peace treaty of Basle of April 1795 marked the end of Prussian participation in the War of the First Coalition†. Basle remained outside the theatre of military operations until the closing weeks of the year 1813, the Swiss hoping that the anti-Napoleonic Allies would respect their assertions of neutrality. Schwarzenberg†, however, induced

Metternich† to send an ultimatum on 19 December demanding passage for Austrian troops through Basle so as to advance into France by way of the Belfort Gap and the Langres plateau. Although the Swiss met the Austrian demand and Schwarzenberg's army traversed Basle on 21–2 December, Metternich's allies were alarmed, believing that Austria had designs on the German-speaking cantons of Switzerland. Alexander I insisted on travelling to Basle and setting up Allied headquarters in the city during the second week of January 1814 so as to preclude any unilateral action by the Austrians. He stayed at Basle only briefly, leaving headquarters to be with his troops on 16 January. Two days later Castlereagh† arrived at Basle after a three week journey from England, the first occasion on which a British Foreign Secretary travelled to the Continent for a summit conference. The Tsar's restless behaviour meant that the first inter-Allied discussions took place without Russian participation, Metternich and Castlereagh forming a close partnership which tended throughout the remainder of the campaign and the subsequent peacemaking to treat the Russo-Prussian combination with suspicion. The Anglo-Austrian talks in Basle continued until the two foreign ministers crossed into France on 22–3 January.

Bassano, Battle of (8 September 1796) The town of Bassano del Grappa lies on the River Brenta nineteén miles northeast of Vicenza. In the autumn of 1796 Bonaparte, pursuing the Austrian commander Würmser down the Brenta valley, attempted to trap the enemy at Bassano by sending Augereau† to envelop the town from the east and Masséna† from the west while Lannes† (then a colonel) and Murat's cavalry led a frontal assault on Bassano itself. Although Würmser escaped, the battle was a disaster for the Austrians, Bonaparte taking over 3,500 prisoners together with 35 cannon, 220 wagons and 2 pontoon bridge trains. On the following day Masséna's division took Vicenza and Augereau occupied Padua. Würmser rallied the survivors of his army and forced his way through to beleaguered Mantua†, where he assumed command of the defences.

Batavian Republic: see *Holland*.

Bathurst, Henry, 3rd Earl (1762–1834) British politician: born in Gloucestershire, the son of North's Lord Chancellor, and educated at Christ Church, Oxford. He was MP for Cirencester from 1793 to 1794 when he succeeded to the earldom. In 1807 he entered the cabinet as President of the Board of Trade, a post he held until September 1812. From October to December in 1809 he was also Foreign Secretary, in Perceval's government. When Liverpool formed his government in June 1812 he appointed Bathurst Secretary for War and Colonies, an office he retained until April 1827. He worked closely with Wellington during the Peninsular War and deputized for Castlereagh† when the Foreign Secretary was on the Continent in 1814, 1815 and 1818. Bathurst's colonial responsibilities gave him authority to determine the conditions of Napoleon's detention on St Helena. Critics – notably the Holland House† set – thought his parliamentary style jocularly irresponsible. His fifteen years at 'War and Colonies' were commemorated by settlement names in Canada, West Africa and Australia, where the town of Bathurst (west of the Blue Mountains, New South Wales) was founded in 1815.

Bausset, Baron de (Louis François Joseph de Bausset-Roquefort, 1770–1830) Prefect of the Imperial Palace: born at Béziers, emigrated in the Revolution but returned with the establishment of the

Consulate and settled at Lyons, where he wrote a couple of comedies. On 1 February 1805 he was appointed Chamberlain and Prefect of the Palace. Three months later he accompanied Napoleon to Milan for his coronation† as King of Italy. During Marie Louise's journey from Austria (March 1810) Bausset was responsible for her personal comfort. In September 1812 he arrived at Napoleon's bivouac on the eve of the battle of Borodino† bringing a portrait by Gérard† of Napoleon's seventeen-month-old son; the Emperor placed the painting outside his tent, where it was respectfully admired by the Old Guard. Bausset arranged Napoleon's accommodation in Moscow†, both before and after the fire, and requisitioned a private theatre in the Poznyakov mansion, where eleven performances of a Marivaux comedy were mounted to entertain the occupying army. After Napoleon's first abdication†, Bausset accompanied Marie Louise back to Vienna and remained in her service until she was established in Parma. He returned to France in March 1816 and spent his last years in local government near his birthplace. His four volumes of *Mémoires anecdotiques*, published in 1827, cover the events of the period from 1805 to 1814 in fascinating detail.

BAUTZEN, Battle of (20–21 May 1813)
Nowadays Bautzen is a manufacturing town in the German Democratic Republic, standing on the River Spree thirty-two miles north-east of Dresden. In 1813 Bautzen was a walled cathedral city in Saxony, held by Russian and Prussian forces under Wittgenstein† and faced by Napoleon's new Army of the Elbe, which was advancing eastwards after checking the Russo-Prussian invasion of Germany at Lützen† on 2 May. Napoleon sought to engage the main defenders of Bautzen in the marshes and fortified woodland on the right bank of the Spree until Ney† and Lauriston† could strike southwards.

Oudinot was to complete the envelopment with an assault on the left of the Allied position. The French were robbed of total success by the slowness of Ney's column and by their lack of cavalry. The Russians and Prussians retreated towards Silesia but the French were unable to pursue them effectively. Austrian mediation brought an armistice (2 June to 17 August): the battles of Dresden† and Kulm† followed the resumption of hostilities.

BAVARIA
Historically Bavaria was the largest German Roman Catholic state outside the Habsburg empire. From 1180 to 1918 the Wittelsbach dynasty ruled in Bavaria, originally as Dukes, from 1623 to 1806 as Electors, and from December 1805 to November 1918 as Kings. Throughout the Napoleonic era the ruler was Maximilian Joseph (1756–1825) who became Elector of Bavaria and Elector Palatine on 16 February 1799. Bavarian troops under General Wrede† fought against the French in 1799–1800 but after the decisive battle of Hohenlinden† they were left to strike the best possible bargain with the victorious French. In August 1801 Max Joseph signed a treaty with Napoleon which guaranteed Bavaria's territories on the right bank of the Rhine while promising Bavaria compensation in the south for lost possessions on the left bank. This agreement set the pattern for twelve years of Franco-Bavarian collaboration, largely at the expense of Austria. A Bavarian army, 25,000 strong, helped France in the Austerlitz campaign; Bavaria received the Tyrol, Vorarlberg and some ecclesiastical lands as a reward for victory, by the Treaty of Pressburg†. Napoleon encouraged Max Joseph to assume a crown; he became King Maximilian I† on 26 December 1805 and joined the Confederation of the Rhine† when it was established in the following summer. The marriage of Max Joseph's daughter, Auguste, to Napo-

leon's stepson, Eugène Beauharnais†, in January 1806 strengthened the Franco-Bavarian alliance. Within Bavaria these were years of reform: new administrative departments of government were set up in 1806 and a single chamber legislature in 1808; a legal code, based on the Napoleonic model, was enacted in 1810; a succession of edicts (1802, 1803, 1805 and 1808) gradually abolished serfdom; and even the predominantly Catholic structure of the state was modified, with the activities of the religious orders curbed in 1804 and the privileged influence of the church on educational policy challenged by further reforms in 1809. During Napoleon's Wagram campaign the Bavarians gained an early victory over the Austrians on the River Inn (19–20 April 1809) but were then fully engaged with quelling the revolt of Andreas Hofer† in the Tyrol. By the Treaty of Schönbrunn† Bavaria received Salzburg, Berchtesgaden and further lands along the Inn.

The Sixth Corps (Gouvion-Saint-Cyr†) of the *Grande Armée†* in 1812 was predominantly Bavarian and fought with distinction in the battles of Polotsk†, again under Wrede's command. Fourteen squadrons of Bavarian cavalry fought under Eugène Beauharnais at Borodino†. Bavarian contingents also supported Napoleon in the early phases of the 1813 campaign. However, on 8 October, Bavaria concluded the Treaty of Ried with Austria: in return for recognition of his royal title, Max Joseph withdrew from the Confederation of the Rhine, and by the end of the month Wrede was leading a joint Austro-Bavarian army against Napoleon as he fell back on the River Main. The Bavarians were badly mauled at Hanau but participated in the invasion of France in 1814. Although Bavaria was forced to return Salzburg, the Tyrol and the Vorarlberg to Austria at the Congress of Vienna, Max Joseph consolidated his kingdom's position as the South German Catholic counterweight to Prussia in the new German Confederation.

Baylen (Bailén), Battle of (19 July 1808) When a national uprising in Spain began in late May 1808, General Pierre Dupont (1765–1840) found that his corps in Andalusia was cut off by an army of 30,000 men raised by the Seville Junta and commanded by General Francisco Castaños†. Dupont's corps was trapped near the town of Baylen, a key position on the road through the Sierra Morena to Madrid, some 200 miles to the north. After making five assaults on Baylen (which was held by the Spanish General, Reding), Dupont's men were caught in the rear by Castaños. Dupont opened negotiations with the Spaniards and on 21 July he capitulated on favourable terms. Some 17,500 Frenchmen surrendered: senior officers were allowed to return to France on parole; most of the men were imprisoned under harsh conditions, and only one in seven survived the ordeal. Dupont's capitulation was a serious blow to French prestige. Resistance movements were encouraged not only in Spain but in central Europe. Castaños's victory induced Joseph Bonaparte† to retreat precipitately from Madrid, where he had recently arrived as King. In the late autumn Napoleon decided he would himself assume command in Spain, but the Spaniards exaggerated the triumph of Baylen; Castaños possessed numerical superiority while Dupont's men were raw conscripts fresh from the depots. Mistakenly the Spaniards assumed that they could win pitched battles against Napoleon's crack regiments; this was a disastrous delusion.

Bayonne

Chief port of the French Basque country, on the river Adour twenty miles north of the Spanish frontier. Bayonne, commanding the main route along the western edge of the Pyrenees, was protected by three fortresses whose defences were devised by the great Vauban in the late seventeenth century. Napoleon used Bayonne as his advance base for operations in Spain. He was there himself from April to July 1808, summoning the Bourbon King of Spain, Charles IV†, and his son, Ferdinand VII†, into his presence at the Château de Marracq and there inducing them to surrender the Spanish crown into French keeping. After long conferences in the Bonaparte family, Napoleon had his elder brother Joseph Bonaparte† proclaimed 'King of Spain and the Indies' at Bayonne on 6 June 1808. The Spanish insurrection forced Napoleon to return to Bayonne on 3 November 1808 and set out on a twelve-week campaign to restore order south of the Pyrenees. Wellington's Peninsular Army reached Bayonne on 9 December 1813 but found the fortresses too powerful for frontal assault. Wellington† duly mounted a siege of the garrison while continuing to pursue Soult† towards Bordeaux. The Governor of Bayonne, General Pierre Thouvenot (1757–1817), maintained resistance to the British even after Napoleon's abdication. Thouvenot only surrendered after making a dramatic and devastating night raid on the besiegers, on 27 April 1814.

BEAUHARNAIS, Eugène Rose de
(1781–1824)
Prince-Viceroy of Italy and stepson of Napoleon I: born in Paris, the son of General the Vicomte Alexandre de Beauharnais (1760–94) and Josephine†. Eugène showed great courage as a boy, effectively protecting his mother and his sister, Hortense (*see below*), after his father's execution during the Terror. He began his military career at the age of fourteen as an orderly to General Hoche in the Vendée†. Eugène's stepfather secured a commission for him in the Hussars in July 1797 and he served as Bonaparte's aide-de-camp in Italy before participating in the Egyptian and Syrian campaigns. Eugène's tact, loyalty and good manners frequently enabled him to reconcile his mother and stepfather. He was in close attendance on Bonaparte during the *coup*

Eugène de Beauharnais, Viceroy of Italy, Napoleon's stepson

of Brumaire† and distinguished himself eight months later as a cavalry captain at Marengo†. In June 1804 he was created a Prince and, at Napoleon's coronation, was Colonel-General of the Guard. Soon afterwards he was promoted to General of Brigade, appointed Arch-Chancellor of State and finally Viceroy of Italy (June 1805). He was a hard worker, ruthless in expecting high standards of administration from subordinate officials; at times he was reproached by Napoleon for his excessive bureaucratic diligence. In January 1806 Eugène married the eldest daughter of the King of Bavaria, Princess Auguste (1788–1851). He was created Prince of Venice in December 1807. He resumed his military career in 1809 as commander-in-chief of the Army of Italy and he fought with courage and initiative at Wagram†. In 1812 he commanded the Fourth Corps of the *Grande Armée†*, fighting at Smolensk† and Borodino† and showing enterprise in capturing Maloyaroslavets†. He succeeded Murat† in command of the rump of the *Grande Armée* in January 1813, retreating slowly from Posen across the Oder and the Elbe so as to join the new forces raised by Napoleon in time for the Battle of Lützen† (2 May 1813). He never saw his stepfather again after Lützen, spending the next eleven months trying to save Italy for the French Empire and refusing an offer from the Allies by which they would have supported him as King of Italy if he deserted Napoleon. Eugène returned to Paris, was received by Louis xviii at the Tuileries while Napoleon was on Elba, and attended the Congress of Vienna. He retired to Munich and was created Duke of Leuchtenberg and Prince of Eichstätt by his father-in-law. In 1818 he appealed in person to Tsar Alexander i to seek an improvement in the conditions of Napoleon's confinement on St Helena. During his final years Eugène was preoccupied with marriage politics: Princess Josephine, the eldest of his seven children, married Prince Oscar, the son of Bernadotte, and was Queen Consort of Sweden from 1844 to 1859. Eugène suffered the first of a series of strokes at Easter 1823 and died in the Palais Leuchtenberg at Munich eleven months later, at the early age of forty-one.

Hortense de Beauharnais, Queen of Holland

Beauharnais, Hortense Eugénie Cécile (1783–1837)

Queen of Holland, stepdaughter and sister-in-law of Napoleon i: was born in Paris, a sister of Eugène Beauharnais (*see above*). As a child, she was a favourite of Napoleon who delighted in showing off her natural charm and versatility. She sketched, painted and composed music: her marching song, *Partant pour la Syrie*, eventually became the national anthem of the Second Empire. In January 1802 she dutifully married Louis Bonaparte†, the third brother of Napoleon. Their union was not happy although Hortense gave birth to three children, the youngest of whom was Charles Louis Napoleon (1808–73) who reigned as the Emperor Napoleon iii from 1852 to 1870. When Louis Bonaparte became King of Holland in June 1806, Hortense spent only a few months with him at The Hague and did not return to the Netherlands until April 1810, less than three months before her husband's sudden abdication. Hortense then retired to Aix-les-Bains where she became the mistress of Count Charles de Flahaut†, the natural son of Talleyrand. In October 1811 Hortense gave birth to a son, of whom Flahaut was the father, at a villa on Lake Maggiore; forty years later he helped plan the *coup d'état* of his half-brother and, as the Duke de Morny (1811–65) held influential posts under the Second Empire. Hortense remained loyal to her mother and to Napoleon. She was with Josephine at Malmaison† in her final illness and was much admired by Tsar Alexander i who persuaded Louis xviii to create her Duchess of Saint-Leu on 30 May 1814. During the Hundred Days† Hortense was virtually the First Lady of France, acting as state hostess for her stepfather in the absence of the Empress Marie Louise. She also gave him refuge at Malmaison for five days after his defeat at Waterloo. Her brave refusal to desert her stepfather forced her into exile after the second Restoration. She eventually settled at Arenenberg, a Swiss lakeside château some six miles west of Constance. She travelled widely, often in the company of the future Emperor, with whom she visited London in the summer of 1831. Six years later she died at Arenenberg. Her fascinating and honest memoirs, written between 1816 and 1820, were not published until 1927.

BEAUHARNAIS, Marie Rose Joséphine de: see *Josephine, Empress of the French.*

BEAUHARNAIS, Stéphanie Louise Adrienne de (1789–1860)
Princess: was born in Paris, a daughter of a first cousin of Josephine's husband. She was therefore a second cousin of Eugène and Hortense de Beauharnais but she was generally known as Josephine's niece. When the Empire was established, Stéphanie was treated with special favour by Napoleon who used her as a pawn in his dynastic marriage diplomacy. In April 1806 she was married to Prince Karl of Zähringen, who succeeded his grandfather as Grand Duke of Baden in 1811. The marriage was not a success; Napoleon sent irate messages to Mannheim reproving Stéphanie for 'petty acts of rebellion' against her husband's social regimen. To Napoleon's dismay, Stéphanie was never able to influence Baden's policy; and the Grand Duke seceded from the Confederation of the Rhine† when fortune swung against the French in the autumn of 1813. Stéphanie outlived her husband by forty-two years.

BEETHOVEN, Ludwig van (1770–1827)
Born in Bonn but settled in Vienna in 1792 and spent the remaining years of his life there. Among his compositions were the opera *Fidelio* (1805), nine symphonies, thirty-two piano sonatas, sixteen string quartets, five piano concerti, ten violin sonatas, two settings of the Mass, an oratorio, a ballet and other theatre music. He depended on the patronage of the Viennese nobility, notably Archduke Rudolf (1788–1831, youngest brother of Emperor Francis† and Cardinal-Archbishop of Olmütz from 1819) and Prince Franz Josef von Lobkowitz. Beethoven at first admired Consul Bonaparte's genius as reformer and man of action. In 1803 Beethoven began to compose his third symphony, conceived on a grander scale than previous work and breaking with tradition by projecting the composer's personality through the discipline of classical form. The score was at first dedicated to Bonaparte, but when Beethoven heard that the First Consul had declared himself Emperor he ripped out

Ludwig van Beethoven

the dedicatory page, exclaiming, 'So he, too, is no more than an ordinary man.' He substituted the new title, 'Heroic Symphony, composed to celebrate the memory of a great man'. This great work, the *Eroica*, was first heard privately in the Lobkowitz Palace and was performed in public for the first time at the Theater an der Wien on 7 April 1805. It was not published until September 1806, ten months after the original dedicatee had entered Vienna at the head of a victorious army.

From 1801 onwards Beethoven was troubled by deafness, but he continued to compose and conduct. His *Wellington's Victory* in 1813 celebrated the fall of Vitoria and quoted national airs. Beethoven personally conducted a performance of this work at a gala concert on 29 November 1814 attended by the Tsar, the King of Prussia and other delegates to the Vienna Congress.

BELGIUM

After the War of the Spanish Succession (1701–14) the Belgian provinces were placed under Habsburg rule and were known as the Austrian Netherlands from 1714 until 1790. An anti-Austrian movement, seeking self-government, triumphed in Brussels in December 1789, but in November 1792 Belgium was occupied by a French army. Apart from fourteen months in 1793–4, when the Austrians recovered their authority, the French remained in occupation until February 1814, formally annexing the provinces in October 1795. Although there was a Flemish revolt against conscription in 1798, no serious national movement challenged French primacy during the Consulate and Empire. Belgian industry benefited from participation in the Continental System†, the towns of Verviers and Ghent flourishing in particular. The former bishopric of Liège, which had enjoyed autonomy under the Austrians, became fully integrated with the other Belgian provinces during the Napoleonic period, largely because it was in character the most naturally French region in the southern Netherlands and could therefore provide Napoleon with his local officials. Yet, despite the linguistic Frenchification of government and popular education, most Belgians remained apathetic over issues of political sovereignty. During the peace negotiations of 1813–14 between Caulaincourt† and the Allies, Napoleon insisted that Belgium would have to remain French as it lay within France's 'natural frontiers'. Austria† and Russia were willing to accept this stipulation but Castlereagh†, for Britain, consistently rejected any peace terms which would have left Antwerp a French port. The first Treaty of Paris† (1814) renounced French claims to Belgium; a protocol concluded by the Great Powers on 21 June 1814 provided for the union of Belgium and Holland† in a Kingdom of the United Netherlands. The vulnerability of France's northern frontier to any invading army ensured that Wellington concentrated his forces on Belgian territory in 1815, a move which confirmed the French desire, during the Hundred Days†, to recover the line of the Rhine and Scheldt. Napoleon's defeat at Waterloo ensured that Belgium continued to be 'Dutchified'. Independence came in October 1830.

BELLEROPHON

The three-decker 74 gun ship-of-the-line HMS *Bellerophon*, veteran of the Nile and Trafalgar, was ordered to patrol off the Charente estuary (see *Rochefort*) on 7 July 1815 when it was thought Napoleon might seek to escape by fast frigate to America. On 10 July Napoleon sent Las Cases† to negotiate with *Bellerophon*'s commander, Captain Frederick Maitland (1777–1839). Napoleon's inclination to seek asylum from his British enemy may have been encouraged by Maitland, an officer of Whig sympathies who had been received in audience by the First Consul

Napoleon, aboard HMS Bellerophon, *watches the coast of France recede, 23 July 1815, from the painting by W. Q. Orchardson*

on 6 October 1802 (during the Peace of Amiens) and who dined at Holland House† shortly before taking command of *Bellerophon*. Maitland nevertheless made it clear that he had no authority to offer any guarantees to the fallen Emperor. Napoleon boarded *Bellerophon* on 15 July; he was well received and became popular with the crew. The ship anchored in Torbay on 24 July and entered Plymouth Sound three days later. Her presence there excited great interest; Maitland himself reckoned that 8,000 people swarmed in hired boats around his ship on Sunday, 30 July, many of them cheering Napoleon when he came on deck. She remained off Plymouth until 4 August. By then Napoleon had learnt that his plea for asylum in England was unacceptable. *Bellerophon* was ordered to sea and on 7 August, some 50 miles south of Start Point, Napoleon was transferred to HMS *Northumberland*, which had sailed hurriedly from Portsmouth to convey him to St Helena†.

BENNIGSEN, Levin August (1745–1826)
Russian general: born in Brunswick and served at first in the Hanoverian army. He entered Russian service in 1773 and fought with distinction in Catherine the Great's wars against Turkey. Tsar Paul's capricious changes of policy exasperated Bennigsen, who played a prominent part in the conspiracy which led to Paul's murder. Alexander I† made Bennigsen Governor-General of Lithuania and, in November 1806, he appointed him effective commander in the field, formally confirming his military primacy two months later after Russia's success at Pultusk†. Bennigsen claimed that Eylau† (8 February 1807) was a strategic victory for Russia since the French could not exploit their tactical gains after the battle. Nothing, however, could conceal the reality of Bennigsen's defeat at Friedland† (14 June 1807). He was present at Tilsit† and was among the senior Russian officers personally decorated by Napoleon as a gesture of reconciliation. By 1812 Bennig-

sen was living in retirement on his Lithuanian estate of Zakret, some two miles east of Vilna. On 24 June 1812 he was host of a grand ball at Zakret, where news was brought to the Tsar of Napoleon's invasion. Bennigsen remained in close attendance on Alexander during the early stages of the campaign and the Tsar appointed him chief-of-staff to Kutuzov† before Borodino†. It was an unsatisfactory partnership: Bennigsen complained that Kutuzov kept too far away from the action to see how a battle unfolded; Kutuzov pretended he could not remember his chief-of-staff's name ('Where is that imbecile, that red-head?'). In late October Bennigsen (like Barclay† before him) was sent on sick leave to Kaluga. He returned to service in May 1813 when he licked new divisions into shape as the Army of Poland. These men he marched through Silesia so as to support Barclay's right flank at Leipzig†, where Alexander commended his initiative. For most of the winter of 1813–14 Bennigsen conducted operations along the Elbe, finishing the war harassing Davout† in Hamburg. He retired from the Russian army in 1820 and settled in Hanover for the last six years of his life.

BENTHAM, Jeremy (1748–1832)

British jurist: born in east London, educated at Westminster School and Queen's College, Oxford, and called to the bar at Lincoln's Inn. He did not go into practice but devoted his intellectual energies to the philosophical problems of jurisprudence and the practical need to reform criminal law. His *Fragment on Government* (1776) was followed in 1789 by his *Introduction to the Principles of Morals and Legislation* and by a series of works on prison discipline. He was the first 'philosophical radical', a Utilitarian who believed in 'the greatest happiness of the greatest number' and who argued that punishment was an evil necessity justified only as a means of checking greater evils.

BENTINCK, Lord William Cavendish (1774–1839)

British soldier and diplomat: the second son of the third Duke of Portland. He was educated at Westminster School and entered the army in 1791 but, after serving under the Duke of York, resigned his commission in 1794. For most of the period 1796–1827 he sat as a Whig MP, except when serving overseas. From 1799 to 1801 he was attached as an observer to the Russian and Austrian armies. Two years later he was appointed Governor in Madras, but he was recalled in 1807 when he was held responsible for a grave mutiny at Vellore. He then returned to active service in Portugal and Spain, but in 1811 he was sent to Sicily as military commander-in-chief in the Mediterranean and envoy to the court of the Bourbon King of Naples, Ferdinand IV†. Bentinck, a vain and ambitious man, behaved at Palermo as though he were a proconsul, embarrassingly independent of the government in London. He induced Ferdinand to grant a constitution on the British model and to send his consort, Maria Carolina, into exile in her Austrian homeland. Bentinck then planned to take a Sicilian expeditionary force to 'liberate' the Italian mainland, but he suddenly changed his plans, sought an accommodation with Murat† and led his Anglo-Sicilian force to Spain (where it was badly mauled at Ordal, 13 September 1813). A month later Bentinck returned to Sicily and, while remaining in secret contact with Murat, called on the people of the peninsula to rise and form a free and united Italy. He also misleadingly gave an assurance of independence to Genoa† although Allied policy favoured the integration of the city in Piedmont. Castlereagh† recalled Bentinck in July 1814 and he was out of public office until 1827, when he became Governor of Bengal. From 1833 to 1835 he was Governor-General of India. He died in Paris in June 1839.

BÉRANGER, Pierre Jean de (1780–1857)
French poet, specializing in light verse:
born and died in Paris. By trade Béranger
was a printer and began writing satirical,
sentimental and occasionally ribald verses
during the Peace of Amiens. Lucien
Bonaparte† secured him a small pension
in 1804 and in 1809 he was appointed to a
minor clerical post at the university†.
These emoluments enabled him to continue bringing out verses which were extremely popular and frequently set to
music. His best known song, *Le Roi
d'Yvetot*, affectionately mocked an easy-
going ruler who set up pleasure as his code
of law. It was first sung at the Parisian
vaudeville club, *Le Caveau moderne*, in
the spring of 1813. His collected songs and
poems appeared in book form as *Chansons morales et autres* in 1815. Six years
later a sequel, *Chansons, deuxième re-
cueil*, ridiculed the ultra-royalists of the
Restoration; the publication earned
Béranger a term in prison and the loss of
his clerical post. When, in 1828, he produced the sentimentally Bonapartist
Chansons inédites he was imprisoned for
nine months and heavily fined. Harassment increased his popularity. With
Chansons nouvelles et dernières in 1833
Béranger became the most widely read
poet in France. More than any other
individual, Béranger lifted Napoleon
down from the pedestal of history to the
folklore of the next generation.

BERESFORD, Lord (William Carr, first
Viscount Beresford, 1764–1854)
British soldier: born in Ireland, an illegitimate son of the Marquis of Waterford. He
attended the military school at Strasbourg
briefly and saw action with the 69th Regiment of Foot at Toulon and in Corsica
before commanding the Connaught Ran-
gers in the West Indies in 1795. After
service in India he participated in the
colonial campaigns which captured the
Cape of Good Hope (January 1806) and
the Spanish colonial settlements at

Buenos Aires and Montevideo in 1806–7.
He was then promoted major-general and
appointed Governor of Madeira in the
name of the King of Portugal. This experience induced Beresford to learn Portuguese, a skill which made him indispens-
able to Moore† and Wellington† in the
Peninsular campaigns. From March 1809
until June 1814 he trained and commanded the Caçadores regiments of the Portuguese army, fighting alongside them at
Badajoz† and Albuera† and enjoying the
status of a Portuguese field marshal. He
was a better administrator than tactician;
disputes over his role at Albuera clouded
his later days. He fought under Wellington at Vitoria and, after the end of the
Napoleonic Wars, helped John VI of Portugal to put down rebellions in his Brazi-
lian Empire. From 1828 to 1830, during
the premiership of his friend Wellington,
Beresford was Master-General of the
Ordnance.

BEREZINA, Crossing of the
(26–9 November 1812)
The Berezina, a tributary of the Dnieper,
was a formidable obstacle to the *Grande
Armée* as it retreated across Byelorussia.
The only bridge on the Smolensk-Vilna
road was destroyed by the Russians at
Borisov†, ahead of the retreating French.
Oudinot's† patrols found a point at
Studenka, some seven miles north of
Borisov, where in normal weather the
Berezina could be forded. Flooding
caused by a brief thaw made this impassable, but when Napoleon reached the left
bank of the river in the early hours of 25
November, General Éblé† and his sappers
were able to begin work on two pontoon
bridges, under an intermittent blizzard.
They had to work speedily because two
Russian armies (under Chichagov† and
Wittgenstein†) were converging on the
river. By the afternoon of 26 November
the bridges were in position but the weight
of artillery caused one of them to collapse
on two occasions. By 28 November Mar-

The crossing of the Berezina; a contemporary print depicts the trestle bridges and the chaos on the banks of the icy, swollen river

shal Victor†, with the rearguard, was desperately fighting off assaults from Wittgenstein's advance troops as well as raids by Cossack patrols. Éblé was forced to destroy the bridges on the morning of 29 November before the stragglers and camp-followers had crossed. By then more than 50,000 men had safely reached the right bank so as to continue the retreat on Vilna†. The skill and ingenuity of the French engineers denied Chichagov and Wittgenstein a decisive victory; but the Russians found 13,000 frozen corpses beside the river and the remains of an even larger number of horses.

BERLIN

The city was founded in the thirteenth century, became capital of the Electorate of Brandenburg at the end of the fifteenth century and capital of the new Kingdom of Prussia in 1701. After his victories at Jena† and Auerstädt†, Napoleon entered Berlin in triumph on 27 October 1806, his troops marching through the newly completed Brandenburg Gate. He remained in residence until 25 November, subsequently appointing Count Daru† as the chief administrative officer of the army of occupation. The people of Berlin received from their French occupiers the benefits of municipal self-government; considerable freedom was granted to academics and intellectuals, Fichte† even delivering in Berlin his famous 'Addresses to the German Nation' in 1807–8, under French occupation. Frederick William III† and Queen Louise† returned to their capital on 23 December 1809 and fostered the nascent intellectualism by supporting the reforms of Wilhelm von Humboldt† and the establishment in 1810 of Berlin university. Arndt† and Jahn† harnessed the wild romantic nationalism of young Berliners so that it served Frederick William's call to arms in March 1813 when the Prussians volunteered for service in the War of Liberation.

BERLIN DECREE (21 November 1806).
In the third week after his triumphant
entry into Berlin Napoleon issued the first
of a series of decrees aimed at ending all
trade between Great Britain and the Continent. He declared that the British Isles
were under blockade and that no vessel
coming directly from Britain or a British
colony would be permitted to trade in any
port under his control. This pronouncement, followed by the Milan Decrees† a
year later, formed the basis of the Continental System†.

BERNADOTTE, Désirée (Eugénie Bernar-
dine Désirée Clary, 1777–1860)
Later Queen Desideria of Sweden and
Norway: born at Marseilles, the younger
daughter of François Clary, a wealthy silk
merchant. Désirée's sister Julie married
Joseph Bonaparte† in August 1794. Napoleon, on St Helena, described Désirée as
his 'first love'; they met early in 1794 and
marriage was discussed in May 1795 but,
writing from Paris later in the summer,
Bonaparte broke with Désirée whom he
considered too young and unsophisti-
cated. Désirée was betrothed to General
Jean Pierre Duphot, who was assassinated
in her presence at Rome on 27 December
1797. In the following August she married
General Bernadotte (*see below*) at
Sceaux. A son was born in Paris in July
1799 and named Oscar at the suggestion of
his godfather, Bonaparte, who had encountered the name in his current
favourite reading, the Ossian epic as
translated by Cesarotti†. After her husband's election as Crown Prince of
Sweden, Désirée travelled to Stockholm
in December 1810 but found court etiquette so inhibiting that she returned to
Paris in June 1811. Throughout the crisis
years of the Empire and the Restoration
the 'Crown Princess of Sweden' lived in
Bernadotte's old house in the Rue d'An-
jou. She only returned to Sweden in the
spring of 1823, five years after her husband's accession. Queen Desideria was

crowned in Stockholm on 21 August 1829.
She survived King Charles XIV John by
sixteen years and her son, Oscar I, by
eighteen months.

**BERNADOTTE, Jean-Baptiste Jules, Mar-
shal of the Empire, later Charles XIV John
of Sweden and Norway** (1763–1844)
Born at Pau, the son of a lawyer, enlisted
in 1780 and was a sergeant-major when
the Revolution began, nicknamed *Belle
Jambe* ('Pretty Leg'). He was commissioned in 1791, became a colonel in 1792
and a general in October 1794, serving
mainly along the Rhine until 1797 when he
collaborated with Bonaparte along the
River Tagliamento. Briefly in 1798 he was
ambassador in Vienna, subsequently
holding commands on the Lower Rhine
and in the Army of the Danube. He was
Minister of War for two months in 1799,
declined to involve himself in the Brumaire *coup* but agreed to become one of
Bonaparte's Councillors of State in January 1800. He was given a marshal's baton
in May 1804 and in 1805 distinguished
himself in the Ulm campaign† and at
Austerlitz†. Napoleon rewarded him with
the title of Prince of Ponte Corvo (June
1806) but he was soon out of favour
through his failure to commit his troops at
Auerstädt† or Jena† in the Prussian campaign. Nevertheless, within four weeks
Bernadotte had pursued Blücher's troops
to Lübeck, where he received the surrender both of the Prussian forces and of a
Swedish division, whose officers were impressed by his leadership and courtesy.
Napoleon remained suspicious of Bernadotte's loyalty, distrusting his ambitions.
He was twice wounded in 1807 and spent
some months recuperating as Governor of
the Hanseatic towns, a post in which he
showed an understanding of Baltic problems. In 1809 he was given command of
the Saxon Corps against Austria; he
showed enterprise at Linz but failed to
check an assault on his positions by
Archduke Charles† at Wagram†. By now

39

Marshal Bernadotte as Prince Royal of Sweden; a contemporary English print

the personal and professional rift between Bernadotte and Napoleon was so deep that he was sent back to Paris in disgrace.

Since King Charles XIII† of Sweden had no surviving children, the Swedish army commanders in August 1810 induced their Diet to offer the right of succession to Bernadotte, whom they respected as soldier and administrator. He arrived in Sweden on 20 October 1810, became a Lutheran and was accepted as Prince Royal. Within a few months he was shaping Swedish policy. Napoleon's entry into Swedish Pomerania in March 1812 made

Bernadotte favour collaboration with Tsar Alexander I, whom he met at Åbo† five months later. In July 1813 Bernadotte led a Swedish army south of the Baltic; he defeated his old colleagues Oudinot†, at Grossbeeren on 23 August, and Ney†, at Dennewitz on 6 September. Subsequently his army engaged Ney's troops again at Leipzig†. But in 1814 he held Swedish forces back from the invasion of France, halting them at Liège, for there seemed a momentary prospect that he might be offered the French throne in succession to Napoleon. As this possibility receded the

Prince Royal gave all his diplomatic skill to securing the absorption of Norway by Sweden in the peace settlement. As King (from 1818 to 1844) he showed himself an enlightened reformer, handing control of the revenue to parliament and encouraging education and the codification of Swedish and Norwegian laws. The descendants of Bernadotte and Désirée Clary (*see above*) remain on the thrones of Sweden, Norway, Denmark and Belgium.

BERTHIER, Louis Alexandre (1753–1815) Marshal of the Empire: born at Versailles, the son of a topographical engineer much respected in Louis xv's army. The young Berthier was a staff officer serving with the French army in America from 1780 to 1783, and he continued to hold staff posts until the summer of 1792 when his royalist loyalties put him under suspicion. Inactive retirement saved his life during the Terror and he emerged to serve in Italy in 1795, becoming chief of staff to Bonaparte in March 1796. Berthier's conscientious staff work, his topographical training and gift for administrative detail ensured that he served as Bonaparte's chief of staff in every major campaign from 1796 to 1814. On the rare occasions when he was given effective command (as on the Danube in 1809) he proved unable to take quick decisions in the field. Napoleon appointed him marshal in 1804 and created him Prince of Neuchâtel and Prince of Wagram as well as giving him honorary posts at court. He was Minister of War from October 1800 to August 1807. In 1814 he accepted a peerage and other honours from Louis xviii whom he escorted to Ghent at the start of the Hundred Days. He then travelled to Bavaria, feeling honour bound to remain a non-belligerent in the new campaign. On 1 June 1815 he fell from a window at Bamberg, where he had been watching Allied troops marching against France. There is no evidence that he threw himself to his death in remorse; he had been wounded in the head at

Marshal Berthier, an engraving, from a portrait by Antoine-Jean Gros

Brienne eighteen months before and it is not unlikely that he suffered an attack of vertigo.

BERTRAND, Henri-Gratien (1773–1844) French general and Grand Master of the Palace: born and died at Châteauroux. He served with the National Guard when the Tuileries was attacked on 10 August 1792 and began his military career in earnest a year later as an engineer officer. He was under Bonaparte's command in Italy, Egypt† and Syria; he was promoted brigadier in 1800 and inspector general of engineers in 1804. While serving with the 'Army of England' at Boulogne† in 1803, Bertrand supervised the creation of a small ancillary harbour at Wimereux, close to the principal encampment of the invasion force. Later he distinguished himself in the Austrian campaigns, especially by the bridges built to span the Danube in 1809. He married an American, Fanny Dillon, in September 1808 and was soon afterwards created a Count of the Empire. He commanded IV Corps at Lützen† and Leipzig†, became Grand Master of the Palace in November 1813 and thereafter remained in loyal attendance on Napoleon in France, Elba† and St Helena†. Countess Bertrand, with three of her eighteen children, shared the exile on St Helena. Her husband was at Napoleon's deathbed and interment.

General Bertrand was politically active in the early years of Louis Philippe's reign and travelled back to St Helena in 1840 to escort Napoleon's remains to Paris. His detailed notebooks, recording Napoleon's conversations on St Helena, were only discovered in 1946. They were published in Paris as the *Cahiers de Sainte Hélène* (1949–59) and are the most valuable source of information for the final phase of Napoleon's life.

BESSIÈRES, Jean-Baptiste (1768–1813)

Marshal of the Empire: born at Prayssac, near Cahors, the son of a surgeon. He was a National Guard captain in 1792 but began his rapid rise in rank under Bonaparte's auspices in Italy and Egypt†, winning praise for courage and initiative at Rivoli†, Acre† and Aboukir†. Bessières returned to France at the same time as Bonaparte, aboard the frigate *Carrère*: as a Guard colonel, he was present at Saint-Cloud during the *coup* of Brumaire. He fought at Marengo†, received his marshal's baton in 1804 and then commanded the Guard cavalry. His charge at Austerlitz† prevented the Russians consolidating ground gained in a surprise counterattack. His cavalry again distinguished themselves at Jena†, Eylau and Friedland. In Spain he was less successful than Soult as a corps commander and by 1809 Napoleon had decided to limit his authority to the cavalry. In this capacity he again showed enterprise at Aspern† and Wagram†, where he was wounded. In May 1809 Napoleon created him titular Duke of Istria. Napoleon always treated Bessières as a personal friend, and his men

admired Bessières's fairness and sense of responsibility. He raised, trained and led the Young Guard† in 1812 and was responsible for advising Napoleon, late in the afternoon at Borodino†, not to risk his Guard '800 leagues from Paris'. His alacrity sent the Guard cavalry to Napoleon's rescue when the Emperor was ambushed by Cossacks at Gorodnya on 25 October 1812. Bessières was killed by round shot on the eve of the battle of Lützen in May 1813.

BEYLE, Henri (1783–1842)

French novelist writing under the pseudonym STENDHAL: born in Grenoble, served briefly in the army in Italy, 1799–1802, and returned to the military commissariat from 1806 to 1813. His letters vividly describe the sight of burning Smolensk† in the 1812 campaign and the

Sketch of Stendhal dancing by Alfred de Musset. As a member of the commissariat, Stendhal took part in the retreat from Moscow

perils of attack by Russian partisans and Cossacks during the retreat. So long as Napoleon ruled France, Beyle was a critic of his policies, sad at the wasteful burden of war and resenting lost liberties. But Stendhal, the novelist, looked back with admiration on the earlier years of French conquest, especially the reorganization of the Italian peninsula. Most of Stendhal's early works were written in Paris between 1821 and 1830, but he then served in the French consular service at Trieste and Civitavecchia. Here he completed *La Chartreuse de Parme* (1839), a novel concerned with the impact of Bonapartist enlightenment on a reactionary Italian state.

BIDASSOA, River

A small river flowing into the southern Bay of Biscay between Irun and Hendaye and forming the western line of the Pyrenees frontier between Spain and France. Wellington established his headquarters in early July 1813 in the village of Lesaca, above the Bidassoa, while his army besieged San Sebastian†. Not until early October did he hear from local fishermen that the river was fordable at low tide. Eventually, on 7 October 1813 Wellington's Peninsular veterans crossed the Bidassoa beneath the village of Fuenterrabia and thus became the first troops to invade metropolitan France in nineteen years of warfare. Soult† retired on Bayonne†; Wellington's army was still 480 miles from Paris. On the day it crossed into France, Napoleon was on the Elbe at Dresden, concentrating his forces for the decisive 'Battle of the Nations' at Leipzig† a week later.

BIGNON, Louis Pierre Édouard, Baron (1771–1841)

French diplomat and historian: born at La Meilleraye and entered the diplomatic service in 1797. He spent most of his official career in the German capitals or at Warsaw but he was an intermediary between Paris and the Emperor's headquarters during the French campaign; he it was who travelled out to Nogent on 7 February 1814 to inform Napoleon that Murat† had gone over to the Allies. During the Hundred Days Bignon was Under-Secretary for Foreign Affairs, with responsibility for presenting Napoleon's cause convincingly to foreign governments. He was elected a Deputy in 1817 and remained a member of successive Chambers until 1837, speaking often on foreign affairs under the Orleanist Monarchy. In his Will, Napoleon commissioned Bignon to 'write the history of French diplomacy from 1792 to 1815' and left him a legacy of 100,000 francs to undertake the task. Bignon's *Histoire de France depuis le 18 Brumaire* appeared in eleven volumes between 1829 and 1842 and fell short of Napoleon's wishes since it chronicled events only between November 1799 and October 1813. Bignon retained a certain independence of mind and was not uncritical of his benefactor, notably over the creation of an Imperial nobility and over the humiliations imposed on the Spanish Bourbons (Charles IV†, Ferdinand VII†) in 1808. From 1829 onwards Bignon was given access to the archives and to Napoleon's correspondence; and it is the combination of personal recollection, pioneer research and near-contemporary judgements of events which makes Bignon's work interesting even today.

BIGOTTINI, Émilie (1784–1858)

French ballerina: born in Toulouse, her father having emigrated from Rome. She first danced in Paris in 1799 making her debut at the Opéra on 20 November 1801 and achieving rapid success as much by her dramatic talents as by the grace and artistry of her technique. She created the title role in *Nina*, a ballet choreographed by her brother-in-law, Louis-Jacques Milon (1766–1845), the ballet master of the Paris Opera. Bigottini was much admired by Napoleon, who once commanded a palace official to present her with a gift. A set of finely bound books was duly sent to her but when the Emperor later asked her if the gift had pleased her, she replied, 'Not very much, Sire: he paid me with *livres*; I would have preferred *francs*'. Bigottini had a long liaison with Eugène de Beauharnais†. Duroc† was the father of two of her four children. Among others who appreciated Bigottini's dancing were the Emperor Francis† of Austria and Castlereagh†; her performances of *Nina* at the Kärntnertortheater were among the social highlights of the Congress of Vienna†. She returned to Paris in the winter of 1815–16 and continued to dance regularly until December 1823.

BLAKE, William (1757–1827)

English poet and artist: born in London and earned a living as an engraver while writing his own poems, which he engraved on copper, surrounded with his own illustrations and published in books bound by his wife. *Songs of Innocence* appeared in 1789 and *Songs of Experience* in 1794 but the last of his prophetic books appeared at the height of the Napoleonic Wars. His apocalyptic symbolism scorned the complacent and conventional with such imaginative genius that his visions had more meaning for later generations than for his own.

BLOCKADE

The Royal Navy resorted to two types of blockade during the Napoleonic Wars: the open blockade of specific naval ports (Brest†, Rochefort†, Texel†, Toulon†) in order to stop French expeditionary forces from putting to sea; and a general blockade of continental Europe so as to prevent French merchant vessels trading with the Americas, the Levant and the Indies. The Orders in Council† (1807) stepped up the blockade so as to hamper foreign trade with Napoleon's empire while, at the same time, smaller vessels such as corvettes were sent closer inshore to check coastal traffic. The British blockade stifled the seaport economy of Normandy, Brittany and the Charente estuary, thereby causing chronic social distress within France, but it was never a decisive weapon in undermining the structure of Napoleon's empire. France was astonishingly self-sufficient and the blockade stimulated the growth of new industries and the cultivation of new crops. It could even be argued that France's counter-blockade – the restrictive aspects of the Continental System†, instituted by the Berlin Decree† – imposed greater harm on Napoleonic Europe than did the British blockade, since it demanded the development of an alternative and unpopular system of trade regulated by the needs of Paris. The Royal Navy's insistence on a right to search neutral shipping as part of the blockade (together with the occasional impressment of seamen from non-belligerent states) aroused general hostility, which manifested itself in the Armed Neutrality† of the North and in the Anglo-American conflict known as the War of 1812†.

BLÜCHER, Gebhard Leberecht von (1742–1819)

Prussian soldier: born at Gross-Renzow, near Rostock, on the Baltic coast. He served at first as a cavalry officer in the Swedish army, but after capture by the Prussians in 1760 he was commissioned by Frederick the Great, retiring to take up farming in 1773 with the rank of captain and a malediction from his King ('Captain von Blücher . . . may go to the devil as soon as he pleases'). He re-entered the army in 1786 and in 1793–4 became famous as an intrepid Hussar officer, reaching the rank of major-general in June 1794 after several successful actions against the French revolutionary armies. He failed to profit from initial gains on the field of Auerstädt† in 1806, retreating in good order to Lübeck where, at Ratkau,

action at Waterloo at the crucial moment to outflank the French position, taking the shock attacks of the last French reserves. The Prussian troops headed the pursuit of the broken French army towards Paris. He then retired to his estate at Krieblowitz, near Breslau in Silesia, where he died on 12 September 1819. He was an intrepid fighting commander, not a great strategist but much loved by his men. In his later campaigns he was fortunate to have as successive chiefs of staff the gifted Scharnhorst† and Gneisenau†.

Blücher; based upon a sketch made by Major-General Reynardson during the visit of the Allied Sovereigns and their commanders to London, June 1814

he surrendered to Bernadotte†. A grave illness in 1807–8, together with the restraints imposed on Prussia after Tilsit†, limited his anti-French activities but, with the outbreak of the War of Liberation, he was given command of the first Prussian army put into the field (28 February 1813). He fought at Lützen†, Bautzen†, at the Katzbach† and at Leipzig†, his greatest triumph. He was promoted to the rank of General Field Marshal and became the great military hero of Germany, *Marschall Vorwärts* ('Marshal Forwards') as he was nicknamed. He suffered a series of rebuffs in February 1814 during the invasion of France (Champaubert†, Montmirail†, Vauchamps†) but gained a strategic success at Laon† and entered Paris on 1 April 1814 after a severe skirmish at Montmartre. He was created a Prince by Frederick William III†, taking his title from Wahlstadt, near the Katzbach in Silesia. During the visit of the Allied sovereigns to England in 1814 he enjoyed great social success. He was summoned to command the Prussian army in Belgium in 1815. After suffering defeat at Ligny† he was able to bring his troops into

BOLIVAR, Simon (1783–1830)

Liberator of South America: born in Caracas (now in Venezuela), the capital of a Spanish colonial captaincy-general. Bolivar came from an upper-class family and was sent to Europe in 1799, spending several months at the Spanish court. He visited Paris in 1801 and in 1804–5. Although greatly impressed by the Napoleonic Codes he was disgusted with the First Consul for creating the Empire and a new hereditary peerage. Bolivar travelled to Italy in the spring of 1805 and

Simon Bolivar, idolized as the Liberator of South America

45

on 13 June watched Napoleon take the salute at a parade at Montechiaro, near Brescia; he later claimed that he noticed Napoleon eyeing him with suspicion. Abortive attempts by Bolivar to lead republican risings in Venezuela and Colombia between 1812 and 1815 were followed by more successful anti-Spanish operations from the Orinoco estuary in 1816–19, Bolivar modelling his tactics on Bonaparte's earlier campaigns. After ensuring the independence of Venezuela in 1821, Bolivar planned a great republican confederation in Spanish America, basing his system of government on the French Consulate and the Napoleonic Codes. Although he was able to gain successes in Ecuador and in the region which was to be named Bolivia in his honour, the separatist movements in his homeland and in Colombia weakened the appeal of his grand design. He died in disillusionment, at an even younger age than Napoleon.

BONAPARTE, Caroline (Marie Annunziata Caroline, 1782–1839)
Queen of Naples: born at Ajaccio, the youngest of Napoleon's sisters. She had a fair complexion, a liking for music, and a liking for Murat† – whom she married at Mortefontaine in January 1800. When she became Queen of Naples in August 1808 she provided the political wisdom which her husband lacked. Caroline was responsible for raising the architectural and social style of court life in Naples, bringing a particular brilliance to the palaces of Portici and Caserta. When Murat sought an accommodation with the Allies so as to save his throne, she gave him every support. Against her advice Murat called on the Italians to rise against Austrian rule during the Hundred Days. When he was faced by a popular revolt against his own authority in Naples itself (21–2 May, 1815), Caroline took refuge on a British warship and never saw her husband again. She called herself the Contessa di Lipona (an anagram of Napoli) and was kept

Caroline Murat, Napoleon's youngest sister, Queen of Naples

under surveillance at Frohsdorf, near Vienna, until 1824. It is possible that in 1817 she married the former Neapolitan Minister of War, General Francesco Macdonald (1776–1837), who was her companion for the remainder of his life. Caroline settled in Trieste for seven years but moved to Florence in 1831 to escape a cholera epidemic. She lived in Florence in some state for her last two years. Two sons emigrated to the United States; two daughters married into the Italian nobility.

BONAPARTE, Charles Louis Napoléon (1808–73
Later Emperor Napoleon III: born in the Tuileries Palace, the third son of Louis Bonaparte† and Hortense (Beauharnais†). He was created a Prince of Holland at his birth. Most of his infancy was spent in Paris, particularly at Malmaison†, and he was present with his uncles at the ceremony of the Champ de Mai† in 1815. After Waterloo his mother took the boy, and his surviving brother, to Switzerland. The elder child was brought up in his

father's care in Italy but Louis Napoleon (having dropped his first name) remained with Hortense at Arenenberg. By 1833 he was the principal Bonapartist claimant to the French throne, which he attempted to seize by *coups d'état* in 1836 and 1840. He settled in Paris after the fall of Louis Philippe and on 10 December 1848 he became President of the Second French Republic, establishing an authoritarian regime by the *coup* of 2 December 1851. Exactly a year later he was proclaimed Emperor of the French. He married Eugénie de Montijo (1826–1920) in January 1853; their only child, the Prince Imperial (1856–79) was killed while serving with British troops in southern Africa. Napoleon III was deposed on 4 September 1870 after being captured by the Prussians at Sedan. He died at Camden Place, Chislehurst in Kent, on 9 January 1873. Napoleon III, Eugénie and their son are buried at Farnborough Abbey, Hampshire.

BONAPARTE, Charles Marie (1746–85)

Father of Napoleon I: born at Ajaccio, became a lawyer and supported Paoli† in his struggle for Corsican rights. When Corsica† accepted French rule in 1768 he changed the spelling of his surname from 'Buonaparte' to 'Bonaparte'. In 1771 he received official recognition of his claim that for two centuries the family had enjoyed a social status among the minor nobility. Two years later he was appointed Royal Counsellor and Assessor in the province and town of Ajaccio. Charles Bonaparte's patent of nobility facilitated the entry of his second surviving son, Napoleone, into the military academy at Brienne†, where he saw him for the last time in June 1784. In the following November Charles left Corsica to seek medical advice for persistent stomach pains. At the end of February 1785 he died at Montpellier where he was receiving treatment for cancer of the stomach. His wife (Letizia Bonaparte†), five sons and three daughters survived him.

BONAPARTE, Elisa (Marie-Anne Elisa, 1777–1820)

Grand Duchess of Tuscany: born at Ajaccio, the fourth and first surviving daughter of Charles and Letizia. At the age of seven she was sent to board at a girl's school at Saint-Cyr, remaining out of touch with her family until she was fifteen, when the school was closed down on the eve of the September massacres. Napoleon, an artillery captain, then escorted her on a dangerous journey by stage coach from Paris to Marseilles (beginning on 9 September 1792) and so on to Corsica. Brother and sister never liked each other, however; Elisa retained from her school days an arrogant manner and sharp tongue. She married a dull but good-looking Corsican, Félix Bacciochi†, at Marseilles in May 1797. Napoleon created her Duchess of Lucca and Princess of Piombino in March 1805. She administered the economy of her state profitably: silk production doubled within three years; the Carrara marble quarries were rapidly de-

Elisa Bonaparte, Napoleon's eldest sister, Grand Duchess of Tuscany

47

veloped; and Lucca became a cultural centre, with Niccolo Paganini (1782–1840) the outstanding musical virtuoso of her court. An *Instituto Elisa*, founded under the Duchess's patronage, revived the type of boarding-school for girls from good homes which she had attended at Saint-Cyr. So successful was Elisa that in March 1809 her brother created her Grand Duchess of Tuscany. She was thus able to hold court at the Pitti Palace in Florence, which she restored and refurbished in competition with her sister Caroline† at Naples. When the French Empire in Italy fell apart in February 1814, Elisa assumed the title Countess of Compignano and spent her last five years of life near Trieste, with a house in the town itself and a villa in the hills at Vicentina, 5 miles away. She died at Vicentina nine months before her brother on St Helena.

BONAPARTE, Jerome (1784–1860)

King of Westphalia: Napoleon's youngest brother, born at Ajaccio and nicknamed 'Fifi', as a spoilt child. The First Consul sent him to sea in 1800, intending him to become a naval commander. He served in the Mediterranean and West Indies until 1802 when he decided that the navy did not suit his temperament. Jerome then visited America and, at Baltimore on Christmas Eve 1803, married Elizabeth Patterson (1785–1879), a Southern belle of Irish descent. The couple remained in America until March 1805, running up considerable debts. They then crossed to Portugal, but Napoleon refused to recognize the marriage and would not allow 'Miss Patterson' to land on territory under French control. While Jerome was escorted to the Emperor in Milan, his wife found her way to London where, in July, she gave birth to a son whom she took back to Maryland in October; in 1905 this son's son became US Navy Secretary.

In the Prussian campaign of 1806 Napoleon gave Jerome command of a Bavarian division. The Emperor was pleased with

Jerome Bonaparte, King of Westphalia, Napoleon's youngest brother and the only member of the family to become a Marshal of France

his brother's military enterprise and, on 8 July 1807, created him King of Westphalia†. A month later Jerome married Princess Catherine of Württemberg (1783–1835), a first cousin of Tsar Alexander. Westphalia became the model Napoleonic state, the Emperor imposing on Jerome and Catherine his hand-picked officials and a German version of the Civil Code†. Jerome spent most of his reign at Wilhelmshohe, near Cassel, where he rapidly acquired a reputation for extravagance. He commanded X Corps in the Wagram campaign†, collaborating with Junot† in protecting the upper Danube. He was given the Third Army in 1812, engaged Bagration† on the Niemen and captured Grodno, but Napoleon thought him slow to follow up his initial success and ordered Davout† to assume authority over Jerome's men. The King of Westphalia accordingly returned to Cassel in disgrace three weeks after the campaign began.

Jerome left his kingdom on 26 October 1813; he and Catherine found temporary refuge at Compiègne. When the Empire fell they hurried to Switzerland. Jerome supported Napoleon during the Hundred Days and fought with tenacity at Waterloo. He escaped to Württemberg but, with his loyal wife, was virtually imprisoned by his father-in-law. Austrian intervention secured for Jerome the title of Prince of Montfort (July 1816) and he eventually settled in Rome in 1823, moving to Florence in 1831. By then he was the father of two sons and a daughter, Princess Mathilde (1820–1904). Cholera forced the family to flee to Switzerland in 1835, where Catherine died. Five years afterwards he secretly married a Florentine widow, Giustina Bartolini-Baldelli (1811–1903). He was allowed to return to Paris in 1847 and was appointed Governor of the Invalides in 1849. A few months later he became the only Bonaparte created a Marshal of France. Napoleon III appointed him President of the Senate and allowed him to live in the Palais Royal. When Queen Victoria made her state visit to Paris in August 1855 he was presented to her: 'An odd old man', she noted in her Journal, 'rather tall and very civil, but not *distingué*-looking'. He died at his country home near Paris in 1860. His great-grandson, Prince Napoleon (b. 1914), is the present Head of the House of Bonaparte.

BONAPARTE, Joseph (1768–1844)

King of Naples and Sicily, King of Spain: Napoleon's elder brother, born at Corte in Corsica and educated at Autun for the priesthood until he was sixteen but returned to Ajaccio and became a lawyer. In August 1794 he married Julie Clary, daughter of a wealthy silk merchant in Marseilles who brought him a dowry of 100,000 livres. He added to comparative fortune by wise investment during the years of his brother's ascendancy. With this wealth he purchased the estate of Mortefontaine, south of Chantilly. He

was elected to the Council of Five Hundred† in 1797 and served on diplomatic missions to Parma and Rome. In Brumaire† he was Napoleon's confidant and adviser, possessing more socially accommodating tact than his brothers. The First Consul used him as a personal envoy in the talks which achieved the Treaty of Amiens†. Joseph ruled in Naples† from March 1806 to June 1808, wooing the church by conscientious fulfilment of his religious observances but failing to impose his will in the towns and villages of the Abruzzi. His apparent success with the church encouraged Napoleon in the foolish notion that Joseph would be an acceptable king to the people of Spain. Reluctantly on 6 June 1808 Joseph abdicated his south Italian kingdom in favour of the Spanish crown; he was proclaimed King in Madrid on 24 July 1808, hurriedly withdrawing to Burgos eight days later. Although troops acting in King Joseph's name conquered Andalusia in January and February 1810 he was never accepted as ruler by his new subjects. He was decisively defeated by Wellington at Vitoria† on 21 June 1813, losing many of his personal treasures and leaving his kingdom for the last time on 28 June, hurrying back incognito to Mortefontaine, where he established himself on 30 July. He formally abdicated on 11 December 1813. Napoleon appointed him principal adviser to Marie Louise during the French campaign. He escaped to Switzerland but returned to Paris during the Hundred Days, accompanying Napoleon to Rochefort† after Waterloo. He then slipped away on an American vessel and was in New York by the end of July, while Napoleon was still aboard *Bellerophon*† off Plymouth. Joseph bought an estate in southern New Jersey where he lived, with his two daughters but not his wife, until 1832 when he travelled to London. After another visit to America from 1837 to 1839 he settled, with his much-neglected wife, in Florence, where he died on 28 July 1844; Julie survived him by eight months.

BONAPARTE, Josephine: see *Josephine, Empress of the French*.

BONAPARTE, Letizia (born Maria Letizia, 1749/50–1836)
'Madame Mère': born at Ajaccio, the daughter of a French army captain. She married Charles Marie Bonaparte on 2 June 1764 and had six sons and six daughters, five of the children dying in infancy. Until 1793 she remained in Corsica but then moved the family home to the vicinity of Toulon and, soon afterwards, to Marseilles. She was a matriarch of iron resolve, indomitable courage and sound common sense. On 1 June 1797 she was welcomed, in considerable state, by her son Napoleon at the gates of Milan, the populace cheering 'the mother of Italy's liberator'. She spent most of his years of imperial primacy in Paris, accorded official status as an 'Imperial Highness' and styled '*Madame Mère de l'Empereur*' from May 1804; 'If only it lasts' ('*Pourvou que cela doure*'), she was heard to remark during the halcyon days of the Empire. Politically she encouraged her son to seek reconciliation with the Church; her half-brother Joseph Fesch† became Cardinal-Archbishop of Lyons. She joined Napoleon on Elba†, returned to Paris in the

'*Mme Mère*', *Marie Letizia Bonaparte*

Hundred Days, finally saying farewell to her son at Malmaison† on 29 June 1815. She left Paris, with Cardinal Fesch, on 19 July and travelled through Switzerland to Rome. There she survived for more than twenty years, living from 1818 to 1836 at the Villa Rinuccini, at the corner of the Piazza Venezia and the Corso. She had acquired great wealth, from jewellery and shrewd investment. Although she dictated a few pages of memoirs, she carefully preserved the historical dignity of the First Empire, trying to ease the misfortunes of her son on St Helena while he was still alive and restraining the internecine feuding of her remaining children in exile.

BONAPARTE, Louis (1778–1846)
King of Holland: third brother of Napoleon, born at Ajaccio. He was commissioned in the artillery in 1795 and served as his brother's aide-de-camp throughout the first Italian campaign as well as accompanying him to Egypt. He later sought to make his own military career, transferring to the cavalry in 1799. On 4 January 1802 he married Napoleon's stepdaughter, Hortense de Beauharnais†. He became a general in May 1804 and was briefly Governor-General of the Départements beyond the Alps before becoming King Lodewijk 1 of Holland† on 5 June 1806. He was extremely conscientious, setting himself to learn Dutch, introducing educational reforms, revising the criminal code and seeking to safeguard the Dutch both from the rigours of conscription and from the burdens imposed by the Continental System†. Louis's sympathy with the Dutch – together with his poor relationship with Hortense (a favourite of Napoleon) – led to friction between the brothers. On 1 July 1810 Louis abdicated, assumed the title of Count of Saint-Leu, withdrew to Austria and settled at Graz, moving to Switzerland when war was imminent between Austria and France in 1813. In January 1814 he returned to Paris as a loyal 'Frenchman wishing to share the

dangers of the moment'. No use was made of his services. He found refuge in Lausanne in May 1814, declined Napoleon's invitation to return to Paris during the Hundred Days, and spent most of his remaining years at Florence, moving to the coast at Leghorn shortly before his death in July 1846. In exile, he was highly critical of the conspiratorial escapades of his only surviving son, Charles Louis Napoleon Bonaparte†, the future Napoleon III.

BONAPARTE, Lucien (1775–1840)
Second brother of Napoleon: born at Ajaccio and, like Napoleon, educated as a cadet at Brienne†. He was, however, not a soldier by nature, showing some skills as a politician and developing a good style of radical oratory. By 1799 he was President of the Council of Five Hundred†, a post which enabled him considerably to help his brother in Brumaire†. As Napoleon's Minister of the Interior he helped draw up the first lists of Prefects†. He served briefly as ambassador in Spain but began to resent his brother's imperial airs. In 1794 he had defied the wishes of his family and married Christine Boyer, an innkeeper's daughter who died in May 1800. He then fell in love with Alexandrine Jouberthon de Vambertie, a stockbroker's widow, whom he insisted on marrying in May 1803, despite Napoleon's disapproval. Napoleon exiled him to Rome, where the family was befriended by Pius VII†. When French troops entered Rome in 1808 Lucien sought to emigrate to America with his wife and eight children. The British refused to allow him passage, his ship was intercepted and the family interned on Malta. At the end of the year they were brought to Plymouth. Lucien was then allowed to live freely as a country gentleman, originally in Ludlow Castle and then, for almost five years, at Thorngrove, a house some four miles from Worcester. The family returned to Rome in April 1814 and Lucien was created

Prince of Canino by Pius VII. During the Hundred Days he was reconciled to Napoleon, who once more accepted him as a political adviser. After Waterloo Lucien vainly tried to rally the Assembly to support the defeated Emperor. While trying to return to the Papal States he was arrested by the Piedmontese and held prisoner in Turin for three months. Pius VII secured his release and he spent his remaining years with his wife and family in Rome, interesting himself in the ancient Etruscans. Alexandrine survived him by fifteen years.

BONAPARTE, Napoleon: see *Napoleon I, Emperor of the French.*

BONAPARTE, Pauline (Marie Pauline, 1780–1825)
Princess Borghese: born in Ajaccio and became Napoleon's favourite sister. Her flirtatious nature, raven hair, blue eyes and sylph-like figure attracted many suitors from among her brother's fellow officers, the best known of them being Junot†. She spent much of her childhood near Antibes, where she met the future General Victor Leclerc (1772–1802), the son of a wealthy mill-owner from Pontoise. They were married at Mombello, Lombardy, in June 1797. For the first year of the Consulate Pauline was queen of social fashion in Paris but in 1802 her brother insisted that she should accompany Leclerc to Haiti, where he had been given command of the expedition to suppress the rising of Toussaint L'Ouverture†. Soon after Leclerc reached the island he contracted yellow fever and Pauline returned to France as a widow of twenty-two, with an unhealthy four-year-old son. Within a few months she married Prince Camillo Borghese† and travelled with him to Rome. Their married life together was brief: Pauline shocked the Borghese faction in Italy, partly by her extra-marital escapades and partly by 'not

Pauline Borghese, the most notorious of Napoleon's sisters

behaving as the Romans' (as Napoleon complained to her). Her willingness in 1808 to pose as a nude Venus for the great sculptor, Canova†, caused further scandal. Her son died in August 1804 and she had no further children.

By 1810 Pauline was back in Paris, delighting Napoleon by an extravagant fête at her Neuilly villa in honour of his marriage to Marie Louise†. Pauline remained loyal to Napoleon; she shared with him four of his ten months on Elba†, enlivening life there with three masked balls and with amateur theatricals in which she herself took part. A week after Napoleon's escape from Elba, she slipped away to the mainland but could travel no further than Compignano, near Viareggio, where she was detained by Austrian guards for more than six months. Pope Pius VII†, whom she had always treated with courtesy and respect, intervened on her behalf and secured a settlement with her estranged husband which allowed her a considerable share of the Borghese properties in Italy. At the same time she sold

her principal home in the Rue Saint-Honoré to the British government for an embassy in Paris. Pauline's health, long plagued with nervous debility and psychosomatic collapses, deteriorated rapidly in 1823–4. Her husband received her again at Florence. She died there from cancer of the stomach in the afternoon of 9 June 1825, having spent that morning dictating a will which disposed of a personal fortune worth well over two million francs.

BORDEAUX

Principal port of south-western France, on the River Garonne, some sixty miles from the sea. Traditionally Bordeaux was concerned with trade to the French colonies and the export of wine. The port suffered a severe recession during the Napoleonic Wars, especially after 1806–7 with intensification of the blockade and of Anglo-French commercial warfare. On 12 March 1814 Bordeaux showed Bourbon sympathies by welcoming back the King's nephew, the Duke of Angoulême†. Subsequently the port served as the principal embarkation base for Wellington's Peninsular army. From Bordeaux, on 14 June 1814, Wellington issued his farewell Order to his troops.

BORGHESE, Camillo Filippo Luigi
(1775–1832)

Prince: born in Rome, a member of a great patrician family, his father being titular Prince of Sulmona and Rossano. Camillo Borghese was a good-looking spineless connoisseur of art, who visited Paris in the spring of 1803, met the widowed Pauline Bonaparte† and married her four months later. They spent less than a year of married life together. Technically from 1808 to 1814 Borghese was Napoleon's Governor-General for the French Départements beyond the Alps (Piedmont and Liguria). He spent most of his later years in Florence, reconciled to Pauline shortly before her death.

BORGHETTO, Battle of (30 May 1796)
Borghetto is a small town on the River Mincio, six miles south of Peschiera and fifteen miles north of Mantua. In his first Italian campaign Bonaparte followed up his victory at Lodi† with a surprise assault on the Austrian-held bridge at Borghetto which was so successful that the Austrians were forced to retreat towards the Tyrol. Thereafter Mantua† and the citadel in Milan† remained the only Italian fortresses in Austrian hands.

BORISOV
Russian town situated on the River Berezina†, some thirty-eight miles north-east of Minsk. The town, held by Poles attached to Oudinot's† Corps, was seized by the Russian Third Army under Chichagov† on 21 November 1812. This surprise Russian action was a serious blow to Napoleon who, with the main body of the *Grande Armée*, was falling back on Borisov from Smolensk and was dependent on the Borisov bridge for safe passage of the river. Oudinot successfully counterattacked two days later and recovered the town but could not prevent the Russians from destroying the bridge. Nevertheless Oudinot's success allowed him to send out patrols as far north as Studenka where work began on improvising bridges for Napoleon's army to cross the Berezina.

BORODINO, Battle of (7 September 1812)
Borodino was a village some seventy miles west of Moscow, a shoulder of high ground broken by ravines, chosen by Kutuzov† as the best defensive position in which to resist Napoleon's advance on Moscow. The opposing armies first faced each other on the afternoon of Saturday, 5 September, when there was a sharp engagement as Murat† sought to take an outlying Russian redoubt above the village of Shevardino. There was a lull on the

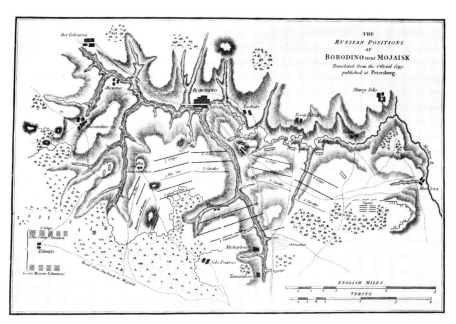

A contemporary print of the Russian positions at Borodino, with the village of Shevardno on the left and the Russian positions at Semionskaya to the south-east of Shevardino

Sunday, as both sides took up their positions: Napoleon with 133,000 men and 590 guns along a four mile front; Kutuzov with 120,000 men and 640 guns along five miles of broken hillocks. The attack began with a heavy French artillery barrage at dawn on the Monday and, although Eugène Beauharnais† soon captured the village itself, the main Russian position in the Raevsky *flèches* withstood wave after wave of attack. Momentarily the Russians wavered when Bagration† was mortally wounded, and Murat's cavalry took the Simyonovskava defences in the centre of the Russian position. The Raevsky *flèches* did not fall until mid-afternoon, and even then the Russians were able to withdraw to another defensive line. Napoleon, whose health was poor all day, was reluctant to risk his Guard regiments so far from Paris, although he threw some of the reserve artillery into the battle when it looked as if the Russians would launch a counter-attack in the late afternoon. The battle died away inconclusively, with the French in command of the original Russian defences but with Kutuzov's men holding new positions on a ridge a thousand yards behind them. During the night Kutuzov withdrew his army towards Moscow rather than risk a new engagement and the French therefore claimed Borodino as a victory. Napoleon failed to rout and destroy the Russian army, as he had hoped and, although he succeeded in capturing Moscow a week later, his troops were unable to force Tsar Alexander to sue for peace. For propaganda purposes the French called the engagement the 'Moskova' and gave the impression that it was fought nearer to Russia's ancient capital: 'The most terrible of all my battles', Napoleon declared on St Helena, 'was the one in front of Moscow. The French showed themselves worthy of victory and the Russians of being invincible.' Nearly one in four of Napoleon's men were casualties; for the Russians the figure was higher than one in three.

BOULOGNE

France's principal fishing port, 150 miles north of Paris. In 1803 Napoleon ordered the concentration at Boulogne of an army to invade England. A camp was established with its centre three miles north of central Boulogne; the 'Army of England' comprised between 160,000 and 170,000 men, under the command of Marshals Soult†, Ney†, David† and Victor†. In the port of Boulogne, and at neighbouring small harbours, some 2,400 vessels were massed. The first troops arrived at the camp in the third week of June 1803. Napoleon paid several visits in 1804 and 1805. He was present at the disastrous naval exercise on 20 July 1804 in which two dozen closely packed invasion sloops were caught in an up-Channel gale which wrecked them on the French shore, drowning more than 2,000 men. The failure of Villeneuve† to gain naval mastery of the Channel over the following year induced Napoleon to begin the despatch of his army towards the Rhine (and the Ulm-Austerlitz campaign) on 25 August 1805. Napoleon left the camp on 3 September. Marshal Soult laid the foundation-stone of a column to commemorate the Boulogne Camp in 1804 and he was Prime Minister in 1841 when the *Colonne de la Grande Armée* was completed. It is 172 feet in height and some two and a half miles north of Boulogne, inland from the road to Wimereux and Calais.

BOURBON DYNASTY

The House of Bourbon inherited the French throne in 1589 when the last Valois king, Henry III, was succeeded by his distant relative, the King of Navarre, who became King Henry IV of France. His grandson, Louis XIV (reigned 1643–1715) put forward the claims of his second son to the throne of Spain when Charles II of Habsburg died childless in 1700. Louis's son duly reigned in Spain as King Philip V from 1700 to 1726. Philip V's seventh son was recognized as King of Naples and

Sicily (Charles VII) in 1735. At the time of Napoleon's birth the Bourbons therefore ruled in France, Spain, and Naples and Sicily. The establishment of the First Republic in Paris in 1792 excluded the French Bourbons until the restoration of Louis XVIII† in 1814. Charles IV† of Spain ceded his crown to the Bonapartes in 1808 at Bayonne† but Ferdinand VII† was restored by the Treaty of Valençay† of December 1813. Throughout the Napoleonic era the Neapolitan Bourbons were represented by Ferdinand IV†, whose reign was marked by frequent violent shifts of fortune. He was effectively restored and styled King of the Kingdom of the Two Sicilies in 1816. The senior line of French Bourbons lost the throne in July 1830 when Charles X (formerly the Count of Artois†) abdicated in favour of the Duke of Orleans, a descendant of Louis XIV's brother. He reigned as Louis Philippe, King of the French, until 1848 when France ceased to be a monarchy; his great-great-grandson, the Count of Paris (born 1908), is the present Head of the Bourbon dynasty in France. The Spanish Bourbons have remained on the throne in Madrid apart from the interlude from 1931 to 1975, but the Neapolitan Bourbons lost their throne in December 1860 when Naples and Sicily were absorbed in a united Italy. From 1748 until the upheavals of 1801 a branch of the Bourbons also ruled as Dukes of Parma and Piacenza. Two of these Dukes (Ludovic I and Ludovic II) were recognized as puppet kings of Etruria by Napoleon between 1801 and 1807. The ducal family of Bourbon-Parma was restored in 1847 on the death of the interloping sovereign, Duchess Marie Louise†, but the dynasty ceased to reign in 1859 when Parma and Piacenza were merged into Italy.

BOURGOGNE, Adrien Jean-Baptiste François (1785–1867)

Sergeant in the Imperial Guard: born at Condé, near Valenciennes. He enlisted in the Imperial Guard† in 1806, fought at Jena†, Pultusk†, Eylau†, Friedland†, Aspern† and Essling† (where he was wounded) and then served in Spain. He is known because of his remarkable *Memoirs* of the Russian campaign, which he wrote in 1835 and which were originally published in 1896 and translated into English in 1926. Bourgogne describes how his regiment of the Guard left Spain in March 1812 and travelled 1,700 miles to Prussian Poland by June, before the campaign began. His narrative has vivid accounts of his experiences in Moscow†, at Maloyaroslavets† and on the retreat, including the crossing of the Berezina†. He was commissioned in the 145th Regiment of the Line in 1813 and fought at Lützen† and Bautzen† before being captured by the Prussians on the Elbe and held prisoner for two years. When he returned home he settled in Valenciennes, at first as a draper, but he accepted a commission from Louis Philippe and became *Major de Place* of the town, the office he held when he set his memoirs down on paper.

BOURRIENNE, Louis-Antoine Fauvelet de (1769–1834)

Bonaparte's first military secretary: born at Sens and studied with Napoleon Bonaparte at Brienne†. He then left the army, perfected his German and planned to become a diplomat. The Revolution forced him to emigrate, but he returned to Paris in 1797 and was appointed military secretary to General Bonaparte, serving with him in Italy, Egypt and Syria. He was competent at his work but embezzled on a grand scale. The First Consul sacked him in 1804. Rather surprisingly he then sent him to Hamburg with a responsible administrative post. Here Bourrienne was guilty of further peculation; he found the illicit sale of passports rewarding and profited even more from a black market in goods rendered scarce by the Continental System†. In 1810 a commission of inquiry found that he had misappropriated 2 million francs at Hamburg. To Bourrienne's anger, Napoleon refused to receive him in private audience and ordered him to repay half this sum. This obligation had still not been fulfilled when, in April 1814, Talleyrand† secured the appointment of Bourrienne as Minister of Posts at the Bourbon Restoration, at the same time arranging a cancellation of his debt to the State. The improvement in Bourrienne's fortunes was, however, short lived. To escape from his creditors Bourrienne settled near Charleroi in Belgium where he began to dictate notes which a ghost writer, Maxime de Villemarest, amplified until they filled ten volumes of dubious authenticity. Bourrienne's mind began to go soon after his sixtieth birthday and he died in an asylum near Caen.

BREAD

Although Napoleon had no great understanding of economic problems, he possessed certain instinctive assumptions which helped determine his policy. Among these was the conviction that bread shortages and high bread prices contributed to political unrest, especially in Paris. The First Consul was concerned when, after Brumaire†, the price of a loaf of bread rose to 13 sous in Paris (about 3p or 5 cents). After a poor harvest in 1802 the price rose in the following winter to 18 sous in Paris, although staying at 7 sous in most country towns and even lower in Brittany. The Paris price was maintained for several years at about 15 sous by state subsidies but Napoleon became extremely alarmed during the bad summer of 1811, refusing to allow the bakers' representatives to increase bread prices. In October he authorized a payment of 100 sous to the bakers for every sack of flour. Nevertheless the bread crisis continued, the price beginning to soar in February 1812, and there were long queues that May when Napoleon set out for Dresden† and the Russian campaign. Outside Paris there were food riots at Issoudun in the Indre region of central France in late April and, more seriously, at Caen† intermittently from March to May. The basic food situation eased in the summer but was still serious at the end of the year. In 1813 the harvest was good and the bread riots which Napoleon had once feared never spread to the capital. In London, the cost of bread was generally higher than in Paris, especially after the Corn Law† of 1804, but exact comparisons are impossible.

BREST

The chief French naval base for operations in the Atlantic. It lies at the mouths of the rivers Penfeld and Elorn in Brittany, some 375 miles west of Paris. The naval port was founded by Richelieu in 1631 and heavily fortified by Vauban, the rocky headland which commands the narrow Goulet de Brest making the broad inner roadstead impregnable. The first shots in Britain's war against revolutionary France were fired when a British warship 'looked into' Brest Roads in January 1793. From 1794 onwards the Royal Navy theoretically maintained a close blockade of Brest, but it was frequently ineffective when there were strong offshore winds blowing from the east. The blockade did not prevent grain convoys from entering or check the sailing from Brest in mid-December 1796 of a convoy of some fifty vessels to land in Ireland. Admiral Lord St Vincent†, as commander of the Channel Fleet in 1800, imposed a stricter blockade, maintaining thirty vessels off Brest. This practice was continued by Collingwood† before and after Trafalgar, frigates even entering the Goulet at times. The blockade prevented Vice-Admiral Ganteaume† from bringing the Brest fleet out to join Villeneuve† on several occasions, notably on 21 August 1805 when Ganteaume had to turn and seek cover under the Brest shore batteries. It is significant that four days after this rebuff Napoleon gave the first order for troops of the 'Army of England' to move from the camp at Boulogne† towards the Rhine and the Ulm-Austerlitz campaign.

BRIENNE

Town in north-eastern France, 125 miles east of Paris and lying between the rivers Aube and Marne, in Champagne. From 1777 until 1790 there was a military academy at Brienne; Napoleon Bonaparte was a cadet there from 13 May 1779 until 30 October 1784. Early in the French campaign of 1814 the small town was seized by Blücher's Prussians. Napoleon sent in a force of young conscripts, backed by veterans from Ney's† corps and Grouchy's† cavalry, and in a fierce day's fighting threw back the Prussians to the east as part of a general counter-offensive (29 January 1814).

BROUGHAM, Henry Peter (1778–1868, created Baron Brougham and Vaux in 1830)
Scottish lawyer and reformer, born and educated in Edinburgh, and was one of the founders of the *Edinburgh Review* in 1802. He entered the House of Commons as a Whig in 1810 and quickly achieved fame as a skilled debater, insistent on legal reforms. He championed the cause of George IV's consort, Caroline† of Brunswick, in 1814–15 and again in 1820. Brougham's conviction that Britain would suffer economic ruin at the hands of Napoleon cost him his seat in Parliament and he was out of the House from 1813 to 1816. He did not share the Holland House† concern for Napoleon's well-being on St Helena. Later he was Lord Chancellor, from 1830 to 1834.

BRUMAIRE

The 'foggy month' in the Revolutionary Calendar†. Bonaparte's *coup d'état* of 18 Brumaire (9 November 1799) established the Consulate† in succession to the Directory†. The military reverses suffered by the French at the hands of Suvorov† and Archduke Charles† so discredited the Directory that a conspiracy was hatched by Sieyès†, Talleyrand† and Napoleon Bonaparte, with Lucien Bonaparte† as intermediary, to overthrow the cumbersome government and replace it by a triumvirate. Sieyès was largely responsible for inducing the Council of Ancients† to agree on 18 Brumaire that the two parliamentary bodies (the Council of Ancients and the Council of Five Hundred) should adjourn to Saint-Cloud†, and that the military command should be given to General Bonaparte in order to safeguard the 'national representatives'. When the Ancients and the Council of Five Hundred met at Saint-Cloud on the following day they found that the Directory had resigned, but they tried to draw up a new Directory, according to the Constitution. Despite Lucien Bonaparte's skill as chairman of the Council of Five Hundred, a neo-Jacobin minority began to threaten Napoleon Bonaparte's life, and at the prompting of Sieyès and Murat†, the General sent troops into the Orangery (chamber) and expelled the dissidents at bayonet point. In the evening the Ancients and a hand-picked rump of the Five Hundred approved a new executive government of three Consuls, Napoleon, Sieyès and Ducos†. Commissions from the two Councils were to prepare a constitution for the new Consulate. Although the coup was bloodless, there could be no doubt that Bonaparte, like Cromwell in 1653, had used force to replace a discredited regime by a powerful executive which had reason to believe that it commanded popular allegiance.

BRUNE, Guillaume Marie Anne
(1763–1815)
Marshal of the Empire: born at Brive-la-Gaillarde on the Corrèze, west of the Massif Central. As a young printer in Paris he joined the National Guard in 1789,

became a captain and received rapid promotion because of his soundly republican views. He ruthlessly repressed counter-revolutionary activities in southern France and Bordeaux and then pursued a more orthodox military career under Bonaparte in northern Italy. He commanded the French forces in Holland† in 1799 and the Army of Italy from August 1800 to January 1801. He was ambassador in Constantinople from 1802 to 1804 and was created a marshal in his absence. Suspicion of his latent Dantonesque republicanism led Napoleon to send him to the Baltic in 1806-7 and then to relieve him of all duties. Brune was reconciled to Napoleon during the Hundred Days, when he was given command of a corps in the Marseilles-Toulon area and saw no action. He was arrested in Toulon at the end of July 1815, sent under escort to Paris but intercepted by a 'White' counter-revolutionary gang at Avignon, who shot him dead as he mocked their political principles and their marksmanship.

BRUNSWICK, Charles William Ferdinand, Duke of (1735-1806)
Prussian general: born at Wolfenbüttel and married his second cousin, Princess Augusta, the elder sister of King George III. After serving under his uncle Frederick the Great, he succeeded as ruling Duke of Brunswick in 1780. At the start of the French Revolutionary Wars he was appointed commanding general of the Prussian and Austrian army which invaded France in 1792 but was repulsed at Valmy. After suffering a succession of defeats in 1793 he retired from active service until 1806 when, somewhat surprisingly, he was given command of the largest of the Prussian armies put into the field against Napoleon. Brunswick was mortally wounded at Auerstädt† on 14 October 1806 and died four weeks later at Altona. Caroline†, Princess of Wales, was his daughter.

BUCHAREST, Treaty of (28 May 1812)
The agreement which ended the desultory war between Russia and the Ottoman Empire†, begun in December 1806 and keeping the Eastern Question† unresolved throughout the years of Napoleon's primacy. The Treaty followed seven months of negotiations between the Turks and the Russian commander, Kutuzov†, at his headquarters in Giurgiu. The agreed terms fell short of Russia's hopes; the treaty provided for the evacuation by the Russians of Moldavia and Wallachia, but it established a Russo-Turkish frontier along the line of the River Prut and the northernmost stream of the Danube delta, thus leaving Bessarabia within the Russian Empire. At the same time Turkey promised autonomy to Serbia†. The Turks realized that Russia had made peace only to allow the Tsar's armies to concentrate in Poland and meet the growing threat from Napoleon. While the Russians were heavily engaged against the French in 1812-13, Turkey took the opportunity to recover mastery of Serbia. It thus soon became clear to both signatories that the Bucharest Treaty was not so much a definitive peace settlement as a truce.

BUDBERG, Andrey (1750–1809)
Russian soldier and Foreign Minister: born, of Swedish descent, near Riga. He served in Catherine the Great's wars and reached the rank of general. Briefly, during Tsar Paul's reign, he was ambassador in Stockholm. Alexander I appointed Budberg Foreign Minister in succession to Czartoryski† in July 1806, but he was not a success in the post. He was too bellicose to take any diplomatic initiative and suffered from chronic ill health. Nevertheless, he was resolutely opposed to any appeasement of France. Sudden illness, feigned or genuine, prevented his attendance at Tilsit† in July 1807. Two months later Tsar Alexander dismissed him in favour of Rumyantsev†.

BULLETINS OF THE ARMY

During the Marengo campaign† Bonaparte developed the practice of sending to Paris communiqués recounting the progress of his army. These 'Bulletins of the Army of the Reserve' were published in the official *Moniteur*‡ and were frequently drafted by Bonaparte himself. Regular bulletins were thereafter issued during all the campaigns of the *Grande Armée*, bolstering morale in Paris or – in later years – preparing the population for grim news. Among the most famous Bulletins of the Army were: Bulletin 32 of the Austerlitz† campaign (published in the *Moniteur* on 17 December 1805) which described how a 'radiant sun' witnessed 'one of the century's most valiant deeds of arms on the anniversary of the Emperor's coronation'; Bulletin 79 of the Polish campaign (published 30 June 1807), reporting the brilliant role of the Emperor in the victory of Friedland†; Bulletin 19 of the Russian campaign (published 3 October 1812) announcing the entry into Moscow† on 14 September; and Bulletin 29 of the Russian campaign (drafted at Molodechno on 2 December and published on 17 December) which revealed the heavy losses of the retreat and ended, 'His Majesty's health has never been better'.

BURGOS

City and provincial capital in northern Spain, almost equidistant from Bayonne† and Madrid† (125 miles). King Joseph (Bonaparte†) found refuge there in September 1808 after his first rejection by the people of Madrid. Napoleon ordered the citadel to be strengthened and, with its outlying fortifications, Burgos successfully withstood a siege by Wellington from mid-September to late-October in 1812. But Wellington made another assault, under better weather conditions, in the following summer and induced the garrison to surrender after only two days of sharp engagement (11–12 June 1813).

BYRON, George Gordon Noel (1788–1824, succeeded his great-uncle as 6th Baron Byron in 1798)

English poet: born in London, spent his early years at Aberdeen, his mother (Catherine Gordon) being a Scottish heiress. When he succeeded to the barony, he also inherited Newstead Abbey, the family seat in Nottinghamshire. He was educated at Harrow and Trinity College, Cambridge, triumphing physically over the disability of a club foot. His first satirical poems appeared in 1809, the year in which he set out on a foreign tour with his college friend, John Cam Hobhouse (1786–1869), a brilliant Whig politician and admirer of Napoleon. Hobhouse and Byron visited Spain, Portugal, Malta and the Ottoman Empire, above all Greece†. Byron was received by Ali Pasha† at Tepelenë in October 1809 and stayed on in Athens until April 1811, identifying himself more and more with the Greeks and their way of life. He arrived back in England on 14 July 1811, took his seat in the Lords and made an impressive maiden speech condemning the death penalty for machine breaking (27 February 1812). Eleven days later the first two cantos of *Childe Harold's Pilgrimage* were published: 'I awoke one morning and found myself famous', he declared later. 5,000 copies were sold in three weeks, and the spring of 1812 marked the acme of his social success, 'my reign', as he called it, a period in which he was pursued by Lady Caroline Lamb and other hostesses. On the night of 23–4 June – in the same small hours that Napoleon's army invaded Russia – Byron was presented to the Prince Regent at a ball, the Regent impressing him by his knowledge of poetry and heaping compliments on him; but Byron was by nature a radical and made little effort in the following years to hide his admiration for Napoleon.

Byron's narrative poems *The Giaour* and *The Corsair* followed in the next two years, *The Corsair* selling 10,000 copies on publication day alone. On 2 January 1815

Byron, as a defender of the Greek cause

Byron married Annabella Milbanke, but the marriage ended in separation a year later with accusations of cruelty and rumours of an incestuous relationship between Byron and his half-sister, Augusta Leigh. Byron left England, scorned by fashionable society, on 25 April 1816. He crossed to Ostend, visited the battlefield of Waterloo and travelled to Geneva, finding inspiration once again in his travels for the third canto of *Childe Harold*. The final canto was written in Venice in 1817, where he also wrote most of *Don Juan*. He spent some months in Ravenna and Pisa before travelling to Greece in August 1823 to serve the revolutionaries seeking to free the country from Turkish rule. He tried to settle disputes between the different Greek factions while living at Missolonghi (from January 1824) but he contracted rheumatic fever and died there on 19 April 1824. His remains were brought home for burial at Hucknall Torkard parish church, near Newstead. More than any other poet, Byron caught the essence of Romanticism† in action. For this reason, despite the fluency of his verse, he was always rated more highly on the European continent than in England.

C

Cabinet Noir

A secret bureau for intercepting and reading correspondence, originally established in France in Louis XIV's reign. It was revived, as a form of postal censorship, in 1800. The *cabinet noir* was controlled by Antoine-Marie de Lavalette, Napoleon's highly efficient Minister of Posts.

CADIZ

Historic seaport, the most southerly provincial capital in Spain, projecting into the Atlantic at the tip of the Isla de León peninsula. Cadiz was the scene of violent rioting in May 1808 against the French occupation of Madrid and the dynastic arrangements reached at Bayonne†. With the recovery of the French in the following winter, Cadiz became the refuge of the Supreme Central Junta, which had fled from Aranjuez to Seville in November 1809 and on to the peninsula two months later. There the Junta resigned, and was succeeded by an ultra-conservative Regency of Five, which was soon in conflict with the patriot democrats of Cadiz. These internal feuds were, however, stilled by the proximity of a considerable French force, under Marshal Victor†, which besieged Cadiz from 5 February 1810 until 24 August 1812. The Spanish defenders were strengthened by British and Portuguese troops, brought in by sea, and the Royal Navy eased the full rigours of the siege by bringing supplies and food from Portugal. On 24 September 1810 the Cortes of Cadiz met in the besieged Isla de León and spent the following eighteen months drafting the famous liberal Cadiz Constitution (*see below*) which was published on 19 March 1812. Long disputes continued (particularly between Liberals and Clericalists) throughout the campaigns which liberated Spain, the Constituent Cortes remaining in session at Cadiz until May 1813. The city was mistrusted, as a centre of radical disaffection, throughout the remaining years of the restored Ferdinand VII†.

CADIZ, Constitution of (1812)

In the spring of 1812 a liberal constituent Cortes meeting in Isla de León, outside Cadiz†, completed the drafting of a constitution which provided for the establishment in a liberated Spain of a single-chamber parliamentary assembly elected by indirect universal manhood suffrage. The constitution also gave guarantees of popular sovereignty, freedom of the press, freedom of legal contract, civil equality and safeguards for property rights as well as local government reform. Spain would remain a monarchy although the king's prerogatives were limited by the authority of a nominated Council of State. This constitution, which owed much to political ideas discussed in Paris in 1791–2, was accepted by Ferdinand VII† on his restoration to the throne on 24 March 1814 but repudiated by him six weeks later in response to a petition from sixty-nine traditionalists. In 1820 a radical revolt forced Ferdinand to restore the Cadiz Constitution although he again repudiated it in October 1823. The constitution was accepted as an ideal model for liberals on the Continent throughout the post-Napoleonic period. It was especially influential in Italy.

A contemporary version of the arrest of Cadoudal, March 1804

CADOUDAL CONSPIRACY(1804)

Georges Cadoudal (1771–1804) was a Breton from the Morbihan peninsula who encouraged militant royalist opposition to the Republic and the Consulate from 1793 onwards, eventually setting up an émigré training camp for anti-Bonapartist terrorists at Romsey in Hampshire. He helped plan the attempt on the First Consul's life known as the 'Rue Saint-Nicaise *Attentat*'† in December 1800. Two and a half years later he began to plan a *coup d'état* which sought, in the first instance, to kidnap the First Consul and replace him by dissident generals who would invite the Bourbons to return to the throne. In the third week of August 1803 Cadoudal crossed the Channel in a Spanish brig from Hastings, landed secretly on the Normandy coast near Biville, made his way to Paris and went into hiding for more than four months. His conspiracy, involving some fifty men including Generals Pichegru† and Moreau†, hinged on the interception of Bonaparte at a parade in the Place du Carrousel. The clumsy conspiracy soon attracted the attention of Fouché† and may even have been encouraged by his *agents provocateurs*. Cadoudal was arrested on 13 February, put on trial and guillotined on 25 June 1804, seven other conspirators dying on the same day. Attempts were made to link the Duke of Enghien† with Cadoudal's plot, but without convincing evidence.

CAEN FOOD RIOTS (March to May 1812)

The most serious riots over food supplies in Napoleon's Europe took place in the old Normandy city of Caen in the spring of 1812 as the army was mustering for the invasion of Russia. Demands for grain and for reasonably priced bread led to major disturbances in the Vaucelles district of Caen, a working-class area south-east of the city and on the right bank of the River Orne. The worst outburst occurred on 2 March. Conscripts joined the rioters and were tried by courts martial when the magistrates began to restore order in the middle of the month: eight rioters were sentenced to death and eighteen others given long prison sentences. Unrest continued until the price of bread began to fall in the early summer.

CAIRO

French troops entered Cairo immediately after the battle of the Pyramids† on 21 July 1798, Bonaparte personally establishing himself in the principal palace of the Bey three days later. He remained in the Cairo area for two months, seeking to improve local administration and to introduce modern government into Egypt† as a whole. The fiscal reforms which he proposed led to an unexpected insurrection in Cairo on 21 October 1798. So widespread

was the killing that Bonaparte ordered a bombardment of the El Azhar Mosque. Before the fighting stopped, on the evening of 22 October, the French had lost some 300 men and probably over two thousand Egyptians perished. Bonaparte showed clemency, formally telling the people of Cairo a month later that he pardoned them. He returned to Cairo from the Syrian campaign in June 1799, finally leaving the city on 18 August. Kléber†, his successor as commander-in-chief, made an impressive entry into Cairo thirteen days later. While he was campaigning in Lower Egypt in March 1800 the people of Cairo rose in revolt and for five weeks held the city. Kléber restored order, imposing heavy punitive financial burdens on the sheikhs. A young religious fanatic murdered him in the palace gardens on 14 June 1800. The French remained in Cairo until the arrival of Anglo-Turkish forces on 22 June 1801 after their successful landing in Aboukir Bay†. The Grand Vizier allowed the French to march out of Cairo with full honours of war.

Cairo, November 1798: Bonaparte pardons the rebels

CALDIERO

Village five and a half miles east of Verona, between the foothills of the Alps and the swamps of the River Adige. Two battles were fought outside Caldiero: (i) 12 November 1796, an abortive attempt by Bonaparte to check the advance of the Austrian commander, Alvintzi on Verona, the French failure redeemed a few days later by the victory of Arcole†; (ii) 30 October 1805, an attack made by Archduke Charles† on Masséna's troops in order to clear his line of retreat towards the main theatre of operations in the Ulm-Austerlitz campaign. Although on this occasion the Archduke saved his baggage train from interception by the French, he could not shake off Masséna, and his army was unable to influence the outcome of the campaign.

CAMBACÉRÈS, Jean-Jacques de (1753–1824)

Second Consul: born at Montpellier, coming from a family of lawyers well known in Languedoc. Before the Revolution he was a tax assessor in his native town. He was then elected to the Convention as deputy for the département of Hérault and in 1793 began work on transforming some 14,000 revolutionary decrees into a draft comprehensive legal code. This task he continued, with constant revision, as a member of the Council of Five Hundred†, at last becoming Minister of Justice in June 1799. He supported Bonaparte in Brumaire† and was appointed Second Consul, with responsibility for formulating the Civil Code†. During the years in which Bonaparte was campaigning in the field, Cambacérès enjoyed great influence and wide patronage. He rapidly acquired a fortune which he invested wisely in real estate, shares, gems and furniture. Napoleon consulted him over the constitutional propriety of establishing the Empire in 1804. Five years later Cambacérès drafted the application to the ecclesiastical court for annulment of Napoleon's marriage to

Josephine†. The Emperor respected his judgement in questions of law although he frequently scoffed at Cambacérès's homosexual proclivities. Under the Empire the former Second Consul served as titular Arch-Chancellor and was created Duke of Parma. He remained in exile in Brussels from 1815 to 1818, returning to France to spend his last years in retirement on his considerable estates. At the time of his death his personal fortune amounted to some $7\frac{1}{4}$ million francs. No other dignitary of the Empire prospered so remuneratively.

CAMPAIGNS OF NAPOLEON BONAPARTE

1. *Italian campaign of 1796–7:* was intended by Carnot to serve as a subordinate campaign, supporting the armies of Jourdan and Moreau, who were to defeat the Austrians by converging on Vienna from the Meuse and the Rhine. Bonaparte gained his first victories against the Piedmontese allies of Austria, defeating them at Montenotte on 12 April 1796 and at Dego five days later; Piedmont-Sardinia withdrew from the war by the armistice of Cherasco (28 April 1796). Lodi (10 May) was a major triumph for Bonaparte, inducing the Austrians to abandon Milan. From July 1796 to February 1797 Bonaparte was faced by four Austrian armies: the main theatre of operations was in the Lombard Plain between Mantua and Verona, the scene of the battles of Borghetto, Bassano, Caldiero 1, Arcole and Rivoli. The victory at Rivoli led to the fall of Mantua and to the collapse of the Austrian position in Upper Italy, Bonaparte's successes having turned upside down Carnot's original plan. In the final phase of the campaign (March-April 1797) Bonaparte's army rapidly drove back the troops of Archduke Charles through Carinthia and into Styria, advancing to Bruck an der Mur, 100 miles from Vienna. Peace preliminaries at Leoben were followed by the Peace of Campo Formio.

Extirpation of the Plagues of Egypt;– Destruction of Revolutionary Crocodiles;– or—The British Hero cleansing ỹ Mouth of ỹ Nile

James Gillray; patriotic cartoon of 1798, 'The British Hero cleansing the mouth of the Nile'

2. *Egyptian and Syrian campaigns, 1798–9*: had, as a strategic objective, the destruction of the British Empire in India. Within three weeks of landing in Egypt, Bonaparte won the Battle of the Pyramids and entered Cairo (21 July 1798). Nelson's naval victory at the mouth of the Nile on 31 July left the French force isolated. Without naval supremacy in the eastern Mediterranean there was no hope of sustaining a major campaign in the Orient and Bonaparte therefore modified his objective, striving to establish an enduring French protectorate over Egypt and to destroy Turkish power in the Levant by defeating the Sultan's army in Syria. Bonaparte's Syrian campaign (6 February to 20 May 1799) opened well but failed to develop, partly because of the persistent resistance of the defenders of Acre but even more because of an outbreak of plague in the French army. Bonaparte personally remained in Egypt until 23 August. Technically the campaign continued until August 1801 when the combined armies of Britain and Turkey forced the surrender of 20,000 French troops.

3. *The Marengo campaign, 1800*: was intended to restore French authority in northern Italy which had been destroyed by Suvorov's successes in the early phases of the War of the Second Coalition. Bonaparte led his army across the Great St Bernard Pass, recovered Milan without difficulty and then headed for the Austrian field headquarters at Alessandria. The decisive battle – Marengo – was fought less than three miles from Alessandria, forcing the Austrians to retreat behind the River Mincio. Although Italy was recovered for the French, the Austrians only made peace (at Lunéville in February 1801) after Moreau's victory at Hohenlinden in Bavaria.

4. *The Ulm-Austerlitz campaign, 1805*: struck at the heart of the Third Coalition. The rapidity with which Napoleon marched his armies from Boulogne to the

Danube made the Austrians miscalculate. Mack's surrender at Ulm was followed by Napoleon's pursuit of Kutuzov's Austro-Russian army from Bavaria down the Danube, Murat occupying Vienna without a struggle while the main armies faced each other in Moravia. Napoleon's decisive victory at Austerlitz (2 December 1805) split the Allied armies, forcing Austria to conclude an armistice and make peace at Pressburg. The Russians withdrew behind the Tsar's frontier.

5. *The Jena campaign, 1806*: was forced on Napoleon by Prussia's demand, made on 26 September, that all French troops should retire from Germany east of the Rhine. Napoleon planned to take advantage of Prussia's slow mobilization to strike across Saxony from the River Main, marching directly on Berlin. He advanced from Bamberg on 8 October. Lack of cohesion in the Prussian command allowed Davout to engage one section of the Prussian army at Auerstädt on the same day upon which Napoleon defeated Prince Hohenlohe's army at Jena, fifteen miles to the north (14 October 1806). This double French victory left open the route to Berlin. For three weeks the French pursued the Prussians northwards into Mecklenburg and eventually to the Baltic coast, separating the main army under Blücher from King Frederick William's small force, which retired eastwards to Küstrin (now Kostrzyn) and the River Oder. When Blücher was captured near Lübeck on 7 November, the Prussians were left with only isolated garrisons in Silesia and East Prussia.

6. *The Polish campaign, 1806–7*, also known as the *Eylau-Friedland campaign*: was a continuation of the Jena campaign, with the Russians giving support to the rump of the Prussian army. Napoleon did not return to France after Blücher's surrender but spent the main winter months in Poland, originally at Poznan (Posen) and later in Warsaw. The Russian army was first encountered by Lannes in the indecisive battle of Pultusk (26 December), but Napoleon did not leave winter quarters until the end of January, bringing the Russians to battle amid the frozen lakes and marshes of East Prussia at Eylau (8 February 1807), a bloodbath which left the French masters of the field but unable to exploit their tactical success. The decisive clash between the opposing armies did not come until almost midsummer, Napoleon defeating Bennigsen in the bends of the River Alle at Friedland (14 June 1807), a victory which soon led to the Peace of Tilsit and the fragile Franco-Russian alliance.

7. *Spanish campaign, 1808–9*: formed a brief episode in the seven years of constant campaigning known as the Peninsular War. Napoleon had not originally intended to fight in Spain himself; he intervened only after learning of the Spanish success at Baylen. He took command at Vitoria on 5 November 1808, galvanized his marshals into action, and advanced by way of Burgos on Madrid, which he entered a month later. His attempt to destroy the small British force under Sir John Moore as it fell back from Salamanca to Corunna was frustrated by the bitterly cold weather and by stubborn rearguard actions. Napoleon left Soult and Ney to finish off the campaign (as he hoped) and crossed back into France on 19 January 1809, leaving his conquest of Spain dangerously incomplete.

8. *The Wagram campaign, 1809*: was Napoleon's response to the decision of Stadion and the war party in Vienna to seek revenge for defeat in 1805. The campaign lasted only thirteen weeks. Napoleon gained a tactical advantage at Eckmühl in the first days of the campaign, following it up with a spectacular success at Ratisbon (Regensburg) on the following day (23 April), but Archduke Charles brought his army back virtually intact along the left bank of the Danube to the Marchfeld, north of Vienna. Napoleon's attacks across the Danube around Aspern and Essling on 21–2 May were beaten off by the Archduke. Fear that Charles's men

would be strengthened by the arrival of considerable reinforcements from Hungary led Napoleon to launch a desperate assault on the Austrian positions at Wagram, outside Vienna, on 5 July. The two-day battle left the Austrians too weak to maintain the war; they signed an armistice on 12 July; the Peace of Schönbrunn followed in October.

9. *The Russian campaign, 1812*: was intended by Napoleon to be a brief military operation, although on a more ambitious scale than any earlier campaign. He hoped to defeat the Russian armies either in one big battle or in a series of engagements fought close to the frontier of the Tsar's Empire. But after Napoleon, without declaring war, had crossed the River Niemen on 24 June, the two main Russian armies under Barclay and Bagration avoided a major encounter, drawing the *Grande Armée* deeper and deeper into old Muscovy, exposing its long supply line to partisan attack and threatening to isolate Napoleon from the government of his Empire. Smolensk was vigorously defended. The great battle came, however, not near the frontier, but at Borodino, 550 miles east of the Niemen, on 7 September. Napoleon entered Moscow a week later, mistakenly assuming Russia would sue for peace. Moscow was fired soon after his arrival and, with the approach of winter, his position became increasingly serious. After five weeks in the old Russian capital he led his army south-westwards towards Kaluga and the Russian arsenal at Tula, intending to find secure winter quarters at Smolensk and Minsk. The Russian troops, under Kutuzov, constantly harried the *Grande Armée* and there was a sharp engagement at Maloyaroslavets before Napoleon left the Kaluga road and sought to retreat directly along the Mozhaysk-Smolensk route which he had followed two months previously. The retreat was hampered, not only by pursuing Russian regular troops, but by Cossack raiding parties and by two other Russian armies, threatening a strategic pincer movement:

Wittgenstein's Army of Finland moved south from the Polotsk region and Chichagov's Army of Moldavia moved rapidly northwards. The retreating French were short of food and fodder, many men had only summer uniforms and their progress was slowed down by the booty they sought to carry with them. Heavy snow began to fall on 4 November. Brilliant improvisation enabled the *Grande Armée* to avoid destruction at the crossing of the Berezina, but the retreat was so costly in men, horses and material that Napoleon brought the campaign to an end. He left the army at Smorgon on 5 December, appointing Murat commander-in-chief. The *Grande Armée* had numbered 450,000 men when Napoleon crossed the Niemen in June. By the time Napoleon reached Moscow he had with him only 100,000 men, through battle casualties, loss of units to hold the supply line, and incompetent provision of maintenance services. Another 80,000 men were lost in the retreat, of whom only a quarter perished during the heavy snowfall. The campaign was already a disastrous failure before the coming of winter.

10. *The German campaigns, 1813* also known as the *Leipzig campaign*: a period of military activity falling naturally into two sections; the Lützen and Bautzen period in April and May, when Napoleon sought to check the westward advance of the Russians and Prussians, gaining victories which he could not exploit through lack of cavalry and being forced to accept an armistice from 2 June to 13 August; and the Dresden and Leipzig phase of the campaign, from mid-August to late October. Napoleon hoped to break the new coalition of Russia, Austria and Prussia by a massive flank attack at Dresden; his tactics won the day, but he could not sustain the offensive, and he twice had to abandon plans for marching on Berlin. Increasing defections by former German puppet states endangered his position on the eve of the largest battle of the Wars, the so-called 'Battle of the Nations' at

Leipzig (16-19 October). His defeat in this terrible engagement cost Napoleon control of Germany; there was no hope that he could put an army in the field again for three or four months.

11. *The French campaign, 1814*: was a brilliant defensive operation by Napoleon who sought to use his much smaller army (young recruits leavened by veteran units) to exploit the wide deployment of the Allied invaders, harassing them in the valleys of the Seine and Marne. In three weeks (29 January to 18 February) Napoleon gained a succession of victories in small engagements at Brienne, Champaubert, Montmirail and Vauchamps. He hoped that these successes would force the Allies to make political concessions in the peace talks at Châtillon so as to save France's 'natural frontiers' and his throne, but his military resources did not match his diplomatic ambitions. The campaign swung in favour of the Allies with Blücher's victory at Laon on 9 March. Napoleon could not prevent the Allies from advancing on Paris, which was covered by Marshals Marmont and Mortier with only 20,000 troops. The Allies entered Paris on 31 March; and Napoleon abdicated at Fontainebleau a week later.

12. *The Waterloo campaign, 1815*: was the desperate gamble of Naopleon's 'Hundred Days'. He wished to destroy the Allied armies piecemeal, picking off the Anglo-Dutch force and Blücher's Prussians in Belgium, before the Austrians and Russians were ready for a new war. He hoped that the occupation of Brussels and an advance to the Scheldt and lower Rhine would enable him to dictate peace. He struck first, with complete surprise, at the point north of Charleroi where Wellington's army and Blücher's army were supposed to join each other. He defeated the Prussians at Ligny but exaggerated Blücher's losses; and he found himself having to fight a static battle against an enemy who remained in carefully chosen defensive positions at Waterloo since Wellington (like Kutuzov at Borodino)

had no intention of exposing himself to manoeuvres in the field. These tactics, together with his miscalculations over the Prussians, cost Napoleon the battle and therefore the campaign, the war and his throne as well. He abdicated a second time on 22 June, not waiting until the British and Prussians re-entered Paris. (See also under individual battles, military commanders etc. Almost every proper name has an entry in the text even though not, in this instance, marked with a dagger for cross reference.)

CAMPO FORMIO, Treaty of
(17 October 1797)

The peace treaty ending Austrian participation in the War of the First Coalition. Austria ceded the Southern Netherlands (Belgium†) to France and secretly agreed to French occupation of the left bank of the Rhine. France retained the Ionian Islands†. The Austrians accepted the primacy of France in northern Italy, formally recognizing the Cisalpine Republic† and the transformation of Genoa into a Ligurian Republic. Austria was allowed to annex Venice† and Venetian territories east of the Adige River and in Dalmatia. Provision was made for a congress to meet at Rastatt†, where the future form of the German lands would be settled. It was secretly agreed that Austria would receive compensation for these losses at the expense of Bavaria and that Prussia would not receive any territorial gains from the Rastatt Conference.

CANALS

To meet the needs of the expanding industrial system in Britain during the third quarter of the eighteenth century merchants and entrepreneurs encouraged the digging of artificial waterways. Many of these canals were planned and engineered by James Brindley, originally a workman employed by the Duke of Bridgewater on his coalfield near Manchester. Brindley, who died in 1772, planned a trunk system linking the Midlands with the Severn and the Thames; and most of his projects were realized during the Revolutionary and Napoleonic Wars. Thus, between 1793 and 1805, the Grand Junction Canal linked London and Warwickshire; the canal enabled goods to be moved faster and more conveniently than by road, and at a third of the cost. The peak of financial speculation in canals fell between 1790 and 1794 but the rewards for all this investment came with the turn of the century: canals facilitated the movement of goods around Birmingham, between the Firth and the Clyde, by locks across the Pennines from Leeds to Liverpool, and from 1803 across Scotland through the 'Caledonian Canal'. Most British canals were private ventures satisfying economic demands; only a few fast-moving barges carried passengers. Pitt in 1804 authorized the construction of the Hythe Military Canal across Romney Marsh as an anti-invasion defensive measure.

French canals had an older history. The earliest industrial artificial waterway was the Briare Canal, constructed in 1642 to serve the Loire ironfield; and a continuous tradition of civil engineering enterprise was revived by Napoleon. Under the Consulate and Empire 130 miles of new waterways were added to the 650 miles of canals completed in France before the Revolution. Napoleon gave priority to the unfinished tunnels between Saint-Quentin and Cambrai so as to bring the Picardy Canal into service. He took great personal interest in the much-publicized Ourcq Canal, bringing barge traffic from the Marne basin to north-central Paris at La Villette. Chaptal‡ ceremonially inaugurated work on the canal at La Villette on 22 September 1802, and the *Moniteur* reported that the First Consul had inspected progress along the canal on two successive days in 1803 (1–2 March). Canal construction, like other public works planned by Napoleon, fell far short of his intentions. Nearly 2,000 miles of pro-

jected canals were unfinished at the Restoration and work continued on programmes originally drawn up in the Napoleonic period until the fall of the Orleanist Monarchy in 1848.

Even before he became First Consul, Bonaparte had shown great interest in the construction of a Suez Canal, as indeed had Louis XIV on three occasions in his reign. Bonaparte visited Suez on 30 December 1798, inspected diggings around the Bitter Lakes dating from Ptolemy II, and appointed a commission of engineer officers to survey the isthmus.

CANNING, George (1770–1827)
British statesman: born in London of Anglo-Irish parentage, his father dying on the child's first birthday and leaving his widow so poor that she went on the stage for a livelihood. Canning was virtually adopted by an uncle, who made it possible for him to be educated at Eton and Christ Church, Oxford. He was called to the bar in 1791 and elected MP for Newport, Isle of Wight, in 1794, marrying a wealthy heiress in 1800. Although Canning never held cabinet office under Pitt‡, he was a warm supporter of his policies and acquired great influence in political society, not least because of his mordant wit. The Duke of Portland‡ appointed him Foreign Secretary in March 1807. While improving efficiency in the Foreign Office, Canning concentrated his efforts on waging the war, encouraging the second Copenhagen‡ expedition of September 1807 and giving vigorous diplomatic support to the Spanish insurrection against French rule. He resigned in September 1809 in protest at the policies of his colleague, Castlereagh‡, as Secretary of War. The two men fought a duel on Putney Heath later in the month, Canning being slightly wounded in the thigh. He then spent three years unsuccessfully trying to convince the Tory Party and the Prince Regent that he would make a good war leader. From 1814 to 1816 he served as ambassador in Lis-

bon. He returned to the Foreign Office in 1822 on Castlereagh's suicide, turning English policy away from the Congress system and participation in Europe's affairs. For the last five months of his life he was Prime Minister, dying while staying at Chiswick, in the room where Fox† had died twenty-one years previously.

CANNING, Stratford (1786–1880)

British diplomat: born in London and educated at Eton and King's College, Cambridge. He was a cousin of George Canning† who sent him, aged twenty, on an important diplomatic mission to Copenhagen in 1807. By the summer of 1809 he was on his way to Constantinople, where he served first as the embassy secretary and became Minister Plenipotentiary a few months later. From 1810 to 1812 he was virtually ambassador, achieving remarkable success in 1812 in mediating between the Russians and the Turks so as to conclude the Treaty of Bucharest†. In later years he became the most famous of all British ambassadors in the nineteenth century, generally remembered by the title he took in 1852, Lord Stratford de Redcliffe. He spent most of his public life in Constantinople, returning there from 1824 to 1829, 1841 to 1845 and for most of the period from 1847 to 1858.

CANOVA, Antonio (1757–1822)

Italian sculptor: born at Passagno, near Treviso, and trained as a mason. By 1774 he was established as a sculptor in Venice, but his delight in neoclassicism led him to move to Rome in 1781 and he soon gained an international reputation. He was in Vienna from 1797 until the end of the century. In 1802 the Pope encouraged him to accept an invitation from the First Consul to visit Paris; his classical style was well suited to Napoleonic grandeur. Busts of Napoleon, two huge statues of him in bronze and in marble, an equestrian bronze and the famous *Pauline Bonaparte as Venus* (1808) were among works commissioned by the imperial family. In 1815 he again travelled to Paris, this time on behalf of Pius VII† to identify and recover art treasures removed from papal collections by the French. He then crossed to London and was commissioned by the Prince Regent to complete two marble groups for Carlton House, both of which are now in Buckingham Palace. Four years later the Regent also commissioned

Engraving after the statue by Canova, 'Pauline Bonaparte Borghese as Venus', completed in 1808

a monument to the exiled Stuarts, which may be seen in St Peter's, Rome. Canova, who was created Marchese d'Ischia by the Pope, was well liked; he was equable in temperament and generous by nature.

CAPE OF GOOD HOPE

The Dutch established a colony around the Cape of Good Hope in 1652, some French Huguenot settlers joining the Dutch burghers, 1690–4. In 1795 the exiled Prince of Orange authorized British forces to garrison the Cape so as to prevent the settlement's falling into French hands. The British administered the region from September 1795 until February 1803 when, in accordance with the Peace of Amiens†, the Cape of Good Hope was handed over to the Batavian Republic. A British expeditionary force of 5,000 men sailed from Cork on 31 August 1805, reached the Cape in the first week of the new year and took over the colony from the Dutch Governor on 10 January 1806. The first Treaty of Paris (30 May 1814) confirmed British possession, and by an agreement concluded ten weeks later in London the Dutch government received £6 million as compensation for their lost colony.

CAPRARA, Giovanni Battista (1733–1810)

Cardinal: born at Bologna. He was sent as Papal Legate to Paris as soon as Pius VII† ratified the Concordat† in 1801. He was a more conciliatory priest than Consalvi†, who had negotiated the Concordat. Caprara eased the difficulties of conscience of priests returning to an allegiance they had cast aside during the Revolution. He also helped Napoleon personally during the transition from Consulate to Empire, notably over the Pope's journey to Paris for the imperial coronation†. As Cardinal-Archbishop of Milan Caprara presided over Napoleon's coronation as King of Italy in Milan Cathedral on 26 May 1805.

CARIBBEAN as a theatre of war: see *West Indies*.

CARNOT, Lazare (1753–1823)

French general and Minister of War: born at Nolay, near Beaune, the son of a notary. He was educated at the school of military engineers at Mézières, commissioned in 1773 but fell foul of authority for his liberal views. He sat in the Constituent Assembly and in the Convention, voting for the execution of Louis XVI. In 1793 he organized the *levée en masse* and drew up the military plans of the fourteen armies raised by the Republic, participating as a captain in the battle of Wattignies, between Dunkirk and Maubeuge, that October. His brilliant staff work won him the reputation of being the 'organizer of victory' and he was, in effect, Minister of War to successive regimes from August 1793 until September 1797. It was under his strategic plan for a three-pronged offensive against the Austrians in 1796 that Bonaparte embarked on his first Italian campaign. After Brumaire he was appointed inspector-general of the army

Lazare Carnot

and was titular Minister of War from April to December 1800. But Carnot, a man of strict republican principles, distrusted the new Consular autocracy and did not hide his criticisms. He strongly disapproved of the transition to Empire and withdrew from public life, achieving distinction as a mathematician who introduced fresh concepts to the study of geometry. Carnot also wrote works on defensive fortification and on balloons. In January 1814 he was hurriedly recalled to the army, promoted to general and sent to defend Antwerp against Bernadotte's Swedish expeditionary force, a task in which he showed all his old skills. He was Minister of the Interior in 1815, urging Napoleon not to abdicate after Waterloo. As a regicide he then went into exile and resumed his writing, first in Poland and, from October 1816 until his death, in Magdeburg.

CAROLINE OF BRUNSWICK, Princess of Wales (1768–1821)
Born at Wolfenbüttel, the daughter of the Duke of Brunswick† mortally wounded at Auerstädt†. She married her first cousin, the future George IV (see *George, Prince Regent*) on 8 April 1795. It was an unhappy union of totally different temperaments; they lived together as husband and wife for only a few months and their one child, Princess Charlotte (1796–1817) was herself to die in childbirth before her father's accession. Princess Caroline's liaisons shocked George III and Tory society but she became a focus for Whig opposition, her wrongs championed by Brougham†. In August 1814 she left England so as to be, in her own words, 'a happy merry soul' on the Continent. She then showed a delight in everything concerned with the Bonaparte family. She was a guest of Marie Louise† in Switzerland, was received by Lucien Bonaparte† in Rome and hoped to see Napoleon on Elba, but he discouraged the proposed visit. The Princess then settled for three months at Portici, six miles outside Naples

where she heaped flatteries on 'King Joachim the Great' (alias Murat†). In April 1815 she crossed to Elba, inspecting Napoleon's house in great detail and taking away, as a 'precious memento', an ebony billiard cue. Her companion, Bartolomeo Pergami (a veteran of the Russian campaign) encouraged her to purchase a villa on Lake Como. After her husband's accession she returned to England in June 1820 and for six months tried to secure recognition of her rights while the government sought to carry through parliament a Bill of Pains and Penalties which would have deprived 'Her Majesty Caroline Amelia Elizabeth . . . of the title of Queen' and declared her marriage 'for ever wholly dissolved, annulled and made void'. Popular support for Caroline led to the withdrawal of the Bill in November; she was granted the right to a royal residence in December but denied participation in the coronation, which took place on 19 July 1821 (a fortnight after London received news of Napoleon's death). Caroline herself was suddenly seized by abdominal pains on 30 July while at Drury Lane theatre; she died in Hammersmith on 7 August, and her body was taken back to Germany for burial, with popular demonstrations honouring her memory as the funeral procession made its way to Harwich.

CASTAÑOS, Francisco Xavier (1756–1852)
Spanish general, created Duke of Baylen: born in Madrid, fought in Germany against Frederick the Great's armies and gained further military experience besieging Gibraltar (1779–82) and participating in punitive expeditions against the pirates of Ceuta and Oran. He became a national hero in 1808 when his Army of Andalusia forced Dupont's Corps to surrender at Baylen†. In the winter campaign of 1808–9 he commanded the Army of the Centre but was defeated by Lannes and outmanoeuvred by Ney†. Castaños was much respected by Wellington, with whom he

collaborated closely in the siege of Bada-joz† and at Vitoria†. In 1825 he was appointed to the Spanish Council of State; and, as an octogenarian, he became principal tutor to the child queen, Isabella II (1830–1904).

CASTIGLIONE, Battle of (5 August 1796) In late July 1796 Bonaparte was threatened by two Austrian armies advancing on either side of Lake Garda to relieve the siege of Mantua†. He broke off the siege and sent Masséna† to check the western advance while seeking favourable ground to meet the more serious menace posed by Würmser's army, which was advancing across the rivers Adige and Mincio. The decisive action was fought at Castiglione, thirteen miles south-west of Peschiera and the southern shores of Lake Garda. Augereau† and Masséna (who had disposed of the threat from the west) sought to lure Würmser forward so that the French cavalry could sweep down on his flank but the manoeuvre failed and, although the Austrians were forced back to Peschiera, Bonaparte was denied the major victory for which he had hoped. A month later, however, he gained more success on the field of Bassano†.

CASTLEREAGH, Lord (Robert Stewart, 1769–1822) British War Minister and Foreign Secretary: born at Mount Stewart, near Newtownards, County Down, the son of Robert Stewart who received an Irish peerage as Marquess of Londonderry in 1789, the courtesy title of Viscount Castlereagh going to his eldest surviving child. Castlereagh was educated at Armagh and St John's College, Cambridge. He was elected to the Irish parliament in 1790, originally holding Whig views. By 1795 he was a Tory and served as Pitt's Chief Secretary of Ireland† from 1798 to 1801, working for the Act of Union while also favouring Catholic Emancipation†,

although he was himself a Protestant. He was the first Irish-born Chief Secretary. From 1794 onwards he also had a seat in the Westminster parliament, successively representing constituencies in Cornwall, Devon, Yorkshire and County Down. He became a cabinet minister in October 1802, as Addington's President of the Board of Control (of Indian affairs). This office he continued to hold under Pitt† from 1804 to 1806, also serving as Secretary for War and Colonies (July 1805 to January 1806). His plan, as War Minister, to hold in readiness a 'disposable force' of at least 10,000 men, with ships to transport them anywhere in Europe where it was possible to engage the French on land, remained unfulfilled because of financial economies. Castlereagh served again as War Minister from April 1807 to September 1809, a period in which he was concerned with the bombardment of Copenhagen†, the beginning of the Peninsular War† and the disastrous Walcheren expedition†. Criticism of Castlereagh's preparations for Walcheren by his cabinet colleague, Canning†, led to a duel between the two men on 21 September 1809. Thereafter Castlereagh remained out of office until 28 February 1812 when he was appointed Foreign Secretary, also becoming leader of the House of Commons when Perceval† was assassinated in May. As Foreign Secretary Castlereagh painstakingly built up the final coalition against Napoleon. In December 1813 he set out from London to meet the Allied sovereigns and foreign ministers at Basle† in order to coordinate policies over peace and war. The journey, by way of Holland, took Castlereagh three weeks; it was the first occasion in seventy years on which a British foreign minister had undertaken a Continental mission. Castlereagh kept the coalition together at Chaumont† and Châtillon†, remaining abroad until after the first Treaty of Paris† was signed on 30 May 1814. He travelled that autumn to Vienna† for the Congress, was in Paris again after the Hundred Days and headed the British delegation to the Congress of Aix-la-Chapelle in 1818. With Wellington, his friend and colleague, he selected St Helena as a suitable place of confinement for the fallen Emperor. An austere manner, and an inability to speak out convincingly in ringing tones, made Castlereagh unpopular in Britain, where he was erroneously identified with the repressive domestic policy of the Liverpool† government. Overwork, and worry over a homosexual scandal in which he had unwittingly become involved, induced a nervous breakdown soon after he succeeded his father as second Marquess of Londonderry; and on 12 August 1822 he cut his throat with a penknife, dying within minutes.

CATECHISM: see *Imperial Catechism.*

CATHERINE PAVLOVNA (1788–1819)
Grand Duchess: fourth daughter of Tsar Paul I†, favourite sister of Alexander I†. She was considered at various times as a wife for both Francis I† of Austria and for Napoleon, but her brother did not favour either of these marriage projects. After a brief affair with Prince Bagration†, she married the exiled Duke George of Oldenburg at Peterhof in August 1809. The married couple remained in Russia, living mainly in Tver, and Catherine was a powerful influence on Tsar Alexander, strengthening his resolve to resist Napoleon but dissuading him from seeking to command the army himself during the critical weeks of the 1812 campaign. Duke George's death on 27 December 1812, and Alexander's long estrangement from his empress, left Catherine virtually the 'first lady' of Russia; she accompanied her brother on his visit to England in 1814 (where she was unpopular at court) and also to the Vienna Congress. There she met, and in January 1816 married, Prince William of Württemberg, who succeeded to the Württemberg throne nine months

later. Catherine died, from a combination of erysipelas and influenza, in January 1819 at Stuttgart.

CATHOLIC EMANCIPATION
The Test Act of 1673 required the holders of public office in the British Isles to receive the sacraments according to the rites of the Church of England. Roman Catholics were thus unable to sit in the House of Commons or hold executive posts in the government. This disability became extremely serious after the Act of Union with Ireland† in 1800, a measure carried through after Pitt† had given verbal assurances that Catholic emancipation would swiftly follow union. George III†, however, considered that the removal of Roman Catholic civil disabilities would be contrary to the pledge he had given at his coronation to maintain the rights and privileges of the Church of England; rather than break that oath 'I had rather beg my bread from door to door throughout Europe', he declared. The King's determination to stick to his principles induced Pitt to resign after eighteen consecutive years as Prime Minister. George IV at first took a similar attitude to that of his father but the threat of civil war in Ireland led him to accept the repeal of the Test Act in 1828 and the passage of a Catholic Emancipation Bill a year later.

CATTARO (Kotor)
The Bocche di Cattaro (Gulf of Kotor), an inlet on the eastern shore of the southern Adriatic, is one of the finest natural harbours in the world. By the Treaty of Campo Formio† of 1797 Cattaro, which with most of Dalmatia had belonged to Venice†, became an Austrian possession but it was ceded to France after Austerlitz by the Treaty of Pressburg†. This transfer was challenged by Austria's former ally, Russia, and the Adriatic squadron of Admiral Senyavin† was sent into the gulf in January 1806, occupying the town of

Cattaro and the fort of Castelnuovo (Hercegnovi), commanding the roadstead. From Cattaro the Russian admiral raided the French settlements in southern Dalmatia. His force was the only Russian fighting unit which engaged the French during the twelve months of nominal war separating Austerlitz† from Pultusk†. Senyavin's presence in Cattaro also encouraged the neighbouring Montenegrins and their co-religionist fellow South Slavs in insurgent Serbia†, thereby opening a new phase of Russian anti-Turkish activity in the traditional Eastern Question†. The Treaty of Tilsit† provided for Russian evacuation of Cattaro which, in 1809, was incorporated in Napoleon's Illyrian Provinces†. In 1813 a joint operation by the Montenegrins on land and a British naval squadron under Admiral Fremantle, ejected the French from the gulf. Montenegro controlled the towns, waters and shores of Cattaro until the whole area was handed back at the Congress of Vienna to the Austrians, who maintained an important naval base there down to 1918 when it passed into Yugoslav hands.

CAULAINCOURT, Armand Augustin Louis de, Marquis de (1773–1827)
French general and Foreign Minister, created Duke of Vicenza: born into a noble family at Caulaincourt, near Saint-Quentin, and reached the rank of captain in the royal army before being dismissed as an aristocrat in 1792. A year later he enlisted as a Republican trooper and by 1799 was a colonel. He was employed on diplomatic missions to Constantinople and St Petersburg, became the First Consul's aide-de-camp in July 1802 and was given command of a brigade in 1803. As *Grand Écuyer* (Master of the Horse) from 1804 onwards he was responsible for the speedy movement of the Emperor throughout his territories, for his personal security and for maintaining an efficient courier service and good stabling. Unjustly he was later accused of planning, and of

carrying out, the kidnapping of the Duke of Enghien†. Caulaincourt became a general in 1805; he was with Napoleon at Austerlitz†, Jena† and Friedland†. From 1807 to 1811 he was ambassador in Russia, sending home shrewd assessments of Alexander I's policies and attaining considerable influence over the Tsar. When, against Caulaincourt's advice, Napoleon embarked on the Russian campaign, he was in regular attendance on the Emperor, accompanying him in carriage and sledge as he hurried back from Smorgon† to Paris. In November 1813 Napoleon appointed Caulaincourt to succeed Maret† as Foreign Minister. He negotiated skilfully with the Allies, especially at Châtillon†. In April 1814 he was the intermediary between Napoleon in Fontainebleau† and Alexander I in Paris. After four long interviews with the Tsar he finally settled the conditions on which the Allies would accept Napoleon's first abdication†. It was Caulaincourt who discovered that the Emperor had tried to poison himself at Fontainebleau and helped him to recover. In 1815 Caulaincourt again served as Foreign Minister. After the Restoration, he was allowed to live in retirement on his estates. Between 1822 and 1825 he compiled valuable Memoirs, using notes he had made in earlier years. The authentic version of these Memoirs was not published until 1933. Like Napoleon, he suffered from cancer of the stomach in his last months.

His younger brother, General Auguste de Caulaincourt (1777–1812), was killed leading a cavalry charge on the Raevsky Redoubt at Borodino†.

CENSORSHIP
Governmental restriction of the printed word and of the theatres had been common in most of the monarchies of the *ancien régime*, although in Austria it dated only from 1753 and elsewhere it was less systematic than in the thirty years following Napoleon's fall. In Britain, govern-

ment interference with the press was generally well concealed; a stamp duty on printed sheets (introduced 1712, amended 1725, abolished 1855) restricted widespread growth of radical newspapers, while prosecutions were instituted for specific crimes such as contempt of court or of parliament, criminal libel or subversion; sentences could be severe as the cases of Cobbett† and Leigh Hunt† were to show. Dramatic productions in Great Britain were subject to the Licensing Act of 1737 which required the approval of the Lord Chamberlain for any theatrical presentation – a stipulation chiefly concerned with imposing a strait-laced public morality but also serving to inhibit political satire. Spain (and much of Italy) relied upon the old restraints of the Inquisition while sometimes having recourse to panic measures, such as the Spanish ban on the importation of all foreign newspapers in 1789–90. Within Russia censorship was the responsibility of the Ministry of Education (or, before 1803, of the Imperial Commissions on Schools); a Special Censorship Committee of the Ministry was set up in 1803 and, at least until Tilsit†, was fairly liberal in its decisions. From 1811 onwards the police authorities could ask the Tsar personally to ban works which, though passed by the censors, seemed to the police 'hostile to public order and security'. When the wars ended in 1815 an attempt was made to give the Russian Censorship Committee a virtuous standing, on the grounds that learned officials were essential to promote the literary quality of the Russian language as well as to protect the state from subversion.

Literary and dramatic censorship was curiously haphazard in pre-revolutionary France, phases of strict censorship alternating with years of relaxation. A licence to print was required from the *Directeur de la librairie* for both newspapers and books; plays needed the approval of the dramatic censor, an official liable for imprisonment in the Bastille for an error

in judgement. Freedom of the Press was proclaimed by the Declaration of the Rights of Man in 1789 and technically censorship was abolished by the Constitution of 1791. But editorial freedom was restricted when the monarchy fell, and dramatic censorship reimposed in 1794. The Directory continued to pay lip-service to press freedom. However, in April 1796, any newspaper agitation for the overthrow of the government was made a penal offence. The Consulate immediately made censorship more rigorous still, Bonaparte believing that the press was essentially an instrument of government propaganda and fearing that journalists would naturally ridicule the theatricality of authoritarian government. New plays needed authorization by the Minister of the Interior, to whom five dramatic censors would report on their moral and political content. From 1806 to 1814 the Minister of Police (successively Fouché† and Savary†) vetted every play, while a theatre could be opened only on the Emperor's orders and the repertoire of the Comédie Française† and the Opéra was subject to close ministerial scrutiny. From September 1800 all newly printed books were examined by the police before publication and might be suppressed. In February 1810 an imperial censor was appointed (the *Directeur Général de l'imprimerie et de la librairie*) with the duty of reading and, if necessary, confiscating manuscripts before printing; he was to reject any matter harmful to the dignity of the throne or the interests of the Empire. Some authors (among them Mme de Staël†) had works approved by the censor but confiscated on publication by the police, under the September 1800 regulations.

Before the *coup* of Brumaire† in 1799 there were 73 newspapers printed and published in Paris. Bonaparte decided that 60 of these publications were superfluous and by the time of the Marengo campaign there were only 13 newspapers on sale in Paris, their contents strictly supervised by the official Press Bureau. The *Moniteur*† served as a government organ, distributed in all the major cities. Outside Paris newspapers were authorized only by the Prefects†. The imperial censor took over supervision of newspapers after the new repressive decrees of February 1810. The crisis† of 1811 produced the most repressive measures of all: Paris to have only four newspapers (*Le Journal de Paris, Le Journal de l'Empire, La Gazette de France* and the *Moniteur*) and no département† allowed more than one newspaper of its own. Despite these restrictions, critics such as Chateaubriand† and Benjamin Constant† found ways of publicizing their views. The stillborn *Acte Additionnel*† of 1815 guaranteed freedom of publication for any work longer than twenty pages.

The French laws on censorship were applied throughout the Empire; Napoleon personally ordered severe measures against Palm† and other German booksellers who, he claimed, had 'spread defamatory writings in places occupied by French armies'.

CESAROTTI, Melchiorre (1730–1808)
Italian scholar: born at Padua. In 1763 he translated the poetic epics of Ossian, the legendary Gaelic warrior, which had recently been published by the Ruthven schoolmaster, James Macpherson (1736–96). Cesarotti's work brought a new range of interest to Italian literature and stimulated the growth of Italian Romanticism†. In 1768 Cesarotti became professor of Greek and Hebrew at Padua University. He was an envoy to the series of peace talks in 1797 which culminated in the Treaty of Campo Formio†. Here he met Bonaparte, who much admired the Ossian translations. Later Cesarotti accepted a pension from the First Consul and, in his last years, was recognized as the foremost champion of Bonapartism among Italy's intellectuals.

Champ de mai (1815)
The principal national fête of the Hundred Days†, celebrated in Paris on 1 June. Napoleon and representatives of the people took oaths of loyalty to the new form of constitutional government, the *Acte Additionnel*†. The fête, for which the Emperor and his brothers wore special robes of purple velvet and white satin, took place in front of the École Militaire in Paris. There were salutes from 600 guns, a parade of 50,000 soldiers, Mass celebrated at an improvised altar, and a *Te Deum*. Yet, though the fête was planned as the most magnificent tableau in Paris since the coronation of 1804, Napoleon failed to impress the crowd of onlookers; the imperial finery made the Emperor appear squat and ungainly.

CHAMPAGNY, Jean-Baptiste de Nompère de (1756-1834)
Diplomat, Minister of the Interior and Foreign Minister: born at Roanne, the son of a cavalry officer, served with distinction in the navy from 1775 to 1786, sat as deputy for the nobility of Forez in the States General and was a member of commissions on marine affairs from 1790 to 1793 when he withdrew from political life. After Brumaire he became a Councillor of State, again concentrating on naval matters, but Talleyrand† sent him to Vienna as ambassador in July 1803. A year later he returned to Paris and from August 1804 to August 1807 he was Minister of the Interior, succeeding Chaptal†. Champagny was a good administrator although not inclined to initiate undertakings himself. As Foreign Minister (August 1807 to April 1811) he consulted his predecessor, Talleyrand, to a greater extent than Napoleon realized. Personal relations between Champagny and the Austrian ambassador (Metternich†) were strained, Metternich barely concealing his contempt for Champagny as the Emperor's sycophant. In 1809 Champagny accompanied Napoleon on the Wagram

campaign and frigidly discussed peace terms with Metternich in Vienna. However the two men collaborated in arranging the marriage with Marie Louise† and Napoleon was sufficiently appreciative of Champagny's services to create him Duke of Cadore. In the spring of 1811 he was blamed by the Emperor for tardiness in alerting him to a war threat from Russia and was replaced as Foreign Minister by Maret†. During the Russian campaign Champagny was Marie Louise's Secretary of State, the chief intermediary between the court in Paris, the improvised administration in Vilna†, and the army in the field. He rallied to Napoleon's support during the Hundred Days and was, in consequence, in disgrace after the Restoration until 1819.

CHAMPAUBERT, Battle of
(10 February 1814)
The first of a series of victories which enabled Napoleon temporarily to halt the Allies in the French campaign of 1814. Champaubert is a village fifteen miles south of the River Marne at Épernay. Napoleon, realizing that Blücher's army was overstretched, mounted a surprise march northwards from the Seine and used Marmont's cavalry to envelop and destroy one of Blücher's Russian corps, left in isolation at Champaubert. Napoleon then turned westwards and gained further successes at Vauchamps† and Montmirail†.

CHAPPE, Claude (1763–1805)
French engineer: born at Brulon (Sarthe), south of Le Mans. He trained for the priesthood at Rouen but the anticlerical phase of the Revolution forced him to retire to his birthplace where, with two brothers, he tried to perfect a method of long-distance signalling, beginning his experiments along the banks of the Sarthe in March 1791. A year later anti-royalists demolished the first signalling devices he erected near Paris, as they believed they were intended to rescue the royal family. He received official backing in the summer of 1793, constructed a system of 'aerial telegraph' (semaphore†) between Paris and Lille in 1794 and was able, that summer, to convey news of the recapture of Le Quesnoy to the capital, 120 miles away, in an hour. During the following ten years Chappe was overworked in seeking to supply France with his telegraphic service, to which Bonaparte gave special attention. Chappe suffered a mental and physical breakdown and in January 1805 threw himself to his death down the shaft of a well.

CHAPTAL, Jean Antoine (1756–1832)
French chemist, entrepreneur and Minister of the Interior: born at Nojaret, of peasant stock from the Cévennes. He was educated by his uncle, a physician in Montpellier, and began to practise as a doctor before becoming interested in industrial chemistry. In 1782–3 Chaptal built up a plant for producing sulphuric and chloric acids on a large scale at La Paillade. Chaptal was the pioneer manufacturer of chemical products in pre-revolutionary France. During the Revolution he held local posts of administrative responsibility in Montpellier and the Hérault district of southern France. Under the Directory he was in charge of the national gunpowder depot at Grenelle, on the outskirts of Paris. The First Consul made him a Councillor of State and he supervised the reform of provincial administration embodied in the Law of 28 Pluviôse† (February 1800). Nine months later he became Minister of the Interior.

Chaptal was an extremely efficient administrator, effectively carrying out public works in Paris, improving hospitals, and setting up state schools for spinning and weaving. In July 1804 he resigned office in a fit of pique when he believed (probably wrongly) that Napoleon was having an affair with his mistress, Thérèse Bourgoin, an actress who owed her career to Chaptal's patronage. He then divided his time between the Senate (of which he became Treasurer) and his chemical industries, particularly a large plant at Neuilly. Napoleon created him Count de Chanteloup and in December 1813 sent him to Lyons with special powers to maintain imperial authority. During the Hundred Days Chaptal became Director-General of Agriculture, Commerce and Industry, a ministerial post of promise rather than of practical value, which left him out of favour at the Restoration. A detailed study of French industry, published in 1819, helped Chaptal recover influence and so, too, did apologetic Memoirs which he circulated in society although they remained unpublished until 1893. From 1820 until his death he was able to sit in the Chamber of Peers, applying his scientific knowledge to the problems of France's growing factory system and the rapidly expanding wine industry.

CHARLES IV, King of Spain (1748–1819, reigned 1788–1808)

Born at Portici, the second son and successor of Charles III. In 1766 he married Maria Luisa of Parma (1751–1819), a much stronger character than her amiably ineffectual husband. Charles IV's coronation in late September 1789 was followed by eight days of celebration. The political peace was shattered not so much by popular unrest as by faction fights at court, from which by 1794 Manuel Godoy‡ emerged as leader. The remaining fourteen years of Charles's reign were dominated by Godoy, who was the queen's lover and a welcome friend to the complaisant king. Discontented nobles, manipulating a mob of peasants and palace staff, forced Charles to dismiss Godoy on 17 March 1808, in the rising known as the Tumult of Aranjuez. Two days later further mob violence induced Charles to abdicate in favour of his son (Ferdinand VII‡), but the instability of Madrid politics led Napoleon to intervene. Both Charles and Ferdinand were summoned to Bayonne‡ where, on 6 May 1808, they ceded sovereign rights to the Emperor of the French, who then passed the crown of Spain to his brother, Joseph Bonaparte‡. Charles IV spent his remaining years in exile, first at Chambord and Compiègne and later in Rome, where he died three weeks after his redoubtable queen.

CHARLES XIII, King of Sweden (1748–1818, reigned 1809–18)

Born at Stockholm, the second son of Adolphus Frederick (reigned 1751–71). Before 1809 Charles was known as the Duke of Södermanland and was the brother of Sweden's enlightened ruler, Gustavus III (reigned 1771–92). Charles became Regent for his thirteen-year-old nephew, Gustavus IV Adolf, in March 1792 when Gustavus III was assassinated at the famous masked ball at Drottningholm. As Regent, Charles was not unsympathetic to France, a policy reversed when Gustavus IV Adolf began to reign in his own right in 1796. A running war with Denmark and total defeat by the Russians in Finland‡ led the Swedish nobility to turn against the young king, who was seized in a palace *coup* on 13 March 1809, abdicating in favour of his uncle sixteen days later.

Charles XIII started his reign with three disadvantages: his age; the military humiliation imposed by the Russians; and his lack of an heir, two children having died in infancy. He speedily made peace with the Tsar and, through Alexander's mediation, recovered a small segment of Swedish Pomerania‡ – a gesture made by Napoleon in return for Sweden's adherence to the Continental System‡. In January 1810 Charles accepted proposals from the Swedish Estates for the election of Prince Christian of Augustenburg as heir. Four months later Prince Christian died from a paralytic stroke. The Estates, eager for a vigorous military leader, then proposed the election of Marshal Bernadotte†, who was duly recognized as Prince Royal of Sweden on 21 August 1810. Throughout the remaining years of the reign, the Prince Royal determined Sweden's foreign policy and led the army, succeeding to the throne when Charles XIII died in Stockholm on 5 February 1818.

CHARLES (Karl), Archduke of Austria
(1771–1847)

Austrian field marshal: born in Florence, the third son of Emperor Leopold II who was Grand Duke of Tuscany at the time of Charles's birth. The Archduke fought at Jemappes in 1792 and a year later was appointed by his brother (the Emperor Francis†) last Governor-General of the Austrian Netherlands. Charles ejected the French from Belgium†, making it possible for Francis to be installed as Duke of Brabant in Brussels in April 1794. Later that summer the French recovered

Belgium, but the Archduke's military gifts led to his appointment as a field marshal in 1796, when he checked the thrusts of Jourdan† and Moreau† across the Rhine. Charles first fought against Bonaparte from February to April 1797, successfully retreating from the Tagliamento River in northern Italy through Carinthia and into Styria, thereby preserving the army in the vain hope of reinforcement from the north. During the War of the Second Coalition, Charles defeated Jourdan on the upper Rhine (March 1799) but then retired from active campaigning, serving as Governor-General of Bohemia from 1800 to 1809. In 1805, however, he returned to active service in Italy, outmanoeuvring Masséna† at Caldiero† and then falling back to cover the approaches to the Hungarian plain along the River Drava. On 10 February 1806 Archduke Charles was appointed 'Generalissimus', virtually reforming the Austrian army after the Austerlitz disaster. Against his better judgement, Charles agreed to risk war in

Napoleon receives Archduke Charles, 1809

1809, counting on the German people to rise against the French. But the appeal Charles issued in April 1809 won response only from Andreas Hofer† in the Tyrol. During the campaign the Archduke brought the main Austrian army back virtually intact from Regensburg along the Danube. He beat off Napoleon's attacks at Aspern† and Essling but his men were too exhausted to go over to the offensive and he was totally defeated at Wagram†, urging Francis to seek an armistice on 12 July 1809. Thereupon Francis relieved him of his command, so as to preserve the dynasty from the humiliation of seeking peace terms from Napoleon. The Archduke, who suffered from epilepsy, held no further commands in the field. He remained a close adviser to Francis, who created him Duke of Teschen in 1822. Charles was highly critical of Metternich's devious policies.

Chateaubriand, at the time of his election to the Académie Française *(1811)*

CHATEAUBRIAND, François René, Vicomte de (1768–1848)

French diplomat and man of letters: born at Saint-Malo, spending most of his boyhood at the neighbouring family château of Combourg. In 1791–2 he was in America but he returned to fight with the émigrés before being wounded in 1793 at Thionville. Over the following seven years he was in exile in the Channel Islands, London and Suffolk, writing a study of history, a prose epic and the first part of his masterpiece on Christian apologetics, *Le Génie de christianisme.* When this work was published in 1802, he had already been back in Paris for some eighteen months and the book won Bonaparte's approval as it coincided with the revived status accorded to Catholicism by the Concordat†. Napoleon appointed Chateaubriand to a diplomatic post in Rome. The execution of the Duc d'Enghien† shocked Chateaubriand and in the spring of 1804 he resigned from French service. For three years he travelled widely in the Mediterranean lands, later de-scribing his journeys in a colourful, poetic prose. By 1807 he was settled near Paris, courageously attacking the repressive character of the regime in a book review in the *Mercure de France* which denounced tyrants. Napoleon hoped to win back Chateaubriand's support and he was elected to the Académie Française in 1811, the year in which the authorities closed down the *Mercure de France.* But Chateaubriand never delivered his inaugural speech of reception, Napoleon having vetoed certain passages which attacked the presence in public life of regicides. When Louis XVIII returned to Paris in 1814, Chateaubriand published a brilliantly invective pamphlet, *De Bonaparte et des Bourbons.* He then resumed his diplomatic career and was ambassador in London in 1822 and Foreign Minister in 1823–4.

Chateaubriand's autobiography, *Mémoires d'outre-tombe*, was partly imaginative and eloquent fiction. It was completed in the 1830s and published in the year after he was buried on the island tomb he had selected for himself, off Saint-Malo. All his work is permeated with the individualism of the Romantic† movement: its love of landscape, self-conscious sense of the past, extravagance of pose and natural arrogance. What is unique to Chateaubriand's Romanticism is the contrast between the flowing, emotional harmony of his descriptive passages and the incisive Tacitean brevity with which he delineates character, as in his description of Fouché's arrival to take office as a minister of Louis XVIII: 'Silently there enters Vice leaning on the arm of Crime: M. de Talleyrand supported by M. Fouché. Slowly this Hellish vision passes before me, makes its way into the king's closet, and disappears.'

CHÂTILLON

Town on the Upper Seine, 150 miles south-east of Paris and 35 miles south-west of Chaumont†. Peace talks were held there intermittently from 5 February to 21 March 1814. Caulaincourt† represented Napoleon: the chief Allied spokesman was Stadion†, the former Austrian Foreign Minister, but Castlereagh† attended the first sessions. The Tsar's delegate, Razumovsky†, was uncooperative as his sovereign wished to march directly on Paris rather than reach any compromise settlement. At the start of the conference it seemed as if Caulaincourt would recommend an armistice provided France retained her 1792 frontiers, but Napoleon's victories at Champaubert†, Montmirail† and Vauchamps† made him raise his terms so that by 21 February he was seeking to retain Belgium and the left bank of the Rhine. These terms were rejected by the Allies on 25 February and Caulaincourt was given a fortnight in which to decide whether to accept a peace in which France was limited to her pre-revolutionary frontiers or to go on fighting to the end. When Caulaincourt returned to Châtillon on 10 March he offered only a minor concession. For another week the Austrians continued to negotiate but they were overborne by the Tsar. A cease-fire was agreed only after the Allied troops entered Paris on 31 March.

CHAUMONT

Town in the Haute-Marne département of France, some 155 miles east of Paris, standing high above the confluence of the rivers Marne and Suize. The town became Allied headquarters during the French campaign on 18 February 1814, after the strategic withdrawal from Troyes which followed Napoleon's victory at Vauchamps†. The British plenipotentiary, Castlereagh†, secured acceptance by Russia, Austria and Prussia of a Treaty of Grand Alliance, signed on 9 March but backdated to 1 March, when it was drafted. The four Powers agreed to make no separate peace; to conclude a final settlement which would restore independence to Switzerland and the Netherlands, establish a confederated Germany and, so far as possible, revive the old order in Spain and Italy; and to continue the Quadruple Alliance for twenty years after the war so as to prevent a resurgent France from seeking revenge. Intermittent peace talks continued at Châtillon† while the Treaty of Chaumont was under discussion. Alexander I†, Frederick William III† and their retinues remained at Chaumont until 23 March when they followed Schwarzenberg's army as it advanced on Paris. Francis I†, Metternich† and Castlereagh moved from Chaumont to Dijon on 21 March and remained there until 7 April, after the fall of Paris.

CHAUVIN, Nicolas (fl. 1790–1820)

Archetypal French patriot soldier: came from Rochefort† and served with valour in the revolutionary and Napoleonic wars, being wounde seventeen times, having three fingers amputated because of frostbite and receiving a sash of honour for his bravery. Chauvin's sentimental patriotism and devoted loyalty to the Emperor made him a legendary figure, with many details of his life remaining obscure. By 1830 his name was associated with a form of exclusive patriotism (*chauvinisme*) which, anglicized as 'chauvinism', crossed the

Channel during the neo-Napoleonic war scare of 1858–62 and was in common journalistic usage by 1870. The opprobrious 'male chauvinism' of today has no obvious connection with the valiant eponymous veteran of the *Grande Armée*.

CHAUVINISM: see *Chauvin*.

CHERASCO, Armistice of (28 April 1796) Ended the opening phase of Bonaparte's first Italian campaign. After ten days of fighting, the King of Sardinia-Piedmont† was prepared to offer Bonaparte peace, withdrawing from the war and granting the French free passage over the River Po to continue their assault on the Austrians. France was also to garrison the towns of Cuneo, Ceva and Tortona. These terms are less important in themselves than the significance of Cherasco in building up Bonaparte's reputation as a successful young general.

CHICHAGOV, Paul Vasilievich (1765–1849) Russian admiral and land commander: served in Catherine the Great's fleet, where he gained a reputation for hotheaded foolhardiness. Alexander I† appointed him Minister of Marine in 1805–6 and, in May 1812, gave him command of 'Moldavia, Wallachia and the Black Sea Fleet', sending him south to succeed Kutuzov† as military custodian of the Turkish frontier. Originally the Tsar expected Chichagov to reach an understanding with Turkey, move Russian troops across the Balkans and strike at the French Empire in the Illyrian Provinces† and Italy. This grandiose scheme was abandoned by Chichagov in July 1812, although he sent a small body of men to Serbia†. In August 1812 Chichagov set off northwards with some 24,000 troops to put pressure on Napoleon's southern flank. By mid-September Chichagov's force had joined the Russian corps south of the Pripet marshes so as to constitute

the Third Army, which threatened Napoleon's tenuous communications with Warsaw. Chichagov captured Minsk on 16 November and, turning eastwards, took Borisov† five days later so that, with Wittgenstein† advancing from the north and Kutuzov pursuing the retreating French westwards, it seemed as if the *Grande Armée* was trapped. Napoleon, however, outmanoeuvred his adversaries on the Berezina† and Chichagov's forces were severely mauled in a succession of actions which continued across Byelorussia until the end of the month. Chichagov pursued the French to the Niemen†. By the spring he had advanced cautiously to Thorn (Torun) where his career as a land commander came to an end.

CINTRA
Town in the hills fourteen miles northwest of Lisbon. After the victory of Wellesley (Wellington†) at Vimiero†, General Junot† sought an armistice and opened negotiations for the withdrawal of French troops from Portugal†. A document was drawn up providing for the evacuation of the French with their arms and equipment in British vessels which would land them at a port in western France. The document was signed by Wellesley and by his two superior officers, General Sir Hew Dalrymple (1750–1830) and General Sir Henry Burrard (1755–1813). Dalrymple sent the terms to London from his headquarters at Cintra and it has always been known as the Convention of Cintra (30 August 1808). News of the convention provoked consternation in London where it was felt that the French had avenged military defeat by a diplomatic triumph. All three generals were recalled to England. Shortly before Christmas a Court of Inquiry grudgingly gave retrospective approval of the convention. Neither Burrard nor Dalrymple received further field commands. Wellesley was soon back in Portugal. Within seven months he won Talavera†.

CISALPINE REPUBLIC (1797–1802)

A political entity, with its capital in Milan†, created by Bonaparte on 29 June 1797 through the absorption of two short-lived French improvisations, the Cispadane Republic (Bologna, Ferrara, Mantua, Reggio) and the Transpadane Republic (Milan, Brescia and other Lombard cities). Many Italian patriots regarded the Cisalpine Republic as an embryonic national state, although after Brumaire† the First Consul treated it as though it were a personal fief. French social reforms benefited the Cisalpiners. The republic was enlarged in 1801 by the incorporation of Verona and Novara. Originally the republic was established with a legislative assembly and an executive triumvirate but in January 1802 450 delegates from the republic were summoned to Lyons where they agreed to accept the transformation of their state into the Italian Republic, under the presidency of the First Consul. Three years later it was renamed 'Kingdom of Italy', with Napoleon crowned in Milan and Eugène Beauharnais† appointed Viceroy.

CIUDAD RODRIGO

Fortress above the River Agueda, commanding the Spanish side of the 'northern corridor' between Spain and Portugal which was guarded on the Portuguese side by Almeida†, some twenty-two miles to the south-west. Ney† and Masséna† blockaded and took Ciudad Rodrigo (February to June 1810). Wellington† ousted the French after an eleven-day siege on 19 January 1812, with heavy fighting in bitter weather. His troops then plundered the town. Possession of Ciudad Rodrigo enabled Wellington to advance through the northern corridor to Salamanca†, fifty miles away, in June.

CIVIL CODE

The basic statement of the reformed legal system in France and its dependencies. The Code was formally proclaimed on 30 March 1804; it was renamed *Code Napoléon* in 1807. Major variations had existed in pre-revolutionary France between legal customs in the north and the south and on five occasions under the Consulate and Directory abortive attempts were made to formulate a uniform code. The First Consul wished to reconcile three different legal strands: Roman law, French customary law and the egalitarian concepts of the revolutionary rights of man. He left the drafting of the code to four lawyers, of whom the most distinguished was François Tronchet (1726–1806) who had defended Louis XVI before the Convention. Cambacérès†, the Second Consul, took a prominent part in the editing of the Civil Code, which was originally prepared in the last five months of the year 1800. The Code was then discussed in detail at more than a hundred sessions of the Council of State†, between July 1801 and January 1802. Bonaparte was present at more than half the meetings, taking great personal interest in the laws dealing with marriage and divorce, civil rights, adoption and disposal of property. The Tribunate and the Legislative Body examined the proposals stage by stage, frustrating the First Consul's hope of having the Code proclaimed as law during a time of general peace. The final version summarized the laws in 2,281 compact articles, some 115,000 words. It was basically a middle-class code, safeguarding property, the headship of the father in a family, and the essential basic unity of family life. It accepted a principle of political equality but recognized the authoritarian right of the state to intervene in the private conduct of affairs. Wherever the French army conquered and changed existing society the Civil Code followed in its wake. The articles of the Civil Code still provide a basis for French jurisprudence and its influence has spread to Belgium, Holland, Switzerland, Italy and, by imitation, to Romania, Haiti, Bolivia, Egypt, Japan, Quebec in Canada and Louisiana in the United States.

CLARKE, Henri Jacques Guillaume (1765–1818)

Marshal of France: born, of Irish descent, at Landrecies in north-eastern France. He entered the *École Militaire* in Paris in 1781 and was commissioned in 1782. Briefly, in 1790, he was attached to the London embassy. By 1793, when he was retired from the army because of suspicion concerning his loyalty, he commanded a brigade. The Directory in November 1796 sent him as an emissary to Bonaparte, primarily to assist in negotiating the 'peace preliminaries' of Leoben, but also to report on the young general's political ambitions. Clarke became a member of the Bonaparte circle and was in Napoleon's personal secretariat from 1802–1806 when he became military governor of Berlin. In August 1807 he took over from Berthier† as Minister of War, holding the post until the fall of Napoleon in 1814. Clarke was a conscientious desk general, rewarded for his diligence by being created Duke of Feltre in 1809. Upon the first Restoration, Clarke gave his support to Louis XVIII whom he accompanied to Ghent during the Hundred Days. Louis gave Clarke his old post as Minister of War, which he held until September 1817, and in July 1816 appointed him a Marshal of France. In retrospect Napoleon complained that Clarke was so inclined to flattery that it was impossible to place reliance on his opinions. Clarke's former companions in arms deplored his severity during the 'White Terror' after Waterloo.

CLARY FAMILY

The Clarys were wealthy silk merchants in Marseilles. François Clary (1725–94) married Françoise Somis, who bore him six daughters and three sons. One daughter, Julie (1771–1845), married Joseph Bonaparte† at Cuges, near Marseilles, on 1 August 1794 in a secret religious service and a civil ceremony. Another daughter became Désirée Bernadotte†, dying as Dowager Queen of Sweden.

CLAUSEWITZ, Karl von (1780–1831)

Prussian general and military theorist: born at Burg, near Magdeburg, entered the infantry as a boy cadet in 1792 and fought against the French on the Rhine, 1793–4. Later he was trained at the Berlin War Academy and was a protégé of Scharnhorst† as a young staff officer. In October 1806 he was taken prisoner by the French although subsequently he was able to help Scharnhorst and Gneisenau† remodel the Prussian army. He served with the Russians in the 1812 campaign (of which he wrote a study, published soon after his death in German and in 1843 in English). After returning to Prussian service in 1814, he was chief of staff to Thielmann, one of Blücher's corps commanders at Ligny† and Wavre†. In 1818 Clausewitz was promoted major-general and appointed director of the staff college in Berlin. There he developed the theories on strategy which were published in 1832–3 as his great (unfinished) study, *On War*. His doctrine that 'war is the continuation of policy by other means' became central to political planning on the Continent in the later years of the century. Clausewitz succumbed to the cholera epidemic of 1831 while serving at Breslau.

COALITIONS

The monarchies of Europe met the military challenge of French revolutionary republicanism and Napoleonic imperialism by a succession of alliances, or coalitions, financially dependent on British subsidies. The First Coalition came into being in 1792–3 when Sardinia-Piedmont, Britain, the Netherlands, Spain, Naples and Tuscany joined the original Austro-Prussian alliance against France. The Netherlands had been overrun and Prussia and Spain had made peace before Bonaparte's first Italian campaign led to the Armistice of Cherasco† and to Austria's withdrawal from the conflict through the Preliminaries of Leoben and the Peace of Campo Formio†. Pitt built up

Pitt secures a larger slice of the pudding, a comment on Britain's acquisition of overseas possessions in a cartoon by Gillray, 1805

a Second Coalition while Bonaparte was in Egypt† and the Directory faced the threat of disintegration. The War of the Second Coalition (1798–1801) was marked by early successes in Italy until the Austrians and Russians fell into dispute, prompting Tsar Paul to withdraw from the war in October 1799. After Brumaire, Bonaparte gave his attention to the Austrians, with whom he concluded the Treaty of Lunéville† in February 1801. The Peace of Amiens†, from March 1802 to May 1803, provided the only interlude in more than twenty years of Anglo-French conflict, and when Pitt† became Prime Minister again in May 1804 he began to build up a Third Coalition, finding an ambitious response from Tsar Alexander I† and his ministers with their 'Grand Design'† of September 1804. The tardy Prussian interest in Pitt's alliance proposals (caused partly by Prussian hopes of acquiring Hanover†) gave Napoleon the opportunity to concentrate against Russia

and Austria in the War of the Third Coalition, which was virtually ended by the great battle of Austerlitz†. It is questionable whether the loose collaboration of Britain, Prussia and Russia in 1806–7 and of Britain and Austria in 1809 ever constituted a coalition, a genuine Allied response to the threat of the *Grande Armée*. In February 1813 the Convention of Kalisch†, which brought Prussia on to the side of Britain and Russia, led to the formation of the Fourth Coalition (originally Britain, Russia, Prussia, Sweden) in June 1813. Austria joined the coalition in August, Bavaria, Württemberg and Saxony in October. Collaboration between the Great Power members of the coalition was strengthened by the Quadruple Alliance of Chaumont† (treaty dated 1 March 1814); and it was this treaty which facilitated the improvised coalition established when Napoleon returned from Elba in the spring of 1815.

COBBETT, William (1763–1835)

English writer: born in Farnham, Surrey, the son of a small farmer. From 1784 to 1791 he served in the 54th Regiment of Foot, mostly in Canada, and reached the rank of sergeant-major. He wrote a pamphlet exposing military corruption (1792), spent six months in France, and was then in Philadelphia until 1800, denouncing what he regarded as the extreme democrat doctrines of the French revolutionaries. On returning to London he opened a bookshop in Pall Mall. From there he published his highly individualistic works, notably the *Weekly Political Register* (January 1803 to June 1835). During the early years of the French Empire Cobbett was violently opposed to Napoleon's re-ordering of Europe but from 1811 onwards he was less hostile. After criticizing the retention of flogging in the army in 1810 Cobbett was fined £1,000 and sentenced to two years' imprisonment. He visited America again in 1817–19. On his return he became a forthright champion of Caroline† of Brunswick and a bitter enemy of the new industrialism which he believed was destroying the yeoman society whose virtues he celebrated. The accounts of his travels through twenty-

William Cobbett, as seen by Gillray

seven English counties during the 1820s were published in his *Rural Rides* (1830), with 'economical and political observations'. In his last years he farmed in Hampshire and sat in the reformed House of Commons, 1832–5, as MP for Oldham.

COBENZL, Ludwig von (1753–1809)

Austrian Foreign Minister: born in Laibach (Ljubljana) but spent much of his early life in Brussels and served Joseph II as administrator in the Southern Netherlands. He helped negotiate the Treaty of Campo Formio†, represented Austria at Rastatt†, and became Foreign Minister in January 1801, in succession to Thugut†. Cobenzl's conduct of foreign affairs was to some extent supervised by Colloredo† and, at least until the proclamation of the French Empire, he seemed to favour the appeasement of Napoleon. Publicists such as Gentz†, and the war party in Vienna, exaggerated the feebleness of both Colloredo and Cobenzl. It was Cobenzl who responded to British and Russian diplomatic overtures in building up the Third Coalition of 1805, but he failed to make certain of Prussian participation and was unpopular in Vienna for apparent subservience to the Russians. He became a scapegoat for the failure of inter-Allied collaboration in the disastrous Austerlitz campaign and was dismissed on 26 December 1805, Stadion† succeeding him as Foreign Minister.

Code Napoléon

The name prefixed in 1807 to the Civil Code† of March 1804.

CODES

Authoritative statements of the reformed laws of the French Consulate and Empire. Between 1804 and 1810 five codes were promulgated in Paris; a sixth, the Rural Code, was never finished. Basic to all of them was the Civil Code† of 1804. The Code of Civil Procedure (1806) revived many of the pre-revolutionary methods of determining non-criminal disputes over litigation but it insisted an effort should be made at finding a conciliatory settlement before a case came to court. The Commercial Code† (1807) sought uniformity in business transactions. The Code of Criminal Procedure (1808) amplified the Law of 27 Ventôse†. It retained the principle of trial by jury but authorized the appointment of juries by Prefects† and the quashing of a jury's verdict by the Senate† if it was held detrimental to the interests of the state. The Code also provided for 'ordinary special courts' (tribunals of soldiers) and 'extraordinary special courts' (tribunals to hear grave political offences). The general effect of the Code of Criminal Procedure was to favour the prosecutor rather than the defendant and to strengthen authoritarian government. The Penal Code (1810) imposed harsher penalties; it restored branding, the iron collar and fetters, the loss of a hand before execution for parricide, the deprivation of civil rights, and other restraints abolished by the more enlightened penology of the Revolution. While the Civil Code and Commercial Code were absorbed into the systems of several European states, the other three codes operated only in France and lands administered directly from Paris.

COLERIDGE, Samuel Taylor (1772–1834)

English poet and critic: born at Ottery St Mary, Devon, and educated at Christ's Hospital and Jesus College, Cambridge. He was a close friend of Southey† and Wordsworth†, with whom he produced the *Lyrical Ballads* (1798) in which appeared Coleridge's *The Ancient Mariner*. In 1798–9 Coleridge went to Germany, where he was greatly influenced by Schiller† and absorbed some of the philosophy of Kant† and Schelling†. Later he travelled in the Mediterranean (Malta in 1805, Naples and Rome 1806) and he therefore had a closer affinity with continental thought than the other Lake Poets with whom he associated at Keswick and Grasmere. In 1808 and again in 1811 he lectured on the English poets in London, and his insight into the nature of Romanticism‡ shows the depth of an intellect whose clarity became increasingly marred by his dependence on opium. Even when, in later years, he ceased to write and settled at Highgate his table-talk stimulated reverence from a small circle of literary admirers. As a journalist, he used powerful invective against Napoleon, notably as assistant editor of *The Courier* in 1811.

COLLINGWOOD, Cuthbert (1750–1810)

British admiral: born at Newcastle upon Tyne, entered the Royal Navy in 1761 and saw much service in the West Indies and in American waters; he was one of the officers commanding a naval detachment which fought beside the army against the colonists at Bunker's Hill (1775). From 1778 to 1805 his career followed that of Nelson‡. He distinguished himself off Brest at the 'glorious First of June' (1794), at Cape St Vincent (1797) and in the blockade of Brest‡ from 1804 onwards. In 1799 he was promoted rear-admiral and, as a vice-admiral flying his flag in HMS *Royal Sovereign*, he was second in command at Trafalgar‡. Early in 1806 he was raised to the peerage as Baron Collingwood. From 1807 until his death he commanded the fleet in the Mediterranean, maintaining a close blockade of Toulon‡ from 1808 onwards, with his base at Port Mahón in Minorca. Frequently he had to exercise diplomacy, especially with local despots in the Levant and north Africa. Such was his skill that the Admiralty consistently refused his requests to return to his much loved Northumberland, even when his health gave way in the winter of 1808–9. He died at sea, one day's sailing out of Port Mahón, having at last in March 1810 been granted sick leave. An over-exacting government belatedly honoured Collingwood with burial beside Nelson in St Paul's.

COLLOREDO, Franz von, Count (1731–1807)

Austrian chief minister: born in Vienna, appointed by Joseph II as chief tutor to his eldest nephew, the future Emperor Francis‡. Colloredo was a clericalist conservative, a natural anti-intellectual who was highly suspicious of the eighteenth-century Enlightenment. Francis appointed Colloredo head of his private secretariat on 2 March 1792, the day following his accession. The special rank of *Kabinettsminister* was created for Colloredo, who remained a powerful influence until his dismissal on 28 November 1805. Colloredo was unpopular with most classes, the Archdukes feeling that the advice which he tended their brother, the Emperor, was almost always lacking in foresight. From 1801 onwards his influence was intensified through the diplomacy of Cobenzl‡, who shared many of Colloredo's prejudices. The repressive system of Francis's later years – generally associated in name with Metternich‡ – originated in Colloredo's obscurantist policies. He was as disastrous an influence on the formation of Francis's views as Lord Bute had been in moulding those of his pupil, the young George III‡.

COMBINATION ACTS, (1799 and 1800)

The chief repressive measures taken by Pitt‡ to curb incipient industrial unrest in Britain. Any union of workmen intended to force employers to increase wages or to shorten working hours was made punishable by summary jurisdiction, before magistrates. These laws were not repealed until 1824. In France, such associations of workers were forbidden by the Loi Le Chapelier of 14 June 1791, a measure reaffirmed under the Consulate by the Law of 22 Germinal, Year XI (12 April 1803).

COMÉDIE FRANÇAISE

The name generally given to the state theatrical company in Paris which can trace its origins back to Molière's players in the middle of the seventeenth century. Officially it dates from 1680, but it was also known from 1799 onwards as the *Théâtre Français*. In 1782 the Comédie Française performed for the first time at the Théâtre de l'Odéon, near the Luxembourg Palace. The Revolution split the company, while also encouraging the growth of new groups of players. Under the Consulate the Comédie Française played mainly in the theatre in the Rue de Richelieu, under state patronage but with its form as an institution left confused by the Revolution. Napoleon personally interested himself in the company's organization. In the second week of October 1812 he spent three of his last evenings in Moscow† perusing and modifying the 101 statutes of the Comédie Française; and he made certain that his decree, signed and dated in Moscow, should be brought back by couriers ahead of the retreating army since he assumed that its publication in Paris would be good for morale, showing that even in distant Russia the Emperor was still sufficiently in control of affairs to give minute attention to settling the future of a great theatrical company. Basically the Comédie Française has retained the form of organization which Napoleon decreed in Moscow. (See also, among individual actors, *Mlle George* and *Talma*.)

COMMERCIAL CODE

The least complete of the Codes† by which the Napoleonic state regulated the functioning of post-revolutionary society. The Commercial Code, promulgated on 11 September 1807, was a blueprint for company law throughout the first half of the nineteenth century in France, Italy, Bel-

The façade of the 'Théâtre Français' in Paris, where the Comédie Française *performed under the Consulate and Empire*

gium, the Netherlands, Spain, Switzerland and much of Germany, but it needed constant updating so as to meet the growing complexities of capitalism. The Commercial Code established the principle that the responsibility of shareholders in a joint stock company should be restricted to their actual holdings, thereby anticipating British legislation by almost fifty years, but the code left so many anomalies that more precise laws on limited liability had to be introduced in France in 1863 and 1867. The code was also incomplete over the issue of promissory notes and the concept of banking. Napoleon's prejudices, against the mortgaging of real property and against usury in general, were strongly reflected in the code.

CONCORDAT

The name given to any treaty between a lay government and the Papacy regulating the relations of Church and State. The anti-clerical sentiments of the Revolution had led the Constituent Assembly to impose a schismatic organization on the Church in France, the 'Civil Constitution of the Clergy' (July 1790). This measure, condemned by the Pope in April 1791, was followed two years later by persecution and 'de-christianization'. Some tolerance was restored by the Boissy d'Anglas decree of 21 February 1795 but, under the Directory, priests were still required to take oaths affirming their 'hatred of royalty and anarchy' as well as their loyalty to the constitution. After Brumaire† the First Consul was eager for reconciliation with the Papacy for five main reasons: to prevent the Bourbons using the Church as an instrument of rebellion, especially in Brittany and La Vendée†; to improve the international standing of the Consulate in diplomatic negotiations, particularly with the Habsburgs; to facilitate the acceptance of Bonapartist beliefs in regions outside France where the influence of the priesthood remained considerable (Italy, Belgium, the Rhineland, Bavaria, and later Spain); to use French bishops as 'moral prefects' in the old provinces; and to have in each village a priest who could represent the established political order.

Bonaparte established contact with Pope Pius VII† through Cardinal Martiniana of Vercelli, with whom he talked on 30 May and 25 June 1800, before and after Marengo†. He told Martiniana that he favoured a restoration of the Church, with a new episcopate and with salaries paid by the state but with no return of dispossessed church land. Negotiations on these terms began in Paris in November 1800 with Pius VII at first represented by Mgr Spina whom Bonaparte had met at Valence thirteen months before, following the death there of Pius VI†. Cardinal Consalvi† went to Paris in late April 1801 and discussed the provisions of the Concordat at great length with Talleyrand† and Joseph Bonaparte† as well as with Napoleon. The Concordat was concluded on 16 July, ratified within seven weeks, but did not become effective until Easter 1802. It then formed part of a general 'Law of Public Worship' which affirmed Huguenot rights as well as the status of Catholicism and imposed upon the Church certain 'Organic Articles'†, to which the Papacy strongly objected.

The Concordat of 1801 recognized Roman Catholicism as the religion of the majority of the French people, left alienated church property in the hands of those who had acquired it, guaranteed liberty of worship, provided for the establishment of a new episcopate with bishops nominated by the state and instituted by the Pope's representative, redrew the boundaries of dioceses, and provided for the stipends of bishops and clergy to be paid by the state. The settlement lasted until 1905 when Church and State were legally separated in France. A special Italian Concordat was negotiated in Milan in 1803, only becoming effective in June 1805 after Napoleon's coronation as King of Italy. The introduction of the Civil Code† to Italy on 1 January 1806 placed a severe strain on Church-State relations in the peninsula because the Code's provisions on divorce ran counter to church teachings on marriage.

Conflict in France over investiture and over the marriage laws threatened the Concordat from 1809 to 1811 and Pope Pius VII was brought first to Savona† and later to Fontainebleau† where Napoleon personally cajoled him into signing a new Concordat which would have given greater spiritual powers to the French episcopate at the expense of Rome. But this 'Concordat of Fontainebleau' of 25 January 1813 was soon disowned by the Pope and never became operative.

CONFEDERATION OF THE RHINE: see *Rhine, Confederation of the*.

CONSALVI, Ercole (1757–1824)
Cardinal: born in Rome, entered the papal service and was briefly imprisoned by the French authorities as an antirevolutionary in 1798. His mastery of detail led Monsignor Consalvi to be appointed secretary of the conclave which met in Venice in November 1799 to elect a successor to Pope Pius VI†. He accompanied the new pope, Pius VII†, to Rome and was made Cardinal Secretary of State in June 1800. Ten months later he travelled to Paris to complete the negotiations for the Concordat†. Consalvi subsequently felt he had been deceived by the First Consul and was especially angered by the Organic Articles†. So marked was his enmity that, under French pressure, Pius VII agreed to accept Consalvi's resignation in June 1806. When Consalvi came again to Paris in the spring of 1810 he angered Napoleon by leading the group of so-called 'black cardinals' who declined to attend the religious ceremony when Cardinal Fesch† blessed the marriage of Napoleon and Marie Louise†. Subsequently Napoleon sent him under restraint to Rheims. Consalvi came back into

Pius VII's counsels at Fontainebleau† in February 1813, strengthening the Pope's resistance to Napoleon's demands. He remained with Pius until the Pope left Fontainebleau for Italy in January 1814. Two months later Consalvi was reappointed Secretary of State, staying in Paris to negotiate with the Allies. In June 1814 he crossed the Channel and became the first Cardinal received in London since 1558. He represented the Pope at the Congress of Vienna† and spent most of the last nine years of his life re-establishing Pius VII's authority in the Papal States.

CONSCRIPTION
The term conscription was first used in 1798 but the practice of making all males in a specified age group liable for military service goes back to the decree issued by Carnot† in August 1793 which established the *levée en masse* obliging *réquisitionnaires* between the ages of eighteen and twenty-five to supplement the volunteer armies defending the Republic. Jourdan's Conscription Law of 5 September 1798 extended Carnot's system, requiring the registering of all men between eighteen and forty, even though those over thirty never became liable for call-up. The register was divided into five categories, according to age, profession and marital status; and it was from this register that Jourdan†, and his successors as Minister of War, found their quotas. The Conscription Law was, from the first, extremely unpopular in France and provoked serious unrest in Belgium† where there were riots in East Flanders in October 1798 and a brief armed rising in West Flanders and around Hasselt a month later. By 1805 some two-thirds of the French Army were conscripts called up for service since Brumaire. Under the Empire, Napoleon varied the system of calling people to the colours, holding back certain categories in any one year until 1809 and even, until 1813, allowing drafted men to find 'volun-

teer' replacements from their district provided that the commune as a whole fulfilled its quota. The increasing strain of the wars – and, in particular, the preparations for the Russian campaign – led to anticipation of call-up; some seventeen-year-old conscripts were fighting in Spain in 1810, and in the 1813–14 campaigns young conscripts of fifteen and sixteen (nicknamed 'les Marie-Louises') fought beside the veterans. 'Refractory conscripts', either youngsters evading the system or deserters, added to the problem of so-called brigandage in the countryside. In the year of Marengo† more than a third of the call-up evaded service, and even in the first year of the Empire it was estimated that a quarter of the conscripts were 'refractory', but by 1813 the figure had fallen to less than ten per cent.

Outside the French Empire and its dependencies Prussia† was the first kingdom to consider universal military service. The Military Reorganization Commission unanimously urged Frederick William III† to introduce conscription in a letter sent to the King on 15 March 1808, repeating the recommendation in December. But the King believed that the swamping of his professional army by conscripts would pose a potential threat to royal authority. On the initiative of Stein†, the East Prussian assembly called out all able-bodied men between eighteen and forty-five in January 1813 immediately after the Convention of Tauroggen†. The King belatedly accepted conscription for all the Prussian lands two months later.

CONSTABLE, John (1776–1837)

English landscape painter: born at East Bergholt in Suffolk, a miller's son. He first exhibited in 1802 but was denied the precocious success of his fellow artist, Turner†, who was a year his senior in age. Not until 1819 did Constable become an Associate of the Royal Academy, with ten more years before he was elected an RA. The church spires, Suffolk mills and water meadows which he painted during the Napoleonic era seem as remote from the struggle as are the novels of Jane Austen†. It is curious that, even though his *Hay Wain* was well received in London in 1824, his reputation was made by success that year in exhibiting in Paris. Ultimately Constable's insistence on painting 'the truth' of what his eyes perceived brought an unprettified discipline to landscape painting which revolutionized tradition in France and Germany as well as in England.

CONSTANT, Benjamin (Henri Benjamin Constant de Rebecque, 1767–1830)

French writer and polemicist: born of Huguenot ancestry in Lausanne, educated in Bavaria and Edinburgh before settling to live by his dextrous pen in Paris under the Directory. From 1794 to 1811 he was dominated by Mme de Staël†, who adv-

Benjamin Constant, leader of the 'Idéologues'

anced his political career in Paris and gave him hospitality at Coppet† and elsewhere on her travels. He entered the Tribunate† after Brumaire and attracted attention by a speech denouncing the first Bill presented to that Chamber for consideration (5 January 1800). Thereafter he was a leader of the opposition group known as the *Idéologues*†. Bonaparte's purge of the Tribunate in March 1802 silenced Constant's political oratory and a year later he withdrew into discreet exile. The following nine years saw the peak of his literary achievements: a single novel, *Adolphe*, written in a fortnight in 1807 but not published until he was in exile for a second time, in London in 1816; a series of political and religious treatises, published only in the last years of his life; and an outstanding pamphlet, written in Hanover in 1813, and denouncing Napoleon's tyranny and usurpation. Constant returned to Paris in 1814, remained there during the Hundred Days, and was so flattered by Napoleon that he agreed to draft the comparatively liberal measures of the *Acte Additionnel*†. This experience induced him to remain abroad after the second Bourbon Restoration until 1817. Two years later he was elected to the Chamber of Deputies and, over the following decade, won considerable respect as a leading liberal spokesman and a brilliant journalist.

CONSTANT, Louis Wairy (1778–1845), Napoleon's valet: see *Wairy*.

CONSTANTINE, Grand Duke of Russia (1779–1831)

Second son of Tsar Paul†: born at Tsarskoe Selo, received a strict military education and served under Suvorov† in northern Italy in 1799. At Austerlitz† he commanded the Russian Imperial Guard, ordering – and bravely participating in – a reckless and tragic cavalry charge late in the afternoon which cost Russia's two best

regiments heavy casualties. In 1806 he was sent on a special mission to Berlin. Thereafter he became critical of his brother, Tsar Alexander†, and was unpopular with the army commanders. Although given command of V Corps of the Reserve at Borodino†, he was prevented by Kutuzov† from taking any rash initiative. He participated in the French campaign, leading impressive cavalry charges against young and raw conscripts during the last week of battle and entering Paris beside the Tsar on 31 March 1814. In 1815 he was appointed to command the Polish Military Commission in Warsaw, where he spent most of his remaining years. An unhappy marriage to Juliana of Saxe-Coburg was annulled in 1820 and he then contracted a morganatic union with a Polish Countess, Joanna Grudzinscy. Constantine decided in January 1822 to renounce his right of accession, after twenty-one years as heir to the throne. The Polish military revolt of 1830 took him by surprise. Before order could be restored in Warsaw, he fell victim to the cholera epidemic, dying at Vitebsk in June 1831.

CONSTITUTIONS OF FRANCE

The first written constitution in France was accepted by Louis XVI on 14 September 1791 after two years of debate by the National Constituent Assembly but it was outdated by the coming of the Republic a year later. A second constitution, agreed in June 1793, never became effective, the Convention decreeing that its operation should be postponed until the end of the foreign war. The *Constitution of the Year III* (22 August 1795) established a bicameral legislature (Council of Five Hundred†, Council of Ancients†) and gave executive power to a Directory† of five members elected by the Ancients from ten candidates proposed by the Five Hundred. This cumbersome system was discarded after Brumaire and the establishment of the provisional Consulate. The Consuls and a committee from the chambers of the Directory began discussing the form of a new and orderly constitution on 10 November 1799. After three weeks, Bonaparte became impatient and summoned a series of private meetings at his residence in the Luxembourg Palace. The resultant *Constitution of the Year VIII* was proclaimed on 15 December 1799 and became operative ten days later. Bonaparte was confirmed as First Consul, for ten years, assisted by two other consuls, appointed by him. Legislative power was shared by the First Consul who proposed laws, the Tribunate† which discussed them and the Legislature† which voted on them. Above the Tribunate and Legislature was the Senate†, eighty officials chosen for life, with the right to decide the composition of the Tribunate and Legislature and to pass other amendments safeguarding the character of the constitution. After a series of popular votes, between mid-December and mid-February, it was announced that 3,011,107 people were in favour of the constitution and 1,567 opposed to it. A plebiscite in the summer of 1802 approved an executive change by which Bonaparte was proclaimed Consul for life by the Senate on 2 August. Two days later the *Constitution of Year X* (4 August 1802) was established by use of the measure known as a *Sénatus-Consulte†* which greatly increased the powers of the Consul to make treaties, grant pardons, appoint the Senate and other officers of state, suspend the constitution, and dissolve Tribunate and Legislature. At the same time the authority of the Senate was enhanced although the senators were dependent upon the Consul's good grace. This fifth written constitution made Bonaparte as much an autocrat as the Tsar. It was only a short step to the Senate's promulgation of the *Constitution of the Year XII* (18 May 1804) which entrusted 'the government of the Republic to a hereditary emperor'. On this occasion there was little change in the government institutions. The Empire was approved by

plebiscite: 3,572,329 for and only 2,569 against. A coronation† in Notre-Dame followed on 2 December 1804.

On the eve of Napoleon's first abdication† the Senate, acting on suggestions from Talleyrand† and drafts from Lebrun†, prepared a constitution by which the restored Bourbons would institute a bicameral system on the British model. This constitution, generally known as the *Charter of 1814* was formally accepted by Louis XVIII on 14 June. During the Hundred Days a constitutional amendment known as the *Acte Additionnel†* (22 April 1815) belatedly asserted Napoleon's passing belief in ordered representative government. Subsequently the restored Louis XVIII tried to observe and implement his 1814 Charter.

CONSULATE

The form of government provisionally introduced in France after Brumaire† (9 November 1799) and consolidated by the *Constitution of the Year VIII (see above)*. The idea of reviving the consulship (extinct since AD 534) accorded well with fashionable neoclassicism. Sieyès† seems originally to have favoured two consuls (as in ancient Rome) and a Grand Elector (a Germanic concept) but Bonaparte transformed Sieyès's plans, securing for himself as First Consul powers more closely corresponding to the authority enjoyed by Augustus as 'Princeps' than to any other Roman precedent. The original provisional consuls, Sieyès and Ducos†, were replaced by Cambacérès† and Lebrun† who were more inclined than their predecessors to accept the thinly-veiled dictatorship of the First Consul. Bonaparte was proclaimed Life Consul with power to nominate a successor on 2 August 1802. The Consulate ended with the *Sénatus-Consulte†* of 18 May 1804 which created General Bonaparte Emperor of the French. Among the achievements of the four and a half years of the Consulate were Marengo† and the defeat of the Second

Coalition, the pacification of La Vendée† and the conclusion of the Concordat† and the Civil Code†.

CONTINENTAL SYSTEM

Was, in the first instance, an attempt to impose a blockade of Britain and ruin British prosperity by closing Continental ports to commerce with the British Isles. The System began with the Berlin Decree† of November 1806 and was extended by the decrees of Fontainebleau† (October 1807) and Milan† (November and December 1807) so that throughout 1808 and early 1809 the French treated any vessel which used British ports or submitted to the search requirements of the Royal Navy as an enemy ship, irrespective of its nationality, and both vessels and cargoes were confiscated. Although the System harmed City interests in London, the European states greatly resented Napoleon's recourse to economic warfare. The Russian trade in corn, timber and naval supplies was hit by the attempts of Napoleon at Tilsit† and Erfurt† to include the Tsar's empire in his System. Portuguese and Spanish evasion prompted French attempts to occupy and police the Iberian Peninsula. The Russian decision to leave the Continental System, announced on 31 December 1810, was welcomed by the Tsar's merchants but led directly to Napoleon's decision to undertake the 1812 campaign. Much smuggling developed along the North Sea coast and in the Mediterranean as France's allies sought means of freeing themselves from the restraints of the decrees. Louis Bonaparte† in Holland connived at evasion and in March 1809 Napoleon began to issue licences for trade, in an effort to save some of the mercantile cities, especially in the Baltic. The Continental System was also intended to stimulate production and manufactures within the Empire and its satellite states. Here the restraints hampered growth, a shortage of cotton in particular preventing the efficient marketing of French textiles. Experiments with crops of rape-seed and sugar-beet were unhappy. Gradually the burdens imposed by the Continental System lost Napoleon support from the French middle classes, natural champions of his system of government so long as it could offer them prosperity and short, victorious campaigns distant from France's frontiers (see *Crisis of 1811*).

COPENHAGEN

Capital of Denmark and the scene of two naval actions in the first decade of the century. On 2 April 1801 a fleet of 26 British ships-of-the-line, supported by 30 smaller vessels, took action against Danish vessels seeking to enforce the Armed Neutrality† of the North. Admiral Sir Hyde Parker commanded the British force, which had originally anchored off Copenhagen on 21 March in the hope of forcing the Danes to withdraw from the Armed Neutrality without any conflict. The van of the naval squadron was led by Vice-Admiral Nelson†, and it was on this occasion that he placed his telescope to his blind eye so as not to observe the signals from Hyde Parker ordering him to break off his engagement with the formidable shore batteries. Both the British and the Danes suffered heavy casualties in five and a half hours of intermittent bombardment, with three of Nelson's twelve ships-of-the-line running aground. The action boosted Britain's naval reputation and was followed by the disintegration of the Armed Neutrality league, a development owing as much to Tsar Paul's death as to Nelson's initiative at Copenhagen.

In August and September 1807 a combined naval and military expedition attacked Copenhagen, with Admiral Gambier commanding the naval squadron and Lord Cathcart landing some 18,000 men to besiege the city, the future Duke of Wellington beating off a Danish counter-attack. Copenhagen was bombarded for

The naval assault on Copenhagen, as depicted by a print in London published four weeks after the action (April 1801)

four days (2–5 September) before the Danish Regent agreed to surrender his fleet so as to ensure that it did not pass into French hands. British troops remained ashore for another month. Technically Britain was not at war with Denmark at the time.

COPPET

Village in the Vaud canton of Switzerland on the shore of Lake Geneva, eight miles north-east of the city of Geneva. In 1784 a château was purchased there by Jacques Necker, the famous Finance Minister of Louis XVI. Necker lived at Coppet from 1790 until his death in 1804. The château was a home for his daughter, Germaine de Staël‡ from 1795 to 1797 and again after her exile from Paris on the First Consul's orders in 1803. Thereafter Coppet (which she inherited on her father's death) became one of the great intellectual centres of the Continent, with Mme de Staël as cultural queen of a salon which included Benjamin Constant‡, August von Schlegel‡ and Mme Récamier‡. The Coppet salon was critical of Napoleon, main-

taining that his desire for authoritarian uniformity cramped the natural vitality of French civilization. Both Mme de Staël and her father are buried at Coppet.

CORFU: see *Ionian Islands*.

CORN LAWS

The first attempts to encourage tillage in England by laws preventing cheap imports of corn date from Richard II's reign, in the late fourteenth century. Once political initiative passed to parliaments in which the landed interest was predominant, the protection of agriculture became a major concern of successive ministries; and Corn Laws regulating imports existed in some form or other from 1673 onwards. War and poor harvests brought the landlords good prices for any corn they could market between 1793 and 1801. Fears that this prosperity would be undermined by peace in 1802–3 led the landowners in parliament to propose the first artificially high price for corn in Britain's commercial history. The Corn Law of 1804 accordingly forbade the import of foreign corn if the home grown price was less than 66 shillings a quarter. Even if it rose to that price, a nominal duty would be imposed on imported corn. When the Peace of Amiens† broke down, these limitations became superfluous for, over the eight years 1804–12, the average price for English corn remained at about 89 shillings a quarter. Renewed efforts to protect war-inflated farming were made by a committee of the House of Commons in 1813–14 but the proposal for a new Corn Law at once aroused hostility in the country, where it seemed as if the landowners wished to keep bread prices at almost famine level. Yet, despite riots in 1814–15, the famous Corn Law of 1815 forbade the import of foreign corn until the price on the home market reached 80 shillings a quarter. This measure intensified postwar distress, mitigated by a sliding scale of duties introduced by Huskisson in 1828. Conditions deteriorated with the general depression and bad harvests in 1839–41, the social suffering being publicized by the Anti-Corn Law League from 1839 onwards. The Corn Laws were repealed in June 1846.

CORNWALLIS, William (1744–1819)

British admiral: born in London, the younger son of the first Earl of Cornwallis and a brother of the distinguished general forced to capitulate at Yorktown in 1781. Sir William Cornwallis entered the navy in 1755 and spent most of the following forty-five years either in the West Indies or as commander-in-chief in the East Indies. He commanded the Channel Fleet in 1801 and again from 1803 to 1805, blockading Brest†, where he was injured by a shell splinter from the shore batteries. Cornwallis had the responsibility of defending southern England from a cross-Channel invasion. He was a gruff, florid, bucolic naval commander – 'Billy-go-tight' to his men.

CORONATIONS

Napoleon crowned himself on two occasions. On 2 December 1804 he placed a specially made open crown, shaped like a laurel wreath, on his head during a three-hour coronation ceremony held in the cathedral of Notre-Dame in Paris. Pope Pius VII† attended the coronation, having arrived in Paris on 28 November after a twenty-six-day journey from Rome. He anointed both Napoleon and Josephine and blessed the insignia. Napoleon subsequently crowned Josephine at the foot of the altar steps. It was argued that a formal coronation helped safeguard Napoleon's life, since an assassin would now be guilty of the sin of regicide, a more grievous act than homicide. On 26 May 1805 Napoleon crowned himself King of Italy with the eleventh-century iron crown of Lombardy in Milan Cathedral in the presence of the papal legate, Cardinal-Archbishop Caprara†. The coronation was followed by a fortnight of festivity.

CORSICA

Island in the western Mediterranean, in the possession of Pisa from the eleventh to the fourteenth century and then part of the Republic of Genoa until 1768 when it was ceded to France. From 1730 onwards the island was in revolt and achieved some degree of independence under the leadership of Pasquale Paoli†. The Corsican struggle attracted widespread interest, even in Britain, and aroused the sympathies of many writers, notably Boswell and Rousseau. Napoleon Bonaparte was born at Ajaccio† on 15 August 1769, lived on the island until December 1778, returned there from September 1786 until September 1787, from January to May 1788, September 1789 to February 1791, September 1791 to May 1792, October 1792 to June 1793 and for three days in October 1799. Corsica was occupied by a British force from February 1794 until November 1796, Nelson† participating in siege operations at Bastia and at Calvi, where his right eye sustained the injuries which deprived it of sight soon afterwards. From 1796 onwards the island remained in French hands, despite ambitious plans by both the British and the Russians to use it as an advanced naval base.

CORUNNA

Provincial capital and historic seaport (La Coruña) in north-western Spain, on a peninsula jutting out into the Atlantic. The port was used as the first British base in the Peninsular War‡ during 1808–9. When, on 1 January 1809, Moore‡ heard that Napoleon, Soult‡ and the main French army was at León, he decided to break off the expedition on which he was engaged in Galicia and to fall back on Corunna. The retreat, over the Cantabrian Mountains, cost 5,000 lives but, ten days later, Moore reached Corunna with some 28,000 men. On 14 January a convoy of twelve ships-of-the-line and a hundred transports arrived at Corunna. Soult's pursuing army approached the town next day, as Moore was embarking cavalry and guns. In the early afternoon of 16 January Soult attacked the British lines seeking, by an enveloping movement, to cut off Moore's army from the harbour. The rocky terrain made the battle primarily a conflict of infantrymen and after three hours Soult gave up his attempt to break through to the harbour in the face of resistance from Highlanders and a Guards brigade. As the fighting died away, Moore was mortally wounded. He was buried next morning, as the ships resumed embarkation. Eventually some 27,000 men reached England. Corunna later became a centre of Spanish liberal sentiment, vociferously demonstrated in 1815 but never so influential as in Cadiz‡.

COUNCIL OF ANCIENTS
(*Conseil des Anciens*)
The upper house of the legislature established by the Constitution of the Year III

(1795) and continuing throughout the Directory‡. The chamber comprised 250 men over the age of forty, a third of the members to be elected each year from 1797 onwards. The Council had powers of deliberation but could not initiate legislation. It was a more conservative body than the Council of Five Hundred‡ and docilely supported Bonaparte at Brumaire‡ in 1799 even though the address he delivered to them in the Gallery of Apollo at Saint-Cloud on 19 Brumaire was hysterically unconvincing. A Senate‡ replaced the 'Ancients' under the constitution of the Consulate.

COUNCIL OF FIVE HUNDRED
(*Conseil des Cinq-Cents*)
The lower legislative chamber under the Directory; it was responsible for proposing and passing laws between 1795 and 1799. Members had to be aged thirty or over and were elected for three years. The Council was more radically Jacobin than the upper house, the Ancients (*see above*). It resented the attempt by Bonaparte and his fellow conspirators to intimidate a hand-picked quorum of the Council during the Brumaire *coup*. Only the masterly chairmanship of Lucien Bonaparte‡ prevented bloodshed when the Council met in the Orangery at Saint-Cloud‡ on 10 November 1799.

COUNCIL OF STATE
The principal advisory body of the Executive in France during the Consulate and Empire. The Council was established in December 1799 and corresponded to the Royal Council of pre-revolutionary days. It was intended as a body of experts, chosen entirely by Bonaparte but given purely consultative functions and therefore allowed greater freedom of dissent and even of opposition than the members of the Senate‡, Tribunate‡ or Legislative Body‡. Twenty-nine men were appointed to the Council on Christmas Day 1799: ten

were lawyers; nine were educational or scientific specialists; and four held high rank in the army or navy. Of these twenty-nine founder members, seven remained councillors until the fall of the Empire in 1814 and the majority held office for more than five years, thus giving to the administration a continuity missing in the experiments of the past decade. The Council was divided into five sections (War, Navy, Finance, Laws, Internal Affairs) and a section on foreign relations was soon set up as well. Occasionally the Council assembled at a general meeting, normally under Napoleon's presidency. More than 60,000 questions are known to have been thrashed out by the councillors with some matters (the Codes†, the Concordat†) given great attention. Slackness led to abrupt dismissal by Napoleon and therefore the loss of a stipend of 25,000 francs a year. A special secretariat was organized to assist the Council of State, while gifted young administrative civil servants were attached to the sections of the Council as supplementary advisers (*auditeurs*). In one form – as a supreme judicial advisory body – the Council of State has survived successive changes of the government system in France.

In Russia a Council of State, on the Napoleonic model, was recommended by Speransky† as an essential administrative reform. It was formally opened by Alexander I† on 1 January 1810 and remained the chief advisory body on legislation throughout the nineteenth century but the Tsars only appointed elder statesmen, wise and experienced in bureaucratic ways, to the Council. In Austria, a *Staatsrat* of six members of the nobility, together with a secretary from the bourgeoisie, advised the emperors from 1780 to 1801 and again in 1808–9 but its functions were never clearly defined.

CRABBE, George (1754–1832)
English poet: born at Aldeburgh in Suffolk and ordained in 1782. He became domestic chaplain to the Duke of Rutland and subsequently rector of two small country livings. His first major work, *The Village*, appeared as early as 1783 but his prolific period ran from 1807 to 1818. He described in simple verse, made impressive through his mastery of heroic couplets, the true character of life for the rustic poor during the aftermath of the English agrarian revolution. His poetry captures both the beauty and the cruelty of natural scenery. In contrast to the lyricism of the early English Romantics it depicts a grim and cold world.

CRACOW
Third largest city of modern Poland (Kraków), on the river Vistula 160 miles south-west of Warsaw. Cracow is among the oldest university cities in Europe and served as Poland's capital from 1305 to 1609. At the Third Partition of Poland in 1795 the city passed into Austrian hands. The Polish Legion of Poniatowski† liberated Cracow in July 1809 and it formed part of the Grand-Duchy of Warsaw† from 1809 to 1813. As the supreme cultural centre of Polish nationalism Cracow became the cause of much diplomatic conflict in 1814–15, with the Russians hoping to secure the area for their satrapy, 'Congress Poland'. Cracow was, however, created a 'Free City', with Russia and Austria exercising joint supervision. A Polish national revolt in February 1846 was suppressed by the armies of the two Powers. Thereafter Cracow remained in Austrian Galicia until 1918.

CRISIS OF 1811
In the last half-century increasing attention has been given to the year 1811 as a critical moment for the economies of both Britain and France. Professor Georges Lefebvre in 1936 emphasized the extent to which the long wars, the blockade and the Continental System† posed unfamiliar problems for the antagonists. Intensifica-

tion of French economic control over Europe, from the Baltic to the Mediterranean, cut British exports from £61 million in 1810 to £39.5 million in 1811. At the same time inflation led to a depreciation in the value of the pound, while gold was needed to support the Spanish and Portuguese war effort. Bad harvests in 1809 and 1810, bankruptcies in Lancashire and panic machine smashing by the early Luddites‡ intensified the social distress. But continental Europe, too, was feeling the strain of interference with a natural trade pattern. The Paris banks were unsteady in the early months of 1811 and there was virtually no commerce in Lyons, Bordeaux or Rouen. The Continental System was crumbling at the edge, with Russia withdrawing from it in the last week of the year 1810. By November 1811 the opposing countries had decided that, to a large extent, they should abandon their rival methods of blockade. Napoleon signed licences for the export of wine and silks and for the import of sugar and coffee. From March 1812 the English issued licences to facilitate trade with the European mainland; British exports rose 28 per cent in 1812, giving the economy a respite at the very moment when Napoleon's Empire was incurring the new burden of successive military defeats and the need to improvise new armies.

CURRENCY

The early years of the French Revolution led to monetary chaos. Few coins were minted and there was confusion because of circulation of the assignats, the resort to bimetallism in the United States in 1792 and the spread of fiduciary paper money to Sweden, Russia, Austria and Spain. The Directory formally established decimal coinage based on the franc as a unit in 1795 but coins from the pre-revolutionary period continued to circulate throughout the first years of the Consulate, together with the new metallic currency. The Law of 17 Germinal, Year XI (7 April 1803) sought to define the value of the franc (4.5 grams of pure

The varied paper currency of France during the 1790s

silver) and compromised with the old coinage: the silver *écu*, which had been worth 6 *livres* in 1789, became a five franc piece, while the twenty franc piece, a golden *napoléon*, replaced the *louis d'or*, worth 24 livres before the Revolution. Uniformity in currency was hampered by the extent to which foreign coinage circulated within the Empire as it expanded into Italy, the Low Countries and Germany; there was some rash speculation in Latin American piastres and gold ingots, and much counterfeiting.

CZARTORYSKI, Prince Adam Jerzy
(1770–1861)

Acting Russian Foreign Minister and Polish patriot: born in Warsaw, a member of one of the historic Polish families. He was held as a virtual hostage in St Petersburg from 1795 to 1799, following the Third Partition of Poland, but he became a personal friend of the future Tsar Alexander I†, who relied on him as his chief foreign adviser for the first five years of his reign. Czartoryski was prominent in the Secret Committee†, became assistant Foreign Minister in September 1802 and was acting Foreign Minister from February 1804 until the spring of 1806. His Polish origins prevented his promotion to the rank of full minister. He was strongly hostile to France and played a considerable part in shaping the Grand Design† of 1804 and in creating the Third Coalition. After the defeat of Austerlitz†, Czartoryski was out of favour until the closing months of 1809 when Alexander began to consult him over ways of winning Polish support. He seemed to have recovered

Prince Adam Czartoryski

much of his old influence when he accompanied the Tsar to London in 1814 and he helped to draft the plans for the 'Congress Kingdom' of Poland at the Vienna Congress in 1815. Although he became President of the Senate in the Congress Kingdom all effective power rested with the Tsar's Russian nominees. Czartoryski, like other members of the Polish nobility, became disillusioned with the settlement of 1815. He was head of the provisional government established in Warsaw during the revolution of 1830–1 but was subsequently forced to flee to Paris. The last thirty years of his life were spent in exile, vainly striving for Poland's complete independence.

D

DANZIG (Gdansk)
A great Hanseatic port in the thirteenth
and fourteenth centuries. It remained a
free city under Polish sovereignty from
1455 to 1793 when it was annexed by
Prussia. After Eylau†, Napoleon sent
Lefebvre's corps to besiege Danzig (18
March 1807). The Russo-Prussian garrison, well-stocked and reinforced from the
sea, successfully defied Lefebvre†. Napoleon was forced to send two more corps
before the defenders capitulated, on
generous terms, on 27 May 1807. Danzig
then recovered its status as a free city but
Napoleon used the port extensively, especially to assemble troops in 1812. When
Prussia concluded the Convention of
Tauroggen†, General Rapp† continued to
hold Danzig for the Emperor throughout
1813. The city returned to Prussian rule in
1815; it became Polish in 1945.

DARU, Pierre Bruno, Count (1767–1829)
French administrative official: born in
Montpellier, a cousin of Henri Beyle†
(Stendhal). Daru was serving in the army
commissariat even before the Republic
was set up and he showed such skill in this
department that he handled major problems of finance and supply until the fall of
the Empire. In 1793 he was briefly imprisoned for allegedly Anglophile sympathies. He then served as chief commissioner to the armies of the Directory, was
secretary-general at the War Ministry during the Consulate, and, after 1804, became Intendant-General of the Imperial
Household and of the *Grande Armée*.
Napoleon appointed him chief administrative official in occupied Berlin (1806)

and he took charge of financial arrangements in each country occupied by the
Grande Armée. In April 1811 he succeeded Maret as Minister of the State
Secretariat and, in this post, was in constant attendance on Napoleon during the
Russian campaign. Had the Emperor lis-
tened to Daru's advice (based on supply
problems) he would have stopped in
Vitebsk† or wintered in Moscow† rather
than attempt the retreat. After the Restoration, Daru amused himself with literary pursuits, notably in writing a ponder-
ous history of the Venetian Republic and a
didactic poem on astronomy. In 1819
Louis XVIII created him a peer; he occasionally participated in parliamentary debates during the 1820s.

DAUNOU, Pierre Claude François
(1761–1840)
French liberal intellectual: born at
Boulogne, the son of a doctor from
Aquitaine. He was ordained priest and
was teaching theology at Montmorency
when the Revolution began. In Paris he
preached the panegyric in the Oratory for
those killed in the storming of the Bastille.
Three years later, having accepted
rationalist beliefs, he sat in the Convention but opposed the execution of the
King. His Girondist sympathies led to
imprisonment in 1793–4 but he afterwards
served the Directory, his orderly administrative mind helping to achieve some of
the legislative innovations of the period.
From 1800 to 1802 he was President of the
Tribunate† – but the First Consul numbered him among the *Idéologue†* 'wets'
and he was purged in 1802. From 1804

onwards he was Keeper of the National Archives. After the Restoration, he edited the influential *Journal des Savants*, was returned to the Chamber on three occasions as a liberal deputy and lectured on the systematic documentary study of history. His teachings were published after his death in twenty volumes.

DAVID, Jacques-Louis (1748–1825)

French painter: born in Paris, studied in Rome but was recognized as a neoclassicist of major importance when his *Oath of the Horatii* was exhibited in his native city in 1785. He became a convinced Republican, sat in the Convention and organized some of the great Revolutionary festivals as well as painting a largely allegorical representation of the *Tennis Court Oath*. In 1794 he narrowly escaped execution as a Jacobin but he regained his eminence as arbiter of pictorial representation under the Directory. He first met Bonaparte in 1798 and became his principal visual propagandist. David, by taste and discipline a classicist, allowed his artistic imagination to create legends on which the Romantics could feed. Thus he portrayed Bonaparte crossing the Great St Bernard Pass† in 1800 on a wild-eyed prancing steed at the head of his men, whereas in reality the First Consul crossed the Alps on a mule some days behind his leading troops. To mark the creation of the Empire David decided to commemorate the placing of the crown by Napoleon on Josephine's head rather than the less dignified act of self-coronation. When Napoleon inspected David's canvas in the studio he had created in the Cluny church, he was delighted with the painting: 'You have guessed my thoughts; you have made me a French knight'. The final version of the *Coronation* contains over a hundred portraits. *The Emperor distributing the Eagles* is also on an epic scale. David settled in Switzerland in 1815 but spent his last years in Brussels.

DAVOUT, Louis-Nicolas (1770–1823)

Marshal of the Empire: born at Annoux in Burgundy, a member of an aristocratic military family. He held a cavalry commission before the Revolution, served with the patriot volunteers in Flanders in 1793 and on the Moselle and Rhine in 1794, much of his early career as a commander being linked with Desaix's fortunes. He accompanied Desaix† to Egypt† in 1798 and distinguished himself at Aboukir† in July 1799. Bonaparte promoted him to command of a division a year later. He led the cavalry of the Army of Italy in 1800–1, was created a Marshal in May 1804 and as a corps commander distinguished himself at Austerlitz†. His most famous victory was at Auerstädt† in October 1806 when he defeated a numerically superior Prussian force. Subsequently he entered Berlin, Poznan and Warsaw, was wounded at Eylau† and captured Königsberg. Napoleon greatly respected his methodical powers of organization and created him Duke of Auerstädt in March 1808. A year later his well-trained corps defeated the Austrians at Eckmühl† and he commanded the French right wing at Wagram†. Napoleon rewarded him with the title Prince of Eckmühl and appointed him Governor of the Hanseatic Cities. During the early phases of the Russian campaign he advanced methodically through Minsk, Borisov and Mogilev to Smolensk, was slightly wounded at Borodino† and successfully countered Napoleon's proposals for a rash advance from Moscow on St Petersburg. Davout, a bald and nearsighted general lacking in outward panache, was a strict disciplinarian who was respected rather than liked by his men. In 1812 he was critical of both Murat† and Ney†; he was nearly captured during the retreat, the Russians seizing maps and letters from his carriage and even sending his marshal's baton as a trophy to St Petersburg. In May 1813 he was ordered to safeguard Hamburg and north-western Germany, a task he performed so well that he was still holding

Hamburg a year later when Napoleon abdicated. From March to July 1815 he was Minister of War, marching the remnants of the army out from Paris to the Loire on Napoleon's second abdication. At first he was kept under police supervision by Louis XVIII's orders and was stripped of rank and titles but within four years he was fully reinstated. He died from lung cancer in Paris early in June 1823, never having lost a battle.

DAVY, Sir Humphry (1778–1829)

English chemist: born in Penzance, making his first experiments while apprenticed to a surgeon in his home town. Important research into the respiration of gases, conducted at Bristol in 1798–9 led to his appointment as a lecturer at the Royal Institution in London in 1801. He concentrated on discovering chemical agencies in electricity and on soil research, eventually becoming the first scientist to identify potassium, barium, strontium and magnesium. His most beneficial invention was a safety lamp, perfected after researches into fire damp in 1815. He was knighted in 1812, created a baronet in 1820 and was President of the Royal Society for the last nine years of his life. From 1812 to 1823 he worked closely with Michael Faraday, researching into gases. The two men much increased popular interest in science through their lectures to the general public at at the Royal Institution.

DEGO, Battle of (14–15 April 1796)

Was fought on similar terrain to Montenotte† (12 April), around the town of Dego in Liguria, which Masséna† took on 14 April, together with 4,000 prisoners. Next morning he was surprised by an Austrian counter-attack and had to be rescued by Bonaparte, who had been pursuing the Piedmontese in the mountains to the west. Heavy losses at Montenotte and Dego induced the Piedmontèse to seek a separate armistice, concluded at Cherasco† on 28 April.

DENUELLE, Éléonore (Louise-Éléonore Denuelle de la Plaigne, 1787–1868)

Mistress of Napoleon: a school companion of Caroline Bonaparte†, she made an unfortunate marriage in January 1805 to Captain Revel of the Dragoons, a quartermaster arrested for forgery eight weeks after the wedding and imprisoned for two years. Éléonore was taken into the household of her school friend (now Princess Murat). After the Austerlitz campaign she became Napoleon's mistress, visiting him secretly at the Tuileries. On 13 December 1806 she bore him a son, known as Léon Denuelle (1806–81). The Emperor acknowledged his paternity but never again met Éléonore, who later married a Bavarian officer, the Count of Laxburg. Mother and child received settlements, Napoleon remembering 'little Léon' when he drew up his will on St Helena. The boy became, in middle age, a gambler but was also an enthusiastic champion of peace societies. The historical significance of the Denuelle affair is that it showed Napoleon he could have an heir. It therefore raised the possibility of divorce and remarriage to a likely mother of royal blood.

DESAIX, Louis Charles (1768–1800)

French general: born in the Château d'Ayat, near Riom, a member of an impoverished aristocratic family. He was commissioned in 1783 but from 1791 to 1796 made his reputation as a brave commander in successive campaigns on the Rhine, often in collaboration with Davout†. He first served under Bonaparte as a divisional commander in Italy in 1797. A year later he participated in the assault on Malta and remained in Upper Egypt while Bonaparte was fighting his Syrian campaign. Desaix conducted remarkable operations against Murad Bey down the Nile as far as Aswan and the cataracts. Early in 1800 he negotiated, with Sidney Smith†, the Convention of El Arish, ending the fighting in Egypt†. After brief internment by the British at Leghorn,

Desaix arrived back in France in late May 1800. He joined Bonaparte at Montebello on 10 June, receiving command of a corps. Four days later he perished at Marengo†, leading the decisive charge against the Austrian position. The First Consul honoured his heroism. 'Desaix was always totally engrossed by war and glory,' Napoleon recalled on St Helena. 'He despised comfort and convenience . . . A man intended by Nature for a great general.'

DESORGUES, Joseph Théodore
(1763–1808)
French revolutionary poet and song writer: born at Aix-en-Provence, achieved passing fame in 1794 when his *Hymn to the Supreme Being* received Robespierre's official approval. Desorgues remained an unrepentant Jacobin and was therefore suspect to Fouché's police spies. In 1804 he was heard to comment, 'Yes, Napoleon is great – a great chameleon.' His robust criticisms led to detention by the police, who declared him to be a mental defective. He died in the asylum at Charenton, on the Seine east of Paris.

DIRECTORY
The system of executive authority in France between August 1795 and November 1799. It was a form of government intended to perpetuate a bourgeois republic, saving France from both Jacobinism and royalist reaction. The *Directoire exécutif de la République française* comprised five men elected by the Council of Ancients† from a list of ten candidates put forward by the Council of Five Hundred†. The original five Directors took office on 27 October 1795. They were: Barras†; Carnot†; Jean-François Rewbell (1747–1807); Louis-Marie de Larévellière-Lépeaux (1753–1824); and Charles Letourneur (1751–1817). One of the five Directors was replaced each year; the only man to hold office throughout the period 1795–9 was Barras. Traditionally the Directory has received a poor press from

The Abbé Sièyes in the full ceremonial costume of a member of the Directory, 1799

historians, who have tended to write as latter-day Jacobins, Girondins or Bonapartists. Some of the Directors were corrupt; public standards were low; provincial administration was chaotic; and the Directory was never popular in Paris, which witnessed the abortive Vendémiaire† *coup* in 1795 and the alleged purge of crypto-royalists in Fructidor†, 1797. Nevertheless, it was under the Directory that France gained the succession of victories which culminated in the Treaty of Campo Formio†. Financial confusion and military defeat in Switzerland and Italy emphasized the inefficiency of the Directory, which was overthrown in Brumaire† 1799 by the uneasy collaboration of two Directors (Barras and Sieyès†) with the military idol newly returned from Egypt, General Bonaparte.

DIVORCE
Was virtually unrecognized by secular law in Europe before the French Revolution,

The preparatory statement of divorce, (14 December 1809), signed by Napoleon, Josephine (note the miniscule handwriting), Louis and Jerome Bonaparte, Murat ('Joachim Napoleon'), Eugène Beauharnais ('Eugène Bonaparte'), Queen Hortense, Catherine (Eugène's wife), Pauline Bonaparte Borghese, Caroline (Murat's wife, Napoleon's sister). Cambacérès signed as Arch-Chancellor of the Empire and Regnault de Saint-Jean d'Angely as a secretary of state.

although people of influence could obtain annulments of marriage. Divorce by mutual consent or on grounds of incompatibility was introduced in 1792 in France, but the Civil Code† limited the main grounds for divorce to cruelty, serious injury or adultery. The church authorities, especially in Italy, regarded the Civil Code as unduly permissive, and from 1804 to 1809 Napoleon tried to discourage divorce, in the interests of State-Church relations. The ground for his own divorce, registered on 14 December 1809, was the ending of the marital union by mutual consent. There were, in all, some 500 divorces in Paris during the ten years 1805–14, some in Lyons and Bordeaux, but very few elsewhere. Divorce was formally abolished in France soon after the Restoration – on 8 May 1816 – and not re-established in law until 1884. In Britain, divorce remained a rarely used privilege of the upper classes throughout the Napoleonic Wars, the first reforms over matrimonial proceedings not coming until 1857.

DOLGORUKY, Peter Petrovich (1776–1806) Russian soldier and courtier: a member of a historic princely family. He won the friendship of the future Tsar Alexander, his near contemporary, when still a junior officer. After serving as adjutant to Arakcheev†, Dolgoruky became Alexander's chief aide-de-camp soon after his accession and was entrusted with important diplomatic missions to Frederick William III† in Berlin. Dolgoruky disliked all Poles and distrusted the acting Foreign Minister, Czartoryski†, who had long enjoyed great influence over the Tsar. On 29 November 1805, three days before Austerlitz†, Dolgoruky was sent by Alexander to parley with Napoleon, in response to a French proposal that the two emperors should meet and seek an end to the campaign. Dolgoruky made a poor impression on Napoleon: 'An impertinent young puppy . . . who spoke to me as he

would have done to a boyar whom he wished to send to Siberia.' Unfortunately Dolgoruky returned to the Russian lines belittling Napoleon's strength and claiming that the *Grande Armée* was war-weary – an assessment which contributed to the disaster of 2 December.

DOMAINE EXTRAORDINAIRE
The name given to the confiscated properties and war indemnities acquired by right of conquest under the Empire. Napoleon sought to finance the campaigns of 1805–12 from the territories which his army occupied. Short, victorious campaigns (notably in 1805 and 1809) produced considerable surpluses which were used to finance prestigious public works projects and to provide rewards for outstanding civilian or military service, including pensions. The Emperor also reserved to himself certain properties, real and personal, in the vassal states which, by 1809, were adding some 35 million francs a year to his civil list. Originally – while in Munich in October 1805 after the capitulation at Ulm – Napoleon established the Army Fund to ensure that war paid for war. When the system became too complex, Napoleon established a special department of the *Domaine Extraordinaire* (30 January 1810), administered by one of his ablest Prefects, the Breton Defermon. Use was made of the profits from the *Domaine Extraordinaire* to invest in the Bank of France† and to advance money to industry during the Crisis of 1811†. Two financially unrewarding campaigns (Spain and Russia in 1812) destroyed the value of the *Domaine Extraordinaire* by imposing a heavy burden of expenditure (possibly as high as 700 million francs for the Russian venture) at the very time when defeat contracted the frontiers of the Empire and so cut off the source of monetary supply.

DOMBROWSKI, Jan Henryk (1755–1818)
Polish general, also known as Jan Dabrowski: born at Pierszowice, near Cracow, and served in the Saxon army for four years before fighting for Poland† in 1791. He then settled in France and raised a Polish Legion which fought under Bonaparte in northern Italy. After Jena† he returned to his homeland with the *Grande Armée* and fitted out a Polish division at Poznan which he led against the Prussians and Russians at Danzig† and Friedland†. He later became deputy commander to Poniatowski† in the Grand Duchy of Warsaw† but during the Russian campaign his division was detached from Poniatowski's Corps to check the advance of Chichagov† from the south. This task

was beyond the Poles; Dombrowski lost Borisov† on 21 November 1812 and was wounded on the Berezina† a few days later. After Leipzig† he succeeded Poniatowski in command of the Polish Corps. He was later reconciled with Tsar Alexander, returned to Poland and became a Senator in the 'Congress Kingdom'.

DRESDEN
City on the River Elbe, capital of Saxony. The wars first came to Dresden in the last week of October 1806 when a Bavarian division commanded by Jerome Bonaparte† occupied the city during the Jena campaign. Napoleon was in residence at

The Polish General, Jan Dombrowski

Dresden after Tilsit†, from 17–22 July 1807; he was mainly concerned with settling Polish affairs. He returned with Marie Louise in great state, on 16 May 1812, determined to impress his allies and his vassals with the magnitude of his power on the eve of the Russian campaign. During his thirteen days in Dresden he received the rulers of Austria, Prussia and most of the German princes and there were spectacular ceremonies and entertainments acknowledging the primacy of the Emperor of the French. Seven months later Napoleon arrived unrecognized on his hurried journey back from Smorgon† to Paris; he rested there for only five hours (14 December 1812), receiving in bed the King of Saxony. Blücher† entered Dresden with his Army of Silesia on 27 March 1813 but the French recovered their position on the Elbe after Napoleon's victory at Lützen† (2 May) and the Emperor made Dresden his advanced headquarters from 8 May until 7 October, although he was frequently in the field, especially during the Bautzen† phase of the campaign. For two months after the signing of the armistice at Plaeswitz†, he was in residence at the Marcolini Palace where he received Metternich† for two important conversations, on 26 June and 30 June. Napoleon ordered a troupe of actors ('not more than six or seven at most') to be sent hurriedly from Paris. 'I want this well publicized,' he said. 'It is sure to have a good effect in London and Spain if it makes them think we are amusing ourselves at Dresden.' The troupe were supplemented by the wayward Mademoiselle George†; they played a repertory of half a dozen classics.

When hostilities were renewed on 17 August the Austro-Russian Army of Bohemia (commanded by Schwarzenberg†) advanced on Dresden at a time when Napoleon was engaging Blücher on the Katzbach†. This threat to French communications brought the Emperor hurriedly back to Dresden where a premature move by Wittgenstein's† Russians began a major battle on 26 August. Against the advice of the Austrians, Tsar Alexander insisted that Schwarzenberg should make a frontal assault on Dresden from hills to the south-west. Napoleon counter-attacked early in the evening, the French recovering almost all the ground lost earlier in the day. Next morning Napoleon took the initiative, Mortier† attacking on the left and Murat† on the right; the Allies retired overnight, pursued across the Austrian frontier to within a few miles of Austro-Russian headquarters at Teplitz. Dresden was the last of Napoleon's major victories. When the Emperor was forced to concentrate around Leipzig† in early October, he left Gouvion Saint-Cyr† to hold Dresden. Saint-Cyr was besieged by the Russians for three weeks before surrendering on 31 October.

Drouot, Antoine (1774–1847)
French general: born at Nancy, the son of a baker. He served as an artillery officer from 1793 onwards, particularly distinguishing himself at Wagram† and Lützen†. After fighting at Leipzig† and in the last battles in France, he accompanied Napoleon to Elba†, where he was Governor of the island. He embarked with the Emperor in the brig *Inconstant* on 26 March 1815 and fought at Waterloo. Subsequently he was charged with high treason but was acquitted. In later years he lost his eyesight but long declined any pension from the Bourbons. Drouot was a staunch Bible-reading Christian, respected for his good sense and integrity.

Ducos, Pierre Roger (1747–1816)
Third Consul: born in Dax, became a lawyer and, as a member of the Convention, voted for Louis XVI's execution. He presided over the Council of Five Hundred† in 1797 and joined his friend, Barras†, on the Directory† in 1798–9. At his best, Ducos was a competent legal no-

nentity, given to hero-worship – Barras, Sieyès†, Bonaparte. He assisted Sieyès in drawing up plans for the Consulate† and was rewarded with the office of provisional Third Consul. This office he held for only a month, finding the First Consul's speed in conducting business uncongenial. He was later a Vice-President of the Senate† and was made a Count under the Empire. At first the restored Bourbons appointed him a Peer of France, but, when it was remembered that he had been a regicide, he hurriedly went into exile in 1816 and was killed in a carriage accident in Bavaria.

Duroc, Géraud Christophe Michel
(1772–1813)
Grand Marshal of the Palace: born at Pont-à-Mousson in Lorraine, a member of an impoverished aristocratic family. After a brief experience of emigration, he served as an artillery lieutenant at Toulon in 1793 and became a personal friend of Bonaparte, who appointed Duroc his aide-de-camp in Italy. Thereafter he remained in close attendance on Bonaparte, often using his tact and good manners to heal rifts caused by Napoleon's tantrums. On several occasions he was sent as a personal envoy on diplomatic missions. Duroc married the daughter of one of the ablest bankers in Spain and built up a personal fortune which was augmented by generous payments from Napoleon when he was appointed Grand Marshal of the Palace in 1805. He was created Duke of Frioul in May 1808, largely in recognition of the skills he was showing at that time in handling Charles IV of Spain at Bayonne†. Duroc was present at almost all Napoleon's battles. On 22 May 1813, the day after Bautzen†, he was mortally wounded by a Russian cannon-ball. Napoleon was deeply moved by the death of one of his closest friends.

E

EASTERN QUESTION
The name given to the problems caused by the weakness of the Ottoman Empire in Turkey and the rivalry between its potential successors. At the close of the eighteenth century the greatest threat to Turkey's integrity seemed to come from Russia and Austria. Until France annexed the Ionian Islands† in 1797 there was a tradition of Franco-Turkish friendship going back for at least 250 years. Bonaparte's expedition to Egypt† and plans to build up French influence in the Levant led to an unnatural phase of Turkish collaboration with Britain and Russia, the Turks and Russians even improvising a vassal republic in the Ionian Islands when they ejected the French in the spring of 1799. Peace between France and Turkey (26 June 1802) was followed by sustained efforts to restore the old relationship between the two states; and by 1806 Napoleon's envoy, General Sébastiani†, had encouraged the Sultan to depose Russophile governors in the Danubian Principalities (Moldavia and Wallachia) and to favour trade with France at the expense of the British. A new phase of the Eastern Question opened with the outbreak of a desultory war between Russia and Turkey in 1806. The British, allied to Russia at the time, sent a naval squadron under Admiral Duckworth which forced the Dardanelles in February 1807 and appeared off Constantinople. This activity aroused disquiet in St Petersburg; and at Tilsit† the Tsar responded to a French suggestion that should the Sultan refuse to make peace with Russia, under French mediation within three months, Napoleon and Alexander I would eject the Turks from Europe and establish a new order in the Balkans and at the Straits. In this policy, however, Napoleon was insincere. He was resolutely opposed to allowing the Russians to re-establish Byzantium. 'Constantinople is the centre of world empire', he remarked privately at Tilsit; and in consequence, he considerably modified his original proposals, ensuring that the Sultan might retain Constantinople and even a foothold in Thrace when it became necessary to partition his empire. Constant suspicion of French activities in the Ottoman Empire worsened Franco-Russian relations during the three and a half years of nominal alliance which followed Tilsit. War between Russia and Turkey continued until abruptly ended by the Treaty of Bucharest† on the eve of Napoleon's invasion of Russia in 1812. By then yet another phase of the Eastern Question had begun, with the spread of Balkan nationalism and with the threat of anti-Turkish revolts in Serbia†, Epirus (under Ali Pasha†) and the islands of Greece. Fear of the complexities of the Eastern Question – and, in particular, the knowledge that Czartoryski† and other eminent advisers of the Tsar favoured partition of the Ottoman Empire – induced Metternich† to keep it off the agenda of the Congress of Vienna† after Napoleon's fall.

ÉBLÉ, Jean-Baptiste (1758–1812)
French general: born at Rohrbach in Lorraine, the son of an artillery sergeant. He enlisted as a boy gunner in 1774 and was commissioned in the artillery in 1785. By 1793 he had risen to command a

division. He was artillery chief of the First Corps of the *Grande Armée* in 1804–5 and was Minister of War for the Kingdom of Westphalia from September 1808 to January 1811, later commanding the guns which bombarded Ciudad Rodrigo† and Almeida†. In 1812 Napoleon gave Éblé responsibility for the bridging train of the *Grande Armée*. His men constructed the bridges across the Niemen which launched the invasion; their pontoons allowed the French to cross the Dnieper at Smolensk† and give speedy chase to Barclay's army on 19 August. Éblé's greatest achievement was bridging the Berezina† under fire on 24–5 November 1812. He then fell back on Vilna† and, on Berthier's† orders, blew up the city's arsenal before retiring to Königsberg. There, on New Year's Eve, he collapsed and died from exhaustion.

ECKMÜHL, Battle of (22 April 1809)
Fought some eleven miles south of Regensburg (Ratisbon) in the first days of what became known as the Wagram† campaign. An attack by the Austrians under Archduke Charles† on Davout's† Third Corps was countered by Napoleon's decision to throw Bavarian and Württemberger troops under Vandamme against the main Austrian position around the village of Eckmühl while using enveloping movements on the two flanks and bringing up a column under Masséna† to complete the manoeuvre. The Archduke lost a third of his men, killed, wounded or captured. Overnight he ordered a retreat, abandoning Regensburg and pulling back along the Danube to the outskirts of Vienna.

EDUCATIONAL REFORMS (of Napoleon)
Before the Revolution, most teaching in France had been a responsibility of the church and, with the breakdown of the parish system during the years of anti-clerical legislation, most schools fell into disuse. Successive reforms proposed by the Convention and the Directory† were little more then superficial palliatives; the First Consul therefore entrusted his brother, Lucien Bonaparte†, with preparing a programme of educational growth in France. Basically Lucien proposed to expand a system originally practised at the former Jesuit college in Paris (now Lycée Louis-le-Grand): high-powered teaching in classics, mathematics and the liberal sciences in what was called (from Greek precedent) a *Prytanée*. In March 1800 seven affiliated *prytanées* were established, not merely around Paris but as far away as Lyons and Brussels, and in the summer of 1801 the First Consul gave detailed instructions to Chaptal† on ways of maintaining disciplined teaching in these schools. A more extensive reform was initiated in May 1802 by Bonaparte's principal educationalist, Antoine Fourcroy†: 45 *lycées* (state-maintained secondary schools, organized on a semi-military basis) and some 700 less élitist *écoles secondaires* were to be set up. During the Napoleonic period only 39 *lycées* were opened but there were some 1,200 *écoles secondaires* established, one in Lyons having more than two thousand pupils. Primary education, left by Fourcroy to the Prefects in the various départements, varied widely from region to region and was frequently entrusted to the bishops and the religious orders; an official report in 1813 gave the figure of primary schools in the French Empire at no more than 31,000. Napoleon was not an enlightened progressive: he wanted good scientists and efficient administrators. The memorandum which he dictated at Finkenstein† on his model girls' school at Écouen, north of Paris, is hardly a manifesto of educational liberalism: for a girl, 'the best education is that which a mother can give her daughters'.

In 1806–7 Napoleon organized France's educational system according to a standard pattern: the curriculum, discipline and hours of teaching reflected the

Emperor's liking for centralized uniformity; pupils were instructed in what to believe rather than in how to think. The system was administered by the *Université impériale*, a hierarchy dominated by a Grand Master (Fontanes†) and a Chancellor with authority over every school and with power to imprison teachers who varied the rules imposed from Paris. Recalcitrant pupils could be locked up, relegated to sit at 'tables of penitence', deprived of the right to wear uniform; but no provision was made for corporal punishment. The Napoleonic system survived the Restoration, contributing to the nineteenth-century reputation of France as a nest of scientific thought; but the eclectic philosophical logicalism which became a hallmark of French educational training is a later creation, owing more to Victor Cousin in Louis Philippe's reign than to Fourcroy or Fontanes.

EGYPT

Was conquered by the Turkish Sultan, Selim I, in 1517 and was thereafter governed by 24 Mamelukes† under a Turkish viceroy who ensured that an annual tribute was paid to the Sultan in Constantinople. In the last week of January 1798 Talleyrand encouraged Bonaparte to suggest to the Directory† that a military expedition to secure Egypt for France would be an indirect means of putting pressure on the British in India†. The Directory approved (5 March) and Bonaparte sailed from Toulon (19 May), with some 35,000 men supplemented by scholars and scientists who were to study and appropriate Egypt's ancient civilization. The expedition surprised and captured Malta†, landed near Alexandria† (1 July) and enabled Bonaparte to enter Cairo† (24 July) after his victory at the Pyramids. Although communications with France were virtually cut by Nelson's victory at the Nile†, the Army of the Orient remained in Egypt, Bonaparte introducing a more equitable system of taxation and more representative government. Resent-ment at the French presence and suspicion of the fiscal reforms led to a rising against 'the infidel' in Cairo (21 October) and there was considerable bloodshed. Desaix† swept aside Mameluke opposition in Upper Egypt as far south as Aswan, Marmont† was left to hold Alexandria while Bonaparte carried his campaign into Syria† (February to May 1799) until forced back by onset of the plague. News of French defeats in the War of the Second Coalition led Bonaparte to sail for France from a beach three miles west of Alexandria in the frigate *Muiron* on 23 August, leaving Kléber† in command. Abortive negotiations with the British and Turks continued intermittently until the eve of Kléber's assassination in June 1800. Menou†, who succeeded Kléber, was forced back on Alexandria after Abercromby's landing at Aboukir Bay†. Terms of surrender were finally settled on 2 September 1801 and some 23,000 Frenchmen were repatriated over the following three months. The French presence in Egypt had three long-term consequences: it stimulated Egyptology, notably by the discovery of the Rosetta Stone†; it broke for all time the effective power of the Mamelukes; and it prepared projects, economic and political, which were used by later Khedives to modernize the country. Uniquely, Bonaparte's virtual protectorate attempted to merge the secular ideas of eighteenth-century Europe with the traditions of Islam, many of his officers (including Menou) accepting conversion to the Moslem faith.

French interest in Egypt continued throughout the Consulate, notably with the mission of Sébastiani† in the autumn of 1802. The Sultan of Turkey's authority was upheld by a largely Albanian force, led by Mehemet Ali from 1805 onwards. With the support of the Sultan, he became Viceroy of Egypt and in 1811 massacred the remaining Mamelukes and their officers in Cairo. Subsequently Mehemet Ali was recognized as Khedive of Egypt, his descendants ruling until 1952.

ELBA

Rocky island, some ten miles off the west coast of Italy, and part of Tuscany† until incorporated in the French Empire in 1802. The Treaty of Fontainebleau† (April 1814) assigned Elba to Napoleon as 'a separate principality which he shall possess in full sovereignty and property'. He landed at the principal town, Portoferraio, on 4 May. The allied commissioners allowed Napoleon a token navy, 400 guards and a flag of his own design. His mother, his sister Pauline Borghese, his Polish mistress Marie Walewska†, and foreign dignitaries visited him at the Mulini 'Palace'. Reports of inter-Allied friction at the Congress of Vienna†, and a belief that he would be welcomed by a French public disillusioned with the Bourbon restoration, led Napoleon to slip away secretly from Elba on 26 February 1815 and begin his attempt to recover the French throne, the 'Hundred Days'†. Elba returned to Tuscan rule.

ELDON, Lord (John Scott, 1751–1838, created an earl 1799)

British Lord Chancellor: born at Newcastle upon Tyne, sat in the House of Commons 1782–99 and was successively Solicitor-General and Attorney-General 1788–1801. As Lord High Chancellor of Great Britain, Eldon presided over the judiciary from 1801 to 1827 except for thirteen months (1806–7). He was much respected by his fellow lawyers but became notorious in the public mind for his illiberalism. Eldon was particularly associated with the repressive measures of the post-war period, 1815–19.

ÉLYSÉE PALACE

Rue du Faubourg Saint-Honoré, Paris: built in 1718 for the Comte d'Évreux, becoming the home of Madame de Pompadour in Louis XV's reign. It was a government printing house at the height of the Revolution and a casino under the

Elba; Napoleon's home, above the sea at Portoferraio

Directory. Murat† and his wife (Caroline Bonaparte†) made it their Paris residence in 1801 but ceded it to Napoleon in July 1808. He liked the garden, found the rooms more comfortable than those in the Tuileries† but complained that the Élysée was cold and damp. Nevertheless, he stayed there often in spring and autumn, 1809–14. During the Hundred days Napoleon made the Élysée his home (17 April to 12 June 1815) while conducting public business from the Tuileries. After Waterloo he returned to the Élysée on 21 June and a day later was induced by his Council of Ministers to sign his second abdication† there. On Sunday, 25 June, he left the Élysée secretly soon after midday by the garden door leading on to the Champs-Élysées, drove to Malmaison† and eventually into exile. Fifteen days later Tsar Alexander I† moved into the Élysée, remaining there until the end of September. The palace, much renovated in 1850, has been the official presidential residence since 1873.

EMANCIPATION EDICT (Prussian, 1807)
A major social reform recommended by the Prussian Civil Organization Commission and published on 9 October 1807, only five days after Stein† became Prussia's Chief Minister. Frederick William III† had already freed serfs on the royal domains, and the edict extended this principle to the whole of Prussia, abolishing the status of serf, providing legal protection for peasant holdings and ending divisions which had prevented the nobility from engaging in commerce, burghers from buying country estates, and peasants from purchasing land (as distinct from possessing holdings). In 1808 supplementary edicts commuted the feudal services on crown lands into money rent and abolished several state monopolies so as to increase freedom of vocation. The edict held out the promise of a changed social relationship in Prussia, thus countering the appeal of the reforms which the French were imposing in the regions of Germany under Napoleon's control.

ÉMIGRÉS
There were three main waves of emigration from revolutionary France: July-October 1789, the flight of aristocrats who feared acts of vengeance for their past way of life; June-October 1791, titled refugees fleeing mainly to Coblenz from fear of war; July 1792 to April 1793, the escape of disillusioned liberals. An émigré army, divided into three corps, was raised in 1791–2, based mainly upon Mainz and Worms; the future French kings, Louis XVIII† and Charles X (see *Artois*) led one of these corps. At its peak the émigré army numbered 20,000 men, but only the Second Corps, commanded by the Prince de Condé (1736–1818), survived for any length of time; Condé received foreign subsidies until 1801. Émigré support for conspiracies against Bonaparte continued until at least 1804, notably through the activities of Cadoudal†. The First Consul sought to win back the loyalty of the less hardened émigrés by establishing a commission in March 1800 to examine requests for permission to return home. Many of the third emigration were allowed back without delay, but other requests were handled so slowly that Bonaparte became impatient. A special council at Malmaison (11 April 1802) drafted an amnesty, published a fortnight later, which permitted the return of anyone not on a proscribed list (with about 1,000 names). The repatriates had to reach France before 23 September 1802, swear loyalty to the constitution and accept police surveillance for ten years. Between 40,000 and 50,000 people took advantage of this amnesty: some retired to what was left of their estates, taking no part in public life; others accepted office in the diplomatic service, the Senate†, the Council of State† and, in due course, at the imperial court. Over the following five

or six years a stream of émigrés continued to return. The irreconcilables and the proscribed remained, for the most part, in British service, many coming back with Wellington's army over the Pyrenees in 1814. Resentment at the arrogance of these veteran émigrés helped revive Bonapartist support in the early months of 1815.

EMPIRE OF THE FRENCH

On 18 May 1804 a *Sénatus-Consulte*† decreed that 'the government of the Republic be entrusted to an Emperor', that 'Napoleon Bonaparte, at present First Consul of the Republic, is Emperor of the French' and that 'the imperial dignity is hereditary'. Only the third of these provisions was submitted to a plebiscite, winning approval from 99.91 per cent of the voters. Napoleon's coronation† was celebrated on 2 December 1804. By then France possessed a new court hierarchy (see *Grand Dignitaries*).

The decision to establish an Empire was taken partly to emulate classical Roman precedent but also to protect the Head of State from royalist plots (see *Pichegru Conspiracy*). The title implied sovereignty over a region greater in territorial extent than the traditional boundaries of the Kingdom of France; and by 1811 the Empire stretched from Lübeck on the Baltic to some seventy miles south of Rome and, in the Illyrian Provinces†, down the Adriatic to Kotor†. Napoleon was declared Emperor 'by the grace of God and the constitution of the Republic'; his coinage bore the legend *République Française* until after the seizure of Spain (1808).

ENCLOSURE ACT (British, 1801)

Although the enclosing of land for improved tillage began in Tudor England, only two-fifths of the cultivated soil in the kingdom was enclosed by 1793, when Pitt† set up the Board of Agriculture. During the war years 1795–1812 parliamentary authority was given for more than 1,500 instances of enclosure, so as to meet demands for corn. The first general Enclosure Act (1801) simplified procedure for enclosing common land. The Act benefited large freeholders, forced some small freeholders to become tenant farmers and threatened the historic rights of cottagers and squatters. Enclosure improved the agricultural yield but at the cost of destroying the communal life traditionally associated with the open field villages.

ENGHIEN, Execution of the Duc d'

(21 March 1804)

The Duc d'Enghien was a great-great-great-great-grandson of Louis XIII, a first cousin of the later king Louis Philippe, and a son of Condé, who commanded the émigrés† until 1801. Enghien had served under his father. In 1802 he settled at Ettenheim in Baden, maintaining tenuous contact with English sponsors of the émigré cause. After frustrating Pichegru's conspiracy†, Bonaparte decided to take action against a prominent émigré in order to discourage further royalist plots. On 10 March 1804, after consultation with Caulaincourt†, Bonaparte ordered a special expedition to enter Baden and seize Enghien; Baden's neutrality was duly violated on 15 March and Enghien brought to the fortress of Vincennes, outside Paris, five days later. A military tribunal condemned him to death for treasonable links with the English. He was shot in the castle moat less than ten hours after reaching Vincennes, the First Consul disregarding pleas from Josephine and from 'Mme Mère'. Napoleon later argued that his harshness saved the Empire from Bourbon or Jacobin plots, but he admitted his responsibility for what (in 1816) he called 'the calamitous Enghien affair'. The execution hardened foreign opinion against him, particularly infuriating Tsar Alexander I†, who had married into the

A propaganda print of the execution of Enghien. In reality he was shot at two o'clock in the morning, in the former moat at Vincennes and beside an already dug grave.

royal family of Baden, and Russia broke off diplomatic relations with France. The cynical Fouché† declared that Enghien's execution was 'worse than a crime – it was a mistake'; but Fouché was one of the six councillors whom Napoleon consulted on 10 March before ordering the expedition to Baden.

ERFURT

Cathedral city now in the German Democratic Republic, sixty-five miles southwest of Leipzig. The town was chosen by Napoleon and Alexander I for a congress in the autumn of 1808 which was intended to strengthen the Franco-Russian alliance, concluded in July 1807 at Tilsit†. Napoleon and the Tsar were at Erfurt from 27 September to 14 October 1808, with the rulers of all the German states apart from Prussia and Austria also present. The congress was intended by Napoleon to impress Alexander and the German princes while providing for Russo-French collaboration against Austria and for a tightening of the Continental System. Expensive spectacles (including nine plays acted by the Comedie Française† company with Talma†) and a series of balls and banquets were followed by an Alliance Convention, which reaffirmed the Tilsit Treaty and appealed to George III to accept a negotiated peace. Despite the splendour of the occasion, the Erfurt Congress failed to achieve anything of lasting value; Alexander's evasiveness emphasized rifts between Russia and France.

ESSLING, Battle of: see *Aspern.*

ETRURIA, Kingdom of: see *Tuscany.*

EXELMANS, Remi Isidore, Count (1775–1852)
French general: born at Bar-le-Duc, volunteered for the army when sixteen

and was a cavalry captain at the time of Brumaire†. He gained a reputation for personal recklessness as Murat's† chief subordinate commander in Spain in 1808 and again in 1811. Napoleon belatedly recognized his value in the French campaign† (1814). He was a corps commander in 1815, serving under Grouchy† and leading the attack which threatened to turn Blücher's† left flank at Wavre†. Subsequently Exelmans protested at Ney's court martial and went into exile for four years. He resumed his army career in 1828, receiving a marshal's baton from Napoleon III shortly before his death.

EXTRAORDINARY DOMAIN: see *Domaine Extraordinaire.*

EYLAU, Battle of (7–8 February 1807) Fought around the town of Preussich-Eylau, just inside the East Prussian bor-

der, twenty-two miles south of Königsberg. Eylau was an indecisive engagement in the Polish campaign. The main French army, checked by nagging attacks from Bagration† and the Russian rearguard, entered the town after a sharp encounter on 7 February, leaving Bennigsen† and his army to hold positions on the plain north of Eylau. Overnight there was more than 30° of frost; next morning a blizzard obscured the movements of both armies, delaying the arrival of Ney† and Davout† to support Napoleon's centre. Despite the terrible weather, a Russian column penetrated the town during the morning and almost captured Napoleon's headquarters. He was saved by a remarkable charge by eighty squadrons of Murat's cavalry against the Russian batteries, giving the French a respite until Ney and Davout arrived in the afternoon. The Russians withdrew that night, with some 25,000 casualties from the fighting and the blizzard; Napoleon lost 10,000 men and at

The battle of Eylau; an engraving after the famous painting by Gros (1808), now in the Louvre

119

least 1,500 cavalry horses. On 9 February Napoleon, who had come close to defeat, dictated the official bulletin; he described the battlefield after the Russian withdrawal and declared, 'Such a sight as this should inspire rulers with love of peace and hatred of war'. Tsar Alexander‡ did not sue for peace but both armies retired into defensive positions until June. When the Red Army entered East Prussia in 1945 and annexed the region to the Soviet Union, Eylau was renamed in honour of the Russian rearguard commander of 1807. As Bagrationovsk, it is the Soviet frontier post between Warsaw and Kaliningrad (Königsberg).

F

FAIN, Agathon Jean François, Baron
(1778–1836)

Secretary to Napoleon: born in Paris, began work for the military committee of the Convention when he was sixteen and remained attached to the War Department and the Foreign Ministry until 1806 when he was recommended to Napoleon by Maret†. He accompanied Napoleon on all the later campaigns, until 1813 as assistant to Méneval†. Fain's memoirs of the years 1812–14 (published as a separate volume for each year in 1823–7) are valuable sources especially for Borodino† and the Berezina†, although at times Fain appears a loyally romantic chronicler. He rallied to Napoleon on 20 March 1815, was with him at Waterloo, became chief secretary to Louis Philippe in 1830 and sat in the Chamber of Deputies for the last two years of his life.

FERDINAND IV, King of Naples and Sicily
(1751–1825)

Born at Naples, the third son of Charles VII of Naples who became Charles III of Spain in 1759. Ferdinand then succeeded him at Naples†, under a Council of Regency until 1767. He was virtually illiterate, ugly and loutish, but in 1768 married Archduchess Maria Carolina of Austria, a sister of Queen Marie Antoinette. Maria Carolina, a formidable personality, inclined her husband's policies towards her native Austria. Husband and wife were driven out of Naples by the French in December 1798, escaping to Sicily aboard Nelson's flagship, HMS *Vanguard*. Ferdinand returned in 1800 and his maladministration was tolerated by Napoleon until 1806,

when he was again forced to find sanctuary at Palermo, protected by the British fleet. From 1809 to 1812 he resigned the active government of his truncated kingdom to his eldest son, but he was encouraged to reassert himself by the British envoy, Bentinck†, who induced him to issue a liberal constitution while sending his Queen back to Vienna (where she died in September 1814). Ferdinand duly married his mistress, Donna Migliaccio, and returned to Naples on the downfall of Murat. He now assumed the title, 'King of the Two Sicilies', it being said by one of his ministers that the chief servant of the restored dynasty was the Public Executioner. Ferdinand survived another ten years, having repudiated Bentinck's constitution and a more liberal one forced upon him by his radical subjects in 1820.

FERDINAND VII, King of Spain
(1784–1833)

Born at San Ildefonso, the son of Charles IV† of Spain and nephew of Ferdinand IV of Naples (see *above*). He succeeded his father on 19 March 1808 when popular discontent against king, queen and chief minister (Godoy†) led to Charles's abdication. Within seven weeks Ferdinand had been encouraged by Napoleon to travel to Bayonne† where, with his father, he ceded the Spanish crown to the Emperor of the French. For five and a half years Ferdinand was interned at Talleyrand's château of Valençay†, where he concluded an abortive treaty in December 1813 restoring his sovereign titles. He returned to Spain on 24 March 1814, abolished the liberal Cadiz Constitution†

Ferdinand vii, King of Spain

within six weeks but was faced by a new radical rebellion in 1820, recovering his throne only with military help from Louis XVIII. Ferdinand lacked courage and good faith, finally throwing Spain into dynastic anarchy by seeking to break tradition so as to ensure the succession of his daughter, Isabella, who was only three years old when her father died.

FERDINAND, Archduke (Ferdinand Karl Josef d'Este, 1781–1850)
Austrian army commander: born in Milan, a first cousin of Emperor Francis and of Archdukes Charles†, John† and Joseph†. In 1805 he successfully led 6,000 men out of Ulm† as the French closed in on the city and tried to reach the main army in Moravia but was at Iglau, ninety miles away, when Austerlitz† was fought. He gained some success ˗ against Poniatowski† in Galicia in 1809. He was entrusted with governorships (Galicia, Transylvania) in the 1830s. The Archduke was an easy-going general, sporadically enterprising.

FESCH, Giuseppe (1763–1839)
Cardinal: born in Ajaccio, a half-brother of Letizia Bonaparte† ('Mme Mère'). He was ordained priest in 1785, took the oath to the Civil Constitution of the Clergy in 1790 but then followed a secular life, joining the war commissariat of his nephew, Napoleon, in March 1796 and prospering financially. By 1802 he was established in a fine house in Paris when, on his nephew's initiative, he was speedily absolved and consecrated Archbishop of Lyons. On 17 January 1803, a fortnight after arriving at Lyons, he was created cardinal. For six months he concerned himself with reviving the ritualistic practices in his archdiocese. In 1804 he undertook the first of many diplomatic missions to Rome, persuading the Pope to come to Paris for Napoleon's coronation†. The Papacy permitted Fesch to act as coadjutor to the Prince-Primate of Germany while remaining a largely absentee archbishop in France, but drew the line at allowing him also to be Archbishop of Paris (1808). Although Fesch bullied Pius VII† when the Pope was under French constraint (1809–13), he did much to restore the priesthood in the empire, particularly by improving clergy training. He was, however, Grand Almoner of the Imperial Household and frequently acted first and foremost in his nephew's interest. Thus, in 1809, he was prepared to support annulment of Josephine's marriage on the grounds that the religious ceremony, of October 1804, had been irregular since it took place in private, without witnesses – and yet he had himself officiated on that occasion. Fesch also blessed the marriage of Napoleon and Marie Louise on 2 April 1810. In January 1811 he presided over a council in Paris which sought to strengthen state control over the institution of bishops. When Napoleon abdicated in 1814 Fesch found sanctuary in the cloisters of Pradines before escorting 'Mme Mère' safely to Rome. He was back at Lyons on 26 May 1815, but again hurried to Italy on Napoleon's second abdication†. Pius VII

treated Fesch generously although, as a Bonaparte, he was not allowed to return to his duties at Lyons. In Rome he resumed his practice of collecting works of art, all of which he bequeathed to Lyons on his death.

FICHTE, Johann Gottlieb (1762–1814)
German philosopher and nationalistic writer: born at Rammenau, near Bautzen in Saxony and educated at the universities of Jena and Leipzig, becoming a devotee of Kant† in the early 1790s. He taught at Jena and Erlangen before helping to found the University of Berlin†, of which he was the first Rector (1810). His development of Kantian philosophy into 'subjective idealism' gave Fichte influence over the formation of German Romanticism†, not least because so much of his teaching was egocentric. Fichte was also an anti-Napoleonic German patriot, author of a series of addresses on national regeneration (*Reden an die deutsche Na-*

tion, 1807–8). He died in Berlin from typhoid, his wife having contracted the fever while nursing in an army hospital.

FINKENSTEIN
A remote castle in Prussian Poland, fifty-five miles south-east of Danzig. Napoleon's headquarters were there for two months between the Eylau and Friedland campaigns† (1 April to 6 June 1807); Marie Walewska† was with him for most of the time. From Finkenstein he tried to control his Empire as closely as from the Tuileries, imposing a great strain on his secretaries, Méneval† and Fain†, and on his courier service to Paris; and he found nothing strange in requiring the Persian ambassador to travel to Finkenstein to negotiate a treaty with him. His correspondence from Finkenstein illustrates the ease with which he switched his mind from war to the problems of civil government: orders to Fouché† on handling the press; advice to Louis Bonaparte† on how to win

Finkenstein Castle, Poland: Napoleon receives the Persian ambassador, 27 April 1807

respect as a king; criticism of Joseph Bonaparte's† dissolution of Naples's monasteries; a memorandum on creating an institute of historical study; an analysis of the Minister of the Interior's reports on the encouragement of literature; and a project to establish a girls' school at Écouen for relatives of members of the Legion of Honour. He also kept abreast of military operations at Danzig† and regrouped his army for the summer campaign.

FINLAND

Became part of Sweden† in the late Middle Ages. In 1721 and 1743 some of southern Finland passed to Russia whose rulers encroached throughout the eighteenth century despite an abortive attempt by Sweden to recover the Karelian Isthmus in 1788–90. A possible Russian campaign in Finland was discussed at Tilsit† and encouraged by Napoleon in a letter to Alexander I† on 2 February 1808. General Buxhowden at once launched a surprise attack on Swedish positions in Finland, the strongest resistance coming from the island fortress of Sveaborg, off modern Helsinki. Sveaborg surrendered on 3 May 1808 and Alexander proclaimed the incorporation of the Grand Duchy of Finland in his empire six days later. Swedish troops, however, held out on the Gulf of Bothnia until the Peace of Frederikshamn in September 1809, when Finland was formally ceded to Russia. In August 1812 a meeting between Alexander I and the Swedish Prince Royal (Bernadotte†) at Åbo† marked acceptance by Sweden of her loss. The Grand Duchy enjoyed considerable autonomy within Russia until 1898; Finland's independence came in December 1917.

FLAHAUT (Auguste) Charles de
(1785–1870)
French soldier and diplomat: born in Paris, nominally the son of General de la

Billarderie, Comte de Flahaut. In reality he was the son of Talleyrand†, one of the beautiful Comtesse de Flahaut's many lovers. Mother and child escaped to London in 1792, the general being guillotined at Arras a year later. In 1797 they returned to Paris. Charles de Flahaut became an aide-de-camp to Napoleon and was a lover of his youngest sister, Caroline Bonaparte†. At Aix-les-Bains in 1810 he met Queen Hortense Beauharnais† and by her had a son, who became the Duke de Morny (1811–65). Flahaut served under Eugène Beauharnais† in the Russian campaign, fighting at Borodino† and Maloyaroslavets† and he was in close attendance on Napoleon during the Hundred Days†, especially after Waterloo. When Hortense spurned his offer of marriage in 1815, Flahaut settled in England and married the English heiress, Margaret Elphinstone, in June 1817; their grandson, Lord Lansdowne (British Foreign Secretary from 1900 to 1906) concluded the *Entente Cordiale* of 1904. Flahaut himself served Louis Philippe as an ambassador in Berlin and Vienna.

FONTAINEBLEAU
Town thirty-six miles south-east of Paris which owes its origin to a royal palace built on the site of a fortified hunting lodge in the mid-sixteenth century. Napoleon first visited Fontainebleau in late June 1804, ordered a refurbishing of the château and, over the next ten years, spent some 165 days in residence, his apartments being on the first floor next to the Orangery. On 25 November 1804 he welcomed Pius VII† to France at Fontainebleau a week before the coronation†. However, from June 1812 to January 1814 Pius VII was kept a prisoner at Fontainebleau; Napoleon visited him there (19–26 January 1813) and concluded the abortive Fontainebleau Concordat†, which modified the 1801 settlement in favour of the French episcopate but never became operative. Napoleon's longest continuous sojourn was in 1810,

Napoleon bids farewell to the Old Guard at Fontainebleau, 20 April 1814

with Marie Louise: the visit began with a stag hunt on 30 September and ended with the baptism of the future Napoleon III on 4 November in the chapel.

On 31 March 1814 Napoleon arrived at Fontainebleau to hear news of the fall of Paris. His plan to march on the capital while Caulaincourt‡ was parleying there with the Tsar and Talleyrand was abandoned when Marmont‡ went over to the Allies. After studying the Fontainebleau Treaty‡, Napoleon swallowed poison in the small hours of 13 April but the capsule was ineffective and Caulaincourt was able to summon medical aid. Napoleon remained at the palace until 20 April when he bade an emotional farewell to his Old Guard‡ assembled on the *Cour du Cheval Blanc*, the principal courtyard in front of the horseshoe staircase; he then set out for Elba‡ in a convoy of fourteen coaches. During his return from Elba eleven months later he spent only four hours at Fontainebleau (20 March 1815), hurrying on to re-enter Paris that evening.

FONTAINEBLEAU DECREE

(18 October 1810)

The last of Napoleon's attempts to make the Continental System‡ effective. The decree ordered the confiscation and sale by the state of intercepted unlicensed colonial goods, the destruction of prohibited manufactured goods, and stiffer penalties (including branding) for smugglers. The chief value of the decree to Napoleon was increased revenue. The tightening of the Continental System contributed to the mounting Crisis‡ of 1811.

FONTAINEBLEAU, Treaty of (April 1814)

The document drawn up by the Allies in Paris on 11 April 1814 setting out arrangements for the fallen Emperor. It was conveyed to Napoleon at Fontainebleau‡ next day by Caulaincourt‡ but not signed until 13 April, after Napoleon's attempted suicide. The treaty had sixteen articles: a renunciation of sovereignty over the French Empire and Italy; the right of

Napoleon and Marie Louise† to retain their rank and titles; assignment of Elba† to Napoleon, and of Parma† to Marie Louise and their son; provision of annuities and pensions to Bonaparte's family, including Josephine† and Eugène Beauharnais†; and provision of a ship to take Napoleon to Elba. Other clauses detailed the size of his bodyguard and gave international maritime recognition to the flag of Elba. No British representative signed the treaty although Castlereagh† duly acknowledged the stipulations regarding Elba and Parma. Napoleon's escape to France in March 1815 invalidated the Treaty.

FONTANES, Louis de (1757–1821)

Grand Master of the *Université impériale*: born at Niort and recognized as a minor poet in the didactic tradition, lauding the efficacy of human reason; he translated Pope's *Essay on Man* and in 1788 published a poetic *Essai sur l'astronomie*. He taught in Paris during the revolutionary years but in 1797 was suspected of royalist sympathies and found refuge with the London émigrés where he became a friend of Chateaubriand†. He now turned away intellectually from rationalism to an emotional hatred of '*philosophaillerie*'. With this conservatism in ideas Fontanes returned to France in 1800, was welcomed at Elisa Bonaparte's salon† and accepted patronage from Lucien Bonaparte†. In 1804 Fontanes became president of the Legislative Body† and virtually public orator; he would welcome Napoleon back to Paris with verbal extravagance on ceremonial occasions, generally after successful campaigns. When the *Université impériale* (see *Educational reforms*) was created in March 1808 Fontanes was appointed Grand Master, with administrative responsibility for education throughout Napoleon's empire. By 1813–14 he was associating himself with the predominantly clericalist salons of the Faubourg Saint-Germain and had con-

tacts with both Talleyrand and his old friend, Chateaubriand. Fontanes readily accepted the Bourbon restoration.

FOUCHÉ, Joseph (1759–1820)

Minister of Police: born near Nantes and was head of a church school in 1789. By 1792–3 he was a zealous Jacobin, notorious for his harshness in stamping out opposition in Lyons. He turned against Robespierre, supported Barras† under the Directory and became Minister of Police. He backed Bonaparte in Brumaire and retained his post under the Consulate, building up a network of informers. Bonaparte always mistrusted him and had his own agents to watch Fouché as a potential leader of the Left. Fouché absented himself from the Council of State on 10 May 1802 which recommended Bonaparte's Life Consulship; and four months later police affairs were placed under the Department of Justice. But in July 1804 internal security was given greater central control and Fouché became Minister of Police again (10 July). He held office until May 1810 when he was dismissed for sending an agent to London to contact the British Foreign Secretary. Napoleon, fearing Fouché's capacity for intrigue, created him Duke of Otranto and sent him on special missions to Italy and Dalmatia.

After the first Restoration Fouché warned the Bourbons that Napoleon might land in southern France. At the same time he conspired with Bonapartist officers in Lille to proclaim a Regency in the name of Napoleon II. During the Hundred Days† he was again Minister of Police but, after Waterloo, he took the lead in contacting Louis XVIII and securing Napoleon's second abdication†. From July to September 1815 he was Louis XVIII's Minister of Police in the Talleyrand government. It was Fouché who drew up the list of (almost) all who had compromised themselves by serving Napoleon on his return: 'One must do M. Fouché the justice to recognize that he has left out none of his friends', commented Talleyrand sardonically. For a year Fouché was Louis XVIII's diplomatic envoy in Dresden before retiring to Trieste where the fortune he had acquired in his years of influence kept him in ample comfort.

FOURCROY, Antoine François, Count (1755–1809)

Educationalist: born in Paris, became distinguished as a chemist at the Museum of Natural History and was given responsibility for reorganizing education under the Consulate. The *Loi Fourcroy* (1 May 1802), creating *lycées*, was basic to the educational reforms† of Napoleon, who appointed Fourcroy director of public instruction in the Ministry of the Interior.

Fox, Charles James (1749–1806)

British Whig leader: born in Westminster, the second surviving son of Henry Fox, Lord Holland. He spent his childhood at Holland House†, was educated at Hertford College, Oxford, and elected MP for Midhurst in 1768. Fox consistently attacked British policy towards the American colonies, showing great gifts as a trenchant debater. With the reform of departmental administration by Rockingham's Whig government in March 1782, Fox became the first ever Secretary of State for Foreign Affairs, but he was back in opposition within four months. He was again Foreign Secretary from April to December 1783 but was then out of office until February 1806, when he returned to the Foreign Office for the last nine months of his life.

The period 1783–1805 saw his long political duel with Pitt†. As virtual Leader of the Opposition, Fox welcomed the early stages of the French Revolution, consistently criticizing British involvement in the wars against France. He declared in parliament after Brumaire that the coming of the Consulate 'made good the past'. On 7 October 1802 he met

Charles James Fox, from a contemporary caricature

Napoleon in Paris, tried to convince him in private conversation that standing armies menaced liberty, and surprised the First Consul by defending the attitudes of the English Tories: 'He fought me warmly in his bad French', Napoleon remarked later. In 1803 he spoke out against renewal of the war and, in his final term as Foreign Secretary, he began abortive peace negotiations. His great achievement in office was to introduce the Bill abolishing the slave trade†. Fox's hostility to George III and his belief in the 'sovereignty of the people' tempted him into political errors; his friendship with Prinny (see *Prince Regent*) puzzled his radical supporters; and his delight in drink and gambling made him the butt of Tory satirists; but he remained throughout the crisis years a consistent champion of the liberties of the subject and of the press, shaping the political values of later parliamentary liberalism.

FRANCIS II, Habsburg Emperor
(1768-1835)

Born in Florence, the son of Emperor Leopold II (reigned 1790-2). Francis was elected 'Holy Roman Emperor of the German Nation' on 7 June 1792 and crowned at Frankfurt† five weeks later. The Imperial Recess† and the establishment of a French Empire† and the Rhine Confederation† made him modify his official style: he became 'Francis I, Emperor of Austria' on 11 April 1804 and abdicated as (last) Holy Roman Emperor on 6 August 1806. From 1792 to 1812 he had to accept successive humiliations at the hands of the French: military defeats in Italy, followed by the peace treaties of Campo Formio† and Lunéville†; the capture of Vienna† twice, with huge territorial losses to his empire; the acceptance of the *parvenu* Napoleon as a husband for his eldest surviving daughter, Marie Louise†; and the condescension shown by his son-in-law at the Dresden† Congress of 1812. He resolutely rejected filial pleas from Paris during the 1814 campaign and insisted on the return of Marie Louise to Austria with her son, whom he sought to educate and train as an Austrian archduke. The strain of the war made Francis prematurely old; his health was poor from 1826 onwards. He was conscientious and self-effacing but lacked sympathetic imagination and was rigidly hostile to innovations in government. From 1809 until his death he retained Metternich† as his Foreign Minister.

FRANKFURT-AM-MAIN.

A free imperial city from 1372 to 1806, famous for trade fairs from 1206 onwards. As early as 1356 Frankfurt became the city in which Holy Roman Emperors were elected; from 1562 to 1792 their coronations were solemnized in the cathedral. Possession of Frankfurt was thus important for prestige, trade and direct political influence over the Rhineland. Rather curiously, Napoleon never stayed for more than a few hours in Frankfurt. He recognized, however, the city's special position and made Frankfurt the seat of the Prince-Primate of the Rhine Confederation†, Karl von Dalberg (1744-1817), an enlightened scholar and patron of Schiller†. After the Allies' victory at Leipzig†, their armies advanced rapidly on Frankfurt, securing the city so that Emperor Francis† could make a ceremonial entry on 6 November 1813. Frankfurt recovered its status as a free city at the Vienna Congress†, retaining its privileges until absorbed by Prussia in 1866, and serving throughout the years 1815-66 as the seat of the Diet of the German Confederation.

FREDERICK, Duke of York: see *York, Frederick, Duke of.*

FREDERICK, Augustus, Elector and later King, of Saxony (1750-1827)

Born at Dresden†, succeeded his father Elector Frederick Christian in 1763, ruling under a regency until 1768. By temperament he was an honest dilettante, much addicted to rose gardens and consistently eager not to offend the greater rulers around Saxony's frontiers. He avoided entanglement in the wars until 1806 when, allied to Prussia, he shared in the Jena débâcle, made a separate peace with Napoleon and joined the Rhine Confederation†. He assumed the title King of Saxony on 11 December 1806 and became nominal Grand Duke of Warsaw† a year later. In May 1812 he was host at the Dresden Congress of Sovereigns, concentrating his tidy mind on the trivia of festivities with the care he lavished on horticulture. He contemplated an alliance with Austria in 1813 but, after Lützen†, veered back to collaboration with Napoleon. He was taken prisoner by the Allies after Leipzig† and insulted in the streets of Berlin where he was detained until the Vienna Congress† decided he might be allowed to rule in a Saxony deprived of some two-thirds of its territory. In Dresden he was long remembered as 'Frederick Augustus the Just'.

FREDERICK WILLIAM III, King of Prussia
(1770–1840, reigned 1797–1840)
Born in Potsdam, the eldest son of Frederick William II and a great-nephew of Frederick the Great. As king, he was not unsympathetic to reform although suspicious of representative government. Characteristically he freed royal serfs (1799–1805), but would not impose an emancipation edict† on the great landowners until backed by reforming ministers in 1807. His remarkable consort, Queen Louise†, committed him to a close collaboration with Alexander I of Russia, symbolized by the dramatic Potsdam

King Frederick William III of Prussia

Oath† of November 1805. The King, however, reacted slowly to external pressures; he failed to enter the War of the Second Coalition† before Austerlitz†, and then rashly provoked war with France in October 1806 at a time which suited Napoleon. After the disasters of Jena† and Friedland†, Frederick William was allowed to retain his throne only by Alexander I's appeals in conversation to Napoleon at Tilsit†. He remained a client king of the French until 1813, unable to reside even in Berlin between October 1806 and Christmas 1809. The civil reforms of Stein† and the military reforms of Gneisenau† raised the capabilities of his kingdom and at Breslau on 17 March 1813 Frederick William issued a proclamation, *An mein Volk*, summoning the Prussian people to rise against France in a war of liberation. He was present at the battles of Bautzen†, Dresden† and Leipzig†, entered Paris behind Alexander I on 31 March 1814 and accompanied the Tsar to London and to Vienna for the Congress. This role of subservience to Russia was continued into the post-war years of peace, although Alexander's successor, Nicholas I, considered Frederick William less repressive than the state of Europe required.

FREEMASONRY
In its modern form originated in the Grand Lodge founded in London in 1717 and spread rapidly through the Continent in the eighteenth century, where it became identified with deism and the rationalistic ideas of the Encyclopaedists. The hostility shown by masonic lodges to Catholicism in France and the Latin countries led to papal condemnation of freemasonry as early as 1738. The French Revolution (and, more precisely, the Directory) accepted freemasonry and it was encouraged by Napoleon. Joseph Bonaparte† became grand master of the Grand Lodge of France in 1805 and during the ten years of the Empire masonic lodges in

France increased from 300 to 1,000; the rising middle-class officials enjoyed wearing honorific regalia. Prominent freemasons included Cambacérès† and the elder Kellermann†. In Italy the Grand Orient of Milan organized the Royal Italian Freemasons, from among whom most of Napoleon's official bureaucracy south of the Alps were recruited. In 1814, when freemasonry was becoming influential in Poland and Italian freemasons remained loyal to Napoleon, Pius VII† renewed old threats of excommunication against Catholic members of lodges.

FRIEDLAND, Battle of (14 June 1807) Fought in East Prussia to the west of the town of Friedland (now Pravdinsk), on a bend in the River Alle, sixteen miles east of Eylau†. After initial success by Bennigsen's Russians against the French flank, Napoleon realized that the Russians had cramped themselves within the river's bend. He therefore launched converging attacks in the evening, taking Bennigsen† by surprise and forcing the Russians back on four improvised bridges across the Alle. Three of these bridges were destroyed by French artillery. There were some 20,000 Russian casualties, about a third of Bennigsen's army and rather more than twice the number of French dead and wounded. These heavy losses convinced Alexander I of the need for peace. An armistice followed a week later; peace talks began at Tilsit† on 25 June; and Friedland therefore marked the effective end of the Third Coalition†.

FRUCTIDOR (4 September 1797) The *coup d'état* in Paris on what was, by the revolutionary calendar†, 18 Fructidor, Year V. The Directory, fearing revolutionary plots initiated by Pichegru† (president of the Council of Five Hundred†), called on the army to arrest possible dissidents. Bonaparte's nominee, Augereau†, assumed command of the army in Paris, carried through the purge, and thereby made the survival of the Directory totally dependent on the army's goodwill.

FUENTES DE OÑORO, Battle of (3–5 May 1811) Two distinct actions fought around a village on the Spanish-Portuguese frontier eight miles south of Almeida†. Wellington successfully prevented Masséna† from breaking through to relieve the French garrison besieged in Almeida.

FULTON, Robert (1765–1815) American engineer: born in Little Britain, Pennsylvania. He was a gunsmith during the American War of Independence but came to Europe in 1786, studying painting in London and later engineering too. His earliest inventions facilitated canal navigation. In 1793 he left London, settled in France in 1796 and published a treatise on canals. A steam-propelled submarine, *Nautilus*, capable of submerging 25 feet, was invented in 1801. Bonaparte was as suspicious of Fulton's inventions as of balloons: according to Bourrienne†, when told of Fulton's invention, he remarked, 'Bah! All these inventors, all these experiment pushers are either schemers or visionaries. Don't mention him again.' Fulton returned to America in 1805, settled in New York, and on 17 August 1807 took the first steam-driven paddleboat, the *Clermont*, up the Hudson River from New York to Albany. Before Napoleon's death the first regular steam packetboat service was running between Dover and Calais and a ship fitted with a steam engine had crossed the Atlantic.

G

GALICIA

Two regions in Europe are named Galicia: (i) the former Kingdom of Galicia in north-western Spain (Pontevedra, Orense, Lugo and Corunna†), the scene of much fighting early in 1809 when Soult† was in pursuit of Moore†; (ii) the historically Polish province north of the Carpathian Mountains. There, in Napoleonic times, Polish landowners had their fields tilled by Ukrainian peasants (Ruthenes) while trading through Jewish merchants and having their carriages and furniture maintained by German-Austrian craftsmen. The Polish Partitions of 1772 and 1795 gave the province to Austria. In 1809 it was liberated by the Polish Legion of Poniatowski† and included in the Grand Duchy of Warsaw†, together with Cracow†. Austria recovered most of the lost lands in 1815 and held the province until 1918. Western Galicia is in modern Poland; Eastern Galicia in the Ukrainian Soviet Socialist Republic.

GANTEAUME, Honoré (1755–1818)

French admiral: born at La Ciotat, served in Louis xvi's navy from 1778 onwards, taking part in the final stages of the American War of Independence. He was Admiral Brueys's chief-of-staff during the battle of the Nile†, safely reaching shore when the flagship blew up. For the Syrian campaign he was attached to Bonaparte's staff. He accompanied Bonaparte back to France in the frigate *Muiron* and from 1800 to 1802 he commanded the squadron at Brest†. Ganteaume was able to evade the blockading vessels and reach the West Indies† with a considerable naval force in 1802, succouring the French garrisons in Haiti† and Santo Domingo†. But during the critical summer of 1805 he was kept closely inshore at Brest, his most notable attempt to break out being frustrated by Collingwood† on 21 August. From 1808 to 1810 Ganteaume commanded in the Mediterranean, running supplies to the French garrison on Corfu†. He served at the Ministry of Marine in Paris from 1810 to 1814.

GAUDIN, Martin Charles (1756–1841)

French Minister of Finance: born at Saint-Denis, the son of a lawyer attached to the Paris parlement. Before the Revolution Gaudin was employed in tax collection and administration (1779–89). Remarkably he continued to handle financial matters throughout the years of revolutionary monetary chaos. He sat as a member of the Council of the Five Hundred and supported Bonaparte in Brumaire†. The First Consul duly appointed Gaudin as Minister of Finance on 11 November 1799; he held office continuously until March 1814 and again in the Hundred Days†. For the most part he was a loyal executant rather than a formulator of policies, and he was rewarded by the Emperor with an Italian dukedom (Gaeta). Gaudin was responsible for establishing the *cadastre*, a survey of lands commune by commune so as to form a basis of local taxation assessment. He wrote his memoirs in exile after the second Restoration.

GAY-LUSSAC, Louis Joseph (1778–1850)
French scientist and pioneer aeronaut: born at Saint-Léonard-de-Noblat, near Limoges. After leaving the École Polytechnique he began his scientific researches while working for Napoleon's Roads and Bridges department from 1801 onwards. He made balloon ascents to collect air samples for analysis, and in 1808 his researches enabled him to formulate the law of volumes. A year later he became Professor of Chemistry at the Polytechnique, but his chemical research on sulphuric acid and on the assaying of silver belong to the period of the Restoration rather than the Empire. Louis Philippe created him a peer of France in 1839.

GDANSK: see *Danzig*.

GENOA
Principal seaport of Italy, a great maritime republic of mediaeval Europe. The last oversea possession of Genoa was Corsica†, ceded to France in 1768. Jacobin republican sentiment was strong in Genoa and the port was secured for Bonaparte by Masséna† in 1796. The Ligurian Republic†, a French puppet state, was established in Genoa a year later. Masséna was besieged there by the Austrians (April to June 1800); garrison and citizenry suffered acutely from scarcities of food and water. In 1805 the Ligurian Republic was absorbed by France and on 30 June Napoleon made a ceremonial entry into the city. During the peace negotiations between the Allies in 1814–15 it was assumed that Genoa would be incorporated in Sardinia-Piedmont†. This proposal ran counter to a plan put forward by Bentinck† on his own initiative for a restoration of the Republic under the 1797 constitution. Castlereagh† disowned Bentinck and Genoa was annexed by Sardinia-Piedmont; but only after vigorous debates in the British parliament (February and April 1815) in which the annexation was condemned as an act of cynical spoliation.

GENTZ, Friedrich von (1785–1832)
Anti-French publicist: born at Breslau, studied under Kant† at Königsberg and entered the Prussian civil service in 1785, transferring to Austrian service in 1802 and becoming the close confidant and diplomatic adviser of Metternich†. He was secretary-general of the Congress of Vienna† and of the later congresses (Aachen, Troppau, Laibach, Verona). Almost every political statement emanating from Vienna in the years 1809 to 1831 was drafted by Gentz; he was feared, respected and occasionally bribed by other statesmen. Among contemporaries only Talleyrand matched his political acumen and knowledge of Europe's affairs. Gentz remained a backstairs man, shunning the limelight.

GEORGE III, King of Great Britain (1738–1820)
Born St James's Square, London, the son of Frederick, Prince of Wales, and grandson of George II, whom he succeeded on 25 October 1760. His personal kindliness and loyalty to his marriage with Charlotte of Mecklenburg-Strelitz were offset by political obstinacy (notably over the American colonies and against Catholic Emancipation†) and by an idealized sense of kingship. Disturbances of the mind in March 1765 and in the winter of 1788–9 foreshadowed a total collapse of mental faculties from December 1810 until his death on 29 January 1820. His eldest son, with whom the King had been perpetually on bad terms, was Prince Regent† from 5 February 1811.

GEORGE, Prince of Wales, later GEORGE IV (1762–1830): see *Prince Regent*.

GEORGE, Mademoiselle (Marguerite Josephine Weymer 1787–1867)
French actress: born at Bayeux, her father being a musician. She possessed a majestic

bearing, a grand tragic voice and a hasty temper. Her debut in Paris as Clytemnestra in 1802 attracted the First Consul's attention and she became his mistress that November, frequently visiting him at Saint-Cloud or the Tuileries until the summer of 1804. In May 1808 she fled from Paris to Russia in pursuit of the future General Benckendorff, who had been her lover while serving at the Paris embassy. For several years she acted with a French company in St Petersburg but appeared suddenly at Dresden† in June 1813 during the Plaeswitz armistice† and was reinstated in the Comédie Française† on Napoleon's orders. Intrigue, and tempestuous scenes backstage, forced her to resign from the company in 1817. She appeared in London, with Talma†, and in the 1830s was acting in the dramas of Romanticism at the Porte Saint-Martin. Extravagant habits reduced her to penury and when Napoleon's nephew mounted the first great Paris Exhibition in 1855 she was grateful to find employment there as a cloakroom attendant.

GÉRARD, François Pascal (1770–1837)
French artist: born in Rome, became a pupil of David†, was an established portrait painter under the Directory and received numerous commissions from the Bonaparte family. In 1801 he was consulted over the interior decoration of Malmaison†. His great canvas of Austerlitz, completed in 1806, extended his range of work. Gérard's portrait of the seventeen-month-old King of Rome was brought by Bausset† to Napoleon's bivouac at Valuevo on the eve of Borodino† in 1812; the Emperor placed his son's portrait outside the tent that evening for veterans of the Guard to admire. Gérard was created a baron by Louis XVIII, remaining in favour under the restored monarchy.

GILLRAY, James (1757–1815)
English caricaturist: born in Chelsea, of Scottish descent. He began publishing satirical engravings about 1783–4 and was famous by 1786, when he pilloried the

Defiance when faced with invasion plans. Gillray portrays 'John Bull offering little Boney fair play'.

attachment of the future Prince Regent†
to Mrs Fitzherbert. Until his mind clouded
over in 1811, Gillray produced some fifty
engraved caricatures each year, mocking
social pretensions and political folly as
well as showing a xenophobic patriotism,
fiercely Protestant in inspiration. His
draughtsmanship reveals savage twists of
humour, often brutal and vigorously
obscene.

GNEISENAU, August Wilhelm Anton Neithardt von (1760–1831)

Prussian field marshal: born near Torgau,
the son of a Saxon officer, fought alongside the English in America (1782–3) and
was commissioned in the Prussian infantry
in 1786. He served in Poland, 1793–4, and
distinguished himself in the Jena campaign and in defence of the Baltic port of
Colberg (1806). For six years Gneisenau
assisted Scharnhorst† in his reform of the
Prussian army, especially organizing the
system of reserves, but he also undertook
secret anti-French missions to London
and St Petersburg in 1809. From 1813 to
1815 he was Blücher's chief of staff,

Gneisenau, Blücher's chief-of-staff

serving him astutely at Leipzig† and between Ligny† and Waterloo†. Gneisenau
became a Prussian count in 1814. After
retiring, with his marshal's baton, in 1816,
he became Governor of Berlin but was
recalled to service in 1831 in order to put
down unrest and restore order in Prussian
Poland. He died at Posen (Poznan), a
victim of the cholera epidemic.

GODOY, Manuel de, Duke of Alcudia (1767–1851)

Spanish politician: born in the Estrema-
dura region, near Badajoz, a member of
the lesser nobility (*hidalgo*). He was commissioned in the king's bodyguard and
became a favourite of both King Charles
IV† and his queen, Maria Luisa. Politically
Godoy was a mildly progressive reformer,
virtual foreign minister from 1792 to 1794
and thereafter Charles's chief minister for
thirteen years, exercising a dictatorial
power which no other Spanish politician
possessed in the nineteenth century. In
foreign affairs Godoy wished to appease
France. His diplomatic initiative took
Spain out of the War of the First Coalition
by the treaty of Basle† in 1795, winning
him the honorific title 'Prince of the
Peace'; but from 1804 to 1807 he collaborated with Napoleon as an ally against
Britain, a conflict which caused economic
hardship in Catalonia and, to a lesser
extent, in other provinces too. Godoy was
unpopular with the old aristocracy and
with the commonalty of Spain; they disliked his deference to France, his anticler-
icalism, his hostility to bullfights and his
personal ostentation. He was said to be
Maria Luisa's lover, although the closest
bond between Queen and First Minister
appears to have been a mutual hypochon-
dria. Napoleon despised Godoy, who in-
trigued with French envoys in the hope of
securing for himself a principality in
southern Portugal. On 17 March 1808
Godoy's life was endangered by a palace
revolution, the so-called 'Tumult of Aranjuez'; he saved himself by hiding in a

rolled-up carpet. Two days later Charles IV abdicated in favour of his son, Ferdinand VII†, long Godoy's enemy. Both kings, and Godoy, were summoned to Bayonne† by Napoleon in April 1808 when the Bonapartes seized the Spanish crown. Godoy spent the rest of his life in exile, with Charles and Maria Luisa until their deaths in Rome in 1819, and thereafter in Paris. Six volumes of memoirs,

published between 1839 and 1841, are a masterpiece of complacency.

GOETHE, Johann Wolfgang von
(1749–1832)
German man of letters: born in Frankfurt am Main†, educated as a lawyer at Leipzig and Strasbourg but lived in his home town until 1775, when he settled under court

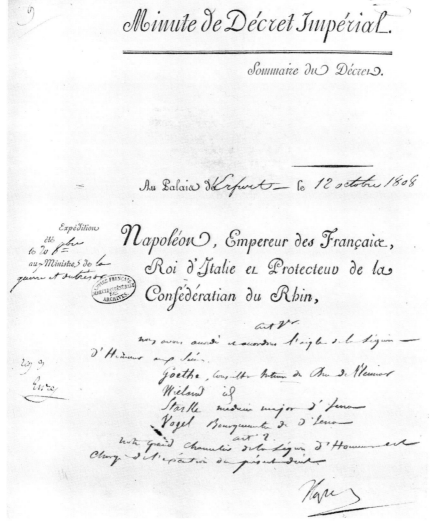

Napoleon creates Goethe and Wieland, 'Grands Chevaliers' of the Legion of Honour.

patronage at Weimar†. His tragedy, *Götz von Berlichingen* (1773), gave an impulse to the short-lived 'Storm and Stress' phase in German literature (*c.* 1771–8). Goethe's short novel, *The Sorrows of Young Werther* (1774) won him wider fame: Napoleon reputedly read it seven times. His literary pursuits at Weimar were combined with administrative duties as a privy councillor and broadened by a growing personal interest in the sciences. A visit to Italy (1786–8) changed his style and his way of life, stimulating an incipient Romanticism† in his basically classicist discipline. *Iphigenie auf Tauris* appeared in verse in 1787, the prose tragedy *Egmont* a year later, and the first fragment of *Faust* in 1790. Goethe accompanied the invading army of Brunswick† in 1792 and was present at the battle of Valmy and the siege of Mainz in 1793. Close friendship with Schiller† from 1794 to 1805 benefited both writers. Goethe published his novel, *Wilhelm Meisters Lehrjahre* in 1795–6, a major influence on German Romanticism, but he was also director of the Weimar theatre, a post he held from 1791 to 1817. When French troops occupied Weimar after their victory at Jena†, looters broke into Goethe's house and he was fortunate to escape with his life. He was, however, held in great respect by Napoleon, who received him in audience at Erfurt† (2 October 1808) and met him at Weimar for a longer conversation four days later. Further work on the Faust legend, together with studies in the aesthetics of light and colour, occupied Goethe during the later phase of the Napoleonic struggle. A collection of pseudo-Eastern love poems, autobiographical fragments, a second novel about Wilhelm Meister, and the final part of Faust followed the return of peace. Goethe retained a certain admiration for Napoleon: 'His life was the stride of a demigod', he remarked in 1828. The supreme humanist polymath of his age died at Weimar six months short of his eighty-third birthday.

GOURGAUD, Gaspard (1783–1852)
French soldier: born at Versailles and became an artillery officer. He was one of Napoleon's aides-de-camp from 1811 to 1815, subsequently accompanying him to St Helena†. There, for three years, he kept a *Journal* in which Napoleon's table talk was recorded with meticulous care. Friction with Montholon† made Gourgaud return to France in 1818. He vainly attempted to secure improvements in Napoleon's conditions of confinement. Later he was accepted as a guardian of the Emperor's historical reputation. Louis Philippe promoted him general and sent him to St Helena in 1840 as one of the escorts for the return of Napoleon's remains to Paris.

GOUVION SAINT-CYR, Laurent (1764–1830)
Marshal of the Empire: born at Toul in Lorraine, the son of a tanner. He was a professional artist who volunteered for the army in 1792, fought along the Franco-German frontier and was rapidly promoted, commanding a division before the end of 1794. Most of his early service was in the Rhineland, but he was in Italy in 1799 and 1805, when he blockaded Venice. He commanded the Army of Catalonia (1808–9) but was reprimanded for leaving his troops without permission, in November 1809. In 1812 he commanded the Bavarians in the *Grande Armée*, achieving such success at Polotsk† that Napoleon created him a marshal (27 August 1812). He was military governor of Dresden in 1813, capitulating in November. From June 1814 he supported the restored Bourbons, Louis XVIII created him a marquis in 1818 at a time when, as Minister of War, he organized a new recruiting system for the royal army and appealed to Napoleonic veterans to serve in the reserve.

Goya depicts the miseries of war, Spain, 1808

GOYA Y LUCIENTES Francisco de
(1746–1828)

Spanish artist: born at Saragossa, studied in Rome and became official court painter to Charles IV of Spain in 1799. As a liberal, Goya continued to work for Joseph Bonaparte† in Madrid, capturing in two famous paintings (*2 May 1808* and *3 May 1808*) the savagery of revolt. His series of etchings known as *The Disasters of War* depicted the horrors of the Peninsular campaign, especially guerrilla† atrocities and reprisals. Ferdinand VII† pardoned Goya for his collaboration with the Bonapartist regime and he remained a court artist in Madrid until 1824, when he settled in Bordeaux. In later years he experimented with lithographs, showing special interest in scenes of bullfighting.

GRAND DESIGN (Russian)

Name given to the ideological plan drafted in the autumn of 1804 by Tsar Alexander I† under the influence of Czartoryski†. It provided Allied 'war aims' to counter the appeal of France's revolutionary principles: peoples liberated from 'the Bonapartist tyranny' were not to have discredited regimes from the past imposed upon them; new frontiers would correspond with natural geographic boundaries and join together 'homogeneous peoples able to agree among themselves'; a German Confederation, independent of both Austria and Prussia, was to be set up; the commerce of neutral states would be safeguarded in any future war by an international code of maritime law; provisional arrangements should be made between Britain and Russia in case the Ottoman Empire collapsed; and the European governments should themselves work out 'a new concept of law among nations' and accept 'an obligation not to wage war unless all means of mediation had been previously exhausted'. Novosiltsov† was sent to London to discuss the

Grand Design with Pitt† and his ministers as a preliminary to a binding Anglo-Russian alliance. Pitt found the Grand Design too comprehensive, imprecise and idealistic; he put forward counter-proposals in January 1805 for the establishment of 'a system of public law among the European nations'. No final agreement was reached on either of these sets of proposals. The moralistic phrases which puzzled Pitt reappeared in a new guise ten years later (see *Holy Alliance*). It is interesting to compare the Tsar's 'Grand Design' with President Wilson's 'Fourteen Points' of January 1918 and the Atlantic Charter of August 1941.

GRAND DIGNITARIES of the Empire

The *Sénatus-consulte†* of 18 May 1804, which created the Empire, provided for an 'organization of the imperial palace suitable to the dignity of the throne and the greatness of the nation'. Six 'grand dignitaries' were appointed: the Second and Third Consuls, Cambacérès† and Lebrun†, became respectively Arch-Chancellor and Arch-Treasurer; Joseph Bonaparte† was appointed Grand Elector, Louis Bonaparte† High Constable, Eugène Beauharnais† Arch-Chancellor of State, and Joachim Murat† Grand Admiral. These dignitaries were followed by officers of an imperial court which included a Marshal of the Palace (Duroc†), Grand Master of the Horse (Caulaincourt†) and a Grand Master of Ceremonies (Ségur†). A decree published on 13 July 1804 regulated court etiquette and procedure. Napoleon later explained that, in creating grand dignitaries and an imperial household, he was rewarding public service while claiming for the new French Empire an equal status with the old monarchies of Europe. He constantly sought the protection of tradition and legitimacy while boasting that his new nobility was free from any dependence on feudal obligations.

GRANDE ARMÉE

La Grande Armée officially came into existence in September 1805 but it had been gradually built up over the previous three years. Napoleon wished to centralize command, a single force replacing the 'front' armies of earlier campaigns. Originally the *Grande Armée* comprised seven corps, with a cavalry reserve, an artillery reserve and the élite Imperial Guard†. There were some 350,000 men in the *Grande Armée* of 1805 but it expanded rapidly, incorporating troops from the satellite states and allied detachments. Thus by June 1812 the *Grande Armée* comprised 630,000 men along the Russian frontier divided into eleven corps, together with four reserve cavalry corps, the Imperial Guard and an independent Austrian Corps, while another quarter of a million men were in Spain. Direction of the *Grande Armée* was left to the Emperor and his personal staff, the so-called *Maison†* of Imperial Headquarters, but planning and administrative organization were the responsibility of the General Staff of the *Grande Armée*, headed by Marshal Berthier† as Minister of War (until succeeded by Clarke† in 1807) and as Chief of Staff. Technically the *Grande Armée* remained in being until March 1814, although badly mauled in the retreat from Moscow. Front armies returned during the Hundred Days†.

GRATTAN, Henry (1746–1820)

Irish politician: born and educated in Dublin, where he spent most of his life. He entered the Dublin parliament in 1775, leading the movement which, seven years later, freed the parliament from dependence on the Privy Council in London. Grattan dominated Irish politics, 1782–1800, refusing any official post under the British crown and exasperating the English ascendancy by encouraging among Ireland's politicians a critical hostility towards Westminster's authority. This non-collaboration, together with the French threat to Ireland, prompted the Act of Union in 1800, which denied Dublin a parliament for more than 120 years. Grattan was MP for Dublin at Westminster from 1806 until his death.

GREAT BRITAIN

Was the most persistent enemy of revolutionary and Napoleonic France, at war from 1 February 1793 until the Treaty of Amiens† (March 1802) and again from 16 May 1803 until 1814, as well as in the Hundred Days†. The small British army played only minor roles in European operations until 1808, when an expedition to Portugal formed a nucleus for the force with which Moore† and Wellington† fought the Peninsular War†: landings in Calabria (see *Maida*) and Walcheren† were ineffectual sideshows. The Royal Navy gained an unparalleled succession of victories (see *Naval Warfare*) despite the administrative bumbling which fired mutinies at Spithead and the Nore in 1797. Outside Europe successive British governments used sea power to build up a maritime commercial empire at the expense of the French and their allies, especially the Dutch. Expeditions to the West Indies†, the Indian Ocean, the South Atlantic and the eastern Mediterranean were mounted whenever the general course of events on the Continent permitted far-ranging enterprises; and Britain's chief gains from the wars were naval or commercial bases (Cape of Good Hope, Ceylon, Malta†, Trinidad etc.) and intangible assets in overseas trade. Friction between Britain and the United States over the Royal Navy's method of enforcing economic warfare eventually drove the Americans to arms (see *War of 1812*) in a conflict independent of events in Europe.

From 1793 to 1815 Britain's main contributions to the wars were subsidies by which France's enemies could be maintained as intermittent allies in coalitions negotiated by British statecraft. The City of London had succeeded Amsterdam as the centre of the European money market some thirty years before the French Revolution and survived both a financial crisis in 1797 and attempts to destroy the value of the pound (1809–11) and reduce Britain to bankruptcy (see *Crisis of 1811*). The wars made little impact on the life of the upper classes; and, especially during the years of Regency†, literature and the arts flourished more remarkably than at any time since the age of Shakespeare and Jonson. Threats of invasion in 1797, 1801 and 1803–5 led to the formation of local militia and volunteers; a French raiding party sailed up the Bristol Channel in February 1797, sacked a farmhouse near Ilfracombe in North Devon and briefly set foot in Fishguard; but no landings were made during the years of Napoleon's primacy. The working classes suffered economic distress from attempts to protect agriculture (see *Corn Laws*); resentment at industrialization and mounting unemployment led to the panic anarchism of the Luddites†. Politically, Ireland† remained the most sensitive area in the British Isles, the problem of Catholic Emancipation† looming disproportionately large in the relations between the sovereign and his ministers.

GREAT ST BERNARD PASS

Over the Alps from Martigny (Switzerland) to Aosta (Italy), a route of some fifty miles and rising to 8,114 feet. In May 1800 Bonaparte decided to send the main body of the newly created Army of the Reserve across the pass at the start of the Marengo campaign†. The route was comparatively short and the army could be supplied by water across Lake Geneva as far as Villeneuve, but in places the track was less than two feet wide and for ten miles the pass was heavily banked with snow. Lannes† led the advance guard over the pass on 16 May; the rest of the army (50,000 men) followed over the next two days; Bonaparte himself crossed on 20

An anonymous contemporary representation of the passage of the Great St Bernard Pass in 1800. This piece of progaganda (associating Bonaparte with Charlemagne and Hannibal) is less romanticized than the famous canvas by David but is little nearer to depicting the real crossing of the Alps.

May. Austrian resistance stiffened around Fort Bard, twenty-five miles south of Aosta and the French were soon forced to transfer their main line of communications to the longer routes through the Little St Bernard and the St Gotthard Passes, which had already been used by detached units, largely as a feint. The passage of the Great St Bernard was romanticized by Bonaparte's propagandists: Napoleon did not cross the Alps on a frightened and rearing charger in the midst of his men (as in the famous canvas by David†); he was led slowly and carefully across the pass astride a mule, guided by local peasants. Nevertheless, the passage of the Alps was a triumph for Berthier's† organizing genius. Milan† was entered on 2 June; the hard-won victory of Marengo† followed twelve days later.

GREECE

Almost the whole of modern Greece was under Turkish rule by the end of the fifteenth century. Subsequently the Greeks gained influential posts in administration and commerce, and enjoyed considerable freedom of worship under Ottoman rule. The spread of French revolutionary ideas stimulated national self-consciousness, much of it expressed by pride in the country's classical heritage and concern for the purity of the written language. Bonaparte sent emissaries to the Peloponnese in 1797, when the French occupied the Ionian Islands†. But, though some peasants joined the French armies, the Greeks looked more naturally for aid to Russia, and Napoleon left little mark on Greek affairs. Ali Pasha† of Janina exploited his contacts with France, while Greek seamen from Hydra and Spetsai took advantage of the fall of the Italian maritime republics to increase their wealth and independence as traders in the eastern Mediterranean. A patriotic secret society, the *Philiki Hetairia*, was founded in Odessa in 1814 and the Greeks hoped for recognition of their national cause by the Great Powers at the Vienna Congress†. In this hope they were disappointed, even though one of Tsar Alexander's closest advisers was a Corfiote, John Capodistria (1776–1831). The Powers preferred not to pose the Eastern Question† in 1815, leaving the initiative to the Greeks themselves, who began their War of Independence in the spring of 1821.

GRENVILLE, William Wyndham (1759–1834)

British Foreign Secretary and Prime Minister: born in London, the son of George Grenville (Prime Minister 1763–5) and a first cousin of the younger Pitt†. He was educated at Eton and Christ Church, Oxford, and sat as MP for Buckinghamshire constituencies from 1782 to 1790, when he was created Baron Grenville. He entered his cousin's cabinet in June 1789 as Home Secretary, moving to the Foreign Office in April 1791. Although he held this post for ten years he was a mediocre Foreign Secretary, naturally conservative, insular and unimaginative, slow to see the inevitability of war in 1792–3 and slower still to accept the need for a negotiated peace in 1800–1. When Pitt died, early in 1806, Grenville formed the 'Ministry of All the Talents'† which abolished the slave trade† but disintegrated over Catholic Emancipation† after thirteen months of uneasy coalition. Although respected thereafter as an elder statesman of moderate Whiggish inclination, Grenville never again held office.

GREY, Charles (1764–1845)

British Foreign Secretary and Prime Minister: born at Fallodon, Northumberland and educated at Eton and Trinity College, Cambridge. He was elected MP for Northumberland in July 1786, while completing the traditional grand tour on the Continent, and held the seat until 1807, when he succeeded his father as Earl

Grey. His political sympathies, originally moderate Tory, responded to the warm humanitarianism of Fox† and by 1792 he was recognized as a 'Foxite Whig' and founder of the modestly radical 'Society of the Friends of the People'. He was First Lord of the Admiralty in Grenville's Ministry of All the Talents (1806–7), succeeding Fox as Foreign Secretary (September 1806 to March 1807). He was then out of office until 1830, the leader of the Foxite Whigs and from 1821 onwards the true Leader of the Opposition. As Prime Minister from 16 November 1830 to 8 July 1834 he saw the passage of the First Reform Act (1832), triumphantly vindicating a cause he had supported for over forty years.

GRIMM, Jakob (1785–1863) and **Wilhelm** (1786–1859)

Prolific German writers, specializing in folklore: both were born in Hanau, studied law at Marburg and served in the library administration of Jerome Bonaparte† at Cassel, when he was King of Westphalia. Both brothers were professors at Göttingen in the 1830s, until suspended for their liberalism; both held academic posts in Berlin when they died. The famous Grimm's Fairy Tales (*Kinder und Hausmärchen*) appeared in two volumes (1812–14) at the climax of the Napoleonic Wars and contributed greatly to Romanticism†, in its German form. The brothers also produced learned studies in folklore and philology; a modern edition of their collected works contains 62 volumes.

GROUCHY, Emmanuel, Marquis de (1766–1847)

Marshal of the Empire: born into an aristocratic family from the Île-de-France, held commissions in the artillery and the cavalry before being retired, as a liberal officer, in 1787 with the rank of captain. Grouchy fought with the revolutionary cavalry in 1792–3, kept order in La Ven-

dée† and Brittany under the Directory and was deputy commander of the expedition to Ireland† in 1798. A year later he was taken prisoner in Italy but was back in France in 1800, fighting as an infantry commander at Hohenlinden† (3 December 1800). Napoleon criticized his handling of the cavalry at Friedland† and sent him to Spain in 1808, where he was Governor of Madrid. In Russia he fought at Borodino† and Maloyaroslavets†; his health suffered so much from the rigours of the retreat that he did not return to the field until February 1814, when he nearly captured Blücher† at Vauchamps†. He was among the first generals to rally to Napoleon in 1815 and received his marshal's baton on 15 April. He fought at Ligny† and Wavre†, but decided not to move his troops westward towards Waterloo as that would have run counter to his battle orders. After Napoleon's departure for Paris he kept the defeated army together and in good order. He then, for four years, lived in Pennsylvania but returned to his French estates in 1820 and was made a Marshal of France by King Louis Philippe in 1831.

GUERRILLAS

Resistance to the French occupation of Spain was continued from the summer of 1808 until 1813 by groups of Spanish soldiers who organized the local peasantry into the first guerrilla bands of modern times. Raids on isolated outposts, and even on small towns, continued in the mountainous regions of the peninsula; there may have been as many as fifty bands operating in the winter of 1812–13. Ambushes, sometimes planned in collaboration with local bandits, hampered French communications and weakened morale; the atrocities committed by both sides in this guerrilla warfare are vividly depicted by Goya†. One in four of French casualties in the peninsula came from guerrilla activities. Similar resistance, on a smaller scale, was offered by supporters of the Neapolitan Bourbons in Calabria and by the Austrians of the Tyrol under Höfer✝ in 1809. Russian guerrillas – 'partisans' – began raiding French communications while Napoleon was in Moscow✝ in 1812. The most successful Russian units were led by regular army officers (Colonels Davidov and Kudaschev, Captains Seslavin and Figner) and peasant resistance was supported by light cavalry and by the much dreaded Cossacks. But Private Chertvertakov, a dragoon who escaped from French custody after Borodino, organized hundreds of peasants who made bitter raids on the retreating French. So barbarous were Chertvertakov's methods that Kutuzov✝ became disturbed at the extent of guerrilla activity and sought to curb the partisans, fearing a general revolt of the serfs against all authority.

H

HABSBURG DYNASTY

The Habsburgs ruled in Austria from the end of the thirteenth century until 1918 and provided the elected sovereigns of the Holy Roman Empire† for almost all of the period 1438 to 1806. In 1740 the male line became extinct with the death of Charles IV: his daughter, Maria Theresa (1717–80), succeeded to the hereditary Habsburg possessions and married Francis, Duke of Lorraine. Their sons, Joseph II (Emperor, 1765–90) and Leopold II (Emperor, 1790–2), were the first rulers of the House of Habsburg-Lorraine; and their eleventh and youngest daughter became Queen Marie Antoinette of France, executed on 16 October 1793. Leopold II's eldest son succeeded his father as Francis II† of the Holy Roman Empire but was styled Emperor Francis I of Austria when he assumed a new imperial title in 1804. His daughter, Marie Louise† (a great-niece of Marie Antoinette) married Napoleon in April 1810. The Habsburgs also had influence in Italy. The dynasty ruled in Modena from 1803 to 1860. The Grand Dukes of Tuscany, too, were members of the dynasty from 1737 to 1860; and Queen Marie Antoinette's sister, Maria Carolina, was the consort of King Ferdinand IV† of Naples and Sicily.

HAITI

The western third of the island of Hispaniola in the West Indies†. The original Spanish colony was ceded to France in 1697 and became a prosperous colony, dependent on slave labour in the cotton and sugar plantations. The Negro leader, Toussaint L'Ouverture†, successfully defied both British naval blockaders and emissaries from republican France so as to secure a unified and slave-free island, in which he was able to maintain order. In December 1801 the First Consul sent his brother-in-law, General Leclerc, to the island in order to reimpose French rule and slavery. Leclerc (accompanied by his wife, Pauline Bonaparte†) landed in Haiti in February 1802 and soon captured Toussaint. Yellow fever killed thousands of French soldiers, including Leclerc. The disease, and persistent Negro resistance, forced Leclerc's successor, General Rochambeau, to withdraw his men in November 1803, the survivors surrendering to blockading British vessels. In twenty months 25,000 French soldiers perished in Haiti. The most successful Haitian general, Jean-Jacques Dessalines, was proclaimed Emperor of an independent Haiti on 8 October 1804 but was assassinated two years later. There was then a power struggle between another general, Henri Christophe ('King Henri'), and the mulatto leader, Alexandre Pétion, who became Haiti's first president.

HAMILTON, Alexander (1755–1804)

American statesman: born in the West Indies, the illegitimate son of a Scottish merchant. After studying law in New York he served as secretary and military aide-de-camp to George Washington. From 1787 onwards he concerned himself with political questions, especially the need for a strong central government. These views he expressed in essays printed as *The Federalist* (1787–8) and in his work at the Federal Constitutional Convention of 1787. He was Secretary of the Treasury (1789–95), establishing the Federal Bank and devising the American system of internal revenue. Hamilton remained hostile to the French Revolution and to the Directory, throwing his influence in favour of war against France in 1798–1800 because of the Directory's clumsy policies in the West Indies† and the suspicion that Spain would retrocede Louisiana† to the government in Paris. The election of Jefferson† eventually eased the foreign crisis but intensified internal political conflict. Friction mounted between Hamilton and the New York Democratic-Republican leader, Aaron Burr (1756–1836). In July 1804 Burr challenged Hamilton to a duel and fatally wounded him.

HAMILTON, Emma, Lady (1765–1815)

Nelson's mistress: born Emily Lyon in Cheshire and led a somewhat dissolute life on the fringe of London society before becoming in 1786 the mistress of Sir William Hamilton, the British Minister at Naples. They were married in 1791 and two years later met Nelson†, whom both husband and wife befriended. Lady Hamilton gave birth to a daughter, Horatia (1801–81), whom Nelson acknowledged as his child. After Sir William's death in 1803, his widow was widely accepted as Nelson's first lady, although the liaison displeased King George III. Despite being left considerable wealth by her husband and by Nelson, Lady Hamilton was heavily in debt within three years of Trafalgar and in 1814 she fled to Calais to escape imprisonment.

HANOVER

Although the Elector of Hanover became King of England in 1714, the union was solely dynastic and Hanover never became a British dependency. In May and June 1803 French troops occupied Hanover. Subsequently Napoleon used Hanover as an enticement to tempt Frederick William III† of Prussia into his alliance system. Prussia at first declined the offer but, after the French victory at Austerlitz, resumed negotiations with France and on 15 February 1806 concluded a treaty of alliance by which the whole of the former electorate became a Prussian possession. The alliance was short lived and, nine months later, French troops reoccupied Hanover after the Prussian defeat at Jena†. From 1807 to 1813 Hanover formed part of the Kingdom of Westphalia†. It recovered its old territorial boundaries at the end of the war and was raised in dignity from an electorate to a kingdom. George IV visited Germany as King of Hanover in 1821.

HARDENBERG, Karl August von
(1750–1822)

Prussian Chancellor: born at Essenrode in Hanover, entered Prussian service as administrator of Ansbach-Bayreuth in 1791, soon transferring to the diplomatic service and representing Prussia in the negotiations for the Treaty of Basle† in 1795. He collaborated closely with Haugwitz† until 1805 but was regarded as a Francophobe by Napoleon and was dismissed during the brief interlude of appeasement in the spring of 1806. Prussia's inability to raise money to pay a war indemnity to France provided an opportunity for Hardenberg's return to office, Napoleon accepting Frederick William III's claim that only Hardenberg had the skill to solve his kingdom's financial problems. Hardenberg accordingly became Prussian Chancellor on 4 June 1810, implementing further reforms begun by Stein†. In 1813 he persuaded his hesitant king to break with France after Yorck's initiative in concluding the Tauroggen Convention†. He conducted the negotiations with the Allies in 1813–14, was created a prince after the first abdication† of Napoleon and subsequently headed Prussia's delegation to the Vienna Congress†. Hardenberg, an astute statesman with a gift for turning his deafness to diplomatic advantage, remained in office throughout the immediate post-war years, showing greater independence of Austrian leadership than Metternich† recognized at the time. He died in Genoa, soon after the Congress of Verona ended.

HARROWBY, Lord (Dudley Ryder 1762–1847)

British Foreign Secretary; born in London and educated at St John's College, Cambridge. He was elected MP for Tiverton in 1784 and, at the outbreak of the French Revolution, was Under-Secretary for Foreign Affairs, becoming a Privy Councillor in 1790. In 1803 he succeeded his father as second Baron Harrowby, becoming first Earl of Harrowby in 1809. From May 1804 to January 1805 he was Pitt's Foreign Secretary but his most effective work was achieved later in 1805 when, while still remaining in the cabinet, he undertook an important mission to Berlin, Vienna and St Petersburg in an effort to realize Pitt's ambition of an effective coalition against Napoleon. This task was beyond his skill and he never again exercised departmental responsibilities. But, over European affairs, he remained a disciple of Pitt and was an influential elder statesman in every cabinet from 1804 to 1827, except for the thirteen months of the Grenville administration (1806–7).

HAUGWITZ, Christian August, Count von (1752–1832)

Prussian Foreign Minister: born at Peuke in Silesia and educated at Frankfurt, where he knew and much admired Goethe† (three years his senior). Haugwitz entered the Prussian diplomatic service in 1791 on a mission to Vienna and was soon given charge of foreign affairs. He believed it essential for Prussia to concentrate on the Elbe and the Oder rather than on the Rhineland and withdrew from the First Coalition (Peace of Basle†, 1795). He resisted all entreaties to oppose France, travelling to French-occupied Vienna in the closing weeks of 1805 to negotiate the acquisition of Hanover†. Against Haugwitz's advice, Frederick William III† changed his policy, taking on the whole strength of Napoleon's armies by a sudden declaration of war in September 1806. The subsequent defeats were blamed by Prussian patriots on Haugwitz, the alleged sympathizer with Napoleon. He was hounded from Prussia, eventually finding sanctuary at Venice where he died a quarter of a century later. His achievement in keeping Prussia at peace for eleven years was never appreciated by his compatriots.

HAUTERIVE, Count Alexandre Blanc de Lanautte (1750–1830)

French bureaucrat: born at Aspres-les-Corps in the Hautes-Alpes and took the first vows in a monastic teaching order before the Revolution. He then entered the diplomatic service and was French consul in New York in 1792, renewing in America an old acquaintance with Talleyrand†, who commended him to the First Consul in 1799. Hauterive produced propaganda works for Bonaparte and was Director of Archives at the Foreign Ministry. More important was his work in organizing the Ministry, which had followed the court from Versailles to Paris in 1789 and had never recovered its old, and much admired, professional efficiency. In 1806 Hauterive completed orderly administrative reforms, begun by Talleyrand in April 1800. He continued to instruct young diplomats in their craft until his death.

HAWKESBURY, Lord (1770–1828)

Title borne by Robert Banks Jenkinson (later the Prime Minister, Lord Liverpool†) when, as Foreign Secretary, he was responsible for British diplomacy during the Peace of Amiens†.

HAYDN, Joseph (1732–1809)
Austrian composer: born at Rohrau in Lower Austria and became a cathedral chorister in Vienna. From 1761 to 1790 he was under the patronage of the Hungarian magnate, Prince Miklos Esterhazy (1714–90), residing first at Eisenstadt and then in the rococo palace of Eszterhaza (now Fertod, in western Hungary). During these years Haydn shaped the accepted form of classical symphonies and string quartets. Despite the mounting European political chaos, Haydn was able to visit

The composer Haydn, in silhouette

England in 1791–2 and 1794–5 where the choral tradition stimulated his interest in oratorio. It was while Bonaparte was travelling to the Paris Opéra for the first performance of Haydn's *Creation* in France on Christmas Eve 1800, that the attempt was made on his life in the Rue Saint-Nicaise†. Haydn spent his last years in the Vienna suburb of Gumpendorf. On 10 May 1809 French troops entered Gumpendorf and stationed a battery of cannon outside the septuagenarian's home, whence they began to bombard the capit-

al. The sudden sound of firing so shocked Haydn that he suffered instant muscular paralysis and died three weeks later. Napoleon mounted a French guard of honour at the gate of his house.

HEGEL, Georg Wilhelm Friedrich (1770–1831)
German philosopher: born in Stuttgart, educated at Tübingen and held a chair of philosophy at Jena from 1800 to 1806 when he fled to Bavaria so as to escape the full rigours of Napoleonic occupation. He was briefly professor of philosophy at Heidelberg in 1817–18 before succeeding Fichte† in Berlin, where he remained until his death from cholera. As early as 1802 Hegel wrote a political tract, *Die Verfassung Deutschlands* (The German Constitution) in which he traced the decline of the Germanic idea since the Peace of Westphalia (1648) and urged the necessity of heroic war so as to give the various German peoples a sense of nationhood. These ideas he developed into a patriotism which showed totalitarian reverence for the state, later propounding a concept of the dialectic, with its claim that progress results from the interaction of conflicting half-truths. The dialectic, together with Hegel's theory of idealism, determined much German speculative philosophy over the following half-century, particularly the conviction that an abstract Spirit, greater than material forms, dominates all historical experience.

HELVETIC CONFEDERATION
French troops occupied Switzerland† in 1798, the Directory imposing a centralized constitution which set up a Helvetic Republic of eighteen cantons. This arrangement did not accord with geographical needs or historical traditions, and as soon as Bonaparte withdrew French occupation forces in August 1802, there was a rising in Schwyz which sought greater cantonal independence. The First Consul

sent Ney† at the head of an army into Switzerland and then summoned Swiss representatives to Paris. An 'Act of Mediation' (19 February 1803) replaced the Helvetic Republic by a Helvetic Confederation which recognized cantonal sovereign rights within a loosely-knit federal union. The Confederation duly signed a fifty-year treaty of alliance with France, undertook to provide 16,000 men to serve under French command and (later) accepted the annexation by France of the Valais canton so as to safeguard communications from Paris to Italy through the Simplon Pass. The Helvetic Confederation survived until 1814 and provided features which were retained in the Federal Pact of Switzerland, accepted by the Vienna Congress† (1815).

HOFER, Andreas (1767–1810)

Tyrolean patriot: born an innkeeper's son at St Leonhard, an Alpine valley southwest of Innsbruck. From 1796 to 1805 he fought as a sharpshooter in the Alpine campaigns of the Austrians against the French. He rose from the ranks to become a captain by 1805. In January 1809 he travelled secretly to Vienna and negotiated with Archduke John† and Stadion†; they agreed to support a Tyrolean rising against the Bavarians, who ruled the province as allies of France. The revolt, in the spring of 1809, was successful; the Bavarians were driven out of Innsbruck by two victories won by Hofer's militia at Berg Isel in the last days of May. When, after Wagram†, Austria sought peace, Hofer continued a guerrilla struggle against a French army under Marshal Lefebvre†. His hiding place, close to the Brenner Pass, was betrayed and he was captured on 27 January 1810, being taken in fetters to Mantua. Napoleon personally ordered him to be shot as soon as possible in order to counter Austrian pleas for clemency with a *fait accompli*. He was executed at Mantua on 18 February, becoming in death the legendary patriot hero of the Tyrol.

HOHENLINDEN, Battle of
(3 December 1800)

Hohenlinden was a Bavarian village some thirty miles east of Munich. A confused battle, initiated by the Austrians but finally causing them to seek peace, was fought there in the War of the Second Coalition. The eighteen-year-old Archduke John†, holding the line of the River Inn against the Army of the Rhine of General Moreau† agreed to proposals from his staff officers for a surprise assault on the French as they advanced in six widely spread columns. The attack caught Moreau off balance. He fell back on the village of Hohenlinden, leaving Ney† to hold the centre while Grouchy† mounted an effective flank attack which forced Archduke John to retire. It was several days after the engagement before Moreau realized he had so mauled the Austrians that he had won an important victory, but in the period 8–23 December he was able to exploit his success, advancing eastwards at a good thirteen miles a day until he reached Melk, where Austrian emissaries sought an armistice. In Paris Moreau's triumph was popularly equated with Bonaparte's victory at Marengo†, to the First Consul's chagrin.

HOLLAND

The United Provinces of the Netherlands were colloquially known as 'Holland' from the late sixteenth century, when William the Silent was recognized as Count of Holland, the central region of the Dutch state. In the years immediately preceding the French Revolution there was a political conflict between the hereditary Stadtholder, Prince William V (1748–1806), and middle-class reformers, organized as the Patriot Party. French troops overran the United Provinces in 1794–5 forcing William V to flee to England. From 1798 until the spring of 1805 the Patriots governed the Batavian Republic, a French vassal state headed by Rutger Jan Schimmelpenninck†. The reluctance of the Dutch to provide funds to aid the French economy induced Napoleon to propose constitutional changes in the winter of 1804–5 and Schimmelpenninck became 'Grand Pensionary' on 22 March 1805, with the right to choose an executive council. This reform benefited the Dutch: the radical Minister of Finance, I.J.A. Gogel (1765–1821), modernized the tax system; and work began on a primary education programme. A suspicion that the Dutch were exercising more independence than he had expected made Napoleon offer the executive council the choice between absorption in the French Empire and acceptance of one of the Bonapartes as king. On 3 May 1806 the executive council, with Schimmelpenninck dissenting, approved the establishment of a Kingdom of Holland, ruled by Louis Bonaparte‡ as King Lodewijk I. To the annoyance of his brother, the new king consistently put Dutch interests before those of France. He implemented the

educational reforms and modernized the criminal code; and his support of the Continental System‡ was half-hearted. Friction between the brothers culminated in Louis's sudden abdication on 1 July 1810; a week later the Kingdom of Holland was annexed to metropolitan France. When French officials began to evacuate the Netherlands early in November 1813, Dutch notables invited William V's son to return from London. He landed at Scheveningen on 2 December 1813, becoming sovereign of a United Kingdom of the Netherlands and Belgium‡ in July 1814.

HOLLAND HOUSE
A seventeenth-century mansion in Kensington, London, which as the home of Henry Fox (first Lord Holland and father of C.J. Fox‡) became social headquarters of the Whig opposition throughout the reigns of George III and George IV. Tory

Holland House, Kensington

propagandists represented the 'Holland House circle' as dupes of the French. The third Lord Holland (1773–1840, Fox's nephew) conducted parliamentary campaigns after 1815 to improve the conditions imposed on Napoleon in exile and also to save the life of Marshal Ney†.

HOLY ALLIANCE

A document drawn up by Alexander I† in September 1815 declaring that 'the precepts of Justice, Christian Charity and Peace . . . must have an immediate influence on the Councils of Princes and guide all their steps'. The alliance was signed by the Tsar, Francis I and Frederick William III† in Paris on 26 September and later by every European sovereign except the Prince Regent†, the Pope and the Sultan of Turkey. It was wrongly identified by contemporary liberals and by Whig historians with the general repressive system instituted by the three autocrats from 1819 onwards. In reality the Holy Alliance was a sincere attempt by Alexander I to reconcile the idealism shown earlier by the Grand Design† with the political mysticism he had recently absorbed from his meetings with Baroness Julie von Krüdener†.

HOLY ROMAN EMPIRE

The supreme form of sovereignty over feudal Germany, Austria and much of northern Italy. It claimed descent from Charlemagne's Imperium and continuity with the Roman Empire. Although the structure of the Empire was based on electoral statutes, it was virtually hereditary in the House of Habsburg† after 1438. From the early sixteenth century the Latin title of the Empire (*Sacrum Imperium Romanum Nationis Germanicae*) gave limited recognition to a concept of German national identity. The successive blows struck by the French at the structure of the Empire, notably the Imperial Recess† of 1803 and the Confederation of the Rhine†, induced Emperor Francis† to renounce his elected title on 6 August 1806. No attempt was ever made to restore the Holy Roman Empire.

HUMBOLDT, Wilhelm, Freiherr von (1767–1835)

Prussian scholar and diplomat: born at Potsdam, a son of Frederick the Great's Court Chamberlain. He travelled widely in his youth, developing original theories on anthropology and the nature of political authority. In 1809 he became director of education in the Prussian Ministry of the Interior and, almost at once, introduced reforms which broadened university teaching, encouraging vocational humanism while also emphasizing the importance of individualism in a school system which stressed the disciplinary value of classical studies. He championed the establishment of the University of Berlin†, which was renamed in his honour in 1945. He was Prussian Ambassador in Vienna, 1810–15, and in London, 1817–18. In his later years he was especially interested in the comparative study of philology and language. His younger brother Alexander (1769–1859) was the distinguished scholar who explored tropical America and central Asia.

HUNDRED DAYS

The name given to the period beginning on 20 March 1815 when Napoleon resumed his rule in Paris after exile to Elba. An attempt was made to establish ordered representative government in France (see *Acte Additionnel* and *Champ de Mai*) but Napoleon's chief concern was to gain a rapid victory in order to secure France's 'natural frontiers'; hence the advance into Belgium, culminating in defeat at Waterloo†. Napoleon signed his second abdication on 22 June (Day 94) and went into exile aboard HMS *Bellerophon†* on 15 July. The phrase 'Hundred Days' seems first to have been used by one of the

RETOUR DE L'ILE D'ELBE, IL RAMENE LA LIBERTÉ !.....

A satirical comment on the Hundred Days in a French royalist cartoon printed soon after the Restoration in 1815

arch-trimmers of the period, the Comte de Chabrol (1773–1843, Prefect of the Seine 1812–30), who greeted the returning Louis XVIII† on 8 July 1815 with the inaccuracy, 'A hundred days have gone since the fatal hour when Your Majesty left your capital'; it was, in fact, 110 days.

HUNGARY

The Napoleonic Wars made little direct impact on the Hungarian lands of the Habsburgs. Only one battle was fought in Hungary, a sharp engagement between the armies of Eugène Beauharnais† and Archduke John† near Raab (now Györ, sixty-eight miles west of Budapest) on 14 June 1809 during the Wagram campaign†. Subsequently Napoleon spent the night of 31 August at Raab after visiting Pozsony (Pressburg†, now Bratislava, in Slovakia) which, like Raab, had been heavily bombarded a few weeks earlier. Hungary was

a constant source of concern to the Emperor Francis†. Police reports of an alleged Jacobin conspiracy, headed by the Franciscan friar Ignac Martinovics in the autumn of 1794, led to a barbarous campaign of repression, with the execution of Martinovics and several members of the lesser nobility on 20 May 1795. Thereafter Francis distrusted the Magyar gentry, even though the Hungarian Diet consistently voted him money and men for the successive emergencies of the war. Landowners in central Hungary made considerable profit by asking high prices for their wheat. Napoleon tried to exploit Hungarian national sentiment in 1809 when (on 15 May) he issued a Manifesto to the Hungarian Nation, drafted in part by the radical poet, Janos Bacsanyi (1763–1845); but the Hungarians remained loyal to their tactful and extremely competent viceroy ('Palatine'), the Archduke Joseph†.

HUNT, (James Henry) Leigh (1784–1859) English essayist: born at Southgate, Middlesex, and educated at Christ's Hospital. In 1808, with his brother John, he founded and edited a radical newspaper, *The Examiner*, which on 22 March 1812 printed a sustained attack on the Prince Regent†. Leigh Hunt described him as 'a violator of his word, a libertine over head and ears in debt and disgrace, a despiser of domestic ties, the companion of gamblers and demi-reps'. For 'traducing and vilifying' the Regent, he was fined £500 and sentenced to two years' imprisonment, as also was his brother. Leigh Hunt thereafter became the darling of the English Romantics, befriended by Byron†, Keats† and Shelley†. His output of literary and social criticism was considerable and spread over forty-five years.

I

Idéologues

Originally a group of intellectuals, mostly men of letters, who extended earlier eighteenth-century rationalism into a general belief in the perfectibility of mankind if governed by those who understood the working of the human mind. They owed much to the logical powers of the philosopher Étienne de Condillac (1715–80) and to the mathematician Condorcet (1743–94), but are best known for their influence on Benjamin Constant† and Germaine de Staël†. Their views were expressed comprehensibly by Destutt de Tracy (1754–1836), who became a French Senator and produced three volumes of his *Éléments d'idéologie* between 1801 and 1805, significantly holding back the fourth volume until 1815, after the fall of Napoleon. At first there was much mutual admiration between the *Idéologues* and General Bonaparte, who, as a young man in Corsica, was impressed by Constantin de Volney (1757–1820), author of a study of Syria and Egypt which combined *Idéologue* disquisition with the fine writing of an early travelogue. The *Idéologues* backed Brumaire† and many were rewarded by selection to serve in the Tribunate† while a few became senators. They remained, however, true to their principles and, unable to understand the First Consul's pragmatism, they became a consistent opposition, especially critical of a reconciliation with the Church. Bonaparte thereafter treated them with contempt; twenty *Idéologue* tribunes were replaced by the First Consul in March 1802, among them Constant† and Daunou†; others survived until the size (and effectiveness) of the Tribunate was reduced five months

later. Only one *Idéologue*, Pierre Louis Roederer†, served on the Council of State†, and he was regarded with some suspicion by Napoleon. During the Empire, *Idéologue* opposition continued in the salons† and, occasionally, through pamphlets (most of which were promptly confiscated on publication).

ILLYRIAN PROVINCES

By the Peace of Schönbrunn† (1809) Austria ceded to France western Croatia, Carinthia, Slovenia and her remaining Adriatic coast. This considerable area, added to Istria and the Dalmatian littoral as far south as Cattaro†, was organized by Napoleon as the 'Illyrian Provinces', a single unit forming part of the French Empire and administered from Laibach (Ljubljana). The Provinces cut off Austria from Italy and the Mediterranean; they also provided France with a springboard to the Near East. French occupation was wholly beneficial to the region. Trade prospered; communications were improved; the *Code Napoléon*† brought uniformity of administration and justice; the South Slav languages, especially Slovene, were encouraged and new schools set up. The union of the Illyrian Provinces ended in 1814 when the Habsburgs restored the old regional divisions, thus keeping the westernized Yugoslav peoples apart until 1918.

IMPERIAL BEES

Heraldic cognizance of the Napoleonic Empire. In establishing the Empire Napoleon made it known to his Council of State that he sought an emblem which would take the place of the *fleur-de-lys*, the traditional heraldic device of the French monarchy. It was therefore suggested to him that, in order to go back before the Capet dynasty in 987, he should assume the golden bee emblem of the earliest Merovingian king, Childeric I (*c.* 458–81), found among treasures in his tomb at Tournai in 1653. The antiquity of this device pleased Napoleon, who adopted it well before his coronation in December 1804.

IMPERIAL CATECHISM

In 1805 Napoleon decided to encourage uniformity in the dioceses of his Empire by recommending to the Minister of Public Worship the teaching of a standard form of catechism, which was to list the duties of Christian believers 'towards Napoleon I, our Emperor' and to describe those 'who fail in their duty towards our Emperor' as 'worthy of eternal damnation'. The additional five questions and answers in the Imperial Catechism never received papal sanction, but they were accepted by every French bishop and approved by the Papal Legate, Cardinal Caprara†. The teaching of this catechism to the young was obligatory in churches in the French Empire from May 1806 to March 1814.

IMPERIAL CORONATION

(2 December 1804): see *Coronations*.

IMPERIAL GUARD

The most prestigious military formation in the Napoleonic armies. It was formed in 1804, having originated in the cavalry Guides, founded to protect Bonaparte in 1796–7, together with a Consular Guard and the Guards of the Legislative Assembly, raised in 1799. There were some 3,000 guardsmen at Marengo in 1800, more than 12,000 at Austerlitz (1805) and over

55,000 in the Russian campaign of 1812. By 1805 the Imperial Guard had become an army in itself. From 1806 onwards the core of the formation was known as the Old Guard, with recruits from other units forming from 1806 to 1809 the Middle Guard and from 1809 the Young Guard, composed mostly of promising and reliable conscripts. The Old Guard consisted of veterans: no one was admitted unless he had served with the army for at least five years and fought in two campaigns. Secondment to the Old Guard was recognized as an honour; it assured supplementary pay and additional rations. Napoleon treated the Old Guard as his 'favourite children' and tended to keep it in reserve in his later battles, notably at Borodino†.

IMPERIAL RECESS

(Reichsdeputationshauptschluss, 25 February 1803)

A drastic reorganization of the map of Germany by representatives of the German states meeting at Ratisbon (Regensburg), with the settlement endorsed by Napoleon, Tsar Alexander I acting as a disinterested mediator. The Recess, which took the form of an Edict, indemnified German princes deprived of Rhineland territory at Lunéville† by providing them with secularized church lands. The ecclesiastical fragments of the old Empire were swept away and almost all the fifty-one 'imperial cities' were mediatized (i.e., they were placed under one of the larger secular rulers and lost their direct allegiance to the Emperor in Vienna). The effect of the Imperial Recess was to destroy more than half the 360 petty states in Germany. It built up Bavaria†, Württemberg†, Baden and Hesse-Cassel and, by a reordering of the Electorates in Germany, gave Protestants a majority over Catholics for the first time, so as to make it unlikely that the Habsburgs† would continue as sovereigns of the Holy Roman Empire, even if that institution survived. The non-Austrian German princes now had an interest in maintaining the structure of Napoleon's Europe since they were beneficiaries from the Imperial Recess which he had authorized.

INDIA

Neither the French Revolution nor the Napoleonic upheaval made any great change in the balance of power in India. The British hold on the sub-continent, built up by the East India Company since 1600, had been challenged by the French in three campaigns between 1744 and 1763. The French threat was posed again during the Directory and the Consulate; French agents continued to encourage rebellions by the native princes. Thus Tippoo, the Sultan of Mysore (who had been educated by French military tutors from Pondicherry), effectively excluded the British from his territories in 1782–3. After being defeated in 1792, established contact with Bonaparte during the Egyptian campaign and waged war again in southern India until killed when his island fortress of Seringapatam was stormed, Colonel Wellesley (Wellington†) participating in the attack. The Mahratta princes of central India continued to resist British expansion and were defeated by Wellesley (by then a major-general) at Assaye (23 September 1803); even so, Mahratta resistance dragged on until 1805. At the same time, the first effective steps were being taken to assert Westminster's control of political affairs in the sub-continent. Pitt's India Act of 1784 left the management of India to a board of privy councillors in London, thus curbing the authority of the East India Company. Lord Cornwallis (Governor-General 1786–93 and in 1805) and Lord Mornington (Wellington's brother and Governor-General 1798–1805) built up an effective Civil Service and achieved British paramountcy over the Indian princes, who retained autonomy for internal administration provided that they did not resist British military penetration. The French islands in the Indian Ocean were taken by expeditions organized by Lord Minto (Governor-General 1807–13): Mauritius, the last colony to owe allegiance to Napoleon and a base for French privateers attacking ships trading with Calcutta, fell in December 1810. Minto also sent expeditions from India to what is now Indonesia, seizing Java in August 1811.

Institut de France

Was created, as the *Institut national*, in 1795 to replace the former learned societies (*Académie française, Académie des sciences*, etc.). On 25 December 1797 Bonaparte was elected to the Institut as a mathematician by 305 votes to 7; he had just returned victoriously to Paris from his first Italian campaign. He took his membership of the Institut very seriously; it encouraged him to invite scholars to accompany him to Egypt†, where he founded an *Institut d'Égypte* to carry out learned (and practical) research in Cairo and along the Nile and its delta. Later, in 1803, the First Consul became critical of *Idéologue†* influence in the *Institut national* (1803), which he renamed *Institut de France* under the Empire. Napoleon's influence encouraged cultural centralization at the expense of provincialism and he emphasized the primacy of science and mathematics among the disciplines. He assumed that members of the *Institut* would advise government departments and the army on matters of public service. It was preserved as a corporate body after the Restoration, although the five old academies were restored as constituent organs of the Institut (housed today, as under the Empire, in the domed Collège Mazarin, across the Seine from the Louvre).

INVASION PLANS (for England).

There were two main occasions when the French threatened to invade England:

155

1797–8; and 1803–5. The first plans were haphazard: there was doubt whether to head for southern England, strike up the Bristol Channel or invade Ireland. The initiative of a small French force which crossed from Brest† in February 1797 in the hope of attacking Bristol ended in fiasco at Fishguard in south Wales. The Directory named General Bonaparte Commander-in-Chief of the Army of England on 26 October 1797 (when he was at Treviso, in Venetia). In Paris, on 4 January 1798, he was told by Schérer†, the War Minister, of the preparations so far made for an invasion, and was not impressed. Between 8 and 14 February he inspected the Channel ports (Boulogne†, Ambleteuse, Calais, Dunkirk, Ostend) and on 23 February reported back to the Directory that invasion without command of the sea was impossible and that the French navy would not be ready for such an operation for several years. The expedition to Egypt† was mounted as an alternative. The First Consul returned to the project in the third week of May 1803 and at the end of the month travelled to Boulogne, staying for the first time at the château of Pont-de-Briques which served as his operational headquarters intermittently over the following two years. He planned a descent on the Kent-Sussex coast by light vessels, crossing on a long and foggy night at a time when the British fleet had been lured away. He calculated that he needed 2,000 barges and began to consider an invasion for the late summer of 1804, when he also wanted an escorting flotilla of a hundred vessels. These demands were beyond the building capacity of French shipyards but he continued to make frequent visits to the ports in the vicinity of Boulogne, occasionally carrying out seaborne inspections by pinnace. The disastrous invasion exercise of 20 July 1804, in which a sudden gale wrecked two sloops and other vessels, emphasized to him the uncertainties of such an operation. In 1804 he was at the Channel ports continuously from 19 July

until 26 August; but in 1805 he was there only from 3 August to 3 September, and decided on 25 August to move the *Grande Armée* eastwards against Austria, having realized that Admiral Villeneuve† was incapable of sailing up Channel and giving him protection. The invasion barges were kept at the Channel ports, where there was occasional shipyard activity to worry the British and distract them from other designs; thus, while preparations were at an early stage for the Russian campaign in November 1811, Napoleon ordered the Minister of Marine to make certain that 500 of the barges were made seaworthy.

IONIAN ISLANDS

Group of islands lying, for the most part, some twenty miles off the west coast of modern Greece, the principal island being Corfu. The archipelago was Venetian until 1797, when it was occupied by the French. Bonaparte tried to convince the Directory of the importance of the islands to France as a stepping-stone to the East, but they fell to a joint Russo-Turkish naval squadron in March 1799. An independent 'Septinsular Republic', dominated by Corfiote Greeks, was recognized by the British, Russians and Turks in March 1800, although bound to pay an annual tribute to the Sultan in Constantinople. The French recovered the Ionian Islands by a clause in the Treaty of Tilsit† of 1807. British naval units occupied Cephalonia, Ithaca, Zante, Zacynthus and Cerigo (Cythera) without much difficulty in October 1809 but Corfu remained garrisoned by the French until April 1814, despite a tight blockade by the Royal Navy. The Ionian Islands were given considerable autonomy, under British protection, from 1815 to 1864 when they were united to the Greek Kingdom.

IRELAND

Was a chronic source of concern to the British governing class, many of whom (including Wellington† and Castlereagh†) came from the Anglo-Irish gentry and were socially isolated from the mass of the population. The gradual awareness of an Irish Problem prompted concessions to the movement for a genuine Irish parliament in 1782 (see *Grattan*), but the successive crises of the French Revolution posed, for the first time, the probability of a radical nationalist movement. Wolfe Tone, a lawyer from Belfast who travelled to Paris by way of America, began to plan an insurrection with French aid as early as 1791. General Hoche sailed for Bantry Bay in December 1796 but was prevented by the Atlantic gales from making an effective landing. A serious uprising from May to June 1798 was suppressed before the French could bring the long awaited military assistance: 900 Frenchmen landed near Killala on 22 August 1798 but were soon captured; as also was Wolfe Tone. Uncertainty over Irish loyalties prompted Pitt† to carry through the Act of Union in 1801, which suppressed the Dublin parliament. Failure to concede Catholic Emancipation† increased latent Irish resentment and Napoleon, in 1804–5, gave serious thought to an invasion of Ireland rather than of England, counting on the backing of a liberated people. English sea power, however, ruled out any such project.

ISABEY, Jean-Baptiste (1767–1855)

French artist: born at Nancy, came to Paris in 1786 and was employed at Versailles on painting snuff boxes, under Marie Antoinette's patronage. He became a pupil of David†, gained recognition as a caricaturist and specialized in ivory miniatures under the Consulate and Empire. The court commissioned designs for coronation robes and ceremonial decorations. His *Le Livre du Sacre* includes lithographs of the coronation procession. Occasionally he produced portraits on a grand scale, one of which was sent by Napoleon to Vienna† in 1810 as a gift for Marie Louise†. Isabey thus became better known in Austria than any other French artist of the day. By 1811 he had a studio in Vienna, returning in 1814–15 to paint fifty portraits of eminent figures at the Congress. When, under Talleyrand's patronage, he was invited to paint the official canvas of the Congress he chose the occasion of Wellington's arrival at the conference table in February 1815. Isabey later returned to Paris, helped design coronation robes for Charles X (1825) and in old age was honoured by Napoleon III. An inclination towards caricature brings touches of irreverent informality to Isabey's most solemn work.

ITALIAN REPUBLIC

The name assigned to the Cisalpine Republic† between 1802 and 1805, at which date it became the Kingdom of Italy.

ITALY, Kingdom of

The Napoleonic Kingdom was basically an upgraded version of the Cisalpine Republic†, whose tricolour flag of red, white and green it preserved and handed down as a symbol of national unity. Napoleon was proclaimed King of Italy on 17 March 1805 and his coronation† was celebrated in Milan† ten weeks later. His stepson, Eugène Beauharnais†, was installed as Viceroy of the kingdom on the following 7 June. The kingdom comprised only the northern and eastern plains of the peninsula, from Lombardy to the Adriatic: Venice† was incorporated in 1806, the March of Ancona, down to the eastern border of Naples, in 1808; the South Tyrol in 1810. Seven million Italian subjects raised an army of 100,000 men for their King (who, after his coronation, made only one visit to Italy, from 21 November to 29 December 1807). The Viceroy was allowed little political initiative and sometimes received as many as three letters of instructions from Napoleon in one day; significantly the kingdom's Secretary of

State, Antonio Aldini, resided in Paris and not Milan. Italy received the benefits of the Napoleonic Codes and other reforms, including the provision of schools and colleges. The economy, however, suffered: high taxes were imposed so as to provide an annual tribute to the imperial authorities in Paris as well as for local needs; and the Continental System† subordinated the silk, fruit and wine of Italy to the needs of French producers. The hard-working Viceroy protested in vain against such blatant exploitation. He was ably assisted by his Minister of Finance, Giuseppe Prina, and served more de-viously by the Grand Chancellor of the Kingdom, Melzi†. An attempt to preserve the kingdom, with Eugène Beauharnais as ruler, was made by a deputation sent to the Allies in Paris in 1814, but rioters in Milan butchered Prina and threatened to kill other representatives of the Napoleonic order; and the Austrians thereupon assumed responsibility for order in the kingdom (see *Lombardy*). However, within a few years Italian patriots had come to recognize that, with all its faults, the *Regno d'Italia* provided them with a cradle of modern nationalism.

JAHN, Friedrich Ludwig (1778–1852)
German nationalist; born at Lanz, dabbled in philology but never completed his university studies and became well known in Berlin in 1810–12 as a teacher who pioneered the virtue of training the body so as to steel the mind. His association of liberal nationalism with physical fitness made him popular with German students in the War of Liberation (1813–14). Many of his supporters later formed *Burschenschaften*, student associations hostile to the established order and Jahn was imprisoned, 1819–25. He was fêted once again at Frankfurt during the revolutions of 1848.

JANISSARIES
The élite infantry corps of the Sultan of Turkey's army from the fourteenth century onwards, originally Christian slaves rigorously trained as fanatic Moslems. By the end of the eighteenth century they were a privileged caste, the Sultan's bodyguard, natural makers of palace revolutions. Local Janissaries frequently indulged in capricious reigns of terror; thus the Serbian Revolt† of 1804–5 was largely directed against Janissary misrule. When Sultan Selim III attempted to replace the Janissaries by a modern westernized army there followed fourteen months of chaos in Constantinople, May 1807 to July 1808. Janissaries deposed Selim, were excluded from power by the reforming Pasha of Rustchuk but believed they had recovered authority with the accession of the young Mahmud II† on 28 July 1808. Mahmud was secretly determined to destroy Janissary power at the earliest moment, but he had to wait until June 1826 when a mutiny led

to the massacre of several thousand Janissaries in their barracks at Constantinople by 'thirty minutes of grapeshot' and the fury of the Turkish mob.

JEFFERSON, Thomas (1743–1826)
Third President of the USA: a Virginian by birth and character, Jefferson drafted the Declaration of Independence in 1776 and was responsible for the American decimal monetary system before going to Paris as American Minister from 1785 to 1789. He was Secretary of State 1789–93, Vice-President from 1797 to 1801 and President from 1801 to 1809. Unlike Alexander Hamilton†, Jefferson was sympathetic towards the French Revolution. Although he warned the First Consul against territorial expansion in the West Indies† and up the Mississippi valley, Jefferson's presidency saw a strict observance of American neutrality. Ultimately Franco-American relations were improved, notably by the Louisiana Purchase†.

JENA
Town on the River Saale, now in the German Democratic Republic, with a university dating from 1558. On 14 October 1806 Napoleon, with a powerful force of some 96,000 men, engaged a much smaller Prussian army under Prince Hohenlohe-Ingelfingen on a plateau immediately north-west of Jena. The Prussians were defeated in some five hours of battle, although in mid-morning Ney's VI Corps was almost cut off by cavalry attacks. At the same time Davout†

defeated the main Prussian army at Auer-
städt†, some fifteen miles to the north.
The combined French victory shattered
Prussian prestige. Traditionally Napoleon's success at Jena is remembered as
the great humiliation of Prussian history,
but it could be argued that Davout's
victory was more remarkable and decisive.

JEWS

The French Revolution advanced the social emancipation of France's Jews, who
were assured of civil rights by the National
Assembly in 1789. The revolutionary
armies facilitated the social and political
integration of Jews and non-Jews throughout much of western Europe and northern
Italy: Jews in Holland and Belgium enjoyed civil rights by 1796; the ghetto gates
of Venice were ceremonially destroyed in
1797; the ghetto of Mainz went a year
later; the ghetto of Rome† not until the
city was incorporated in the French
Empire (1810). The spread of civil equality through the Napoleonic Codes meant
that, by the time the Kingdom of West-
phalia† was established in 1807, most
German Jews outside Prussia and Austria
were emancipated, although in Bremen,
Hamburg and Lübeck they had to wait
until their cities were absorbed into the
French Empire in 1811.

Between 1805 and 1808 Napoleon gave
considerable thought to the problems of
Judaism as a sect, especially in relation to
the religious settlements made already
with Catholics and Protestants (see *Concordat*; *Organic Articles*). In May 1806 he
agreed to permit the summoning of a
Jewish assembly. Two months later representative Jews, chosen by the Prefects†,
met in Paris to answer specific questions
on the Jewish attitude towards other
faiths, to the state and to business transactions. While the Assembly was in session
Napoleon proposed to summon a Great
Sanhedrin, a parliament representing
three-quarters of Europe's Jewish community, then under direct or indirect
French rule. The Sanhedrin was to draw

The battlefield of Jena, 14 October 1806

up a code, adapting the law of Moses 'to the customs and usages of the present'. The Sanhedrin – 45 rabbis and 25 laymen – opened in Paris on 9 February 1807, to be presented with instructions dictated by Napoleon while snowed up in Poznan ten weeks before. This procedure limited the Sanhedrin's scope. There was no new guiding law, only a rubber-stamp on Napoleon's call for the Jewish community to accept civil marriage, conscription and any commercial licences which the government might impose. By an Imperial Edict of 18 March 1808 Jewish worship was organized through a central consistory in Paris and a consistorial synagogue in each département with a Jewish community. Special licences limited interest rates and, in 1810, all Jewish believers in the French Empire were compelled to choose a family name.

Jews outside France and her dependencies criticized Napoleon's attempt to impose a reform of Jewish customs. Russia's Jews supported the Tsar rather than Napoleon in 1812. Many Jews fought alongside the Prussians in 1813: some thought Bonapartism threatened their purity of faith: others welcomed the Prussian promise in 1812 to give immediate emancipation, a pledge unfulfilled for fifty years. The Rothschild† family was consistently anti-Napoleonic.

JOHN, Archduke of Austria (1782–1859)
Austrian field marshal: born at Florence, the ninth of Emperor Leopold's twelve sons. He was eight weeks short of his nineteenth birthday when, overconfidently, he allowed staff officers to persuade him to attack Moreau† at Hohenlinden† and was defeated by the tenacity of Ney† and the enveloping skill of Grouchy†. In 1805 he commanded the army in the Tyrol but was forced back by Ney and Augereau†, away from the main theatre of war, and was fortunate to escape encirclement, eventually joining his brother, Archduke Charles† at Mari-

bor on the River Drava (26 November 1805). Neither brother could influence the decisive operations in Moravia (see *Austerlitz*). When Charles began to reorganize the Habsburg army 1806–7, John prepared schemes for a people's militia (*Landwehr*) and in January 1809 he met Andreas Hofer† to plan a Tyrolean rising†. In the Wagram campaign John stood on the defensive in northern Italy, gradually falling back on the Sava and into western Hungary† where he was badly mauled by Eugène Beauharnais† at Raab (Győr) on 14 June 1809. In February 1813 he again contacted dissident Tyrolean patriots and planned to force his brother Francis's ministers to support a general war of national liberation. Such ideas seemed dangerous to Metternich† and Archduke John was placed under house arrest in Vienna. He retired to Styria, interested himself in Slovene culture, morganatically married the postmaster of Bad Aussee's daughter and was reckoned the most liberal of the Habsburgs. In 1848 he helped to unseat Metternich from office and facilitated the accession of his great-nephew, Francis Joseph (Emperor 1848–1916).

JOMINI, Antoine Henri (1779–1869)
Swiss-born soldier: came from Payerne, near Lausanne and helped to organize the army of the Helvetic Confederation before serving on Ney's staff at Austerlitz. Napoleon was impressed by Jomini's ability and he was on the Emperor's staff in the Jena campaign. For some years he was the equivalent of a military attaché at St Petersburg. He was Military Governor of Vilna† in 1812, later of Smolensk†. After fighting under Ney at Lützen†, he went into Russian service in August 1813 and was a military aide-de-camp both to Alexander I and to Nicholas I. His *Précis on the Art of War* (1836) was a rival to the famous *On War* of Clausewitz† as an authoritative study of strategy and tactics.

JOSEPH, Archduke of Austria (1776–1847)
Palatine of Hungary†: born in Florence,
Emperor Leopold's seventh son. He was
appointed Captain-General and Palatine
of Hungary in 1795, an office he held for
fifty-two years, rarely leaving the kingdom. Joseph was popular with the
Magyars, whose cultural interests and
traditions he encouraged; his personal
qualities promoted loyalty to the Habsburg connection. He played less part than
his brothers in military affairs but raised
an army of 19,000 Hungarians to defend
the river-fortress of Komarom when it was
threatened by Eugène Beauharnais's
army in July 1809.

JOSEPHINE, Empress of the French
(1763–1814)
Born Marie Josephine Rose de Tascher de
la Pagerie in Martinique where she spent
much of her infancy with the son of a
colonial governor-general, Alexandre,
Vicomte de Beauharnais whom she married in December 1779. Their two children, Eugène and Hortense (see *Beauharnais*) were born in Paris (1781, 1783) but
Josephine returned to Martinique with
Hortense in 1788, coming back to a revolutionary France in November 1790.
The Vicomte was guillotined in Paris on 23
July 1794; Josephine herself was held in
prison in the former Carmelite convent in
Rue Vaugirard from 21 April to 6 August
1794 and was released through the mediation of Tallien†. During the early phase of
the Directory† she remained the friend of
Tallien and his wife, became the mistress
of Barras†, and met General Bonaparte in
the second week of October 1795. Napoleon, six years her junior, became her
lover before the end of December; they
were married at a civil ceremony in the
Rue d'Antin on 9 March 1796; but were
canonically married in the chapel of the
Tuileries only on the day before their
coronation† in 1804. She joined Bonaparte for the climax of his Italian campaign in July 1796, remaining south of the

*A detail of the sketch of the Empress
Josephine made by David for his canvas of
the Coronation in Notre Dame*

Alps until November 1797 and undertaking a ceremonial visit to Venice† for three
days in September. Josephine never again
accompanied Napoleon on a campaign.
Her liaison with Captain Hippolyte
Charles (1772–1837), which had begun in
the early summer of 1796, strained marital
bonds during Bonaparte's absence on the
Egyptian campaign, but there was a reconciliation on the eve of Brumaire†.
Josephine purchased Malmaison† on 21
April 1799; and her home became a
favourite retreat of the First Consul. She
was a patient hostess and accompanied
her husband on long inspection tours in
France and the Netherlands in 1802 and
1803 as well as travelling to Plombières
and other spas whose waters encouraged
hope of pregnancy. On 2 December 1804
Josephine was anointed and crowned
Empress but she was never crowned
Queen of Italy, although present in Milan
Cathedral for Napoleon's second coronation. The need for an heir made Napoleon
begin to consider divorce† and remarriage

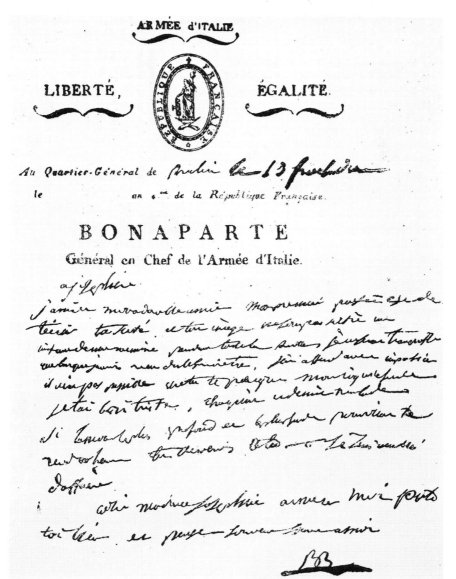

Love letter from Napoleon to Josephine, sent from Brescia on 30 August 1796

in 1807 but he did not take a final decision until 30 November 1809. The civil marriage was dissolved 'by mutual consent' sixteen days later; Cardinal Fesch† secured an ecclesiastical annulment on 10 January 1810. Thereafter Josephine lived mainly at Malmaison, where she was visited for the last time by Napoleon on 10 July 1810. After the fall of Paris in 1814, Tsar Alexander I† paid a courtesy call on Josephine and was captivated by her charm. The strain of unaccustomed hospitality to the cream of Russian imperial military society in the following weeks weakened her health and she died suddenly on 29 May 1814. Russian guards of honour lined the route from Malmaison to Rueil, where she was buried.

JOURDAN, Jean-Baptiste (1762–1833)

Marshal of the Empire: born at Limoges, fought in the ranks in America (1778–9) but won rapid promotion in the revolutionary armies, commanding the *Armée du Nord* in 1793–4, his troops entering Brussels, Cologne, Coblenz and Düsseldorf. Under the Directory† he presided over the Five Hundred† and was responsible for the conscription† law of 1798. After being defeated by Archduke Charles† at Stockach in March 1799 he held no field command for five years, but the First Consul was eager for his support and appointed Jourdan inspector-general of cavalry and infantry in 1800 and he was one of the original marshals† created in May 1804. From 1806 to 1813 he was chief military adviser to Joseph Bonaparte† in Naples and in Spain. He was a competent tactician but poor strategist: Wellington defeated him at Vitoria†, capturing his marshal's baton which was sent as a gift to the Prince Regent. In 1814 Jourdan, as military governor of Rouen, ordered his troops to wear the white cockade of the Bourbons as early as 9 April and, although present at the *Champ de Mai*† in 1815 he did not take part in the Waterloo campaign. Louis XVIII made him a peer in 1819.

JUNOT, Androche (1771–1813)

French general: born near Dijon, was a law student when he volunteered for the army in 1792. At Toulon† he was one of Bonaparte's sergeants and greatly admired his commander, who promoted him rapidly. In Egypt† Junot was wounded in a duel by an officer whom he had challenged for criticizing Bonaparte. He

General Junot as Governor of Paris, sketched by David

married Laure Permon (*see below*) at the start of the Consulate and, as Governor of Paris, lived in fine state just off the Champs-Elysées, gaining a reputation for good food and rare books. He fought beside Napoleon at Austerlitz and particularly distinguished himself in Portugal† in 1807, capturing Lisbon; his success was commemorated by the place name of Abrantès, which he was accorded on becoming a Duke in 1808. Although defeated at Vimiero†, he secured good terms (see *Cintra*), returned to France and was commanding again in Spain within fifteen months. His health was failing when he received command of VIII Corps in the Russian campaign: he made a major map-reading error near Vitebsk† (15 August 1812), was slow to reach Smolensk†, and was roundly abused by Napoleon. After Borodino† Junot was left to clear the battlefield and protect the wounded in the field hospital at Kolotskoe. He successfully led his Westphalian troops in the retreat, crossing the Berezina† in good order. Three months later he was sent to govern the Illyrian Provinces† but by early July 1813 he had lost his sanity. He died before the end of the month, probably by suicide.

JUNOT, Laure (1785–1835)

Became Duchesse d'Abrantès: born Laure Permon in Montpellier, her mother being a Corsican friend of Letizia Bonaparte†, 'Mme Mère'. Laure married Junot (see *above*) in 1800. Her relations with her husband were tempestuous; both had su-percharged tempers and Laure also possessed a cutting tongue. She fell foul of Mme Mère and of Pauline Bonaparte†, both of whom urged Napoleon to keep her out of Parisian society. In 1807–8 she was Metternich's mistress, delighting in the general scandal. After Junot's death she wrote some novels and she made a small fortune from her *Mémoires historiques*, published between 1831 and 1835. They are a racily spicy collection of fantasized reminiscences enlivened by some vivid phrases, which may owe something to her friendship with Balzac.

K

KALISCH, Treaty of (28 February 1813)
Completed the reversal of alliances begun at Tauroggen† by providing for Russo-Prussian military collaboration on the understanding that Alexander I† would assist Frederick William III† to recover the pre-Tilsit frontiers of Prussia.

KANT, Immanuel (1724–1804)
Prussian philosopher: born and died at Königsberg (now Kaliningrad), having entered the university there at the age of sixteen and held the professorial chair of logic and metaphysics for the last thirty-four years of his life. His speculative idealism provided a philosophical basis for Romanticism†, both by asserting the importance of individuals as beings seeking to realize a concept of duty and by his recognition that there are 'things in themselves' which cannot be identifiably experienced but which determine a person's perception of the physical world and the community to which he or she belongs. Constant (see *Wairy*) records a conversation between Cambacérès† and Napoleon shortly after Kant's death: Cambacérès raised a metaphysical speculation made by Kant; Napoleon brusquely replied that Kant was obscure and he did not like him, thus ending all discussion.

KARADJORDJE ('Black George'), 1752–1817)
Leader of the Serbs: born George Petrović, a pig-dealer from the Šumadija region, south of Belgrade. He rose to the rank of sergeant in the Austrian army against the Turks in 1787 and was twice decorated for bravery. He led the anti-Turkish Serbian Revolt† of 1804, set up a Serbian state assembly in liberated Belgrade and founded Serbia's first high school. Although confirmed as Governor (*Gospodar*) of Serbia in 1811 by a national assembly and accorded hereditary rights to rule the country, he was forced to flee to Austria when the Turks recaptured Belgrade in 1813. In the summer of 1813 he returned to Serbia but, on 13 July, was murdered by supporters of his rival, Miloš Obrenović (1780–1860) at Radovanje. Karadjordje's grandson, Peter I, was King of Serbia 1903–18 and first King of the Serbs, Croats and Slovenes (Yugoslavia), 1918–21.

KATZBACH RIVER
A small tributary of the Oder, some fifty miles east of Dresden†. On 21–22 August 1813 Napoleon forced Blücher's Army of Silesia back across the Katzbach. The Emperor then concentrated on checking Schwarzenberg's Army of Bohemia which was advancing on Dresden from the south. Marshal Macdonald† (with some 100,000 men) was left to hold the Katzbach defences against Blücher†, whose Prusso-Russian force was slightly superior in numbers. On 26 August while Napoleon was fighting the battle of Dresden, Macdonald sent three columns across the Katzbach and was trapped by the Prussians on high ground east of the river, his visibility hampered by pouring rain. Although Macdonald escaped in the bad weather, nearly a sixth of his army were killed or captured. The defeat, caused by Macdonald's cavalier disregard of his

orders to stay on the defensive, nullified Napoleon's attempts to exploit his Dresden victory.

KEATS, John (1795–1821)
English poet: born in London, educated at Enfield and trained as a surgeon at Guy's Hospital. Leigh Hunt† introduced him to Shelley† and in 1817 he published his first volume of *Poems*, which went largely unrecognized. The long poem in heroic couplets *Endymion* appeared in 1818; his final volume, *Lamia and Other Poems* in 1820. He suffered from consumption, dying in Italy two months before Napoleon on St Helena. His poetry – probably the purest lyric Romanticism† in the English language – appeals primarily to the senses.

KELLERMANN, François Étienne Christophe (1735–1820)
Marshal of the Empire: born in Strasbourg, became a gentleman cadet in a crack regiment at the age of fifteen, fought in the Seven Years' War and became a general in 1784. He checked the advance of Brunswick† at Valmy in 1792 and commanded in the Alps in 1793 but was kept under frequent surveillance as a royalist suspect, retiring from active service at the age of sixty-two in September 1797. Bonaparte appointed him President of the Senate†, created him a marshal in 1804, later making him Duke of Valmy. Frequently he was given military commands in the rear of the armies, so as to safeguard communications, notably along the Rhine (1806–7, 1809, 1813) and north of Bayonne (1808). He was reconciled to the Bourbons in 1815.

KELLERMANN, François Étienne (the Younger, 1770–1835)
French general: son of Marshal Kellermann, commissioned in the cavalry in 1785 but, as he was in America in 1791–2,

he did not see active service until 1794. He distinguished himself at Arcole† and Rivoli, becoming a brigadier in 1797. His famous cavalry charge at Marengo† endeared him to Napoleon, who promoted him major-general. Under the Empire his personal life was frequently marked by scandal, sometimes involving the extortion of money, but Napoleon excused his waywardness, respecting his courage and initiative as a cavalry commander, especially in Portugal and in the battles of 1813. He gained some tactical success at Quatre-Bras† in 1815 but was wounded at Waterloo†. Louis XVIII acknowledged him as second Duke of Valmy in 1820 and he held various administrative posts over the following twelve years.

KLÉBER, Jean-Baptiste (1753–1800)
French general: born in Strasbourg, served in the Bavarian army (1777–85), before fighting with the Alsatian volunteers on the Rhine in 1792–3 and commanding a division of the revolutionary army at Fleurus in 1794. As a divisional commander in Egypt and Syria, he gained striking victories, decimating the Turkish cavalry at Mount Tabor during the siege of Acre†. When Bonaparte returned to France, he left Kléber in command of the Army of the Orient. He defeated a large Turkish army outside Cairo† on 20 March 1800 (battle of Heliopolis) but was assassinated in Cairo by an Aleppan religious fanatic on the following 14 June.

KLEIST, Heinrich von (1777–1811)
German dramatist: born into a Junker military family at Frankfurt on Oder, serving as a Guards officer 1793–9 until inner spiritual doubts turned him against Potsdam's traditional way of life. He fled with his half-sister to Paris and Switzerland and, under Kant's influence, began to write plays. Personal depression and political disasters kept him in chronic mental instability. After seeking to settle near

Heinrich von Kleist, a sensitive mind harassed by the unpredictability of momentous events

Weimar†, he suddenly travelled to Boulogne and tried to enlist in the invasion army for England. After Tilsit his hostility to Napoleon aroused the interest of the French police and he spent the winter months of 1807–8 in solitary confinement at a fortress on the Marne. On his release he dabbled in journalism in Vienna and Berlin, accomplishing some of his best work in 1809–10: the nationalistic tragedy *Hermannsschlacht* in blank verse and *Prinz Friedrich von Homburg*, a classical study of expiation in a Prussian setting. The failure of the public to recognize the greatness of this poetic drama intensified Kleist's personal uncertainty. In November 1811 he entered a suicide pact with a young woman suffering from cancer; they were found shot on the shore of the Wannsee outside Berlin. Kleist's work has considerable historical interest in showing the struggle of a sensitive mind harassed by the unpredictability of

momentous events, but his genius was not recognized until some twelve or fifteen years after his death.

KOCHUBEY, Victor Pavlovich (1768–1834) Russian statesman: born near St Petersburg, the nephew of Catherine the Great's foreign affairs' adviser, Count Bezborodko. Kochubey studied at Uppsala, was in London 1788–9, Paris 1790–1 and Constantinople in 1793 and was much respected by the future Alexander I†, although he found life in St Petersburg unbearable under Paul I† and went into voluntary exile. After Alexander's accession he joined the unofficial Secret Committee† and became Russian Foreign Minister in October 1801. His wish to keep Russia free from continental entanglements so as to concentrate on internal reform conflicted with Alexander's wish for a Russo-Prussian dynastic understanding and Kochubey resigned after eleven months. From October 1802 to October 1807 he was Minister of the Interior but was once again disappointed with the Tsar, who failed to carry out domestic reforms. He was frequently consulted by Alexander in the crisis of 1812, was again Minister of the Interior in 1820, and was respected as an adviser on internal affairs by Alexander's successor, Nicholas I.

KOSCIUSZKO, Tadeusz (1746–1817) Polish patriot leader: born at Mereczowszczyzna, receiving military training in Prussia and France before fighting as a colonel for the Americans at Yorktown. He led the Polish insurrection against Russia in March 1794, gaining a victory at Raclawice in early April but suffering defeat outside Warsaw in October. Two years later, as an honorary American citizen, he was deported from Russia, but in 1798 settled in France rather than in the United States. Both Napoleon and Tsar Alexander I tried to win his support for their respective puppet states in Poland†, but he refused to accept anything short of an independent Poland with a parliamentary constitution. He died, still in exile, in France.

KOTOR: see *Cattaro*.

KRASNOE

Small town, thirty-one miles west of Smolensk† and forty-nine miles southeast of Vitebsk†. It was the scene of two battles in the 1812 campaign: a skirmish on 14 August, when Grouchy's† cavalry attacked the Russian rearguard falling back on Smolensk; and a more serious engagement on 17 November, in which Napoleon sent the Old Guard† to clear Miloradovich's men from a ravine, east of the town, where they threatened to ambush Davout's† First Corps as it approached Krasnoe. This first counterattack by the retreating French surprised Miloradovich†, but could not prevent a flank assault on Davout's column in which some of the Marshal's personal baggage was seized.

KRÜDENER, Baroness Julie von
(1764–1824)
German evangelical prophetess: born Barbara Juliane von Vietinghoff at Riga, married a Russian diplomat, Alexis von Krüdener, in 1782 and accompanied him on missions to Vienna and Copenhagen. They had a son and a daughter before they separated in 1792, Alexis dying in 1802. The Baroness was on the fringe of Mme de Staël's circle at Coppet† in 1801, coming later under the influence of pietists and developing a unique form of mystical religion. Her two-volume semi-autobiographical romance *Valérie* (French edition 1803, German in 1804) attracted wide attention; it was admired by Tsar Alexander's consort, Elizabeth; and Mme von Krüdener was received by Queen Hortense (Beauharnais†) at

Baden in May 1809. Her peak period of influence came in the summer of 1815 when she inspired Alexander I† in Paris with a sense of divine mission to establish a Christian Commonwealth of Princes. These ideas, together with the theosophic mysticism of Franz Baader†, bore fruit in the Tsar's much misunderstood Holy Alliance† of September 1815. Soon afterwards Alexander, while respecting her pietism, began to doubt the authenticity of her divine inspiration. She met the Tsar twice more – at Pechory, near Pskov, on 21 September 1819 and outside St Petersburg on 19 September 1821 – but he was puzzled by her mixture of sibylline warnings and elated nonsense and encouraged her to settle in the Crimea. She died there, on Christmas Day 1824, at Karasubazar (now Belogorsk).

KULM, Battle of (30 August 1813)

Fought in the Erzgebirge Mountains (Krušné Hory in Czechoslovakia), on the Austro-Saxon border some twenty-five miles south of Dresden† where Napoleon had gained his victory three days earlier. Unexpectedly Vandamme†, harrying Schwarzenberg's left flank in difficult terrain, met stiff Russian resistance and was trapped by Prussian units brought hurriedly to the battle on personal orders from Frederick William III†. Casualties on both sides were heavy, more than half of Vandamme's corps being killed or captured. Vandamme was among the prisoners. The Kulm victory restored allied morale after the defeat at Dresden.

KURAKIN, Alexander Borisovich, Prince
(1759–1829)
Russian diplomat: born in St Petersburg, became a foreign policy adviser to Tsar Paul† and was Vice-Chancellor of State for the first eighteen months of Alexander's reign, being regarded as a Francophile. After assisting Alexander at Tilsit† and serving briefly as envoy to Vien-

na, he became ambassador in Paris (1808–12). At Napoleon's birthday reception on 15 August 1811 the Prince was subjected to a forty-minute tirade from the Emperor because of the Tsar's alleged encouragement of Polish nationalism. Kurakin sought a compromise settlement of Franco-Russian relations even after Napoleon's departure from Paris for his armies in the East on 9 May 1812.

KUTUZOV, Michael Ilarionovich
(1745–1813)
Russian field marshal: born at St Petersburg, the son of a military engineer of Tartar descent. He was commissioned in the artillery before transferring to the light infantry. Kutuzov distinguished himself under Suvorov† against the Turks in the Crimea (1770–4), losing his right eye at Alushta. Later he was commended for his assault on the fortress of Izmail (1791). With his wife, Kutuzov was one of Paul I's dinner guests on 23 March 1801 a few hours before the Tsar was murdered; Kutuzov could see for himself how ill-at-ease the heir to the throne (Alexander I†) seemed to be that evening. In November 1805 Kutuzov commanded the Russian army which successfully retired from the River Inn. to Moravia but, against his better judgement, he was induced to give battle at Austerlitz†. After the defeat he regrouped the stragglers and retired to Poland in good order. In 1811 he commanded the Southern Army against Turkey, seeking a speedy end to the war (see *Bucharest*). With great reluctance and under pressure from his family and advisers, Alexander dismissed Barclay† in August 1812 and made Kutuzov commander-in-chief against Napoleon. After giving battle at Borodino† (7 September), Kutuzov retreated on Moscow†. On 13 September, in conference at Fili outside

Kutuzov; an engraving published in London in 1813 and based on an original Russian drawing of the Field Marshal

the city, he ordered the army to pull back through Moscow towards Kaluga as a strategic device to tempt Napoleon to disaster ('Napoleon is a torrent which as yet we are unable to stem; Moscow will be the sponge to suck him dry'). He rejected armistice proposals brought by Lauriston† and for five weeks waited at Tarutino for Napoleon to begin his retreat. Kutuzov's troops then harassed the *Grande Armée* from Maloyaroslavets† back to Vilna†, where he re-established Russian headquarters in mid-December. Tsar Alexander, who created Kutuzov Prince of Smolensk at Vilna, ordered him to advance into Germany in January 1813 although Kutuzov thought it too soon to mount an offensive. The old man's health gave way in the spring; he suffered a stroke and died at Bunzlau in Silesia on 28 April.

LABOUCHÈRE, Peter Caesar (1772–1839)
Banker and secret envoy: born in The Hague and became head of the Amsterdam banking house of Hope and Labouchère and a son-in-law of Sir Francis Baring (1740–1810), the co-founder of the financial House of Baring and a friend of Pitt†. On the French side, Labouchère had close contact with the Parisian financier, Gabriel Ouvrard†, and indirectly with Fouché†. In May 1805 he took over from Ouvrard responsibility for transferring the 71 million silver piastres of the Mexican treasury to European coffers, a plan which Napoleon believed was helping the economy of France but which, thanks to Labouchère's international connections, brought silver temporarily into the vaults of the Bank of England while shaking the stability of the Bank of France†. In 1810 Labouchère made contact with his father-in-law in London to forward a peace plan from Fouché by which Britain would give up all interests in Spain, Naples and Sicily in return for the cession of Malta and an eventual alliance with Napoleon for a Franco-British expedition against the United States. Labouchère settled in England in 1821 and died in London.

LA HARPE, Frédéric César de (1754–1838)
Swiss liberal: born in the French-speaking Vaud canton at Rolle and educated at neighbouring Lausanne. In 1783 he went to Russia as tutor to a noble family and, a year later, was chosen by Catherine the Great to tutor her grandsons, Alexander† and Constantine†. He remained in St Petersburg until spring 1795, Catherine coming in later years to distrust his republican liberal sentiments. Throughout Tsar Paul's reign Alexander secretly corresponded with La Harpe and invited him back to Russia in the summer of 1801. During the months that he was in Russia La Harpe was consulted by the Secret Committee† on ways of reforming the empire. In 1814 Alexander re-established contact with La Harpe, who represented Vaud canton at the Vienna Congress† and advanced the cause of Swiss independence and neutrality with the warm backing of his old pupil.

LAKE POETS
The name given, as early as 1817, to the three earliest masters of Romanticism† in England because of their residence in the Lake District: Wordsworth† at Grasmere and Rydal; Coleridge† and Southey† at Keswick.

LAMARCK, Jean-Baptiste (1744–1829)
French naturalist: born in Picardy, at Bazentin. While serving in Louis XVI's army at Toulon he became interested in Mediterranean flora and fauna. His first work on botany was published in 1773 but it was under the Consulate that he advanced his zoological studies, not publishing his pioneer evolutionary *Philosophie zoologique* until the year of Wagram (1809), and further studies on invertebrates did not appear until Louis XVIII's reign. Lamarck first suggested the influence of environment as a reason for transformation of species. It was his colleague at the Jardin des Plantes, Geoffroy

Saint-Hilaire (1772–1844) who put forward the theory that all vertebrates are attached to the same stock. Lamarck and Geoffroy between them advanced the concept of evolutionary descent, but their ideas were attacked by the fashionable anatomist, Baron Cuvier (1769–1832) who had once collaborated with Geoffroy. Cuvier was a friend of Napoleon but the Emperor continued to show interest in Geoffroy's ideas, as he had been the chief naturalist on the Egyptian expedition.

LANNES, Jean (1769–1809)
Marshal of the Empire: a Gascon farmer's son from Lectoure, commissioned in the volunteers in 1792 for service in the Pyrenees, becoming a colonel by 1795 and serving alongside Bonaparte at Lodi†. He was wounded at Acre† and again at Aboukir† before returning from Egypt at the same time as Bonaparte and commanding the infantry at the Tuileries during the *coup* of Brumaire†. In 1800 he won Montebello, the preliminary action to Marengo† and checked the Austrian attacks at the height of the main battle itself. A diplomatic mission to Portugal in 1801 was a failure and he spent much of 1803–4 at Ambleteuse in expectation of a high command in the invasion of England. Napoleon, who regarded him as a personal friend, made him a marshal in 1804. At Austerlitz† he halted Bagration's cavalry and he launched the opening attacks at Jena† and at Friedland†. He was created Duke of Montebello in 1808 but next year was wounded at Essling†, dying nine days later. Napoleon mourned him deeply, often recalling his courage and loyalty. The astringent Laure Junot†, on the other hand, recalled how Lannes 'could always storm a fortress more easily than he could a woman'.

LAON, Battle of (9 March 1814)
The final attempt by Napoleon to destroy Blücher's Army of Silesia, which he had forced northwards over the Marne and the Aisne after his victories around Montmirail†. Laon was indecisive, its timing determined by Blücher† who inflicted heavy losses on Marmont's corps. Napoleon, anticipating renewed attacks next day, took up defensive positions south of Laon, but on that morning Blücher's health gave way and his chief-of-staff (Gneisenau†) found his orders so incoherent that he broke off the action. Napoleon, unaware of this chaos in the Prussian camp, lost his opportunity, turning south to intercept Schwarzenberg† as he advanced methodically down the Seine.

LA ROTHIÈRE, Battle of (1 February 1814)
A bitter engagement fought in heavy snow three miles south-east of Brienne†, whence Blücher† had been ejected two days before. A Prussian force of 53,000 men, supported by Barclay's 34,000 Russians, attacked Napoleon's largely inexperienced army which was outnumbered two to one. Although the French held their ground, Napoleon had already decided before the battle that he would regroup his troops so as to meet the mounting threat from Schwarzenberg† and he withdrew during the overnight snowstorm. This success made Blücher over-confident and he bungled his subsequent advance south of the Marne, sustaining defeats around Montmirail†.

LAS CASES, Emmanuel Augustin, Comte de (1766–1842)
Publicist: born in the château of Las Cases, south-east of Toulouse and served in the pre-revolutionary navy before coming to London as an émigré in December 1792, having walked through Luxembourg and Belgium to Rotterdam to make his escape. He participated in two abortive royalist raids on the French coast before becoming a tutor in London where he made valuable contacts (including a meeting with the Prince of Wales), and in

1800 he produced a historical atlas, with charts of recent history not unfriendly to Bonaparte. In 1802 he returned to France, held minor office at Napoleon's court and helped defend Walcheren against the British in 1809. Five years later he was back in England but he served Napoleon in the Hundred Days and volunteered to accompany him to exile. Las Cases encouraged Napoleon to appeal to the Prince Regent for asylum in England under the protection of British law. Las Cases remained a year on St Helena, where he took down an important statement of Napoleon's ideas, published in 1823 as the *Mémorial de Sainte-Hélène*, influential in the spread of the Napoleonic Legend. After succeeding in getting himself expelled by the British from St Helena (1816) he was briefly imprisoned on the Cape of Good Hope but by June 1818 he was in Baden, where he met Eugène Beauharnais and gave him information about St Helena. Las Cases sat in the Chamber of Deputies (1830–42) and accompanied the Emperor's remains back from St Helena to Paris in 1840.

LAURISTON, Jacques Alexandre Law
(1768–1828)
French soldier: born in Pondicherry, of Scottish descent, and commissioned in the artillery in 1785. Although he had risen to the rank of colonel along the Rhine by 1795, suspicion of his royalist sympathies left him inactive until after Brumaire†. He fought at Marengo† but was sent by Bonaparte as an envoy to London to discuss preliminaries to the Peace of Amiens†. In 1805 he commanded the division of troops afloat with Villeneuve† on his expedition to Martinique. A year later he was at Ragusa (Dubrovnik) where he beat off a Russian attack in May 1806. After commanding the artillery at Wagram, he succeeded Caulaincourt† as ambassador in St Petersburg in May 1811, genuinely seeking to ease Franco-Russian tension. He joined Napoleon at Smolensk in 1812 and undertook two abortive peace

missions to Russian headquarters from occupied Moscow. At Leipzig he was taken prisoner and from 1814 onwards loyally served Louis XVIII who created him a marquis in 1817 and a Marshal of France in 1823, when he led French troops across the Pyrenees to capture Pamplona in support of Ferdinand VII of Spain. Five years later he collapsed and died in a dancer's dressing-room at the Paris Opéra.

LA VENDÉE: see *Vendée*

LAW OF 28 PLUVIÔSE, Year VIII
(17 February 1800)
Codified arrangements for the administrative organization of France. While retaining départements and communes, the Law created the new middle-sized unit known as the arrondissement. It also provided for the appointment of a Prefect in every département, a subprefect in the arrondissement and a mayor in every commune. The effect of the reform (prepared by a commission chaired by Chaptal) was to extend the practice of appointing officials from above rather than accept earlier revolutionary ideas of popular election.

LAW OF 27 VENTÔSE, Year VIII
(18 March 1800)
Completed the reorganization of the judiciary. New courts were created for the arrondissements and twenty-nine courts of appeal were set up, assuming some of the judicial functions of the parlements before the Revolution. The Law allowed the First Consul to appoint almost all judges, notaries and bailiffs, a characteristic move towards administrative centralization. In practice, Bonaparte looked for advice to his ministers, Cambacérès in particular having great influence over appointments to the judiciary.

LAW OF 18 PLUVIÔSE, Year IX
(7 February 1801)

A repressive measure aimed at re-establishing control in country districts threatened by brigandage, sometimes planned by political dissidents. The Law abandoned the jury system (for fear of local intimidation) in any region which the First Consul might specify. Special criminal courts, composed of nominees chosen by the Consul, would judge cases concerned with arson, armed robbery, murder or sedition. Anyone convicted in these courts had no rights of appeal. Bonaparte ordered the Law to be enforced in thirty-two départements, almost a third of metropolitan France.

LAWRENCE, Thomas (1769–1830, knighted 1815)

British portrait painter: born in Bristol, first exhibiting at the Royal Academy aged eighteen. So impressive was his draughtsmanship that in 1792 he succeeded Joshua Reynolds as Painter to George III. He basked in royal favour for the rest of his life, gaining a European reputation in 1814 when he was commissioned by the Prince Regent† to paint portraits of the allied military and political leaders. Further commissions followed in Rome and Vienna. The 'Waterloo Chamber' in Windsor Castle houses the finest examples of Lawrence's work.

LEBRUN, Charles François (1739–1824)

Third Consul: born at Saint-Sauveur-Landelin in Normandy on the Cotentin peninsula. Under Louis XVI he served as a payments officer, inspector of crown lands and royal attorney before becoming a deputy to the States-General in 1789. Robespierre imprisoned him but he then sat in the Council of Ancients† and was chosen by Bonaparte as Third Consul after Brumaire†, holding office from 1799 to 1802, principally supervising financial reform. From 1804 to 1814 he was Arch-Treasurer of the Empire and administered the annexed Dutch départements from 1810 to 1813, having been created Duke of Plaisance (Piacenza). In his spare time he translated Tasso and Homer. He was a patient and shrewd administrator. His exercise of patronage – particularly over the appointment of Prefects† – brought him wealth and a lasting influence, especially in Normandy. Although out of favour at the Restoration, he was pardoned when he reached the age of eighty.

LEFEBVRE, François Joseph (1755–1820)

Marshal of the Empire: born at Rouffach in Alsace, a miller's son. In 1789 he was a sergeant in a Guards regiment but by the end of 1793 commanded a brigade and fought in most of the campaigns in western Germany 1794–9. As commandant of Paris he sent guards to rescue Bonaparte when the Council of the Five Hundred became hostile at Saint-Cloud (see *Brumaire*). He was, for a time, President of the Senate and received his marshal's baton in May 1804. After fighting at Jena†, he successfully besieged Danzig (Gdansk) and took its name for his dukedom in 1808. He was in Spain (1808–9) before commanding Bavarian troops in the Wagram campaign, and therefore was responsible for stamping out the Tyrolean revolt of Andreas Hofer† (October 1809 to January 1810). At Borodino† he commanded the Old Guard, leading them again at Dresden, Leipzig and Montmirail†. Lefebvre was with Napoleon at Fontainebleau for the first abdication† and supported him in the Hundred Days but held no command. His wife, Catherine, who had reputedly been a washerwoman, brought a touch of jolly vulgarity to Napoleon's court; the Duchess of Danzig was nicknamed Mme Sans-Gêne (Madame Free and Easy).

LEGION OF HONOUR

Was instituted, as a reward for loyal

service to the nation in the spring of 1802, but the first crosses were not distributed by the Emperor until 15 July 1804, outside the Invalides in Paris, after a Mass celebrated by Cardinal Caprara† at Notre Dame. Two thousand more légionnaires were decorated by Napoleon at the camp outside Boulogne† a month later (16 August). Originally the Legion was to have comprised 5,250 soldiers and civilians, selected by the Emperor and organized into fifteen cohorts. They were to pledge themselves to serve the Republic, oppose the restoration of feudalism, and work together to maintain liberty and equality; they were to be graded into five classes, receive suitable stipends and be guaranteed special privileges. The oath and the five classes were retained, and there were certain privileges, particularly in schooling for the légionnaire's family, but the stipend was replaced by decorations attached to a red ribbon. By 1814 there were some 32,000 members of the Legion, 30,500 of whom were in the army or navy. The concept and basic structure of the Legion survived Napoleon's downfall.

LEGISLATIVE ASSEMBLY (*Corps législatif*) (see also *Constitutions of France*)
The Constitution of the Year VIII (December 1799) declared that the First Consul proposed laws, the Tribunate† discussed them and a *Corps législatif* voted on them; the constitutions of 1802 and 1804 made little change in the character of the legislative assembly, membership of which was reckoned an honour and a duty rather than a source of political influence. There were 300 members of the Assembly, all of whom had to be aged at least thirty. They were selected by the Senate† from 6,000 names on a *liste nationale*, drawn up by a three-stage process of indirect election, the first stage of which (in a local commune, or arrondissement†) was based upon universal male suffrage over the age of twenty-one. The Senate had to ensure that each département had at least one member in the assembly, which normally met for four months each year. Delegates from the Tribunate and the Council of State† made speeches to the Assembly, whose members voted for or against measures without ever commenting on them. Negative votes were rare. The *Acte Additionnel*† provided for a more representative legislature in 1815, which at once proved less accommodating.

LEIPZIG
City in Saxony, on the River Elster and its tributary, the Pleisse, seventy-four miles north-west of Dresden†. Napoleon had only visited Leipzig briefly in 1807 and 1812 before establishing his headquarters in the eastern suburb of Reudnitz on 14 October 1813, organizing defensive positions which made use of the swampy terrain and the intersection of the two main rivers and three smaller streams. There he awaited what became known as the 'Battle of the Nations' (16–19 October 1813). A quarter of a million Allied troops (Austrian, Russian, Prussian, Swedish) converged on 175,000 French, massing some 1,000 pieces of artillery against Napoleon's 700 guns. The battle began on 16 October with piecemeal attacks by Barclay† de Tolly on the south of Leipzig, Blücher's Prussians attacking from the north soon afterwards. Interior lines of communication gave the defenders an advantage, and by nightfall the French had gained limited successes. On 17 October there was a lull: Napoleon received 20,000 men as reinforcements, but these were offset by the arrival of 115,000 Allied troops, under Bernadotte† and Bennigsen†, who also increased the artillery fire-power until the Allies had twice as many guns as the French. The decisive day was 18 October when, after Napoleon had shortened his line, the Allies launched concentric attacks on the defences, but made little headway except in the north-eastern sector. By midday, however, the

battle of attrition was shifting in favour of the Allies and Napoleon began an orderly withdrawal through Leipzig to the western village of Lindenau, on the left bank of the Elster. Chaos came on the following morning when a frightened corporal, temporarily in charge of demolition, blew up the bridge between Leipzig and Lindenau while French troops were still retiring across it and a rearguard of 20,000 men was inside the city. Napoleon's defeat cost him control of Germany and over 70,000 casualties, many of whom (like Marshal Poniatowski†) were drowned seeking to swim the Elster.

LIECHTENSTEIN, Johann, Prince of (1760–1836)

Austrian general: born in Vienna, commanded the Austrian cavalry on the right flank at Austerlitz†, his troops being caught in Bernadotte's assault on the village of Austerlitz itself. Next day Liechtenstein was sent to Napoleon to seek a cease-fire. In 1809 he fought with distinction at Aspern† and Wagram† and was appointed commander-in-chief on 12 July, only to be given once more the task of making peace. After three years as Governor of Upper and Lower Austria, he resumed his military career and fought at Leipzig†. He was the richest man in the Habsburg Empire, with a baroque palace in Vienna's Herrengasse and huge estates in four provinces. From 1805 until 1836 he was also sovereign ruler of the Principality of Liechtenstein, which he never once visited.

LIGNE, Charles, Prince of (1735–1814)

Cosmopolitan: born in Brussels, his chief estate being in Belgium, at Beloeil. He rose to the rank of field marshal in the armies of both Austria and Russia. The Prince was a man of wit and culture who knew Voltaire, charmed Frederick the Great and Catherine the Great by his good talk, frequented the salon of Mme de

Staël† and, between 1795 and 1811, acutely observed the changing life of Europe and noted what he saw in a series of letters. He was present at Vienna† in 1814 for the peacemaking. Even before the Congress opened, he studied the social preparations and political intriguing and commented, 'The Congress dances, but isn't going anywhere'; he died before the end of the year, well content with his often repeated exit line.

LIGNY, Battle of (16 June 1815)

A preliminary action to Waterloo†, fought on the same day as Quatre-Bras†, six miles to the west. Ligny was a neighbouring village to Fleurus, where Napoleon established his headquarters that day, and where major battles were fought in 1622, 1690 and 1794, some French writers calling Ligny 'the fourth battle of Fleurus'. Napoleon, seeking to drive a wedge between the British and Prussians, launched an assàult on three Prussian corps holding Ligny. The Imperial Guard routed the Prussians in the evening, nearly killing Blücher†, who was thrown from his horse. Technically Ligny was the last Napoleonic victory. Gneisenau† restored order in the Prussian lines and pulled back to Wavre† on the River Dyle. The French lacked the resources to exploit their tactical advantage.

LIGURIAN REPUBLIC

The French puppet state established in Genoa† in 1797 and absorbed into the French Empire in 1805.

LIVERPOOL, Lord (Robert Banks Jenkinson, 1770–1828, becoming Lord Hawkesbury in 1803 and Earl of Liverpool in 1808)

British Prime Minister: born in London, educated at Charterhouse and Christ Church, Oxford, and undertook the grand tour of Europe on the eve of the French

Revolution. He entered the Commons as Tory MP for Appleby in 1790, changing to Rye in 1796 until he went to the Lords in 1803. Except for fourteen months in 1806-7, he held government office from 1793 to 1827, entering the cabinet as Foreign Secretary under Addington† in February 1801. He was at the Foreign Office until May 1804, conducting the negotiations which led up to the Peace of Amiens† and accepting the need to re-sume the war in 1803. After two terms as Home Secretary (1804-6, 1807-9) he be-came Secretary for War and Colonies under Perceval† (1809-12), loyally back-ing Wellington and the Peninsular War†. On Perceval's assassination in May 1812 he became Prime Minister, heading the government for almost fifteen years. Liverpool, a poor public speaker, was remarkably able at keeping together a government of strong personalities, often in conflict with one another.

LIVRET OUVRIER

A workbook, supplied by the local author-ities, which every worker was obliged to carry. Employers were forbidden to give work to anyone who could not produce this job record. The *Livret* was instituted after a decree issued on 1 December 1803 sought to tighten police powers over wage-earners throughout France.

LODI, Battle of (10 May 1796)

Famous action in Bonaparte's first Italian campaign, an attempt to secure the cros-sing of the River Adda at the Lombard town of Lodi, eighteen miles south-east of Milan. Bonaparte, eager to trap the Au-strian rearguard west of the Adda before securing Milan, placed several batteries to control the far bank of the river and sent Masséna† and Berthier† forward to storm the bridge, which was taken at a cost of 400 casualties. For purposes of morale the Directory publicized Lodi as a victory of greater importance than the action mer-ited. The popular impression of Lodi – a

coloured print showing Bonaparte as a standard-bearer leading his men across the bridge – originated in a Genoese artist's imagination; but in later years Napoleon contentedly basked in the glory of the legend. It is questionable if there was any sound reason for so costly an assault on the bridge.

LOMBARDY

Region of Italy south of the Alps, north of the River Po, west of Venetia and east of Piedmont. In 1790 Lombardy was the Duchy of Milan†, acquired by Austria in 1714 from Spain and ruled by a Viceroy (Archduke Ferdinand†, brother of the Emperors Joseph II and Leopold and of Queen Marie Antoinette of France). The Duchy was overrun by Bonaparte in his first Italian campaign and formed part of the Transpadane Republic (1796) soon becoming the Cisalpine Republic†. Lom-bardy was recovered by the Austro-Russian forces under Suvorov† in 1799 but Bonaparte's passage of the Great St Ber-nard Pass† in May 1800 and the subse-quent battle of Marengo† left Lombardy under French dominance until 1814. When the Kingdom of Italy† was set up in 1805 Napoleon was crowned with the mediaeval iron crown of Lombardy. In 1815 Lombardy was united to Venetia and the two provinces were ruled by the Habsburgs until, in 1859, Lombardy was finally incorporated in the new Italy.

LOUIS XVIII, King of France

(1755-1824 reigned 1814-24)
Born at Versailles, becoming the elder surviving brother of Louis XVI. He was created Count of Provence at birth. In June 1791 he emigrated and with his brother, Artois† (Charles X), organized émigré armies in the Rhineland, especial-ly at Coblenz. He assumed the Regency of France in January 1793 on Louis XVI's execution. On 16 June 1795 he was proc-laimed King at Mülheim, Baden, since it

was assumed that his imprisoned nephew (Louis XVII) was dead. After exile in Brunswick and Warsaw, Louis XVIII came to England: he lived at Gosfield Hall, near Halstead, Essex, from 1807 to 1809 and thereafter at Hartwell House, Aylesbury, until he crossed to Calais on 24 April 1814. He then negotiated a compromise constitution with Talleyrand†, entering Paris on 3 May. Napoleon's return in the Hundred Days† forced him to seek refuge at Ghent (20 March to 24 June 1815) but he returned to Paris a second time on 8 July. Louis XVIII followed a moderate policy, seeking to curb the vengeance of ultra-royalists who gathered around Artois.

LOUISE, Queen Consort of Prussia
(1776–1810)
Born at Hanover, the daughter of the Grand Duke of Mecklenburg-Strelitz. In December 1793 she married the future Frederick William III† of Prussia, who acceded in December 1797. Louise was an ideal mother, wife and patriot queen. She heartened her husband, countering the apathetic defeatism of the Prussian court after Jena† and Auerstädt† and seeking to influence Tsar Alexander I†, who greatly admired her. Extracts from her private letters, found when the French occupied Berlin, were published by Napoleon in the official army Bulletins so as to discredit her – a propaganda trick which infuriated the Tsar. Reluctantly, on 6 July 1807, she went to Tilsit† hoping to save her husband's throne by exercising her charm on Napoleon, as well as on Alexander; and the Tilsit settlement did indeed allow Frederick William III to retain the heart of his kingdom. Her health gave way under these years of campaigning. Seven months after returning to Berlin, she collapsed and died at Hohen Zieritz, Mecklenburg (19 July 1810). In 1871 her second son became the first German Emperor, William I (1797–1888).

A hostile French representation of the flight in 1806 of Queen Louise of Prussia, whom Napoleon rightly considered one of his most resolute opponents

LOUISIANA

Until 1762 Louisiana was a French possession. It was then ceded to Spain but retroceded by the Treaty of Madrid (1801). The prospect of Bonapartist colonization of the Mississippi alarmed President Jefferson† who, throughout 1802, encouraged his minister in Paris, Robert Livingston, to seek guarantees of free trading rights along the river. Bonaparte, on reflection, considered New Orleans and its hinterland too difficult to hold against British attack and he therefore authorized an offer to sell the French possessions to the United States. Final details of the Louisiana Purchase were worked out by the future President Monroe, who travelled to Paris in January 1803. For 15 million dollars France sold to the United States the whole of the Mississippi valley, up to the Rocky Mountains. This area of 828,000 square miles more than doubled the size of the USA.

L'OVERTURE, Toussaint: see *Toussaint L'Ouverture*.

LOWE, Sir Hudson (1769–1844)

British soldier and colonial governor: born in Galway, the son of an army surgeon, and spent most of his early years accompanying his father's regiment, particularly in America, and having only brief schooling in Salisbury. He was gazetted ensign in 1787, becoming captain in 1795 and thereafter seeing service mainly in the Mediterranean, including Corsica†, where he remained on garrison duty for two years and picked up a smattering of French and Italian. In 1810 he was military governor of two of the Ionian Islands† retaken from the French, Cephalonia and Ithaca. He was attached to Blücher's army as a senior liaison officer in 1813–14, first catching sight of Napoleon through his spyglass on the battlefield of Bautzen†. Lowe was humane but unimaginative, insensitive and pedantic. When appointed Governor of St Helena† in the autumn of 1815, he was advised to take a wife with him as hostess and quickly found a convenient widow. He arrived on St Helena in April 1816, tightened restrictions on Napoleon's movements and had five interviews with the Emperor ('General Bonaparte' to Lowe) before Napoleon refused again to receive him; their relations worsened when the obtuse Lowe declined to allow a marble bust of Napoleon's son, which had arrived from Europe, to be delivered to his distinguished prisoner. Lowe arrived back in London in September 1821 and was much criticized by the Whig Opposition for his conduct of affairs on St Helena. He became Governor of Antigua in 1823 and held a high administrative post in Ceylon from 1825 to 1830, when he was retired with the rank of lieutenant-general.

LUDDITES

The most desperate manifestation in England of the discontent caused by the Crisis of 1811†. The Luddites were manual workers who, fearing they were being displaced by machinery, resorted to wrecking power looms, gig mills, stocking frames and other inventions. 'Ned Ludd', their eponymous unknown leader, came from Leicestershire. In March 1811 hosiers in Nottinghamshire, Derbyshire, and Leicestershire began the first wave of wrecking, which soon spread to Lancashire and Yorkshire. In these two counties twenty-four Luddite rioters were sentenced to death in January 1813. Luddism died down in 1818, giving way to a more specifically political form of radical protest.

LUNÉVILLE, Treaty of (9 February 1801)

Ended Continental participation in the War of the Second Coalition†. The Austrians, defeated at Marengo† and Hohenlinden†, sued for peace and received generous terms: ratification of the Campo Formio† settlement, so far as Austria was

179

concerned; the cession by Austria of Tuscany† to the Duke of Parma†, whose lands had been included in the Cisalpine Republic; recognition by Francis† as Holy Roman Emperor that the left bank of the Rhine should be incorporated in France, with an undertaking that the disinherited German princes would receive indemnities (see *Imperial Recess* and *Mediatization*). Although the Treaty of Amiens† did not follow for another thirteen months, Lunéville encouraged the movement among the commercial classes in London in favour of a general peace.

LÜTZEN, Battle of (2 May 1813)

The first major engagement of the 1813 campaign was fought around the villages of Gross Görschen and Kaja, twelve miles south-west of Leipzig and four miles south of the small town of Lützen, already famous for the battle of 6 November 1632 in which Gustavus Adolphus of Sweden was killed. Wittgenstein's Russians attacked what they believed to be isolated units of Ney's corps but found themselves unexpectedly engaged by the XI Corps (Macdonald†), VI Corps (Marmont†) and by the Imperial Guard†, too, with Napoleon himself arriving on the battlefield in the early afternoon, some three hours after the fighting started. Prussian reinforcements were severely mauled: Blücher† was incapacitated and Scharnhorst† so badly wounded that he died two months later. Successive attacks by the Young Guard and the Old Guard in the early evening thrust the Russo-Prussian forces back towards Dresden†, duly entered by the French five days later. For the first time, however, Napoleon was conscious that his shortage of cavalry horses limited his chances of turning an Allied defeat into a rout.

LYCÉES: see *Educational Reforms*.

M

MACDONALD, Jacques Alexandre
(1765–1840)
Marshal of the Empire: born at Sedan, his father being a cousin of the romantic Jacobite heroine, Flora Macdonald (1722–90). Alexandre Macdonald served in the Dutch army before being commissioned by Louis XVI in 1787. During the revolutionary campaigns he won steady promotion but saw service mainly in Germany and had little contact with Bonaparte who, in 1804, became prejudiced against him because of his friendship with the unfortunate Moreau.† Eugène Beauharnais† advanced his career from 1807 onwards and Macdonald won Napoleon's favour by his attack on the second day of Wagram†, an action which led to an immediate elevation to the marshalate. Five months later he was created Duke of Taranto and, after service in Spain, commanded X Corps in the Russian campaign, which he spent mainly around Riga and along the Baltic coast. At Lützen† Macdonald led an outflanking attack on the Russo-Prussian left, and it was his reconnaissance in force which enabled Napoleon to plan the enveloping movements of Bautzen†. Macdonald disobeyed orders on the Katzbach† and was defeated by Blücher†, but he showed great courage at Leipzig†. After the Restoration he supported Louis XVIII, whom he escorted into Belgium as Napoleon approached Paris. Macdonald supervised the dispersal of the remaining Napoleonic units after Waterloo.

MACK, Karl (Baron Mack von Leiberich 1752–1825)
Austrian general: born at Nennslingen in Bavaria, enlisted as a cavalry trooper in 1770 and was commissioned seven years later. He was in Joseph II's personal service from 1778 to 1788, being ennobled in 1785 and suffering a bad head wound in the Turkish wars. He was a courageous hard worker, a good chief of staff in Belgium in 1793, but unlucky in seeking to rouse the Neapolitans to defend their lands in 1798, when he was captured by the French, escaping in 1800. As Quartermaster-General from 1804 onwards, he was given joint command with Archduke Ferdinand† of the principal Austrian army in 1805. Napoleon's brilliant enveloping manoeuvres in front of Ulm† perplexed the defenders; there were serious differences between Mack and Ferdinand which were followed by Mack's confinement with 27,000 men in the city of Ulm. There, isolated for a week without hope of relief, Mack negotiated the surrender of his army. In 1807 he was court-martialled on the initiative of Archduke Charles†. Although sentenced to death he was reprieved and served eighteen months of imprisonment. In 1819 Schwarzenberg† secured his reinstatement. The archdukes treated him shabbily.

MADISON, James (1751–1836)
Fourth President of the United States: born in Virginia, helped framed the US

Constitution in accordance with views he had developed while writing papers for *The Federalist* (see *Hamilton*). He was Secretary of State, 1801–9, seeking to uphold neutral rights at sea threatened by both Britain and France. As President (1809–17) he was weak and vacillating, forced into the War of 1812† by the widespread anger in his home state at British impressment of American seamen and interception of American merchantmen. The misfortunes of the war lost him much prestige, only partially redeemed by the American victory at New Orleans after the peace terms had been signed at Ghent.

Mahmud II, Sultan of Turkey
(1785–1839, reigned 1808–39)
Was a nephew of the reforming sultan, Selim III (dethroned in July 1807) and the son of a French Creole mother brought to Constantinople by Barbary pirates. She had much influence on her son, educating

Mahmud II, Sultan of Turkey

him in western ideas; he owed his life, however, to a canny comprehension of Ottoman palace murder politics (see *Ottoman Empire*). Mahmud put down rebellious pashas in outlying provinces by playing off rival factions against each other, although he could not prevent the more distant provinces from breaking away in areas where Turkish control had long been weak, such as Serbia and Greece. He brought some vigour to the central government, destroying the powerful Janissaries† in a military *coup* (June 1826). His mental faculties failed rapidly from 1831 onwards.

MAIDA
Small Italian town in the foothills of Calabria, seven miles inland from the Gulf of Sant'Eufemia where, on 1 July 1806, 5,000 British troops landed in support of Ferdinand IV† of Naples†. The British commander, Sir John Stuart (1759–1815), defeated a French force at Maida on 6 July but failed to exploit his victory, heading southwards and returning to Sicily rather than encouraging a general insurrection against Joseph Bonaparte†. Maida showed the steadiness and musketry power of British infantry; it was the first tactical defeat sustained by the French imperial army.

MAISON
Napoleon's military household organization, his personal headquarters staff. From 1804 to 1813 the most important officers attached to the *Maison* were Berthier†, Duroc† and Caulaincourt† as well as aides-de-camp (Mouton†, Rapp†, Savary†, Flahaut† and others), personal 'secrétaires de cabinet' (originally Bourrienne†, later Méneval† and Fain†), the Topographical Office – which was headed by a former professional painter, General Bacler d'Albe (1761–1824) from 1804 until the close of 1813 – and personal servants, notably Constant (see *Wairy*) and

Roustam†. There was also attached to the *Maison* a field library with appropriate geographical studies of the battle areas and Napoleon's notebooks (*carnets*), with intelligence details of his own and his enemy's military units.

MAISTRE, Joseph de (1753–1821)

Diplomat and Christian philosopher: born at Chambéry (then in Sardinia-Piedmont). He bitterly opposed French ideas, his writings deploring nationalism, extreme monarchism, physical science and the rationalism of the *Idéologues†*. From 1803 to 1817 he was Sardinia's diplomatic envoy in St Petersburg, where, though respected, he was mistrusted for his 'jesuitical' proselytizing among the Russian nobility. His posthumously published *Soirées de Saint-Pétersbourg* are witty and paradoxical dialogues set in the Russian capital; they provide a strictly Catholic explanation of the role of Evil in Divine Providence, as revealed in the conversations of a French émigré, a Russian senator, and a count (Maistre himself). His extreme views on the impiety of his age complement the prejudices of Chateaubriand†. To some extent he was the apostle of the Ultramontanes, with their championship of papal supremacy over the rule of secular princes.

MALET CONSPIRACY

General Claude de Malet (1754–1812), a convinced republican despite his origins in the minor nobility, was arrested in 1808 for conspiracy but the affair was hushed up, largely through the intervention of Fouché†, who may well have been implicated. After a term of imprisonment, Malet was interned in a private asylum outside Paris. From there he escaped on 22 October 1812. Next day he published a forged Senate pronouncement that Napoleon had died in Russia; he then called on the people of Paris to support his own provisional republican government. He shot and wounded the commander of the Paris garrison and held the Minister of Police and the Prefect of Police under arrest. So great was the confusion that the Minister of War swore an oath of loyalty to the King of Rome† as Napoleon's successor. General Laborde marched troops from Saint-Cloud† into the centre of Paris, captured Malet and restored order with the assistance of Cambacérès†. Malet and fourteen accomplices were executed on 29 October; Napoleon did not hear of the conspiracy until 6 November when his retreating army reached Mikhailevska on the upper Dnieper. The affair emphasized to him the political instability in Paris so long as the sovereign of the Empire was snowbound in Russia, still east of Smolensk. He determined to shake off the peril of isolation as soon as possible ('My presence in Paris is essential for France') but it was not until 5 December that he was able to set out from Smorgon† for the capital.

MALMAISON

A country house some eight miles west of central Paris, purchased by Josephine† on 21 April 1799 and used frequently by Napoleon until 1805, less often during the peak years of the Empire and not at all between 21 March 1809 and 25 June 1815. Napoleon had the original, somewhat undistinguished, château improved in 1800 so as to include a large dining-room, a council chamber in his former bedroom on the ground floor, and a compact library. Josephine delighted in the gardens (considerably larger than they are now); the château was assigned to her after the divorce and she died there on 29 May 1814. The house then became the property of Hortense Beauharnais who was hostess there to her stepfather from 25 to 29 June 1815, after his second abdication† and before his departure for Rochefort† and ultimately St Helena. The château remained in private hands for most of the nineteenth century; it was restored, and

Napoleon in the gardens of Malmaison

presented to the French Republic in 1904. It is now the most attractive of Napoleonic museums.

MALOYAROSLAVETS

Town seventy-five miles south-west of Moscow† on the route to Kaluga; five roads converged there on a crossing over the River Lutsa. On 24–25 October 1812 Eugène Beauharnais† and the Army of Italy encountered two regiments of Kutuzov's main army. Town and bridge changed hands seven times before the Italians drove out the Russians, who suffered heavy casualties. Napoleon, who had left Moscow on 19 October to march on Kaluga and find a more southerly (and not 'scorched') route back to Poland, spent the night at Gorodnya, five miles north of Maloyaroslavets, and was nearly captured by Cossacks. The stiff resistance encountered by Eugène made him abandon his plan to march on Kaluga; he turned north and fell back along the route by which the *Grande Armée* had come two months before. The Russians claim that the battle of Maloyaroslavets was 'the beginning of the enemy's rout and ruin'.

MALTA

The island was a possession of the Knights of St John from 1530 until it was occupied by Bonaparte's *Armée de l'Orient* in a surprise assault on 12 June 1798. The pretext for seizing the island was a refusal by the knights to allow the French to replenish water supplies in Valetta as their fleet sailed to Egypt†. Bonaparte personally stayed in Valetta for five days, leaving a garrison of 4,000 men under the command of General Vaubois (1748–1839) to hold the island. Nelson† instituted a naval blockade of Malta two months later and attempts were made to aid Maltese rebels against the French occupation troops; but the blockade only began to affect the French forces in the summer of 1800. Vaubois capitulated on 5 September 1800 and was allowed to take his troops back to France, the British garrisoning Malta in place of the French. Meanwhile Tsar Paul† of Russia had made the French seizure of Malta one of the principal reasons why he entered the War of the Second Coalition†, since the Knights of St John, who held a priory in Russian Poland, had offered him the

Grand Mastership of their order when the island fell. Paul and his successor, Alexander I✝, continued to support the claims of the knights, against both France and Britain. By the Treaty of Amiens✝ the British undertook to restore the island to the knights, but declined to do so while the French were allegedly planning renewed war in the eastern Mediterranean. The first Treaty of Paris✝ of 1814 recognized the annexation of Malta and her dependencies by the British Crown.

MAMELUKES
Originally a name, derived from an Arab word for slave, given to the Circassian bodyguard of the rulers of twelfth-century Egypt✝. When the French landed in 1798, Egypt was governed by twenty-four Mameluke Beys, nominally under a Turkish viceroy; and Bonaparte claimed that he had come to liberate the Egyptian people (and French merchants) from the capricious tyranny of the Mamelukes. But Bonaparte was greatly impressed by the skill and bearing of 6,000 caparisoned Mameluke cavalry who, attended into battle by their own slaves, vainly charged the French positions at the pyramids✝. He accepted the gift of a Mameluke servant, Roustam✝, from Sheik El-Bekri in June 1799 and ordered General Rapp✝ to raise a squadron of Mamelukes who, from 1804 to 1814, were attached to the Imperial Guard as a picturesque and intimidating personal escort. In Egypt the last Mameluke Beys were massacred by Mehemet Ali in 1811.

MANTUA (Mantova)
Key fortress in Lombardy✝, set among lakes and marshes formed by the River Mincio. In 1796–7 an Austrian garrison held out for eight months against a French blockade and siege, thus delaying Bonaparte's victory in his first Italian campaign. The city was blockaded from 4 June 1796 until 31 July, when Bonaparte had to withdraw his troops to meet the Austrian challenge at Castiglione✝. He imposed a strict siege on 24 August. The defenders, strengthened after Bassano✝, attempted an unsuccessful sortie in mid-September, but were too ravaged by disease to take advantage of the movement of French forces to fight at Arcole✝ and Rivoli. Some 14,000 Austrians had perished from disease when Mantua capitulated (2 February 1797) although another 16,000 survived. The fall of Mantua enabled Bonaparte to concentrate his full strength against Archduke Charles✝.

MARENGO, Battle of (14 June 1800)
The first victory won by Bonaparte as First Consul. Marengo was a village two and a half miles east of the citadel of Alessandria✝, held by the Austrian commander, Friedrich von Melas. Bonaparte, seeking to re-establish his control of northern Italy, decided to divide his forces, sending two divisions north to cover the Po and a corps commanded by Desaix✝ to cover the River Scrivia. Within hours of Bonaparte's decision, Melas's troops emerged and surprised Victor✝ who, despite support from Lannes✝ and Murat✝, was forced back on Marengo itself, about midday. At the same time an Austrian enveloping movement threatened the whole of Bonaparte's position. He was saved by Desaix who, having heard the gunfire in the morning, brought his column back to give the commander-in-chief support in the late afternoon. Desaix, supported by Marmont✝ and the younger Kellermann✝, mounted a counter-attack in which Desaix himself was killed outright. The explosion of an ammunition waggon threw panic down the Austrian line; and the defeated Melas pulled back to Alessandria, agreeing on an armistice next day. For propaganda purposes, reports of Marengo were romanticized in detail and the battle was given a predetermined place in the strategy of the war which it never really possessed.

MARET, Hugues Bernard (1763–1839)

French diplomat and Foreign Minister: born at Dijon and was practising as a lawyer when the Revolution began. He was sent on a diplomatic mission to London in 1792, reported the Convention debates for the *Moniteur†*, set out for Naples† in June 1793 authorized to offer Marie Antoinette's life for a negotiated settlement, but was thrown into prison in Milan by the Austrians as he journeyed south. He was freed only by the arrival of Bonaparte's army in May 1796. After Brumaire† he was appointed Secretary of State, the government minister responsible for all communications between the First Consul (Emperor) and military and civilian administrative departments; he held this key post from 1799 to 1811 and again in 1814 and 1815. From the beginning of 1800, he also directed the *Moniteur*, giving it the stamp of official authority as a government organ. Napoleon created him Duke of Bassano in 1809. In April 1811 Maret replaced Champagny† as Foreign Minister and within four months was assisting Napoleon in the diplomatic preliminaries to the Russian campaign. From early July 1812 until the first week of December Maret was at Vilna†, accompanied by the six foreign envoys accredited to the Emperor. Napoleon replaced Maret by Caulaincourt† in late November 1813, largely because he thought Maret too warlike for peace negotiations. While Napoleon was on Elba, Maret secretly kept him informed on the state of French public opinion. After serving in the State Secretariat in the Hundred Days, Maret went into exile for five years before retiring to his native Burgundy.

MARIE LOUISE, Empress of the French (1791–1847)

Born at Vienna, eldest surviving daughter of Emperor Francis I† of Austria and therefore a great-niece of Queen Marie Antoinette. Metternich†, anxious to save Austria from Franco-Russian collaboration which might have ended Habsburg rule, urged Francis to offer his daughter as a second wife for Napoleon, when it was known that the Emperor of the French was hesitating whether to choose a Russian or an Austrian princess to be the mother of the heir his dynasty needed. A proxy marriage took place in Vienna on 11 March 1810, Napoleon meeting his bride for the first time on 27 March at Courcelles, east of Soissons. The religious ceremony was celebrated in the Louvre on 2 April, Cardinal Fesch† officiating. A son (see *Napoleon II*) was born on 20 March 1811. Marie Louise was empty-headed and sensual, never popular in France, and treated by Napoleon with an affection she did not return. She attended the royal congress at Dresden† in May 1812 and remained loyal to her husband until after his first abdication†. She left Paris with her son for Orleans on 29 March 1814. Emperor

The Empress Marie Louise, after a canvas by Gérard

Francis ignored suggestions from Napoleon that Marie Louise might head a Regency for 'Napoleon II' and she returned to Vienna. While she was taking the waters at Aix-les-Bains in July, General Neipperg† was sent from Milan to serve as her personal aide-de-camp. By September they were lovers. Marie Louise became sovereign Duchess of Parma†, Piacenza and Guastalla, technically reigning from 10 April 1814 until her death. She married Neipperg at Parma in September 1821; they had two sons and two daughters. In February 1834, five years after Neipperg's death, she married Count Bombelles (1785–1856). She became prematurely old, her figure made gross by dropsy, and she died in Vienna in December 1847 while Metternich, who had shaped her adult life, still had four more months of office at the Foreign Ministry.

MARMONT, Auguste Frédéric Louis Viesse de (1774–1852)
Marshal of the Empire: born at Châtillon-sur-Seine and, having fought at Toulon, became one of Bonaparte's inner circle of military aides throughout the Italian and Egyptian campaigns. In 1800 he commanded the artillery at Marengo† and, before he was twenty-seven, he held the equivalent rank to a major-general. After fighting before Ulm†, he captured Dubrovnik (then known as Ragusa) from a Russian force in 1805 and was Governor of Dalmatia until the region was incorporated into the Empire as the Illyrian Provinces† in 1809. He was responsible for the only good roads around Dubrovnik between the Roman Empire and the Tito dictatorship; and in 1808 he took the name Ragusa as the title of his dukedom. In 1809 he defeated Archduke Charles† at Znaim five days after Wagram and received his marshal's baton in recognition of his victory. After another eighteen months in Illyria, he was sent to Portugal† in May 1811. Wellington† outmanoeuvred him at Salamanca† (22 July 1812), an

action in which Marmont was badly wounded. In 1813–14 he commanded VI Corps at all the major battles but was censured by Napoleon for ineptly handling his troops at Laon†. He surrendered VI Corps independently to the Allies on 5 April 1814 at a time when Napoleon, in Fontainebleau†, was allegedly hoping to lead it in an effort to recover Paris. For this apparent treachery – and for voting in favour of Ney's execution in December 1815 – Marmont has had a bad press from patriotic French historians. He served the restored Bourbons as a Peer of France until 1830, spending the last twenty-two years of his life in exile, mainly in Venice. Prejudice has done less than justice to Marmont's imaginative skill and administrative talent.

MARSHALS
The Bourbon kings traditionally honoured esteemed commanders with the title 'Marshal of France', the last appointment of the *ancien régime* being that of the Duke de Broglie (1718–1804). On 19 May

Marshal Marmont

1804, the day after becoming Emperor, Napoleon revived the marshalate by creating, at Saint-Cloud†, eighteen Marshals of the Empire. Fourteen were his close companions in arms: Augereau†, Bernadotte†, Berthier†, Bessières†, Brune†, Davout†, Jourdan†, Lannes†, Masséna†, Moncey†, Mortier†, Murat†, Ney†, Soult†. The others were distinguished elderly commanders, 'Senatorial Marshals': Kellermann†, Lefebvre†, Pérignon†, Sérurier†. After Friedland† (July 1807) Victor† was made a marshal; Macdonald†, Marmont† and Oudinot† after Wagram† (July 1809); Suchet†, for services in Spain and Portugal, in July 1811; Gouvion Saint-Cyr† on 27 August 1812, after Polotsk†; Poniatowski† on 16 October 1813, in the Leipzig campaign; and Grouchy†, during the Hundred Days, on 3 June 1815. The marshals received grants of money as well as enjoying the prestige of the new aristocracy. In the imperial family only Jerome Bonaparte† received a marshal's baton, from his nephew Louis-Napoleon as Prince-President of France in 1850.

MARTINIQUE

Island in the Lesser Antilles group of the West Indies†, forty miles long and fifteen miles wide. It was colonized by the French in 1635, the principal crops being sugarcane and bananas. The future Empress Josephine† was born there, near the settlement of Trois-Îlets, in June 1763. Black rioters demanding slave emancipation brought anarchy to the island in 1790. Sir John Jervis and a British naval force occupied Martinique in 1794 but it was returned to France by the Treaty of Amiens† and its defences were then strengthened. Villeneuve†, with a powerful naval squadron, used Martinique briefly as a base in the summer of 1805, Nelson† pursuing the squadron across the Atlantic and back again. Early in 1809 a British force of 10,000 men from Barbados captured Martinique as part of the general policy of mopping up France's colonies in the West Indies. French sovereignty was restored in 1815; Martinique became an overseas département of France in 1946.

MASSÉNA, André (1758–1817)

Marshal of the Empire: born at Nice, ran away to sea in 1771, subsequently rising to the rank of sergeant-major in Louis XVI's army. By 1792 he was a lieutenant-colonel of volunteers fighting along the Italian borders, near his birthplace. He rose rapidly to high command and fought at almost all the battles in the Italian campaign, playing a decisive role in the victory of Rivoli and in the capture of Mantua†. His most remarkable achievement was to have checked the run of Russo-Austrian victories in September 1799 by his success at Zurich†. His army suffered considerably during the siege of Genoa† in 1800

André Massena, holding his Marshal's baton

and he was temporarily discredited a year later by the blatant plundering which he encouraged in northern Italy, an aspect of his character which gave credence to tales that he had been a smuggler during his youth. After becoming a marshal in 1804, he returned to Italy, first to engage the Archduke Charles† at Caldiero† and later to invade Naples. He fought with distinction at Aspern† and Wagram† (1809), was created Prince of Essling in January 1810 and, in the spring, was sent to command in Portugal†. His year in the Peninsula marked an unsatisfactory closing of his military career: after successes at Ciudad Rodrigo† and Almeida†, he was unable to breach Wellington's defences at Torres Vedras† and was roundly defeated at Fuentes de Oñoro†. He found it difficult to collaborate with Ney† and Junot† and offended his senior officers by taking with him on his campaign his mistress, Henriette Leberton, disguised as a dragoon officer. He took no part in the campaigns of 1813–15. By temperament he was a cunning, lecherous, unlearned natural fighter, who by 1810–11 had become a Franco-Italian Kutuzov. His reputation has suffered from the spiteful memoirs of Laure Junot† who jealously resented the apparent charms of Henriette Leberton.

MAXIMILIAN I, King of Bavaria
(1756–1825)
Born at Mannheim and generally known as Maximilian Joseph. He became Elector of Bavaria† and Elector Palatine on 16 February 1799, and followed an astute policy by which, from 1801 to 1813, Bavaria collaborated with France and made territorial gains at the expense of Austria, while Maximilian left himself ready to bargain with France's enemies so as to retain his influence and status in south Germany's affairs. He was raised to the dignity of King on 26 December 1805 and secured Allied recognition of his title before changing sides in the first week of October 1813. He was also able to keep most of the reforms which he had introduced into Bavaria during the period of French primacy. In the last years of his reign he showed a typically Wittelsbach dynastic delight in patronizing the arts, particularly in Munich.

MEDIATIZATION
The process proposed in the Treaty of Lunéville† and prescribed in detail in the Imperial Recess†, by which between 1803 and 1810 most of the ecclesiastical and small secular states of the Holy Roman Empire† surrendered their rights to the jurisdiction of the larger rulers. The families deprived of territorial authority retained their rank and titles as Princes, Counts, etc. and continued to fight for compensation and, notably in 1813–15, for restitution. They gained only token success even though many of the most distinguished families in Habsburg service were among the mediatized: Esterhazy, Metternich†, Schwarzenberg†, Stadion†, and others.

MÉHUL, Étienne Nicolas (1763–1817)
French composer: born at Givet in the French Ardennes, became an organist and was commissioned to write for the Paris Opéra in 1789. He composed five symphonies and several musical dramas (notably *Joseph*) as well as piano sonatas and choral music. Much of his work reflected the political mood of the time: a *Hymn to Reason* in 1793; the famous *Chant du Départ* on 4 July 1794; *La Prise du pont de Lodi*, a propaganda musical tableau lauding Bonaparte as early as 1796; a highly original cantata for two full-sized choirs and known as the *Chant national du 14 juillet 1800*; a choral work to celebrate the return of the *Grande Armée* in 1808; and a cantata to mark Napoleon's marriage to Marie Louise. Not surprisingly, Méhul was Napoleon's favourite French composer.

MELZI D'ERIL, Francesco, Count
(1753–1816)

Milanese politician: born in Milan† and for a time a court chamberlain to the Empress Maria Theresa. Although a member of the lesser nobility, he took a leading part in the foundation of the Transpadane Republic and its conversion in 1797 into the Cisalpine Republic†. He was one of the triumvirs of the Republic and, in January 1802, became Vice-President of the Italian Republic, a post which made him effective head of the executive. A French-influenced judicial system, a concordat, a gendarmerie, and a Ministry of Finance were introduced by Melzi, who was, however, suspected by Napoleon in 1803 of seeking independence and national recognition from Austria. When Napoleon, in May 1804, notified Melzi of his wish to transform the Italian Republic into a Kingdom of Italy†, the Vice-President devised a constitutional scheme which would have given greater independence to the administration in Milan than the Emperor desired. Napoleon set aside these proposals and appointed his stepson, Eugène Beauharnais† as Viceroy rather than Melzi, who became Duke of Lodi (1807) and Grand Chancellor. He deputized for the Viceroy during Eugène's absence at the wars in 1809 and 1812–13. His conduct in 1814 was devious, Melzi having developed a form of gout which regularly left him incapacitated on his estate at Como during periods of turmoil in Milan. He did not long survive the restoration of Habsburg rule.

MÉNEVAL, Claude François de
(1778–1850)

Napoleon's secretary: born into an aristocratic family. His industry and discretion commended themselves to the First Consul in 1802 on the disgrace of Bourrienne† and Méneval served Napoleon continuously from 1802 to 1813, when he was succeeded by Fain†, who had assisted Méneval from 1806 onwards. In his memoirs Méneval describes how he would take dictation from Napoleon, normally at seven in the morning, occasionally as early as four or five o'clock. From 1813 to 1815 he was attached to Marie Louise's suite; he accompanied her back to Vienna, but left her in disgust when it was clear that she was emotionally dominated by Neipperg†.

MENOU, Jacques (1750–1810)

French general: born, a marquis's son, at Boussay in Touraine and was a colonel when the Revolution began. His military career was undistinguished and he was distrusted by the Directory. Bonaparte, however, gave him a divisional command in Egypt† in 1798; he was wounded during the assault on Alexandria†. Thereafter he served as Governor of Rosetta, taking no part in military operations. He was a fanatical believer in France's need to colonize Egypt. To Bonaparte's satisfaction he became a Moslem, adding 'Abdallah' to his first name and marrying Zobeida, daughter of a bath-keeper in Rosetta. On Kléber's murder, he took command of the army in Egypt, was defeated by the British outside Alexandria and capitulated (August-September 1801). By the end of the year he was back in France, with wife and child. He never again commanded in the field, but he held several administrative posts; he was Governor of Venice at the time of his death.

MERCANTILISM

A term used to describe the normal theory of trading practice in the seventeenth and eighteenth centuries which assumed that one nation's gain was another nation's loss and that prosperity could be reckoned by the amount of silver and gold flowing into a country. This theory favoured tariffs and protectionism and therefore corresponded closely to Napoleon's natural inclination, reaching its most organized form in the Continental System†. Against mercantilism were the doctrines of Adam Smith (1723–90), assuming that the 'wealth of nations' depends upon free international commerce. Under Pitt†, Britain was moving away from mercantilism at the moment when Napoleon was seeking to give it new life, but wartime conditions necessarily imposed artificial restraint, postponing the era of free trade by several decades.

MÈRE, Mme
Title by which Letizia Bonaparte† was known from May 1804.

METRIC SYSTEM
Under the *ancien régime* weights and measures varied in name and meaning from region to region, and from one country to another. A metric system (grams, metres, litres) was proposed in the National Assembly in 1791, Talleyrand being among its champions. Although attempts were made to establish the system during the Revolution, it was another eight years before scientific commissions reported on the correct size of the basic units, which were settled by law early in the Consulate (December 1799). The metric system was officially introduced in France in 1801, although alternative weights and measures survived for another thirty years. The conveniently standardized system was spread over the Continent by Napoleon's armies and survived the fall of his Empire, assisting the internationalization of science and mathematics.

METTERNICH, Clement Wenceslas Lothar von (1773–1859)
Austrian statesman: born in Coblenz, the son of a diplomat in Habsburg service. He was educated at the universities of Strasbourg and Mainz, undertook a special mission to London in 1792–4, assisted his father at the Congress of Rastatt† in 1798

Prince Metternich in 1815, based on the portrait by Lawrence

and was appointed Austrian envoy to Saxony in 1801. From 1803 to 1805 he served in Berlin and then held the important post of ambassador in Paris from August 1806 until April 1809, establishing close relations with Talleyrand† and coming to know Napoleon well. Francis I† appointed Metternich Foreign Minister on 8 October 1809; he held the post continuously until 13 March 1848. From 1809 to 1813 Metternich favoured collaboration with France; he promoted Habsburg-Bonapartist marriage (see *Marie Louise*) and was himself in Paris from March to September 1810. Metternich kept Austrian support of France to a minimum during the Russian campaign, withdrawing the expeditionary force under Schwarzenberg† from active operations in February 1813 and seeking a general negotiated peace over the following six months. His efforts culminated in a dramatic meeting with Napoleon at the Marcolini Palace in Dresden† on 26 June 1813 in which he claims to have realized that nothing could save the French Empire. Metternich then collaborated with Prussia and Russia; his relations with Tsar Alexander I† were frequently tense; from January 1814 he found Castlereagh† a more natural ally. The Austro-Russian rift was even more marked during the Vienna Congress†, largely through Metternich's distrust of Russian policy in Poland† and Saxony†. Napoleon's return from Elba restored inter-Allied cohesion. The peace settlement of 1815 was a triumph for Metternich, leaving the Austrian Empire almost half as large again as when he took office and extending Habsburg influence throughout the new German Confederation and Italy. He sought to perpetuate the settlement for the rest of his career, favouring joint Great Power action to check manifestations of 'Jacobin' liberalism. Although the revolutions of 1848 technically ended his system of Great Power diplomacy and forced him to flee to England, Metternich returned to Vienna in September 1851 and exerted great influence as Austria's 'elder statesman' until a few weeks before his death. Emperor Francis created him a Prince after Leipzig† (October 1813) and gave him the coveted rank of Chancellor on 25 May 1821. Personally Metternich regarded the years of Napoleonic upheaval as the climax of his life.

MILAN

Capital of Lombardy† and successively of the Transpadane, Cisalpine and Italian Republics† (1796–1805) and of the Napoleonic Kingdom of Italy† (1805–14), remaining the second largest city in Italy today. Masséna† entered Milan at the head of the French army on 14 May 1796, four days after Bonaparte's victory at Lodi†; Bonaparte himself received a delegation of Milanese dignitaries, headed by Melzi d'Eril†, at Melegnano on 13 May and entered the city to a triumphant welcome on 15 May, seeking in eight days to organize a republican form of government in the void left by the withdrawal of Austrian authority. Milan became his chief residence; he lived, with Josephine†, in great state at the Serbelloni Palace or at Mombello until November 1797, when

not campaigning. Napoleon's mother, Letizia Bonaparte†, was welcomed by the Milanese on 1 June 1797. At the end of April 1798 the Austro-Russian Allies captured Milan; when Bonaparte recovered the city on 2 June 1800, he was received less rapturously for fear of Austrian reprisals, but his popularity increased after his victory at Marengo†. From 12 May to 10 June 1805 Napoleon and Josephine were at Milan for his coronation† in the cathedral (26 May), a time of great festivity. Eugène Beauharnais†, as Viceroy, preferred to live at neighbouring Monza but received Napoleon formally in Milan in November and December 1807 on the Emperor's last visit to Italy. When the Empire fell in 1814, there was rioting and bloodshed in Milan (20 April) and the city was occupied by the courteous Austrian commander, Marshal Bellegarde.

MILAN DECREES (23 November and 17 December 1807)

Regulations which intensified economic warfare by expanding the Berlin Decree† of 1806. The First Milan Decree provided for the confiscation of ships, with their cargoes, if they had touched at British ports, and threatened confiscation of any goods not accompanied by a certificate indicating that they had originated outside Britain and her dependencies. The Second Milan Decree declared that any neutral vessel which had submitted to British naval orders would no longer be considered neutral, and might therefore be confiscated as a prize of war. Neither decree was totally enforceable.

MILORADOVICH, Mikhail Andreevich (1770–1825)

Russian general: born in St Petersburg, saw service against the Turks and in Poland and by 1799 commanded the Aspheron Regiment under Suvorov† in the Alps. He again led the regiment at

Austerlitz†. In 1812 he commanded the rearguard after Borodino†, delaying Napoleon's advance on Moscow and, eventually, negotiating the surrender of the city. During the retreat from Moscow Miloradovich harried the French from the north, launching a ferocious flank attack on Davout's† Corps three miles east of Vyazma (3 November 1812) and another one a fortnight later at Krasnoe†. He almost cut off Ney† as the French rearguard pulled away from Smolensk. In May 1813 he checked an advance by Eugène Beauharnais† at Colditz, three days after the Allied defeat at Lützen† and he contributed considerably to the victory at Kulm† in August. At the end of the wars he became Governor of Kiev and was appointed Military Governor of St Petersburg in 1819. When some of the garrison mutinied in support of the Decembrist radicals, Miloradovich was fired on as he tried to restore order and fell mortally wounded in Senate Square (26 December 1825). His courage, horsemanship and generous pride induced his brother officers to refer to him as 'our Murat'.

MINISTRY OF ALL THE TALENTS
Name given to the coalition government established in London on 10 February 1806 after the death of Pitt†. It was headed by Grenville†, though the dominant personality was, at first, Fox†. The coalition was not as broad as the name suggests: it comprised two groups of Tories (the followers of Grenville and of Addington†) and the Foxite Whigs. When Fox died seven months after taking office, the rift between the factions began to widen, although 'the Talents' won a general election in December 1806. Its greatest achievement was legislation ending the slave trade†. The coalition disintegrated over the vexed issue of Catholic Emancipation†, and the government fell on 24 March 1807. George III invited Portland† to form a new government; no Foxite Whig held office again until 1830.

MIRANDA, Francisco de (1750–1816)
Latin American general: born in Caracas (now in Venezuela) of Creole descent. He gained military experience in the American War of Independence, came to Europe, was promoted general in the Army of Belgium and fought at Valmy (1792); his troops occupied Antwerp in November 1792. Accusations of treason brought him under suspicion in 1794 and he was fortunate to escape from France and find refuge in England, where he began to work for Venezuelan independence. The British decision to send an expeditionary force to Portugal† rather than to South America in 1808 dashed his hopes, but it was not until 1811 that he arrived back at his birthplace. For eight months he led the Venezuelan rebels in their struggle against Spanish rule. In July 1812 he was forced to surrender to the Spanish irregular commander, Monteverde. Miranda was eventually brought to Cadiz, where he died in prison.

MONCEY, Jeannot de (1754–1842)
Marshal of the Empire: born at Palise, in central France. He enlisted as a private when he was fifteen years old, and was commissioned by Louis XVI in 1779. Most of his military experience was gained in Spain. In the Pyrenees, 1793–5, he rose from captain to the equal of a major-general and he received his marshal's baton from Napoleon in May 1804. In 1808–9 he was in Spain again, besieging Saragossa†, becoming Duke of Conegliano in June 1808. Moncey's greatest skill was in mountain warfare. He also had administrative ability and was used occasionally by Napoleon as an itinerant inspector general. He later served the Bourbons, commanding the troops that occupied Catalonia in 1825. Technically, from 1824 until his death, Marshal de Moncey was Governor of the Invalides. In this capacity he received Napoleon's remains when they were brought back from St Helena† in December 1840.

Moniteur (In full, *Le Moniteur universel*) Founded as a liberal national gazette on 24 November 1789 under the direction of the publisher Charles-Joseph Panckoucke (1736–98). It reported, with semi-official detachment, the debates in the Constituent Assembly, the National Assembly and the Convention as well as all decrees and military bulletins. 'Buonaparte' is first mentioned on 14 October 1793, as a captain who had distinguished himself at Toulon†. From 28 December 1799 the *Moniteur* became, in effect, the Bonapartist official journal, soon passing under the direction of the Secretary of State, Maret†. Copies of the *Moniteur* were circulated to armies in the field and sent to foreign capitals for propaganda purposes. Occasionally Napoleon dictated an article himself, an anonymous statement of policy. He ordered the *Moniteur* to be read aloud at mealtimes in the lycées† so as to introduce pupils to current affairs. On 19 April 1807 Napoleon explained to the Minister of the Interior (Champagny†) that he 'saw no reason why the back page of the *Moniteur* should not be set aside for literary articles or criticism, written by men selected by the Minister'. By 1811 it was one of only four newspapers allowed in Paris, the others being *Le Journal de l'Empire*, *Le Journal de Paris* and *La Gazette de France*, all subject to censorship†. The prestige of the *Moniteur* ensured that it continued, as a government-inspired publication, under the restored Bourbons. In 1868 it fell foul of Napoleon III's government and was replaced by *Le Journal officiel*.

MONTENOTTE, Battle of (12 April 1796) Fought on high ground some eleven miles inland from Savona† on the Ligurian coast. Bonaparte employed Masséna's mountain brigade to drive a wedge between his Austrian and Piedmontese enemies, gaining tactical successes which he failed to exploit because he had not foreseen the difficulties of a night march in this terrain. Montenotte was Bonaparte's first victory as an army commander.

MONTHOLON, Charles Tristan, Comte de (1783–1853) French soldier: born in Paris, was successively aide-de-camp to Augereau†, Macdonald† and Berthier† before becoming an imperial chamberlain at the age of twenty-six. Next year he was briefly attached to the suite of the Empress Josephine† when she resided at the castle of Navarre in Normandy. Although popularly known as 'General de Montholon', he was in fact a colonel when he became Napoleon's aide-de-camp in 1815 on the eve of Waterloo. Together with his wife, Montholon accompanied Napoleon to St Helena†. She returned to France in poor health in 1819; he remained with Napoleon until the end. It was Montholon who addressed a 'remonstrance' to Hudson Lowe† complaining of the indignities inflicted on Napoleon; the remonstrance was smuggled to England and published by sympathizers with the fallen Emperor in March 1817. Montholon was unpopular with Napoleon's suite, some of his colleagues suspecting he was a royalist agent. Memoirs, based allegedly on Napoleon's small talk, were published in 1823; his better-known (and unreliable) *Récits de la captivité de Napoléon à Sainte-Hélène* came out in two volumes in 1847. By 1838 he was in London with Louis Napoleon Bonaparte†; he participated in the abortive coup at Boulogne in 1840 and shared captivity with the future Napoleon III until 1847. A year later Montholon was elected to the National Assembly and supported the gradual transition from Second Republic to Second Empire.

MONTMIRAIL, Battle of (11 February 1814) A sharp rebuff inflicted by Napoleon on a Russian corps in Blücher's army and on a

Prussian advance guard under Yorck†, the action immediately following the French victory at neighbouring Champaubert†. Napoleon, with the Old Guard† and young conscripts, marched westwards through the small town of Montmirail along the valley of the Petit Morin, to strike at the Allied force advancing carelessly through the mud towards Paris, sixty miles to the west. Yorck was able to save the Russian corps from destruction, but Blücher† ordered the Allied troops to fall back north of the River Marne and regroup before resuming the offensive. This check to the Allied advance gave Napoleon an opportunity to turn and face Blücher himself three days later at Vauchamps†, east of Montmirail.

MOORE, John (1761–1809)

British soldier: born in Glasgow, the son of a physician who was also a distinguished writer. Moore was commissioned in the infantry in 1776, fought in the American War of Independence and entered the Commons as a Whig MP in 1784. As a colonel in 1794–5 he served in Corsica, attached to Paoli†; a year later he commanded a brigade in the West Indies. He distinguished himself when, as a major-general, he commanded the landing of Abercromby's army at Aboukir†, an event vividly recorded in his published diary. A fortnight later he was wounded in the night battle of 21 March 1801. From 1802 to 1805 he was in charge of infantry in England, mainly at Shorncliffe in Kent, where he would have been in a position to meet the challenge of invasion. He was then sent to Portugal and on 27 October 1808 set out from Lisbon, with 30,000 men, to help the Spaniards resist Napoleon's invasion. By mid-December he was at Salamanca†, thus threatening French communications from Bayonne to Madrid. On hearing that Napoleon had turned back to deal with this menace, Moore conducted a masterly retreat through mountains deep in snow to reach Corun-

na†, where he successfully defied Soult's† attempts to prevent the evacuation of the British army. In the final phase of the battle Moore was mortally wounded.

MOREAU, Jean Victor Marie (1763–1813)

French general: born at Morlaix in Brittany, his father being a prominent lawyer, who was guillotined. Moreau became a brigadier in 1793 with only two years' military experience behind him, and commanded the Army of the Rhine from 1795 to 1797, when he was dismissed for conniving at the royalist conspiracy of Pichegru. After assisting Bonaparte in Brumaire†, he again fought along the Rhine in 1800, gaining a striking victory at Hohenlinden†. He could, however, never shake off the suspicion of royalist intrigue, and was seen by Bonaparte as a rival contender for power. Moreau was arrested in February 1804, allegedly for having contacts with Cadoudal† and Pichegru. He was acquitted on a charge of treason but was subsequently sent into exile. He settled on the Delaware River, living at Morrisville for over eight years before returning to Europe as an adviser to the Tsar during the 1813 campaign in Germany. He was wounded at Alexander's side during the battle of Dresden† and died five days later. To some extent his ambitions were fired by his Creole wife, envious of her compatriot and former friend, Josephine.

MORTIER, Édouard Adolphe Casimir Joseph (1768–1835)

Marshal of the Empire: born at Cateau-Cambrésis in the extreme north of France, the son of a wealthy linen merchant who married an Englishwoman. He fought in the early battles of the Revolutionary Wars, served under Masséna† and Soult† and commanded a division in 1799–1800. Bonaparte sent him to occupy Hanover†, gave him his marshal's baton in May 1804 and appointed him commander of the infantry of the Imperial Guard‡. His imperturbability under stress at Friedland‡ won Napoleon's admiration and he was created Duke of Treviso in 1808. After participating in the sieges of Saragossa‡ and Badajoz‡ he accompanied Napoleon on the Russian campaign, deliberately failing to carry out orders to blow up Moscow‡ when left as Governor of the city on Napoleon's withdrawal (19 September 1812). Mortier rejoined the main body of the *Grande Armée* before the Berezina‡ and fought in every major battle of the 1813 campaign. In 1814 he showed inventive improvisation at Montmirail‡ and Laon‡. Illness prevented him from serving in the Waterloo campaign. In 1834 he became Louis Philippe's Minister of War and was assassinated during a bomb attempt on the King's life (28 July 1835).

Moscow

The national capital of Russia from the sixteenth century until 1703 and thereafter the spiritual centre of Orthodox Christianity. The defence of 'Holy Moscow' in 1812 was, in the first instance, the responsibility of the Governor-General, Rostopchin‡, who made a great show of expelling the French émigré community from the city and parading wretched 'French spies' through the streets. The decision not to fight on the hills outside Moscow was taken by Marshal Kutuzov‡ in a conference at Fili, to the west of the city, on 13 September 1812. Kutuzov believed the occupation of Moscow would overstrain French resources, provided Russia kept what remained of her army intact and refused to make peace. Rostopchin, though disagreeing with Kutuzov, ordered fire-raisers to remain in Moscow

A French propaganda representation of the burning of Moscow on the orders of 'Governor Roptoskin' (sic)

after it was evacuated by most of its people. Napoleon entered the city on 15 September, took up residence that night at the Kremlin but next day was forced to find refuge in the Petrovsky Palace, north of the city which was in flames. The Great Fire of Moscow burned for four days and destroyed three-quarters of the old city; drunken carousing by the occupying troops added to the work of the arsonists. Napoleon was disappointed in his hopes that the fall of Moscow would bring peace. He evacuated the city on 19 October. Mortier† remained, with 8,000 men, to blow up what remained of the city, a task he did not attempt, withdrawing his forces four days later. Over the following three months deaths from infectious diseases in the ruined city decimated the army and the civilians who returned to Moscow. Rebuilding had advanced sufficiently for Alexander I† to be received in state at the Kremlin in the autumn of 1817.

MOSCOW, RETREAT FROM

Should technically be called the 'Retreat from Maloyaroslavets'†, as Napoleon did not order the *Grande Armée* to break off contact with the enemy and retire along the main Smolensk road until 26 October, after the fierce engagement at that small town above the Lutsa. Slightly less than 100,000 men accompanied Napoleon on the retreat, which began in fine autumn weather. Flank attacks by Miloradovich† near Vyazma on 3 November and later at Krasnoe† harried the French. Snow began to fall on 4 November and was severe by 6 November, three days before Napoleon reached Smolensk†, where there were relief supplies for less than a week. Cossack raids, attacks from partisans†, and the worsening frost took a heavy toll, but the French were able to avoid the trap set by converging Russian armies, crossing the River Berezina† on pontoon bridges (26–9 November). Napoleon left the *Grande Armée* at Smorgon† on the night of 5–6 December.

When Ney† led the rearguard across the Niemen† and out of Russia on 14 December, the army had an effective strength of a thousand men, not counting stragglers and the temporarily non-combatant sick. The retreat lost Napoleon prestige throughout his Empire; the gamble of the Russian campaign had cost nearly half a million men and over 150,000 horses. It was possible, after the retreat, to raise new armies; it was not possible to find and to train the new cavalry horses.

MOUTON, Georges (1770–1838)

French general: born at Phalsbourg in Lorraine. He was successively aide-de-camp to Joubert (1798), Masséna† (1800) and Napoleon (1805–9), fighting beside the Emperor in all the major battles of the period. He was a senior staff officer in Russia in 1812, following Napoleon back from Smorgon† mainly on a sledge, so as to help plan the next phase of the wars. At Dresden† he was taken prisoner but he was with Napoleon at Waterloo, where he was wounded. Napoleon admired his loyalty and courage ('*Mon mouton est un lion*') and created him Count of Lobau (1809). King Louis Philippe gave him a baton as a Marshal of France in July 1831.

MURAT, Joachim (1767–1815)

Marshal of the Empire, King of Naples; born at Labastide-Fortunière in the Guyenne, between the Dordogne and the Lot. He was the youngest of the eleven children of an innkeeper, who hoped Joachim would be a priest. Instead, he entered the army in 1787 as a trooper, becoming a cavalry officer in October 1792. He supplied the guns which Bonaparte used at Vendémiaire† in October 1795 and was his chief aide throughout the early stages of the Italian campaign. By 1797 he was already respected as a cavalry leader of great courage, a quality he showed again in Egypt†. He helped Bonaparte in Brumaire† and was made first

Detailed sketches by David's friend and pupil, Baron Gros, of Murat

commander of the Consular Guard; his panache attracted Caroline Bonaparte†, whom he married in January 1800. He fought with astonishing bravery at Marengo†, remaining in Italy for operations against Ferdinand IV† of Naples until June 1802. In 1804 he became a marshal, was given the title of Prince in February 1805 and commanded the cavalry in the Austerlitz† campaign to such effect that on 13 November 1805 he occupied Vienna. Although he became a sovereign ruler as

Grand Duke of Berg and Cleves in March 1806 he continued to serve Napoleon as the finest cavalry commander in Europe, distinguishing himself at Jena† and Eylau† in particular. As Napoleon's deputy in Spain he savagely suppressed the Madrid insurrection of 2 May 1808. Two months later he succeeded Joseph Bonaparte† as ruler of Naples† (King Gioacchino Napoleone, ruled 1 August 1808 to 19 May 1815), and he resided in his kingdom until 1812 when he joined Napoleon again to command the cavalry, and generally the advance guard, in the invasion of Russia. He was prominent in the battles of Smolensk† and Borodino†; and, just as he had been the first general to enter Vienna, so, too, he led the *Grande Armée* into Moscow a day ahead of Napoleon. During the French occupation of Moscow, Murat was frequently engaged with Russian troops some thirty miles outside the city. His relations with Davout† were strained during the campaign, but Murat was idolized by his troops and feared by the Russians and he was therefore given command of the *Grande Armée* when Napoleon left it at Smorgon† for Paris. This was not the type of warfare to which Murat was accustomed; at Vilna† there was complete administrative chaos; his nerve seems to have cracked and he prematurely evacuated the city, but he brought what remained of the *Grande Armée* back to Prussia before handing over command to Eugène Beauharnais† on 18 January 1813

and returning to Naples. Murat fought beside Napoleon again at Dresden† and Leipzig†. He then sought to come to terms with the British and Austrians to save his Neapolitan kingdom and signed a treaty with Austria on 11 January 1814; he did not take any action against French troops but remained on his throne after Napoleon's first abdication†. Fear that Britain would back Ferdinand IV and exclude his claims, led Murat to call on all Italians to fight under his leadership for the national cause when Napoleon escaped from Elba. But Murat had few troops and was defeated at Tolentino on 2 May 1815. He escaped to France but Napoleon foolishly declined his offer to lead the cavalry in the Waterloo campaign. Murat then made a last attempt to raise rebellion in Italy, landing in Calabria on 8 October. He was soon captured, court-martialled and shot by a firing squad at the Castello di Pizzo (13 October 1815).

N

NAPLES

Was united with the Norman duchy of Sicily to form a kingdom in the eleventh century. This was governed by Spanish viceroys from 1504 to 1707 and thereafter by Austria until conquered by Don Carlos, son of Philip V of Spain, in 1734. Don Carlos became the first King of Naples and Sicily (Charles I) in 1735 and was succeeded by his son, Ferdinand IV† in 1759. In December 1798, with Austrian military aid and British naval support, Ferdinand attempted to overthrow the puppet republic set up by the French in Rome†. This action proved disastrous; the royal court fled to Sicily while the French entered Naples and in January 1799 set up the Parthenopean Republic†. When six months later the French forces left Naples to meet the threat from Suvorov† in northern Italy, Ferdinand sent Cardinal Ruffo to the mainland with the 'Army of the Holy Faith', a motley force of 40,000 men which included the notorious brigand, Fra Diavolo (Michele Pezza, 1771–1806). In two days of arson and looting Ruffo's army so devastated the city of Naples that the Parthenopean commander, Admiral Francesco Caracciolo, agreed to capitulate in return for a safe conduct for his supporters to Marseilles. These terms were ignored by the British naval commander, Nelson†, who hanged Caracciolo from the yard-arm of his own flagship; more than a hundred of the republicans were also executed. Ferdinand remained ruler of Naples until 1806 when Napoleon, fearing that Britain would take Calabria and use it as the base for a movement to liberate Italy (see *Maida*), declared 'the dynasty of Naples

has ceased to reign'. A French army again marched south, Ferdinand fled to Palermo and Joseph Bonaparte† became King, to be succeeded on 1 August 1808 by Murat†. Reforms were introduced and Murat sought to avoid complete integration of his kingdom into the Continental System†. In 1814 he tried to save his kingdom by negotiations with Metternich†. The British, however, stood by their commitments to Ferdinand IV who, in Sicily†, had been backed by the highly individualistic British envoy, Bentinck†. A series of miscalculations in 1815 cost Murat not only his crown but his life. Ferdinand returned to Naples and reigned until his death in 1825. Naples and Sicily were annexed to the newly unified Italian Kingdom in December 1860.

NAPOLEON I (1769–1821)

Emperor of the French; born at Ajaccio in Corsica on 15 August 1769, the second surviving son of Charles and Letizia Bonaparte. He was baptized in Ajaccio Cathedral by his great-uncle, Archdeacon Lucien Bonaparte. Napoleon's principal education was at Autun in Burgundy and at the military college in Brienne. He was commissioned in the artillery in 1785 and was on garrison duty in Auxonne in July 1789. For most of the following four years he was in Corsica but he witnessed the attack on the Tuileries (10 August 1792). His first military expedition was an ill-planned and unsuccessful raid on the Sicilian island of La Maddalena (February 1793) in which Lieutenant Bonaparte commanded a battery of three guns. Toulon, later in the year, brought him success, recognition

Bonaparte, as a young officer, witnesses the defence of the Tuileries by the Swiss Guards in the last months of the old monarchy (10 August 1792)

and rapid promotion to brigadier. As a nominal supporter of Robespierre he fell from political favour in the summer of 1794, but when he arrived in Paris (25 May 1795), he came under the military patronage of Barras, whom he assisted to keep order in Vendémiaire (5 October 1795). A few days later he met Josephine Beauharnais, whom he married on 9 March 1796, a week after receiving command of the Army of Italy. The Italian campaigns established his reputation, the actions at Lodi and Arcole in particular being romanticized. The Peace of Campo Formio and the strategic concepts behind the Egyptian campaign marked him out as an original thinker. On returning from Egypt he used the widespread disillusionment with the Directory as an opportunity to seize power (Brumaire, 9 November 1799) and establish the Consulate, promising to give France orderly government and a victorious peace. The Civil Code, the Concordat and reforms in education, finance and commercial life offered the French their best government for more than a century; victory at Marengo and the treaties of Leoben and Amiens brought a respite from war. Royalist and Jacobin plots (see *Cadoudal, Rue Saint-Nicaise, Pichegru*) made Napoleon seek the greater security of a dynastic succession. He was proclaimed Emperor on 18 May 1804 and crowned in Paris in the Pope's presence on 2 December 1804; a second coronation in Milan (26 May 1805) made Napoleon nominal King of Italy.

Despite the abandonment of his invasion plans against England, the War of the Third Coalition brought him a succession of victories – Austerlitz, Jena and Friedland among them – and he was able to establish a French Empire from the Baltic to the Adriatic, with client states in Warsaw (1807) and Germany (see *Rhine Confederation*) as well as in Italy.

His recourse to economic warfare in the Continental System from 1806–7 onwards put considerable strain on France's allies and dependencies in Europe while his attempt to absorb Spain by a dynastic *coup* at Bayonne (June 1808) turned the rising spirit of nationalism against him for the first time. The Wagram campaign of 1809 was the last occasion on which Napoleon achieved a succession of military triumphs, the humbling of Austria being followed by the Habsburg marriage, in which Napoleon took Archduchess Marie Louise as his second wife in order to secure an heir (see *below*).

The invasion of Russia in 1812 was the biggest-scale military operation of the Napoleonic era: the loss of half a million seasoned troops and of his best cavalry horses made it impossible for Napoleon to exploit the victories which he was to gain in 1813 when he was faced by a union of the old dynasties (Habsburg, Romanov, Hohenzollern) with the radical nationalism of Germany's 'War of Liberation'. Tactical victories in the early months of 1814 in France itself were exaggerated by

A French royalist cartoon depicting the rapidity of Napoleon's fall in 1815, from Mont St Jean at Waterloo to captivity aboard a British warship

Napoleon and led him to reject any possible compromise over peace terms in the negotiations at Châtillon. Napoleon was cut off from Paris, which fell on 31 March 1814; he was forced to abdicate at Fontainebleau a week later, becoming ruler of Elba.

His attempt to recover his throne and the natural frontiers of France during the Hundred Days of 1815 ended in defeat at Waterloo (18 June 1815). By 16 October 1815 he was at St Helena, the rocky island in the South Atlantic where 'General Bonaparte' spent the last five and a half years of his life subjected to humiliating vexations imposed by the island's governor, Hudson Lowe. Napoleon died at Longwood at 5.51 in the afternoon of 5 May 1821. His remains were brought back for interment in the chapel of the Invalides, Paris, on 15 December 1840. The coffin was placed in its present sarcophagus under the dome of the Invalides on 2 April 1861, in the presence of Napoleon III. (See also under *Campaigns*. Most proper names mentioned above have entries in the text even though not, in this instance, marked with a dagger for cross reference.)

NAPOLEON II (Napoléon François Charles Joseph, 1811–32)

King of Rome, later Duke of Reichstadt: born on 20 March 1811 in the Tuileries Palace, the only child of Napoleon I and Marie Louise†. From his birth the child was styled 'King of Rome', a city he never saw. His birth was the cause of great rejoicing in Paris, the news being spread around the towns and villages of the Île-de-France by a balloonist, the widowed Mme Armant Blanchard (1778–1819), who ascended from outside the École Militaire forty minutes after he was born. Napoleon lavished affection on his son; he ordered the clearing of the hilltop at Chaillot for the building of the 'King of Rome's Palace' in Paris, and in January 1813 began preparations for the boy's

Engraving after Gérard's famous painting of the 'King of Rome' (Napoleon II)

coronation by the Pope. Neither enterprise was accomplished. Napoleon last saw his son on 24 January 1814, having on the previous day dressed him in National Guard uniform and presented him at a parade outside the Tuileries. Mother and son left Paris on 29 March 1814 and from May the boy was brought up at his grandfather's court in Vienna, Francis I† creating him Duke of Reichstadt on 22 July 1818. Loyal Bonapartists acknowledged him as Napoleon II, the title being proclaimed by Napoleon I on his second abdication† in 1815. The boy was a favourite grandson of Francis I. Although he was highly intelligent, his health was poor and Metternich† excluded him from all political activities. He died from tuberculosis at Schönbrunn on 22 July 1832. In December 1940, on Hitler's orders, his remains were brought from Vienna to lie close to his father's tomb in the Invalides.

NAPOLEON III (1808–73)

Emperor of the French, 1852–70: nephew of Napoleon I. (See *Bonaparte, Charles Louis Napoléon*.)

NARBONNE, Count Louis Marie de
(1755–1813)

French general and diplomatic envoy: born in Parma, reputedly an illegitimate son of Louis xv. He was commissioned in 1771 and remained at court in 1789, being trusted both by the king and the constitutionalists. For a time he was the lover of Mme de Staël†. From December 1791 to March 1792 he served as Minister of War, fleeing to England after denunciation by the Jacobins. He returned to France with the pardoned émigrés† of 1800. In 1809 he undertook difficult marriage negotiations for Napoleon with Metternich†. Early in 1812 he was a special envoy from Napoleon to Frederick William III†, encouraging Prussian participation in the forthcoming Russian campaign. He then travelled to Vilna† where he was received by Alexander I† at Russian headquarters (18–20 May 1812) but failed to ease the mounting war tension. On his return to Dresden†, Narbonne emphasized to Napoleon the purposeful resolve which he had noticed among the Russians. He accompanied the *Grande Armée* to Moscow and was one of Napoleon's aides in 1813. After the battle of Leipzig† Narbonne was left with some 25,000 men to hold Torgau on the Elbe. Typhus spread rapidly; Narbonne succumbed in November and there were 19,000 deaths before Torgau surrendered in January 1814.

NATIONAL GUARD

Originally a citizen's militia raised in Paris on 13 July 1789. The militia was formed by a quota of 200 men, later increased to 800, provided by each of the sixty electoral districts. The system spread throughout revolutionary France, although control remained local. The 'volunteers' who responded to the national emergency when Brunswick† invaded France in 1792 were drawn from the National Guard. The militia remained basically a radical force; Bonaparte distrusted the National Guard after watching them assault the Tuileries in August 1792, but it was guns from the National Guard reserve that he used in Vendémiaire† and he cultivated the support of forty Parisian National Guard commanders (*adjudants*) on the eve of Brumaire. Under the Consulate and Empire the National Guard became a general reserve of men between the ages of twenty and sixty, organized in 'legions' (regiments) and 'cohorts' (battalions). On 11 January 1813 the National Guard was absorbed into the army, 80,000 men being shared between 88 battalions, with experienced NCOs and units of the Imperial Guard associated with them in order to bring them up to fighting strength. The National Guard was revived in 1815 and called out by the Chamber of Deputies in Paris to keep order in the capital at the time of Napoleon's second abdication†.

NAVAL WARFARE

There were no major innovations in strategy at sea during the Napoleonic Wars. The British sought to protect the homeland by mastery in the Channel, safeguarding trade routes by reviving a convoy system, and seeking to secure as many colonial possessions as possible from the enemy. At the same time, the Royal Navy mounted a close blockade† of ports in France and in the French dependent states and collaborated with the army in amphibious operations, disastrously at Walcheren†, but successfully at Copenhagen†, in Calabria (see *Maida*) and the Ionian Islands†. Attempts were also made to isolate French expeditions overseas, most dramatically in Nelson's victory at the Nile† but also in the West Indies†.

French naval strategy was based on plans to lure British vessels away from vital waters and to secure mastery of a limited region so as to mount expeditions which would cause disproportionate alarm, such as the attempts to land in Ireland†. Russia, as earlier in the eighteenth century, sought to maintain naval

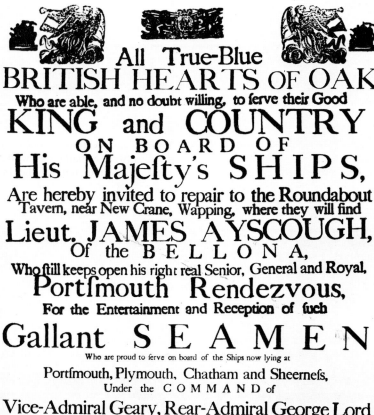

All True-Blue

BRITISH HEARTS OF OAK

Who are able, and no doubt willing, to ferve their Good

KING and COUNTRY

ON BOARD OF

His Majefty's SHIPS,

Are hereby invited to repair to the Roundabout
Tavern, near New Crane, Wapping, where they will find

Lieut. JAMES AYSCOUGH,

Of the BELLONA,

Who ftill keeps open his right real Senior, General and Royal,

Portfmouth Rendezvous,

For the Entertainment and Reception of fuch

Gallant SEAMEN

Who are proud to ferve on board of the Ships now lying at

Portfmouth, Plymouth, Chatham and Sheernefs,

Under the COMMAND of

Vice-Admiral Geary, Rear-Admiral George Lord Edgcumbe, and Commodore Hill; viz. The

Centaur	74	Prince of Wales	74	Bell-Ifle	70	Portland	54
St. Antonio	74	Defence	74	Buckingham	64	Minerva	32
Bellona	74	Temeraire	74	Achilles	ditto	Rainbow	44
Ajax	74	Fame	—	Yarmouth	—	Cerberus	28
Arrogant	74	Prudent	74	Rippon	—	Mercury	20
Hero	74	Ramallies	ditto	Firm	64	Garland	24
Cornwall	ditto	Albion	—	Augufta	—	King's Fifher,	16

With a Number of Frigates and Sloops at the above Ports.

Lieut. Ayfcough will be damn'd happy to fhake Hands with any of his old Ship-mates in particular, or
their jolly Friends in general.—Keep it up, my Boys!—Twenty may play as well as one.

Able Seamen will receive Three Pounds Bounty, and Ordinary Seamen Two Pounds, with Conduct-Money,
and their Chefts, Bedding, &c. fent Carriage free.

N. B. For the Encouragement of DISCOVERING Seamen, that they may be impreffed, a REWARD of Two Pounds will be
given for Able, and THIRTY SHILLINGS for Ordinary Seamen.

Succefs to His Majefty's NAVY! With Health and Limbs to the Jolly Tars of Old England—JAMES AYSCOUGH

GOD SAVE THE KING.

Printed by R. HILTON, in WELLCLOSE-SQUARE

Naval recruiting poster, London, late eighteenth century; several of the ships listed were to contribute to Nelson's famous victories

squadrons in distant ice-free waters, notably the Mediterranean, where Admiral Senyavin† had remarkable success. The Dutch and Spanish fleets were important in estimating the effective strength of the rival navies: until 1795 they were allied to the Royal Navy: from 1796 until Trafalgar† and beyond, they supplemented French naval power. Napoleon gave France a good navy; he encouraged the construction of fast vessels and the modernization of Brest†, Rochefort† and other bases. His pleas to the Ministry of Marine to improve sea-going artillery went unheeded. Despite the competence of such admirals as Allemand†, Ganteaume† and Villeneuve†, there was a resigned defeatism in the French fleet. Nevertheless the French introduced a significant tactical innovation: they assumed that to destroy masts and rigging by gunfire would more rapidly immobilize an enemy than any attempt to sink the vessel. The tactical improvisations of Nelson† were generally risky manoeuvres which succeeded, as at Trafalgar, because the enemy could only slowly adjust preconceived plans to meet the unexpected. Not every British commander had the 'Nelson touch' and it could be argued that the determination of Collingwood† and St Vincent† more faithfully reflects the endless naval obligation of the period – the wearisome upkeep of a close blockade and the enforcement from 1807 onwards of the Orders in Council†. (See also *War of 1812*.)

NEIPPERG, Adam Adalbert, Count von (1775–1829)
Austrian general: born in Vienna and became an aide-de-camp of Francis I. In March 1814 he tactfully negotiated with Eugène Beauharnais† on behalf of Marshal Bellegarde, the Austrian commander in northern Italy, and Neipperg led the first units of Bellegarde's army into Milan† on 28 April 1814. Three months later Francis sent Neipperg to Aix-les-Bains to escort his daughter, Marie Louise†, back to Vienna. Neipperg was a dashing cavalry officer of charm and social grace. Marie Louise became his mistress in September and married him at Parma† on 7 September 1821, four months after Napoleon's death. Two sons and two daughters were born to them before Neipperg died, at Parma, in February 1829.

NELSON, Horatio (1758–1805)
British admiral: born at Burnham Thorpe, Norfolk, the son of a country rector, entered the Royal Navy in 1770 and served mainly in the West Indies† until 1787 when he retired from active service for five years which he spent with his wife at his birthplace. He took part in the occupation of Corsica† (1794), losing an eye during an assault on the defences of Calvi. In 1795 he participated in the Toulon† operations and in 1797 was promoted rear-admiral because of the courage with which he intercepted Spanish vessels after the battle of Cape St Vincent (February 1797). He lost his right arm when the elbow was shattered by grapeshot during a raid on Santa Cruz (July 1797). From the spring of 1798 until the autumn of 1800 he commanded HMS *Vanguard* in the Mediterranean, at first blockading Toulon and subsequently pursuing Bonaparte to Egypt†, destroying the French fleet at the battle of the Nile†. He also gave material assistance to Ferdinand IV of Naples†, taking severe measures against the former leaders of the Parthenopean Republic† (July 1799). It was during these two years in Naples and Sicily that Nelson first became the friend of Emma Lady Hamilton† and her husband. After serving as second-in-command in the Baltic to Admiral Sir Hyde Parker, Nelson led the British vessels in their attack on the Danish fleet at Copenhagen†. Nelson, who had been raised to the peerage as a baron in 1798, was created viscount after Copenhagen. When war was renewed after the Peace of Amiens†, Nelson com-

*Nelson; a contemporary drawing by
Charles Grignon*

manded the blockade of Toulon for eighteen months. Villeneuve†, however, succeeded in evading the British squadron on
30 March 1805 and headed westwards out
of the Mediterranean to reach Martin-
ique† on 14 May. Nelson followed the
French to the West Indies, reaching Barbados on 4 June, five days before Villeneuve left Martinique for the Bay of
Biscay in the hope of securing French
naval mastery of the Channel. Nelson
returned to Gibraltar by 19 July and,
finding Villeneuve blockaded in Cadiz,
took a month's leave in England. His
flagship HMS *Victory* sailed from Portsmouth on 15 September and was off
Lisbon ten days later. The combined
Franco-Spanish fleet was finally brought
to battle at Trafalgar† on 21 October 1805.
In the moment of triumph a French sniper
aboard the *Redoutable* perceived Nelson,
resplendently decorated with his four
orders of knighthood, on the quarterdeck
of *Victory* – and shot him; he died some
three hours later and was interred in St
Paul's Cathedral on 9 January 1806.

NESSELRODE, Karl Robert (1780–1862)
Russian foreign minister: born in Lisbon
of German parentage. He entered Russian service at the age of sixteen as a
midshipman in Catherine the Great's
navy, later transferring to the army. Soon
after Alexander I's accession he began his
diplomatic career and was stationed in
Berlin and The Hague before going to
Paris in 1810 and 1811. There he was
commended by Napoleon as 'the one man
of talent in the Russian embassy', but he
secretly established links with Talleyrand†
and the anti-Bonapartist opposition. During the 1812 campaign he joined Alexander I's personal staff, accompanying the
Tsar across Germany and France in 1813–
14 and going with him to London before
being created 'State Secretary for Foreign
Affairs' in August 1814. He shared control
of Russian foreign policy with John Capodistria until 1822 but was then sole Foreign
Minister until May 1856 and titular Chancellor from 1844 until his death. Nesselrode, a conservative bureaucrat who believed in Russo-Austrian collaboration,
thus shaped foreign policy for over forty
years, a longer span than any other minister, Tsarist or Soviet.

NEY, Michel (1769–1815)
Marshal of the Empire: born at Sarrelouis
in western Germany, the son of a cooper.
He was a sergeant-major of Hussars in
1792, fought in the Army of the North and
was rapidly promoted becoming a colonel
in 1794 and a brigadier in 1796. By 1799 he
was respected as a light cavalry commander, serving with distinction in Switzerland and in 1800 helping Moreau† to win
Hohenlinden†. He received his marshal's
baton in May 1804 before ever he had
collaborated closely in the field with
Napoleon, and in later years he found it
difficult to co-operate with two of the
Emperor's most famous veterans from
Italy, Masséna† and Murat†. He impressed Napoleon in 1805 by the tactical skill
with which he outmanoeuvred the Au-

strians at Elchingen, near Ulm, on 14 October, and then by the rapidity with which he occupied the Tyrol, capturing Innsbruck in the first week of November. He was cut off by the Prussians at Jena† and was rescued by Lannes† but distinguished himself at Eylau† and Friedland†. In 1808 he was created Duke of Elchingen but there followed a difficult campaign in Portugal, marked by disputes with Masséna over operations at Ciudad Rodrigo† and Torres Vedras†. As commander of III Corps in Russia in 1812 Ney was in the centre of the fighting at Smolensk† and Borodino† and, when cut off during the retreat, held the rearguard together until he re-established contact with Napoleon. Ney, reputedly the last fighting soldier of the *Grande Armée* to leave Russian soil, was honoured by Napoleon as Prince of the Moskva and hailed as 'the bravest of the brave'. He was wounded at Lützen†,

led the left wing as it enveloped the enemy at Bautzen† and was wounded again at Leipzig†. In 1815 he was appointed commander-in-chief of Louis XVIII's cavalry, boasted that he would intercept Napoleon and bring him back captive 'in an iron cage' to Paris but went over to the Emperor's side when the two men met at Auxerre (18 March). In the Waterloo campaign he engaged Wellington† at Quatre-Bras† and was given overall battle command at Waterloo† itself even though he was an abler corps commander than a mastermind at handling the various sectors of a major action. To his surprise he was arrested by the restored Bourbons, charged with treachery, tried by a court of peers, and shot in the Luxembourg Gardens, Paris, on 7 December 1815.

Marshal Ney awaits his fate in the courtyard of the Conciergerie prison, Paris, December 1815

NIEMEN

Russian river some 550 miles long, now shown on many maps as Neman. It rises south-west of Minsk and flows west-north-west, passing Grodno and Kaunas to enter the Baltic by a delta. Napoleon first encamped beside the river from 19 June to 9 July 1807 for the meeting of sovereigns at Tilsit†. By 1812 the Niemen formed Prussia's north-eastern frontier with Russia. In the two months preceding his invasion of Russia Napoleon concentrated 430,000 men of the *Grande Armée*† along the lower Niemen. At midnight on 23–4 June 1812 the cavalry of Davout's† 1 Corps began to cross three pontoon bridges erected by the engineers under General Éblé†; they were protected by light infantry ferried across the river two hours earlier. Napoleon crossed one of the bridges at five in the morning (24 June) and by the afternoon was established in the nearest Russian town, Kaunas. He re-crossed the Niemen 166 days later, travelling hurriedly from Smorgon† to Paris. Murat† led the survivors of the *Grande Armée* back over the river a week later (13–14 December), Ney† commanding the rearguard. Kutuzov's Russians crossed the Niemen to invade Prussia on 15–16 January 1813.

NILE, Battle of (1 August 1798)

Decisive naval action fought in Aboukir Bay†, some ten miles west of the principal mouth of the River Nile. Nelson†, flying his flat in HMS *Vanguard*, led a squadron of thirteen ships of the line into the bay, where he succeeded in placing Admiral Bruey's French fleet between his two main divisions of warships. Bruey himself was killed on his flagship, *Orion*, which subsequently blew up. Nine French warships were captured and two others sunk; only two French battleships and two frigates escaped. Nelson's victory deprived Bonaparte of his supporting naval squadron, thus cutting him off from France and limiting the effectiveness of his mastery of Egypt†.

NOVOSILTSOV, Nikolai (1761–1836)

Russian statesman: born on family estate near Moscow. He was an aristocrat of liberal views who became a friend of the future Tsar Alexander I† in the spring of 1797 and, four years later, belonged to the 'Secret Committee'† of Alexander's advisers. He was sent as the Tsar's personal envoy to London in 1804 and discussed with Pitt† the programme of war aims known as the 'Grand Design'†. Illiberal tendencies in Alexander's government made Novosiltsov reluctantly resign office in 1806 and withdraw from active political life, but he returned to favour in 1814 and became the Tsar's first commissioner in Warsaw after the withdrawal of the French. In 1819–20 Novosiltsov was given the unrewarding task of preparing a draft constitution for a federalized Russian Empire with consultative elected assemblies; but Alexander soon lost interest in this project and Novosiltsov's preliminary work was in vain.

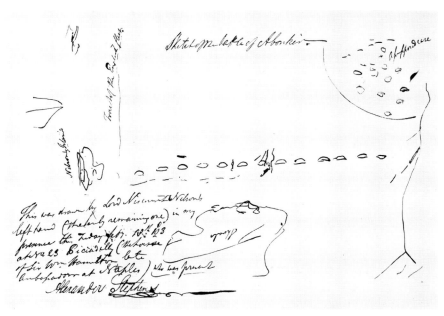

A sketch drawn by Nelson at Sir William Hamilton's house in Piccadilly in February 1803 to describe the battle of the Nile, four and a half years previously

O

ODESSA

Chief Russian grain exporting port on the Black Sea. It was founded in 1794–5 close to the site of the classical Greek colony of Odessos. The prosperous development of the port owed much to the efforts of the émigré French nobleman, the Duke of Richelieu†, who was Governor-General of the Odessa region from 1804 to 1814. There was a strong Greek nationalist movement among the Odessa seamen and merchants. (See *Greece*.)

OLDENBURG, Duchy of

Today part of Lower Saxony, in the German Federal Republic, but was formerly a German state covering an area of some 2,000 square miles on the left bank of the River Weser, with a North Sea coastline. The ruling dynasty was Holstein-Gottorp, the family into which Catherine the Great of Russia was born. Both Paul I† and Alexander I† treated Oldenburg as a remote fief of Russia. The Russian connection was strengthened in August 1809 by the marriage of Grand Duchess Catherine Pavlovna† to the son of the reigning Duke of Oldenburg. When Napoleon annexed the northern coast of Germany, including Oldenburg, in December 1810 to January 1811 his action was regarded in St Petersburg as a deliberate affront. It became one of Alexander's chief complaints against France and an indirect cause of war in 1812. Oldenburg became part of the new German Confederation after 1815.

OLD GUARD

The nucleus of the Napoleonic *corps d'élite*, the Imperial Guard†.

O'MEARA, Barry Edward (1786–1836)

Physician: born in Ireland and served as an army doctor until 1808 when he was dismissed for participating in a duel. In 1815 he was ship's surgeon aboard HMS *Bellerophon*† when Napoleon surrendered off Rochefort. O'Meara could talk to Napoleon in French and Italian. He was invited to accompany him to St Helena† as his personal doctor. O'Meara became a channel of communication between the fallen Emperor and his London sympathizers at Holland House†; he consistently supported Napoleon in his disputes with Hudson Lowe†. In 1818 O'Meara's activities led to his abrupt departure from the island, where Lowe thought him an undesirable presence. He maintained constant harassment of Lowe, both in letters to the Admiralty and in his book *A Voice from St Helena* (1822). O'Meara was dismissed from naval service for allegations that Lowe had tried to win his support in poisoning Napoleon. Yet at times O'Meara seems to have been a double agent, encouraging Napoleon to contact his European sympathizers but also quietly ingratiating himself with Lowe.

OPERA

Traditionally dates from about 1600 in Italy, with Venice and later Naples as the chief centres of the art form, although it flourished in Vienna by the 1660s. Between 1762 and 1787 the influence of the Bavarian composer Christoph Gluck reformed opera, subordinating music to drama and thereby raising the standards of presentation in Vienna, Milan, Munich, Dresden and Paris. Mozart

(1756–91), during the last ten years of a short life, completed the transition to a style which combined vocal virtuosity and sensitive musicality with stage craftsmanship. The French Revolution liberated opera from classical mythology and, at the turn of the century, Paris was shaping operatic fashion. Napoleon attended operatic performances a dozen times a year, on the average, preferring Italian works to anything French. He liked grandiose productions, encouraging Gasparo Spontini (1774–1851) who, in 1809, brought fourteen horsemen on the stage to add verisimilitude to his *Fernand Cortez*. Napoleon bestowed decorations on the principal singers, commending the versatile Pierre Garat, whose voice ranged from tenor to bass, the castrato Girolamo Crescenti, and the contralto Giuseppina Grassini (who was briefly his mistress in Milan and Paris in 1800 and 1802). Napoleon insisted that the Paris Opéra should keep the price of seats down to a reasonable level, but he also made it clear that 'no opera may be given without my order'. Few of the works by his favourite composers – Spontini, Méhul†, Paisiello† – survive. It is possible that he had no great appreciation of opera, liking military bands to use operatic music for regimental marches and sometimes to encourage his troops into battle. More enduring operas appeared outside France. Thus Beethoven† conducted the first performance of *Fidelio* at the Theater an der Wien on 20 November 1805, in the eighteen-day interlude between the fall of Vienna† to the French and the battle of Austerlitz†; and the premières of Rossini's *Silken Ladder*, *Tancred* and *The Italian Girl in Algiers* all took place in Venice between 1810 and 1813 while the city was part of Napoleon's Kingdom of Italy.

OPORTO

Second largest city and seaport in Portugal, 214 miles north of Lisbon and on the north bank of the Douro, 4 miles from its mouth. Soult† seized Oporto in March 1809 while advancing on Lisbon. He halted there to refit his army but was surprised by Wellesley (Wellington†) on 12 May. The British assaulted Oporto from the south-east, having crossed the Douro on barges provided by townsfolk who had fled before the French advance. Soult was forced to retreat through the mountains and into Spanish Galicia†, harassed by a ferocious peasantry. The French never returned to this region of Portugal.

ORDERS IN COUNCIL

In response to the Berlin Decree† and the Continental System† of 1807, the British government issued a series of 'Orders in Council' designed to hamper neutral ships seeking to trade with enemy ports. The first Order (7 January 1807) merely prohibited neutral shipping from trading between one French held port and another. The more famous Orders (11 November and 25 November 1807) declared that any ship with a cargo for a French (or French dominated) port would have to unload its cargo and would be required to pay duty and purchase a special licence from the British before being allowed to bring goods or produce into France. This British move in the chronic trade war of attrition produced a swift French response, the Milan Decrees†. American resentment at enforcement of the Orders in Council by the Royal Navy intensified with the passage of the years and contributed considerably to Madison's declaration of war on Britain in June 1812. (See *War of 1812*.)

ORGANIC ARTICLES (1802)

The *Articles organiques du culte catholique* were provisions added by the First Consul, on Talleyrand's suggestion, to the Concordat†. Bonaparte regarded them as supplementary regulations defining the relations of Church and State; in reality, they were concessions to anti-clericals in the Senate† and Tribunate†. The articles asserted government control over papal documents entering France and over all church councils and synods; they gave limited state control of seminaries, allowed the government to regulate clerical dress, bell ringing and open air processions; and they provided for state regulation of clerical stipends and parochial boundaries. At the same time seminarists were to be taught the need to accept Louis XIV's Gallican Articles of 1682, which limited the authority of a pope in temporal matters within France. The Papacy never accepted the Organic Articles; they were however implemented by the authorities under both the Consulate and the Empire. The *Articles organiques des cultes protestants*, also published in 1802, asserted similar state control over the salaries and administrative organization of the Reformed Churches.

ORTHEZ, Battle of (27 February 1814)

A delaying action fought thirty-five miles east of Bayonne†. Soult† sought to check the advance of Wellington on Toulouse†. The French held high ground above the River Gave de Pau, checking Beresford's first assault with concentrated artillery fire. Wellington drove a wedge between the French positions so as to threaten Soult's line of communications and the French withdrew. Wellington was wounded when a bullet struck his sword hilt, thrusting it into his thigh. He insisted on remounting and remaining in the saddle until the end of the battle.

OTTOMAN EMPIRE

The Ottomans, descendants of the Emir Osman (d. 1326), formed the ruling dynasty in the Turkish Empire from the capture of Constantinople in 1453 until 1922. By 1800 the Ottoman Empire had receded considerably from its zenith in the early seventeenth century and its apparent weakness was already posing the 'Eastern

Question'†. Even so, the Sultan in Constantinople was still sovereign of all the Balkans, of Asia Minor as far as the Persian Gulf and the Red Sea, and overlord of Egypt†, Cyrenaica and Tripolitania (Libya), and Tunisia. Outlying provinces were administered by local 'pashas' with the help of the Janissaries†, often with capriciously cruel inefficiency (see *Serbian Revolts*); the only genuine reforming Sultan of the period, Selim III (Sultan 1789–1807) was deposed and later murdered when he tried to create a western-style army. His successor, Mahmud II†, was fortunate to avoid a similar fate. The Ottoman Empire was at war with France from 1798 until 1802, largely because of Bonaparte's ambitions in Egypt and Syria. There was then a period of Franco-Turkish collaboration until 1807, with amicable relations continuing until the fall of Napoleon. Trade concessions to France and hostile acts along Russia's frontier in Bessarabia led to war with Britain and Russia in 1806, a British naval squadron under Admiral Duckworth forcing the Dardanelles in February 1807. Peace between Britain and Turkey was concluded in January 1809 but the Russians remained at war with the Sultan, steadily encroaching on Ottoman lands in modern Romania until preoccupation with the threat from Napoleon induced them to make peace in 1812; the resultant Treaty of Bucharest† ceded Bessarabia to Russia. The general peace settlements of Paris and Vienna in 1815 made no change in the frontiers of the Ottoman Empire.

OUDINOT, Nicolas Charles (1767–1847)

Marshal of the Empire: born at Bar-le-Duc, the son of a brewer, saw service in the royal infantry and cavalry before becoming in 1790 the *adjudant* (commander) of the National Guard† in the département of the Meuse. His battle experience over the following ten years was almost entirely in the Rhine-Moselle regions and in Switzerland; and by April 1799 he commanded a division at Zurich†. He was then Masséna's chief-of-staff at Genoa†. Serious wounds in the Austerlitz campaign left him incapacitated for over a year but he fought with reckless bravery at Friedland†, Aspern† and Wagram† and was created a marshal in July 1809 and Duke of Reggio in April 1810. He was twice wounded in Russia, at Polotsk† and the Berezina†, and had to fight off an attack by Russian guerrillas† as he was being brought back to France for medical treatment. During the enveloping tactics at Bautzen† Oudinot commanded the right wing, as Ney† did the left. In 1815 he remained loyal to the Bourbons, refusing to leave France and travelling to Paris to tell Napoleon why he felt obliged to keep his oath to Louis XVIII. As Oudinot had suffered eighteen wounds while fighting for the Consulate and Empire, Napoleon merely ordered him to remain on his country estate. He campaigned in Spain (for the first time) in 1823 and was Governor of the Invalides for the last five years of his life. His son, Nicolas Charles Victor Oudinot (1791–1863) was the commanding general of the French expeditionary force which suppressed Garibaldi's Roman Republic in 1849.

OUVRARD, Gabriel Julien (1770–1846)
French banker: born near Clisson in southern Brittany. He acquired a considerable fortune as principal handler of contracts for the navy under the Directory. So dubious were his methods that, on the establishment of the Consulate, he was put under surveillance and his papers were confiscated for inspection. Ouvrard, however, was protected by Fouché† and was soon again serving as contractor for the navy. He also made valuable contacts with the Dutch financier, Labouchère†, and the Spanish bankers, Cabarrus and Hervas, father-in-law of Duroc†. By 1803 Ouvrard was supplying the Spanish navy, too, and in 1804 he founded the 'Company of United Brokers', which rested on funds

supplied without any sure guarantees from the Bank of France†. The United Brokers undertook to supply provisions for the French and Spanish armies and navies as well as advancing money to the treasuries of the two countries. Ouvrard also sought to bring to Europe the silver piastres from Spanish colonial vaults in Mexico and Cuba, a financial operation which would have brought profits to himself and, as he convinced Napoleon, would bring bullion reserves into France. The scheme failed, as also did the United Brokers. The Bank of France faced a crisis of confidence and the Minister of the Public Treasury, Barbé-Marbois†, fell into disgrace for having accepted Ouvrard's assurances. Napoleon summoned Ouvrard and his partners into his presence on the day after his return from the Austerlitz campaign in January 1806 and threatened to have them shot; he contented himself with confiscating their assets. Ouvrard, however, had been warned in advance by an influential member of the Emperor's *Maison*† and safely disposed of some of his possessions. He was imprisoned for debt in 1809, but was soon free and active again, thanks to Fouché's protection. A strange project, dependent on Franco-British collaboration, led Ouvrard through Labouchère to make contact with London. When Napoleon heard of this initiative, by a chance remark of King Louis Bonaparte† at Antwerp on 27 April 1810, he had Ouvrard thrown back into prison (and also dismissed Fouché). With the Restoration, Ouvrard soon reasserted his influence as a financier and made immense profits in supplying the needs of the Army of the Pyrenees with which the Duke of Angoulême† invaded Spain in 1823; and Ouvrard's banking concerns prospered, too, under Louis Philippe.

OWEN, Robert (1771–1858)
Pioneer British socialist: born at Newtown, Powys, and became a draper's

apprentice in 1781. He set up a workshop in Manchester on borrowed capital, became a partner in a Scottish mill and in 1800 established an 'ideal' working community in the factory which he managed at New Lanark; he employed no young children, limited the hours of work, provided further education for adolescents and set up a cooperative store. These social experiments attracted much attention and he developed his cooperative theories in his book, *New View of Society*, which appeared at the height of the 1813 campaigns. His greatest influence did not come until the 1830s, after he had experimented with the settlement of a socialist community at New Harmony, Indiana (1825–9); but even in 1818 he was sufficiently well known to be received by Gentz‡ at the Aachen Congress and discuss with him the social problems raised by industrialization.

P

PAISIELLO, Giovanni (1740–1816)
Italian composer: born and died in Naples†. From 1776 to 1784 he was in St Petersburg under Catherine II's patronage, completing in 1782 the earliest operatic version of *The Barber of Seville*. By 1784 he was back at Naples, later visiting Vienna where he was on friendly terms with Mozart. He supported the short-lived Parthenopean Republic† in 1799 and, after its fall, was welcomed in Paris, Bonaparte having already declared that Paisiello was one of his favourite composers. To celebrate the Concordat† he completed a *Te Deum* for two choirs and two orchestras which was sung at the Pontifical High Mass in Notre-Dame on Easter Day (18 April 1802), an occasion treated with great solemnity by the First Consul. Paisiello remained Director of Choral Music in Paris for another two years and composed elaborate settings for the coronation† (2 December 1804). He returned to Naples under the patronage of Joseph Bonaparte†. As well as choral music and symphonies, Paisiello probably composed as many as a hundred operas; among them, as early as 1789, was a version of *Nina* from which Napoleon was known to hum recognizable arias.

PALAFOX Y MELZI, José (1780–1847)
Spanish patriot general: born into the Aragonese aristocracy near Saragossa†. He was commissioned in the Spanish Royal Guard and became on good terms with King Ferdinand VII† whom he accompanied to Bayonne in June 1808. Having avoided internment by the French, Palafox then returned to his native Aragon, led the epic defence of Saragossa for the following two months and, although no democrat, put himself at the head of the popular insurrection against the French, collaborating with Castaños†. After defeat by Lannes† at Tudela (23 November 1808) he again fell back on Saragossa where he inspired a second heroic defence until Lannes took the city street by street in February 1809. For five years Palafox remained a prisoner in France but was later made Captain-General of Aragon and Duke of Saragossa.

PALM, Johann Philipp (1768–1806)
Bavarian bookseller: born at Schorndorf, setting himself up as a bookseller in Nuremberg. In 1806 he published and sold an anonymous pamphlet, *Germany in her Deep Humiliation* which deplored the fate of the old German free cities under the weight of French occupation. Napoleon sent orders from Saint-Cloud to Berthier† on 5 August that 'booksellers who spread defamatory writings in districts occupied by French armies' must be tried by court martial and shot. Palm and two Augsburg booksellers (Schoderer and Meikle) were brought before a French military court at Braunau on 25 August; Palm was shot immediately after sentence; Schoderer and Meikle were spared. Booksellers from Vienna and Linz were condemned to death *in absentia* for spreading works which libelled Napoleon. News of the sentences was, on the Emperor's orders, 'published all over Germany'. Palm's death aroused anti-French feeling, especially in Prussia where there was already a strong German patriot war party.

PAOLI, Pasquale (1725–1807)

Corsican patriot: born on the island at Morosaglia, spending his youth in the armed struggle of the Corsicans against Genoese rule. He was proclaimed chief of the island in 1755 and won a high degree of independence for the Corsicans until defeated by a French force under the Comte de Vaux in 1769. He then escaped to England where he was introduced to London society by Boswell, who had visited him in Corsica†. For fifteen years Paoli was frequently in the company of Samuel Johnson, Joshua Reynolds and other eminent figures in British cultural life. Paoli returned to Corsica on the outbreak of the French Revolution but favoured British naval protection and was formally outlawed by the Revolutionary Convention in 1793. The Bonapartes had supported Paoli on his return to Ajaccio† in November 1789 but were at loggerheads with Paoli and his political nominees (see *Pozzo di Borgo*) as early as October 1791; and threats of death from the Paolists induced Napoleon to escort his family from Calvi to the mainland at Toulon† in June 1793. Paoli again found sanctuary in England in 1796.

PAPAL STATES

Under the pontificate of Innocent III (1198–1216) the Papacy established rights of sovereignty over central Italy including Ancona, Ferrara, Ravenna and Spoleto. These Papal States were expanded in the seventeenth century. Their existence was challenged by the advance of French armies as far south as Bologna and Ferrara, which Bonaparte visited in October 1796 and included in the Cispadane Republic when it was established three months later. Rioting in Rome† led to the occupation of the city by Berthier† early in January 1798 and the Papal States were organized as the Roman Republic. This creation collapsed in June 1799 and Austrian troops then occupied most of the Papal States, although Rome itself was held by the Neapolitans. After the Peace of Lunéville† the northern possessions (the 'Papal Legations' of Bologna, Ferrara and Ravenna) were included in the Italian Republic but Pius VII† was once again sovereign ruler of Ancona and the lands around Rome. In October 1805 the French seized and fortified the port of Ancona, which was incorporated in the Kingdom of Italy† in 1808. Rome and the remaining Papal States were annexed by Napoleon in June 1809. The Papal States were restored at the Congress of Vienna† (1814–15) although Austria retained rights to garrison the Papal Legations.

PARIS

Napoleon spent about nine years and three months of the fifteen and a half years in which he was Consul or Emperor resident in Paris, including Malmaison† and Saint-Cloud†. He lavished greater attention on the city than any previous ruler of France. The Arc de Triomphe†, the Arc du Carrousel, the Madeleine, the Vendôme column, four Seine bridges, the Bourse, a wing of the Louvre, the cemetery of Père Lachaise, quays along the Seine, and the Ourcq canal survive, although some have been restored or extended. About seventy-five new roads were paved, not entirely to the Emperor's satisfaction. Many were on the left bank but the most important road building project created a west-east route, along the arcaded Rue de Rivoli. The city was given more than 4,000 gas street lamps and over three miles of sewers in ten years. These projects fell short of the Emperor's plans. He wished the capital to stretch westwards beyond the Invalides and the Concorde to Saint-Cloud. Work began in 1811 on a huge palace for the King of Rome†, descending in terraces down the hill of Chaillot to the Seine. Grandiose government buildings were to house ministries from the Quai d'Orsay to the Champs de Mars. He gave Parisians plenty of public spectacles, celebrations of

GLORIOUS NEWS.

THE

ALLIED SOVEREIGNS

With their Armies of 150,000 Men,

ENTERED PARIS,

On the 31st Ult. after

HAVING TOTALLY DEFEATED

BUONAPARTE,

WITH THE LOSS OF

10,000 MEN and 100 PIECES of CANNON,

AMMUNITION, BAGGAGE, &c. &c. and

TEN GENERALS.

The EMPRESS and Her SON fled with Precipitation from

PARIS.

A poster brings Londoners 'glorious news', April 1814

victory, a coronation, the *Champ de Mai*† in 1815 and military reviews in the Place Vendôme, on the Carrousel or beside the Invalides. Although censorship† limited the press and the theatre, he was deeply concerned over the standard and style of the Comédie Française† and the presentations at the Opéra†. There was opposition to the Empire in the fashionable salons†, but the city as a whole remained loyal to Napoleon, despite his repeated fear that the rising price of bread† would cause unrest. In March 1814 he belatedly sought to reach Paris ahead of the advancing Russians, but the fate of the capital was decided in a sharp engagement on 30 March around Pantin and on the northern slopes of Montmartre before the Emperor could arrive. In 1815, after Waterloo, no attempt was made to defend the city, which surrendered on 3 July.

PARIS, Treaties of

There were two Treaties of Paris at the end of the Napoleonic Wars: (i) Treaty of 30 May 1814; France was treated leniently, retaining the 1792 frontiers (including areas along the Belgian frontier and in Savoy which had not belonged to France before the Revolution) and recovering most of her colonies, except for Mauritius, St Lucia and Tobago. Louis XVIII† recognized the independence of the United Netherlands, Switzerland and the states of Germany and Italy. He also undertook to abolish the slave trade†. No claims were made by the Allies for a war indemnity. (ii) Treaty of 20 November 1815; France was treated more severely after Waterloo. The frontiers of 1790 were restored, with territorial concessions to Prussia, Bavaria, Sardinia-Piedmont and the Netherlands (Belgium). Seventeen fortresses in northern and north-eastern France were to be garrisoned by the Allies for five years; France was to pay a war indemnity of 700 million francs and restore the art treasures† taken from other countries by the revolutionary and Napoleonic armies.

PARMA

City in north-central Italy, east of the Apennines, south of the Po; capital of the Duchy of Parma 1545–1859. It was occupied by the French in 1801 and annexed to the Italian Republic in 1802, the reigning Duke being temporarily compensated in Tuscany† ('Etruria'). In 1814 Parma came under Austrian influence; Marie Louise† was sovereign Duchess from April 1814 to December 1847, when the traditional Ducal House of Bourbon-Parma was restored. Napoleon spent only one night in the city (26 June 1805).

PARTHENOPEAN REPUBLIC

French puppet state established in Naples† on 23 January 1799. When French troops withdrew in June 1799 to meet the challenge from Suvorov† further north, the Republic was easily overthrown by an Anglo-Neapolitan force supporting Ferdinand IV†. Severe reprisals were taken against republican sympathizers in Naples.

PAUL I (1754–1801)

Tsar of Russia 1796–1801: son and successor of Catherine the Great. He was a militaristic martinet who suffered from vagaries of the mind. Hostility to the ideas of the French Revolution together with concern for his unexpected status as Grand Master of the Knights of St John induced Paul to join the Second Coalition† after Bonaparte had seized Malta†. The Russian armies gained remarkable successes under Suvorov†, but envy and suspicion made the Tsar turn against his 'Prince of Italy'. He took Russia out of the war in 1800, and in December 1800 and January 1801 wrote three personal letters to the First Consul, proposing a meeting and ways of putting pressure on Britain to conclude a general peace. The Tsar's conduct was so strange that a conspiracy was formed by a group of officers who wished to force his abdication in favour of his son, Alexander†. Officers of the Semeonovsky Regiment entered the Mikhailovsky Palace in St Petersburg on 24 March 1801 with Alexander's connivance. When Paul refused to abdicate he was struck on the head by a heavy snuff-box and strangled. Alexander had not foreseen that the conspirators might kill his father.

PENINSULAR WAR

The chief theatre of operations for British land campaigns against Napoleon's France. The War arose from the decision of the government of the Duke of Portland† in London to send an expedition to the Iberian Peninsula in order to support the Spaniards and Portuguese against Napoleon. But the first action in the Peninsula occurred in October-November 1807 when Junot† marched into Spain† and down the River Tagus so as to occupy Portugal†, a move which met partisan resistance and was, to some extent, countered by prompt decisions of Sidney Smith† at Lisbon. The British expeditionary force landed at Mondego Bay, 110 miles north of Lisbon, in the first week of August 1808; Wellesley (Wellington†) defeated Junot† at Vimiero† three weeks later, and, by an agreement known as the Convention of Cintra†, the French withdrew from Portugal. News of this defeat, of the Spanish insurgent victory at Baylen†, and of mounting resistance throughout Spain, made Napoleon take over personal command at Vitoria† on 5 November 1808. He campaigned in Spain for only 77 days, with no major battles; Madrid capitulated on 3 December. Sir John Moore†, commanding in Portugal, penetrated the Spanish mountains as far as Salamanca† and threatened French communications. There followed, in January 1809, his famous retreat to Corunna† and the temporary withdrawal of British troops from the Peninsula apart from a garrison holding the base of Lisbon. Soult† advanced as far south as Oporto† and the River Douro. Wellesley (Wellington) returned to Lisbon on 22 April and began to build up an Anglo-Portuguese army. The French were soon cleared from Oporto and most of Portugal. Advancing into Spain, Wellington defeated Jourdan† and Joseph Bonaparte† at Talavera† before falling back on defensive positions at Torres Vedras† when Masséna† launched a counter-offensive in 1810. The Spanish liberals held out at Cadiz†, where a considerable French army was tied down in Andalusia until August 1812. Spanish guerrillas† continued resistance in the mountains while Portuguese and Spanish regular troops increasingly contributed to the battle plans drawn up by Lord Beresford† and Wellington himself.

In the spring of 1811 Wellington emerged from the Torres Vedras lines to blockade Almeida† and gain an important victory over Masséna at Fuentes de Oñoro†. Further south, Badajoz† proved an unassailable fortress but Beresford gained another victory at Albuera†. During 1812 Wellington went over to the offensive, capturing Ciudad Rodrigo† and

Badajoz and in June beginning the steady advance which won the battle of Salamanca on 22 July, captured Madrid three weeks later but failed to take Burgos† in the autumn. After a largely inactive winter and spring, the second Allied advance began in June 1813 with Wellington's triumph at Vitoria carrying the war to the Pyrenees. Despite the resistance of San Sebastian†, the Bidassoa† was crossed into France on 7 October. The French continued to resist, at Bayonne† in the west and Orthez† further east, Soult fighting in defence of Toulouse† six days after Napoleon's first abdication†. The Pensinsular Army finally occupied Bordeaux†, where Wellington issued his farewell message to his troops on 14 June 1814.

Continental and American historians maintain that the British have traditionally exaggerated the importance of the Peninsular War in Napoleon's downfall, pointing out that the Emperor's Spanish campaign was brief and that he never fought a major battle on Spanish or Portuguese soil. Nevertheless, by maintaining a British army which never numbered more than 50,000 men and was supported by Spanish and Portuguese regulars and guerrillas, Wellington forced Napoleon to keep in the Iberian Peninsula some quarter of a million trained troops at the peak of his main Continental campaign.

PERCEVAL, Spencer (1762–1812)

British prime minister: born in London, the second son of the 2nd Earl of Egmont, educated at Harrow and Trinity College, Cambridge. He became a highly successful barrister and was elected Tory MP for Northampton in 1796. From 1802 to 1806 he was Attorney General, without a cabinet seat. He entered Portland's government in 1807 as Chancellor of the Exchequer, an office he continued to hold when he succeeded to the premiership on 4 October 1809. Perceval was a dedicated man of unspectacular industry, calm

enough to handle the temperamental Prince of Wales during the passing of the Regency† Act in 1811 and confident that he would, in time, solve the mounting economic crisis† of 1811. Prosecution of the war he tended to leave to others in the cabinet, notably Liverpool† and Bathurst†. On 11 May 1812 he was shot dead in the lobby of the House of Commons by John Bellingham, a bankrupt Lancashire broker with a grievance against the government. Liverpool succeeded him.

PÉRIGNON, Dominique Catherine (1754–1818)

Marshal of the Empire: born into the landed gentry at Grenade-sur-Garonne, near Toulouse. He was commissioned in 1780, became a colonel in the National Guard in 1789, and from 1792 to 1795 held high rank in the army which was holding the eastern Pyrenees against Spain. From 1795 to 1797 he was ambassador in Madrid. He was a corps commander at Novi, where he was wounded and taken prisoner. In 1800 he was able to return to France, became a senator a year later, Vice-President of the Senate† in 1802 and (rather surprisingly) received a marshal's baton in 1804. Thereafter he held administrative posts, entirely in Italy. From 1813 onwards he was suspected of royalist sympathies. He remained loyal to Louis XVIII in 1815 and was deprived of his marshalate by Napoleon. A few months later Louis XVIII created him Marshal of France and made him a marquis in 1817.

PICHEGRU CONSPIRACY (1797)

General Charles Pichegru (1761–1804) distinguished himself as an army commander on the Rhine and in Belgium in 1793–4 and became President of the Council of Five Hundred† under the Directory. He was believed to have organized a *coup d'état* by crypto-royalists in Fructidor† 1797, was arrested by troops led by Augereau† and transported to Guiana. From

The arrest of Pichegru in the Rue de Chabanois, Paris 'at three in the morning' on 28 February 1804

there he escaped a year later, reached London and began to plot the overthrow of the Consulate. He became so involved with the planning of the Cadoudal Conspiracy‡ in 1803 that it, too, has sometimes been called the 'Pichegru Conspiracy'. After Cadoudal's secret crossing to Normandy, Pichegru followed him and tried to win the backing of General Moreau‡. He was arrested in Paris but was found dead in his cell on 5 April 1804, having either hanged himself or been strangled.

PIEDMONT: see *Sardinia-Piedmont.*

PITT, William ('the Younger' 1759–1806) British prime minister: born at Hayes, the second son of the Seven Years' War leader, Lord Chatham. He was educated at Pembroke College, Cambridge, and Lincoln's Inn, becoming a barrister in 1780 and MP for Appleby from 1781 to 1784, sitting as member for Cambridge University for the remainder of his life. In July 1782 he entered Shelburne's administration as Chancellor of the Exchequer, but the government only lasted seven months. Pitt himself formed a minority government in December 1783, won the general election of 1784 and remained Prime Minister until 3 February 1801, eventually resigning because of differences with George III over Catholic Emancipation‡. During the years of peace Pitt was responsible for reforms in the tariff and financial system, improvements in criminal administration, the remodelling of government in India and Canada and the relaxation of anti-Catholic penal laws. War with revolutionary France in 1793 made him introduce a succession of repressive measures, notably the Traitorous Correspondence Act (1793), the Seditious

Meetings Act (1799) and the suspension of Habeas Corpus. In Ireland†, the shock of rebellion in 1798 induced him to persuade the Irish parliament to vote its own dissolution, thus enabling him to carry through an Act of Union (1800) which left Ireland governed from Westminster from 1 January 1801 onwards. As war leader, Pitt followed the principles of his father, for the most part subsidizing coalitions for campaigns in Europe while concentrating on overseas expeditions to acquire the colonial possessions of France and her allies. The inadequacies of Addington† during the crisis months following the breakdown of the Peace of Amiens† led to Pitt's return as Prime Minister in May 1804. He negotiated the alliances with Russia and Austria which made possible the War of the Third Coalition†, giving a practical twist to the idealism of the Tsar's 'Grand Design'† so as to provide the Allies with a programme of war aims. Pitt was a fine orator and, in his parliamentary tussles with Fox†, a good debater and shrewd party manager. Three days after news of Trafalgar† reached London, Pitt delivered his famous speech at the Guildhall: 'Europe is not to be saved by any single man', he declared on 9 November 1805. 'England has saved herself by her exertions and will, as I trust, save Europe by her example'. He was already physically worn out from his own exertions and died only twelve weeks later on 23 January 1806.

PIUS VI (Giannangelo Braschi 1717–99)
Pope from 1775 to 1799: born at Cesena in the Romagna, south of Ravenna. He succeeded Clement XIV at a time of mounting anti-clericalism, first under Joseph II in Austria and later in revolutionary France. He condemned the Civil Constitution of the Clergy and encouraged Italian resistance to Bonaparte's armies. The Papal States† were invaded in 1796–7 and Rome† occupied by Berthier† at the beginning of 1798. Pius VI was then escorted

as a prisoner to Valence, on the Rhône south of Lyons. He died there on 29 August 1799, the mayor of the commune formally recording the death of one 'Jean Ange Braschi, exercising the profession of pontiff'.

PIUS VII (Gregorio Barnaba Chiaramonti, 1742–1823)
Pope from 1800 to 1823: born, like his predecessor Pius VI (see *above*), at Cesena. He became a Benedictine monk in 1756, Bishop of Tivoli in 1782 and Cardinal-Archbishop of Imola (near Bologna) in 1785. Wartime conditions made the papal conclave after Pius VI's death gather in Venice rather than in Rome, electing Chiaramonti after three months of voting. His principal concern was the relations of the Papacy with France and he was fortunate to have as his chief adviser, Cardinal Consalvi†. The Concordat† of 1802 was followed by Pius's acceptance of Napoleon's invitation to consecrate him at his coronation† in Paris; but Pius's hopes of

Pope Pius VII, drawn by David, a detail sketched for the Coronation canvas

being able to win concessions from the French by his show of collaboration were disappointed. A French army entered Rome in 1808 and incorporated the city in the French Empire a year later. When Pius excommunicated those responsible for this act, he was arrested and deported to Grenoble and later to Savona†. From June 1812 until January 1814 he was held prisoner at Fontainebleau†. Napoleon visited him there for a week in January 1813 extracting from him the abortive Fontainebleau Concordat. Pius was taken back to Savona at the end of January 1814, travelled on to Parma in late March and made his way slowly to Rome through Imola and Cesena. His carriage was escorted in triumph into Rome on 24 May 1814. The Papal States were restored and new agreements over Church-State relations were concluded with Bavaria, Sardinia-Piedmont and Naples and with non-Catholic Prussia and Russia. Pius treated the Bonapartes generously in their misfortunes, especially Mme Mère† and Cardinal Fesch†.

PLAESWITZ, Armistice of

(4 June to 12 August 1813)

The French victories at Lützen† and Bautzen† left the Russo-Prussian allies needing a breathing space in which to reorganize their armies (and curb the mounting friction between rival commanders). Napoleon, for his part, was short of cavalry horses and ammunition, and, fearing Austrian intervention, he wanted to build up reserves in Germany and northern Italy. Both sides therefore accepted a cease-fire on 2 June which, after a conference at Plaeswitz, was converted into an armistice two days later. Originally the armistice was to last until 20 July. Peace proposals from Metternich† were examined and, after a famous meeting between Napoleon and the Austrian Foreign Minister at Dresden† on 26 June, the armistice was extended until 10 August while the Austrians sought to mediate at a conference

in Prague. Little effort was made at Prague to find a compromise settlement; the Austrians formally joined the coalition against Napoleon on 12 August. During the armistice, Sweden had concentrated an army of 110,000 men under the Prince Royal (Bernadotte†) around Berlin; and Napoleon's position was thus far worse after the ten week interlude in the 1813 campaign than before it. Nevertheless, it was Napoleon who won the first battle (Dresden†), fought after a resumption of hostilities.

PLEBISCITES

Bonapartist political theory emphasized the importance of individuals voting by name directly for or against constitutions†. This 'plebiscitary democracy' may be criticized as liable to intimidation and easy manipulation, and the high figures of *Oui* votes in 1800, 1802 and 1804 make it suspect. Moreover, the wording of the question on which the vote was taken was hardly impartial; thus the plebiscite on the transition to Empire in 1804 was a vote not on the assumption of the title of Emperor but on whether or not the Empire should be hereditary. Officially in the plebiscite of February 1800 on the establishment of the Consulate there were 3,011,307 in favour and 1,562 against; but half a million votes were added to the *Ouis* for members of the army and navy unable to vote in their own communes. Even so, there were large numbers of abstentions, notably in Marseilles and Belgium. There is no reason to think that the figures in the later plebiscites, which, proportionately, were uncannily similar to those of 1800, are any more reliable as a guide to public opinion.

POLAND

By the eighteenth century the Kingdom of Poland had become politically enfeebled by the problems of an elective monarchy and by rivalry between some of the great aristocratic families. Poland's three powerful neighbours (Russia, Prussia and Austria) took advantage of the kingdom's weakness to partition the Polish lands. A third of Poland was divided between the three Powers in August 1772. Russia acquired a considerable area in the Second Partition of January 1793, which led to a rising under Kosciuszko†. The rest of Poland was divided between the three autocracies in the Third Partition (October 1795). Napoleon encouraged the Polish exiles to believe that he would support their cause, in 1806–7 and in 1812; but he complained that 'they seek too many guarantees before committing themselves'. Some leading Poles did, however, fight for Napoleon, notably Dombrowski† and Poniatowski†, both of whom raised 'Polish Legions'. Poniatowski's men freed Cracow† from Austrian rule in July 1809 and the city formed part of the Grand Duchy of Warsaw† which Napoleon established as his chief contribution to the Polish national cause. Other Poles – notably Czartoryski† – hoped for national recognition under Alexander I's patronage. On 12 February 1811 Tsar Alexander† told Czartoryski he was willing to proclaim a Polish Kingdom, with a liberal constitution and a Polish government, provided all the Polish gentry and aristocracy would pledge themselves to support a Russian war against Napoleon. This pledge they could not give. Military events in 1813 left Russia in occupation of almost all Poland and Alexander sought to proclaim a Polish Kingdom of which he would be sovereign. Disputes over a new partition of Poland continued for the first three months of the Vienna Congress† (1814–15). Eventually, by the Treaty of Vienna, Austria retained Polish Galicia†, Prussia recovered Poznania, Cracow became a 'Free City', and the rest of Napoleon's former Grand Duchy, including Warsaw, was recognized as a kingdom ruled in perpetuity by the sovereign of Russia. Alexander I was greeted as King in Warsaw in November 1815; he issued a Constitutional Charter for 'Congress Poland'

which provided for internal self-government. The Poles, however, were disillusioned by Russian primacy in the administration of the new Viceroy, Grand Duke Constantine†. There were anti-Russian revolts in Congress Poland in 1830–1 and 1863; an independent Poland was reconstituted in 1918.

POLOTSK

Town on the River Dvina, sixty miles north-west of Vitebsk†. On 30 July 1812 Wittgenstein† checked an advance by Oudinot† east of the town, forcing the French to fall back on Polotsk itself and allowing the Russians to claim their first victory in the campaign. Less than three weeks later (18 August) Gouvion Saint-Cyr's VI Corps gained striking successes against Wittgenstein outside Polotsk, Oudinot having been wounded in the early phases of the battle on the previous evening. Heavy fighting around the neighbouring village of Smolyan on 14 November 1812 is sometimes also called the battle of Polotsk. It was an indecisive encounter, tactically a victory for the French IX Corps (Marshal Victor†); but it only delayed Wittgenstein's southward thrust towards the Berezina†.

POMERANIA

A geographical region extending along the Baltic coast from Danzig in the east to Rostock and the Warnow estuary in the west. Possession of the Duchy of Pomerania became one of Sweden's chief objectives in the Thirty Years' War (1618–48) and much of western Pomerania passed into Swedish hands. Incursions by Brandenburg-Prussia in 1679 and 1720 left only an area around Stralsund by the end of the eighteenth century. Napoleon sent Mortier† to seize this last Swedish foothold south of the Baltic in November 1806. He agreed to evacuate Swedish Pomerania in 1809, provided Sweden† joined the Continental System†, but in March 1812 he annexed the whole region. It was largely in response to this action of his former master that the Swedish Prince Royal (Bernadotte†) sought reconciliation with Russia and landed on the Baltic coast in 1813 to join the Allied armies in Germany. At the Vienna Congress† in 1815 it was accepted that Sweden's sliver of territory should join the remainder of Pomerania within Prussia, where the whole region constituted the province of Pommern until 1945. Most of Pomerania is now in Poland but the former Swedish foothold is in East Germany.

PONIATOWSKI, Jozef Anton (1763–1813)
Polish Prince, Marshal of the Empire: born in Vienna, the son of a high-ranking officer in the Austrian army and a nephew of the last King of Poland. Poniatowski himself fought with the Austrians against the Turks intermittently from 1778 to 1788 and was wounded in Croatia. From 1792 to 1794 he was in the Polish army fighting the Russians in the Ukraine but was later allowed to settle on the family estates near Warsaw†. Briefly in 1806 he accepted office as Governor of Warsaw under the King of Prussia but he welcomed Napoleon's invitation to command the first Polish Legion of the *Grande Armée* in 1807 and became Minister of War in the Grand Duchy. He liberated Cracow† from the Austrians in July 1809 and founded new military institutions around Warsaw. Napoleon gave him V Corps in the *Grande Armée* of 1812, merging Saxon and Polish troops. Poniatowski took part in the storming of Smolensk†, was heavily engaged around the village of Utitsa at Borodino† and was seriously wounded crossing the Berezina†. After his recovery, Napoleon gave him the command of VIII Corps (July 1813). He was again wounded in the actions preceding Leipzig†. On the morning of the 'Battle of the Nations', he received his marshal's baton from Napoleon. Next day, while covering Napoleon's retreat, Poniatowski was

drowned in the River Elster as he tried to reach the French bank after blowing up the last bridge.

PORTLAND, 3rd Duke of (William Henry Cavendish-Bentinck, 1738–1809)
British prime minister: born in London, educated at Westminster School and Christ Church, Oxford, succeeding as third Duke in 1762 and as leader of the Whigs† in 1782. He was briefly Prime Minister from April to December 1783. Dislike of the French Revolution led his faction of Whigs (unlike the Foxites) to collaborate with Pitt† after the coming of war with France. Portland was Home Secretary (1794–1801) and minister without portfolio under Addington† and in the second Pitt ministry. In March 1807 (at the age of 69) he became Prime Minister again, in succession to Grenville†. George III† believed Portland could hold the Pittites together without conceding Catholic Emancipation†. But Portland was too old to lead a nation at war effectively. Muddled military thinking produced second naval action at Copenhagen† and the expedition to Walcheren†. Rifts between members of his cabinet, notably Canning† and Castlereagh†, discredited his government. In September 1809 Portland suffered an apoplectic stroke, resigned office and died six weeks later. Spencer Perceval†, his Chancellor of the Exchequer, succeeded him as Prime Minister.

PORTUGAL
Apart from the 'Sixty Years' Captivity' – the period 1580–1640, when the kingdom was absorbed by Spain – Portugal has been an independent state since the twelfth century, ruled from 1640 until 1910 by the Bragança dynasty. During the eighteenth century the economy of Portugal was in decline and the nation's independence was maintained with some difficulty by close Anglo-Portuguese col-

laboration. The enlightened despotism of King Joseph I and his Chief Minister, Pombal, in the years 1750 to 1777 was followed by a recovery of political initiative on the part of the Portuguese nobility after the accession of Joseph's daughter, Queen Maria I (ruled nominally from 1777 to 1816). Maria's insanity from 1792 onwards, and internal rifts between clericalists and 'liberals', left Portugal open to a Spanish invasion in 1801. Napoleon at first supported Spanish ambitions in Portugal ('England's oldest ally'), approving a partition plan in 1807 and authorizing Junot† to march on Lisbon, with Spanish support, in November 1807. The unfortunate Queen Maria and her son John (Prince Regent 1799–1816) escaped to Portugal's richest colony, Brazil. A British expeditionary force landed at Mondego Bay in August 1808 and defeated Junot at Vimiero†, compelling France to evacuate the country (Convention of Cintra†). The British raised a Portuguese army, loyal to Prince Regent John. When, in the second French invasion, Soult† advanced as far south as Oporto† in March 1809, the Anglo-Portuguese forces drove him from the kingdom. A third French invasion, in 1810, by Masséna† in the north and Soult in the south was countered by Wellington† and Beresford† in some of the main actions of the Peninsular War† (Torres Vedras†, Almeida†, Fuentes de Oñoro†, Albuera†, Ciudad Rodrigo†). These successive campaigns left Portugal impoverished. In the absence of the legitimate ruler in Brazil, Portugal was effectively administered by a Council of Regency headed by Beresford until 1820, when a liberal revolt, followed by the return of King John VI from Rio de Janeiro marked the start of seventy years of dynastic confusion and civil strife.

POTSDAM OATH (4 November 1805)

A dramatic climax to the ten day visit of Tsar Alexander I† to Frederick William III† in Berlin. Tsar and King concluded a secret treaty pledging Prussia to join Russia within six weeks in the War of the Second Coalition†. The two sovereigns and Queen Louise† then descended into the crypt of the garrison church at Potsdam and, over the wooden coffin of Frederick the Great, swore an oath of eternal friendship, assuring God and each other that the interests of Russia and Prussia would never again run in conflict. The immediate effect of the oath was negligible: Alexander's defeat at Austerlitz† four weeks later postponed Prussia's entry into the war. But the pledge of friendship influenced both Russo-Prussian relations for the next thirty-five years and dynastic diplomacy throughout the nineteenth century. Alexander was especially conscious of the oath at Bartenstein†, Tilsit† and during the peacemaking of 1814–15.

POZZO DI BORGO, Count Charles André (1764–1842)

Corsican general in Russian service: born at Alata, a few miles north of Ajaccio†. He became a supporter of Paoli† and in 1791 began a family vendetta with the Bonapartes. Pozzo followed Paoli to England but travelled to Russia in 1804 and served Alexander I† on a series of special diplomatic missions: Naples in 1805, Venice 1806 and Constantinople in 1807. After Tilsit he settled in Vienna although secretly maintaining contact with St Petersburg. He returned to Russian service in 1812 and was sent as the Tsar's personal envoy to Stockholm in the early months of 1813, encouraging the Prince Royal (Bernadotte†) to intervene. In December 1813 Pozzo travelled to London secretly to persuade Castlereagh† to come to the Continent and promote inter-allied collaboration at headquarters. At the Vienna Congress† Pozzo was the chief supporter of the Bourbon Restoration in the Russian delegation and was critical of the decision to send his personal enemy, Napoleon, to Elba†, which he thought too near to Italy and to Corsica. During the Hundred Days Pozzo attached himself to Wellington's staff as personal commissioner of the Tsar and was thus the only 'Russian' general at Waterloo†. From 1815 to 1835 he was Russian ambassador in Paris.

PRAGUE CONFERENCE (1813)

A half-hearted attempt by Metternich† to impose Austrian armed mediation on France so as to convert the Armistice of Plaeswitz† into a basis for peace. Metternich's chief concern was to convince Emperor Francis† that everything had been done to avoid entangling Austria in a war to dethrone his son-in-law, Napoleon. Caulaincourt† represented France, but with instructions not to make concessions and never to accept the terms offered in the Reichenbach Convention†. Informal talks were held in Prague from 28 July until 10 August 1813 but the French attitude was so rigid that the conference never met in plenary session. Metternich formally dissolved the conference and Austria declared war on France two days later.

PREFECTS (Préfets)

The office of Préfet de département was instituted by the First Consul as part of the general reform of provincial administration embodied in the Law of 28 Pluviôse† Year VIII (17 February 1800). A Prefect was appointed by the central government as executive head of each département, giving local affairs a clear directing hand missing since long before the Revolution. The first 98 Prefects were appointed in March 1800, their number increased to 102 with the four départements created after the Treaty of Lunéville† in 1801 and to 130 when the Empire reached its fullest extent in 1810. The original list of Prefects was supervised by Lucien Bonaparte† while Cambacérès† and Lebrun† exercised patronage over a dozen prefectures,

and other appointees benefited from contacts with the Beauharnais family or from having known the First Consul at school or in his days as a junior officer. Even so the general level of administration attained by the Prefects was high, particularly in the Seine-Inférieure, the Seine-et-Oise and the Rhin-et-Moselle départements. Prefects had the assistance of a nominated council, but efficient holders of office took the decisions themselves. The Prefects provided better roads, bridges and policing, greater security from bandit attacks, efficient collection of taxes and a more equitable response to the demands of conscription. Many Prefects came from the nobility, old or new, and one in six had served as army officers, but most of those appointed in 1800 were already experienced in provincial administration, mainly during the Directory. The system gave France such good local executive government that it was retained after Napoleon's fall and survives today.

PRESSBURG, Treaty of

(26 December 1805)

The peace settlement which took Austria out of the War of the Third Coalition†, three weeks after Napoleon's victory at Austerlitz†. It was concluded at the castle above the Danube in the city known in German as Pressburg, Magyar as Pozsony and Slovak as Bratislava. The Austrians surrendered to the Napoleonic puppet Kingdom of Italy all the Venetian lands gained at Campo Formio†, including Istria and Dalmatia. France's ally Bavaria† gained the Tyrol, Vorarlberg and other south German possessions from Austria as well as the free city of Augsburg. Both Bavaria and Württemberg† were recognized as independent kingdoms. Further Habsburg enclaves in south Germany were handed over to Württemberg and Baden although, as compensation, Austria gained the former ecclesiastical possessions of Salzburg and Berchtesgaden. The general effect of the

Treaty was to destroy Habsburg rule in most of Italy and Germany, thereby making the Holy Roman Empire† an archaic concept which was finally abandoned eight months later.

PRINCE REGENT (of the United Kingdom) The title borne by George, Prince of Wales (1762–1830) from 5 February 1811 until his accession as King George IV on 29 January 1820. The mental state of his father, George III†, deteriorated rapidly in November and December 1810. On the last day of the year the Prime Minister, Perceval†, introduced a Regency Bill which for twelve months limited the Prince's power to dissolve parliament or dismiss the government but thereafter gave him full powers of sovereignty unless the King recovered his health. As the Prince had admired Fox† in earlier years, the Whigs† hoped they would be asked to form a government by the Regent. He, however, decided against any change of leadership in 1812 because he wanted full political backing for the Peninsular War; Grey† (the Whig leader) favoured a negotiated peace and turned down the Regent's suggestion that Whigs should serve under Tories in a coalition pledged to continue the war. The Prince Regent's alleged treacherous treatment of his former political allies ensured that, for the rest of the century, he received a bad press from Whig historians and writers. They portrayed him as a corpulent adulterer, selfishly extravagant, frequently drunk and habitually mendacious; this impression owed much to the verbal onslaught of Leigh Hunt† printed in *The Examiner* at the end of the 'probationary' year of the Regency†. Popular sympathy for the Regent's wayward wife, his first cousin Caroline† of Brunswick, led to hostile demonstrations in London and southern England. In reality, however, the Prince Regent was a man of wit and culture, a great patron of the arts who left to the nation a magnificent collection of paintings as well

as such architectural gems as the Royal Pavilion in Brighton and the restored state apartments at Windsor. He possessed a better understanding of European affairs than his father or most English politicians, and he was aware of the need for the British monarchy to win support in the more distant parts of the United Kingdom; he made successful visits to Dublin and Edinburgh.

PRUSSIA

A unitary German state, having as a nucleus East Prussia and Brandenburg, with its capital in Berlin†. The Prussian Kingdom was established in 1701 when the Elector of Brandenburg was crowned King-in-Prussia at Königsberg. Under Frederick the Great (1740–86) Prussia challenged Habsburg dominance of Germany and central Europe, acquiring Silesia, western Poland and other enclaves and creating a legend of military strength through Frederick's victories at Hohenfriedberg (1745), Rossbach (1757) and Leuthen (1757). Frederick's successors, his nephew Frederick William II (reigned 1786–97) and his great-nephew Frederick William III†, relied excessively on what they believed to have been the Frederican tradition. Thus Frederick William II was too eager to complete the partition of Poland with Russia and Austria to give his attention to the campaign against the French revolutionary armies, which had begun in 1792 with the invasion of France by the Duke of Brunswick† but ended ineffectually in the Peace of Basle† (April 1795). Under the influence of his foreign minister, Count von Haugwitz†, Frederick William III stayed out of the wars for eleven years although inaugurating the friendship with Russia symbolized by the Potsdam Oath† of 1805. When Prussia belatedly went to war with France in September 1806 the King's armies were defeated at Jena† and Auerstädt† and the kingdom dismembered at Tilsit†. The skill of Stein† and Hardenberg† in domestic affairs and of Scharnhorst† and Gneisenau† in rebuilding the army enabled a modernized Prussia to emerge from the Napoleonic disasters. A Prussian corps under Yorck† von Wartenburg participated in Napoleon's invasion of Russia but on 30 December 1812 Yorck concluded a truce with the Russians at Tauroggen† and popular German patriotism led Prussia to take the lead in February 1813 in calling for a German 'War of Liberation'. By the Treaty of Kalisch† Russia and Prussia became allies and the armies of Blücher† successfully withstood Napoleon's assaults at Bautzen† and Dresden†, gaining victories at the Katzbach† and, above all, at Leipzig† before advancing through France in the early months of 1814. Blücher's presence at Waterloo† gave Prussia greater bargaining power in the peacemaking of 1815 than of 1814. Prussia recovered all her lost territories apart from the Warsaw region of Poland; she gained additional lands in Saxony and extensive territory in the west, particularly along the Rhine frontier with France and in Westphalia. These gains enabled Prussia subsequently to become the most industrialized state in Germany. Under Bismarck between 1862 and 1871 Prussia was recognized as the nucleus of a new German Empire. Prussia was formally broken up after the Second World War by the Potsdam Decrees of 1945.

PULTUSK, Battle of (26 December 1806)
Was fought, thirty-two miles north of Warsaw, in sleet and thick mud on the slopes of wooded heights commanding the approach to the Polish town of Pultusk, on the River Narew. The Prussians, falling back after Jena-Auerstädt†, had made contact with their Russian allies, under Bennigsen†. This army was attacked by Lannes† in the mistaken belief that it was merely a rearguard retiring northeastwards. The Russo-Prussian force outnumbered the French by two to one and was superior in artillery, with guns well placed behind defensive ridges. The French occupied Pultusk but were thrown out by the end of the day, retiring to their original positions with heavy casualties on both sides. Bennigsen reported to St Petersburg that he had defeated Napoleon – who was forty miles from Lannes – and a victory was celebrated in the Russian capital. Overnight Bennigsen made a strategic withdrawal. Napoleon arrived at Pultusk on 29 December and spent three nights there in the bishop's palace. The even more costly battle of Eylau† followed six weeks later.

PYRAMIDS, Battle of the (21 July 1798)
Was fought by Bonaparte's Army of the Orient (25,000 men) nineteen days after it landed in Egypt†. A Mameluke† host of 6,000 good horsemen with some 34,000

Bonaparte encourages his army before the battle of the Pyramids, 1798; detail from a painting by Baron Gros, who was with the army in Egypt

primitive infantry was stationed along both banks of the Nile, guarding the approach to Cairo† from the north. The main body, under Murad Bey, was entrenched through water melon fields on the left bank with the pyramids of Giza visible some miles behind them. The French, deployed in echelon squares, fought off the Mameluke horsemen with musket fire backed by case-shot. Most of the Egyptian infantry ran in panic from the battlefield, many drowning in the Nile. Bonaparte's victory enabled him to enter Cairo in triumph next day. There is no reference to his over-quoted eve of battle address ('Soldiers, forty centuries look down on you') earlier than 1817 when he was reminiscing on St Helena†.

QUATRE-BRAS, Battle of (16 June 1815)
A preliminary engagement to Waterloo†, fought on the same day that Napoleon engaged Blücher† at Ligny†, six miles to the east. Quatre-Bras was a village twenty-one miles from the Belgian capital, at the point where the Namur-Nivelles road crossed the main route from Brussels to Charleroi. In the forenoon Ney† launched a desultory attack on the predominantly Dutch defenders of the village. The main action took place in the afternoon after the arrival of 9,000 British reinforcements. Wellington† and his staff reached Quatre-Bras having come from the Duchess of Richmond's famous ball in Brussels which they left at three in the morning. The battle was indecisive: Ney failed to receive reinforcements, which went instead to Ligny; and in the evening Wellington regained ground lost to a cavalry charge by the younger Kellermann† earlier in the day. But Quatre-Bras slowed down the French advance on Brussels. It allowed the Allies to retire to their chosen defensive positions along the ridge at Waterloo, some nine miles north of the crossroads.

R

RAPP, Jean, Count (1772–1821)
French soldier: born at Colmar into a Huguenot family. He enlisted in the cavalry in 1788 and over the next twenty-five years was wounded on at least twenty-five occasions. He fought along the Moselle and Rhine, was aide-de-camp to Desaix† throughout the Egyptian campaign and was beside him at his death at Marengo†. Rapp led a cavalry charge at Austerlitz† against the Russian Imperial Guard, taking prisoner the distinguished General, Prince Nicolas Repnin. In 1809 Rapp was created a count and, with Mouton†, fought his way through to Napoleon when the Emperor was threatened with encirclement at Aspern†. In December 1800 Rapp had been in attendance on Josephine during the attempted assassination in the Rue Saint-Nicaise† and he retained a sentimental attachment to the Empress which made him critical of Napoleon's divorce and remarriage. He remained, however, in Napoleon's immediate circle of aides during the Russian campaign, helping to fight off Cossacks who nearly captured the Emperor at Gorodnya on 24 October 1812. He defended Danzig† in 1813 but was then held prisoner by the Russians for twelve months. By 1815 he was back in France and commanded the Army of the Rhine (23,000 men), gaining a minor victory against the Austrians in his native Alsace on 28 June, ten days after Waterloo. Rapp was allowed back to Paris in 1817, wrote his memoirs but died from cancer four years later.

RASTATT, Congress of (1798–9)
On 27 November 1797 Bonaparte made a ceremonial entry into the Habsburg town of Rastatt, between the Rhine and the Black Forest. He stayed there for five nights as delegates arrived for a congress to determine the form of compensation for German princes dispossessed of the left bank of the Rhine by the Treaty of Campo Formio†. Formally the congress sat from 19 January 1798 until 21 March 1799. It achieved nothing. The Austrians successfully played for time, negotiating a new coalition which took the field against France when Bonaparte was in Egypt†. Historically the congress is interesting because of the skill with which the young Metternich† (and his bumbling father) perfected prevaricating diplomacy. It is noteworthy that neither the French nor the Austrians were prepared to settle changes in the map of Europe during the absence of Bonaparte.

RATISBON
The city of Ratisbon (now generally known as Regensburg) lies on the upper Danube in Bavaria, sixty-five miles northeast of Munich. Early thirteenth-century charters recognized Ratisbon as a 'Free City' and its independence commended it as a seat for the perpetual commission (*Immerwährender Reichstag*) of the rulers of the Holy Roman Empire†. This 'Diet of Ratisbon' survived in the city from 1663 until 1 August 1806 when it accepted the dissolution of the old Empire. Territorial

changes within Germany were customarily discussed at the Diet. The city was stubbornly defended by the Austrians, under Archduke Charles†, on 23 April 1809, before being stormed by Lannes†. During this action Napoleon was slightly wounded on the right ankle by a spent musket-ball.

RAZUMOVSKY, Count Andrey Kirillovich
(1752–1836)
Russian diplomat: born in St Petersburg, the son of a field marshal. Much of his life was spent in Vienna, where he was ambassador from 1801 until succeeded by the Francophile Prince Kurakin† in 1807. Even then Razumovsky continued to live in the Austrian capital where he was respected as a patron of music, the dedicatee of three of the string quartets of Beethoven†, composed in 1806–7. Razumovsky served at Allied headquarters in 1813–14 and was chief Russian spokesman to the conference at Châtillon†, February and March 1814. At the Congress of Vienna† (where he entertained liberally until his house was burnt down in December 1814) Razumovsky was the only native-born Russian in the Tsar's cosmopolitan delegation. Even so, he would never write the Russian language and he was a convert to Catholicism. His brother, Aleksey Razumovsky (1748–1822), was Alexander I's Minister of Education from 1810 to 1816.

RÉCAMIER, Jeanne-Françoise, Mme
(1777–1848)
Literary hostess: born Jeanne-Françoise Bernard at Lyons, marrying an elderly banker at the age of fifteen. Her beauty and her capacity for listening, as well as for stimulating conversations, made her the natural creator of one of the Paris salons†. During the Directory she was associated with the Palais Luxembourg set, which included Mesdames Tallien† and Josephine† Bonaparte, but her interests were in music, drama and litera-

ture rather than in politics. She was a friend of Germaine de Staël†. Although she remained on amicable terms with Josephine, she inclined increasingly towards the Bourbons. She seems only once to have met Napoleon, at a reception given by Lucien Bonaparte† on 26 January 1800. Her literary lion was Chateaubriand†, who dominated her salon at the Abbaye-aux-Bois during the Restoration. She was admired by Benjamin Constant†, but she often found his starry-eyed enthusiasm slightly ridiculous.

REGENCY
In Great Britain the period from February 1811 to January 1820 (see *Prince Regent*). Socially the period is associated with a somewhat feverish frivolity at variance with the strain of military campaigns and with the economic distress which produced the Luddites†. Yet 'Regency' bucks and dandies flourished in a slightly earlier period, the fashion being set by George 'Beau' Brummel (1778–1840) who had lost the favour of the Prince before July 1813, when the Regent attended the last 'Dandy Ball' given by Lord Alvanley at the Argyle Rooms. While Romanticism† was the prevailing form of literary expression and women's clothes became simpler and less constrained, Regency furniture and architecture were neoclassical, although adding light-hearted adornment to a fundamental dignity of style. John Nash (1752–1835), who made his reputation by country house designs and rebuilt Brighton Pavilion, was responsible for the great town planning scheme, the 'metropolitan improvements' of the Regency which enriched London's West End, even though Regent Street and Regent's Park are only a small part of the comprehensive design which Nash put forward in 1812. The Prince Regent himself warmly supported Nash, wishing to make certain that the planning scheme eclipsed Napoleon's ambitions for Paris†. Many aspects of Regency culture contri-

Regency London; the realization of Nash's plans. Cumberland Terrace, Regent's Park

buted to English social life long after the Prince had succeeded to the throne. Victorian critics frowned on the ostentatious gaiety of the Regency years.

REICHENBACH, Convention of

(27 June 1813)

An agreement concluded in the town of Reichenbach (now Dzierzoniow) in Silesia between Russia, Prussia and Austria and embodying verbal arrangements reached in talks between Alexander I† and Metternich† in the Moravian castle of Opočno on 18–19 June. Napoleon was to be invited to accept a peace based on four fundamental points: dissolution of the Grand Duchy of Warsaw†; the restoration of Prussia's frontiers of 1805; the withdrawal of French military backing for the Confederation of the Rhine†; and the return to Austria of the Illyrian Provinces†. If Napoleon rejected these terms, Austria would enter the war against France. At the Prague Conference† Caulaincourt† indicated that Napoleon would not even consider these terms.

Austria declared war on France on 12 August 1813.

RÉMUSAT, Claire Élisabeth, Countess of

(1780–1821)

Lady-in-waiting to the Empress Josephine: born in Paris, the daughter of an aristocrat, Gravier de Vergennes, who was guillotined during the Revolution. At sixteen she married Auguste de Rémusat, a lawyer from Aix-les-Bains, having already been befriended by the future Empress Josephine†. She was Josephine's chief attendant from the establishment of the Consulate until the divorce and her husband was First Chamberlain of the Empire. From 1802 onwards Mme de Rémusat was a friend of Talleyrand†. His influence makes the *Mémoires* which she wrote after the Restoration unreliable even though they are good reading. Her letters (published in 1881) and covering only the years 1804 to 1814 provide some interesting character sketches, and are more generous in their treatment of Napoleon than the memoirs.

233

REVOLUTIONARY CALENDAR

A new calendar, rejecting the traditional Gregorian form and nomenclature, was imposed on France by the Revolutionary Convention on 5 October 1793. It was antedated to Proclamation Day of the First Republic (22 September 1792) but did not come into use until 26 November 1793. The mathematician Gilbert Ronne (1750–95) devised a chronology which made the year consist of 12 months of 30 days each, divided into three ten-day weeks. To complete a year of 365 or 366 days, five additional national festival days (nicknamed *sansculottides*) were included in the calendar, six for 1796, 1800 and 1804. The days were named in numerical order; the months were called after seasonal characteristics with names devised by the poet Philippe Fabre d'Eglantine (1755–94), who was guillotined on what he reckoned as 16 Germinal, Year II. The months were: Vendémiaire (beginning the year on 22 September); Brumaire (22 October); Frimaire (21 November); Nivôse (21 December); Pluviôse (20 January); Ventôse (19 February); Germinal (21 March); Floréal (20 April); Prairial (20 May); Messidor (19 June); Thermidor (19 July); Fructidor (18 August). The *sansculottides* began on 17 September. The revolutionary calendar, unlike the Gregorian, reckoned that 1800 was a leap year; and any comparative table between the two calendars must be changed by one day after 22 October 1800. This extraordinary system remained legally in use until 31 December 1805; it had long since disappeared from private correspondence.

REYNIER, Jean Louis Ébénézer
(1771–1814)

French soldier: born in Lausanne, Switzerland, into a Huguenot family. He was a junior artillery officer in the early campaigns of the revolutionary wars but soon showed himself a first-rate planner and was chief of staff to Moreau† on the Rhine and Moselle with the rank of General. He served in Egypt† in 1798, fought at the Pyramids† and along the Nile but was sent back to France because of his scornful criticisms of Menou†. Verbal attacks on his fellow commanders culminated in a duel outside Paris in which Reynier killed General Destaing. Thereafter he served Murat† as Minister of War in Naples but returned to Napoleon's favour in 1809 and showed masterly detail in planning marches and counter-marches of the French armies in Spain and Portugal. After serving in the Russian campaign, Reynier helped Eugène Beauharnais† reorganize the armies in 1813 and fought at Bautzen† and Dresden†, commanding the predominantly Saxon VII Corps. He was captured at Leipzig†, returned to France in February 1814 in an exchange of prisoners but died from exhaustion a fortnight later. Napoleon admired his intelligence but thought him too reserved to inspire his men.

RHINE, CONFEDERATION OF THE

A protectorate of the French Empire, established by the Treaty of Paris of 17 July 1806 and intended to consolidate the French mastery of western Germany attained by the Ulm-Austerlitz campaign. The President (*Protektor*) of the *Rheinbund* was Napoleon himself. Bavaria, Württemberg, Hesse-Darmstadt, Baden and twelve other small states of the Holy Roman Empire joined the original Confederation. Westphalia† became a member in 1807, as also did Saxony, Mecklenburg and several petty principalities. By 1808 the Confederation contained thirty-six German states who were expected to furnish contingents for the *Grande Armée*†, originally 63,000 men but considerably more on the eve of the Russian campaign. The Confederation was an essential part of Napoleon's Continental System†, closing important trade markets to Britain. Most states in the Confederation adopted the French Civil Code and other reforms, some such as Hesse-

Darmstadt and Anhalt in flatteringly close imitation of the Parisian model. The Confederation disintegrated in the autumn of 1813, falling apart rapidly after the Allied victory at Leipzig†.

RICHELIEU, Armand Emmanuel du Plessis, Duke of (1766–1822)

French statesman: born in Paris, a great-great-great-nephew of the famous cardinal. As an émigré, he entered Russian service and from 1804 to 1814 was the Tsar's Governor-General of 'New Russia', building up the port of Odessa†, where his statue still stands today. He was Louis XVIII's Prime Minister from September 1815 to September 1818 and again from February 1820 to December 1821. His connections with the Tsar enabled him to restore France's prestige in Europe with astonishing rapidity.

ROADS

The foundation of France's road system was laid by the Romans but it was not until the early seventeenth century that Sully prepared a network radiating specifically from Paris. Sully's *routes royales* were used by Napoleon as a basis for the *routes impériales*, which have survived under the more familiar designation *routes nationales*. There were 229 of these routes, linking Paris with the chief provincial cities and strategic towns with one another. The routes were the direct responsibility of a 'Director-General of Roads and Bridges' under the Minister of the Interior; they were built and maintained by state funds and followed a standard pattern, being straight paved roads about five metres wide. These tree-lined avenues survive across the plains of France. Non-trunk roads (*routes départementales*) were the responsibility of the Prefects† and not directly of central government. The road system was geographically unbalanced, with a much greater density in the north and north-east for strategic reasons. Trunk routes were few in south-western France. Napoleon's road programme was not limited to metropolitan France. On St Helena in September 1816 he told Las Cases† that he reckoned among his great achievements 'the splendid roads from Antwerp to Amsterdam, from Mainz to Metz, from Bordeaux to Bayonne, the carriage routes over the Simplon, Mont Cenis and Mont Genèvre Passes and the Corniche road, opening the Alps to access from four sides . . . mountain roads . . . which link the Pyrenees with the Alps, Parma with La Spezia, Savona with Piedmont', and he might have added the remarkable road programme of Marmont† in the Illyrian Provinces†. Inevitably Napoleon's engineers were also great bridge builders, in Paris† as well as in such distant cities as Lyons, Turin and Bordeaux. The 1814 campaign ruined many of the recent roads and cut short Napoleon's programme of development. As with canals†, work on Napoleonic projects in France continued well into the railway age.

On the Continent outside the French Empire and its dependencies the road system was almost non-existent and the road surfaces abominable. The first metalled roads in Prussia were laid down in 1788 around Berlin, but there were no good surfaces at all east of the capital or in the sandy and muddy areas of Poznania as late as 1815. Catherine the Great had ordered the construction of the 'Big One', a surfaced highway from Vilna† to Moscow through Minsk and Smolensk†, a route of importance to French staff officers planning the invasion of Russia; a so-called 'grand road' also ran from Moscow to St Petersburg, but it was in places little more than a dirt track, thick with mud from autumn to early summer if not impassable with ice. In Spain, Charles IV† undertook a road-building programme which was cut short in 1808, although there was a reasonably good route from Burgos southwards through Madrid to Ciudad Real. In the Iberian Peninsula in general, reported a

French engineer officer in 1809, 'travelling is very difficult, attended with inexpressible fatigue and sometimes with peril'. Roads of some importance ran from Badajoz† to the Tagus opposite Portugal's capital and from Lisbon inland northwards to Coimbra and Oporto†. By contrast, Great Britain had developed the turnpike system of roads so effectively in the period 1750–90 that by the outbreak of the French Revolution mail coaches covered 120 miles between London and Bristol in seventeen hours. Further improvements, dating from the scientific surveys of Thomas Telford in 1803, ensured that even before 'macadamizing' of the road surfaces began in 1819 it was customary for carriages to average ten miles an hour along a comprehensive trunk system.

ROCHEFORT

French naval base ten miles up the River Charente from the estuary in the Bay of Biscay, developed as a port by Colbert between 1665 and 1674. The port itself was protected by a fort on a chalk bluff overlooking a long meander in the river, but the principal anchorage was in the roadstead at the estuary between the islands of Aix and Oléron. A loose blockade by British vessels did not prevent several expeditions from sailing into the Atlantic during the Wars of the First and Second Coalitions. Even when a tighter blockade was mounted by Cornwallis† after the breakdown of the Peace of Amiens†, Admiral Missiessy was able to give the Royal Navy the slip in a snowstorm on 11 January 1805 and head for the West Indies†. Napoleon inspected the base in the first week of August 1808 and ordered the construction of new trunk roads to serve the port. However on 11–12 April 1809 a British raid with fireships on the Aix roadstead – though not entirely successful – caused such alarm in the Ministry of Marine that the naval authorities thereafter gave preference to the more secure anchorage of Brest†. After his second abdication†, Napoleon reached Rochefort on 3 July 1815 hoping for a safe conduct to the United States aboard one of two frigates lying in the Charente. He remained at Rochefort until 8 July, spent four days aboard the frigate *Saale* and then landed on the Île d'Aix, finally embarking on HMS *Bellerophon†* in the roadstead on 15 July.

ROEDERER, Pierre Louis, Count (1754–1835)

French journalist and economist: born in Metz, the son of a magistrate. As early as 1779 he was a member of the parlement in Lorraine, displaying the liberal principles to which he consistently adhered. He sat in the Constituent Assembly 1789–91 and became a great admirer of Condorcet. Roederer was a natural *Idéologue†* but, unlike other members of that group, he consistently supported Bonaparte, became a member of the Council of State† and a Senator. He was one of the ablest of administrators, a skilful financier who showed respect for constitutional forms, drafting with great care the resolution inviting Bonaparte to assume the Life Consulship. From 1815 onwards Roederer was engaged in historical studies, but his most interesting work is probably the *Journal*, not published until 1909 but giving a vivid picture of the Consulate. At times Roederer appears to have been what would today be considered a speechwriter for the Emperor, elegantly editing bulletins and proclamations.

ROMANTICISM

A revolt against classical formality and restraint, seeking to express transcendent qualities of imagination rather than obey rational discipline. Romanticism showed itself in literature, drama, music and most of the visual arts, especially painting. The Romantic revolt began by evoking Graeco-Roman themes, exemplified by

Napoleon's neoclassical admiration for a consulate and his liking for the laurel wreathes of a Roman triumph rather than for an ornate crown at his coronation†. By 1804, however, the Romantics were harking back to an idealized Middle Ages. This movement was exemplified by Schiller† who published his *Wilhelm Tell* that year, and in the appearance of Walter Scott's† first collection of Border ballads. Bonaparte's principal visual propagandist, David†, had, like his master, moved from neoclassicism to a subjectivity of expression which allowed the imagination to shape his work. Beethoven†, although in many respects a classicist in technique, found in the *Eroica Symphony* one of the supreme expressions of Romantic intensity. For, as the Lake Poets† discovered, Romanticism was in part the communication as vividly as possible of an emotional state held in deep passion. Goethe† and the brothers Schlegel† helped shape German Romanticism at Jena† and Weimar†; but the principal forerunners of the literary Romantic Movement in France, Mme de Staël† and Chateaubriand†, had a totally different emotional appeal from that of the early German Romantics. So, too, did Byron† and Shelley†. Once military events turned against Napoleon, Romanticism became a liberating force in politics, helping to inflame Germany and other lands with a mood of national patriotic emotionalism. Yet, within a decade, the frustrations of the Metternich era and the sentimental appeal of Prometheus on his rock in the South Atlantic turned the Romantic Movement back to Bonapartism. From 1828 to 1848 the cult of the Napoleonic Legend (see *Béranger*) was a potent force in politics. Romanticism, the least rational of cultural creeds, remained consistent only in its inconsistency.

ROME

Despite the incursions of Bonaparte's armies into the Papal States† in 1796 no attempt was made to seize Rome until riots in the city culminated in the assassination of the French General, Jean-Pierre Duphot, by a corporal in the Papal Guard on 27 December 1797. Soon afterwards Berthier† occupied Rome and a Roman Republic was proclaimed in February 1798, Pope Pius VI† being taken as a prisoner to Valence. Neapolitan troops overthrew the Republic and occupied Rome at midsummer of the following year. Pius VII†, elected pontiff at a conclave in Venice, arrived in Rome in July 1800 and maintained reasonably normal relations with Bonaparte until the French fortified Ancona in October 1805. On 2 February 1808 General Miollis seized the fortress of Sant'Angelo and put Rome under French military occupation, although with no more than 300 men. A war of nerves continued until 17 May 1809 when Napoleon, at Schönbrunn†, announced the annexation of Rome and the Papal States; Rome was proclaimed the 'second city' of the French Empire, although Napoleon never visited it. The Pope was arrested by Miollis's deputy, General Radet, and deported to France. Miollis remained in control of Rome until January 1814 when Neapolitan troops loyal to Murat† took over the city. They surrendered authority to Pius VII on his return in triumph on 24 May 1814.

ROME, King of

Title bestowed at birth on the only child of Napoleon and Marie Louise (see *Napoleon* II).

ROSETTA STONE

The principal discovery of the Artistic and Scientific Commission which Bonaparte insisted should accompany his expedition to Egypt†. In July 1799 a basalt slab was discovered at Rosetta, on the western mouth of the Nile, by Captain Bouchard of the French corps of engineers. He realized that the triple parallel version of a decree of Ptolemy V written in Greek, and Egyptian demotic and hieroglyphic might provide a key to the decipherment of hieroglyphics. The slab passed into British hands when General Hutchinson's Anglo-Turkish force occupied Rosetta in April 1801; but it was a Frenchman, Jean Champollion (1790–1832), who deciphered the hieroglyphics, three years after Napoleon's death. The stone is on display in the British Museum and has formed the basis of Egyptology during a century and a half of scientific study.

ROSTOPCHIN, Fedor Vasilievich, Count (1763–1826)

Governor-General of Moscow: born in Moscow†, travelled widely as a young man, visiting England in 1788. He later tried to introduce English farming techniques on his estate at Voronovo, thirty miles south of Moscow. Paul I† liked Rostopchin and he was briefly in charge of foreign affairs but he remained out of favour with Alexander I† until the spring of 1812 when the Tsar, on the prompting of Grand Duchess Catherine Pavlovna†, made him Governor-General of Moscow. During the first weeks of the campaign Rostopchin energetically encouraged patriotic resistance, especially while Alexander was visiting Moscow in July. But Rostopchin was not liked by the Moscovites; they thought him a braggart, a bully and a coward. As the French approached the city, he ordered the removal of all fire fighting equipment and encouraged police agents to lay trails of combustible materials, thus making certain that any fires begun as the French entered the city would speedily spread. Rostopchin then withdrew to Voronovo where he entertained Sir Robert Wilson† and General Bennigsen† on 1 October 1812, inviting them to watch him fire his home rather than risk its fall to the French. Subsequently he retired to Vladimir but was reinstated as Governor-General in Moscow in 1814. Catherine the Great had nicknamed him 'crazy Theo', perhaps with good reason.

Rostopchin, Governor-General of Moscow, and the Kremlin

ROTHSCHILD FAMILY: bankers

Meyer Amschel Rothschild (1743–1812), born in Frankfurt, founded a moneylender's business which became a bank, Meyer himself becoming financial adviser to the ruler of Hesse. The house prospered by assisting the transmission of money from London to the army in the Iberian Peninsula, by advancing subsidies to anti-French rulers on behalf of the British and by negotiating loans for Denmark. Meyer Amschel's five sons spread the banking network wider. Nathan M. Rothschild (1777–1836) settled originally in Manchester but opened his London bank in 1803 and handled Britain's war subsidies to her allies, in collaboration with his father. He was also able to supply funds for the hastily improvised expeditionary force which fought at Waterloo. Solomon Rothschild (1774–1855) controlled the Vienna bank, bolstering Austria's shaky post-war finances. Charles Rothschild (1783–1855) established the bank in Naples, James (1792–1868) in Paris after the Restoration. Meyer Amschel's eldest son Anselm M. Rothschild (1773–1855) continued the banking house in Frankfurt. The family connection allowed the Rothschilds to play a more international role than the banking houses of the previous century.

ROUSTAM, Raza (c. 1780–1845)

Napoleon's personal bodyguard: born in Armenia but was kidnapped at the age of seven and sold as a Mameluke† slave. He belonged first to Salih Bey (who was murdered at Acre in 1797 on returning from a pilgrimage to Mecca) and then to the leading sheik in Cairo, El-Bekri, who presented him to Bonaparte as a gift in June 1799. Roustam was Napoleon's bodyguard and valet for nearly fifteen years, continuing to dress as a Mameluke at his master's command and constantly at his side, even during the retreat from Moscow. At Fontainebleau† in 1814 he

deserted Napoleon, probably fearing for his life, and went into hiding. Later he married a French girl, gave his name to a collection of *Mémoires*, spent some years in London and reappeared publicly in Paris on 14–15 December 1840 for the interment of Napoleon's remains in the Invalides.

RUE SAINT-NICAISE PLOT (1800)

On Christmas Eve 1800 the First Consul set out in a carriage procession from the Tuileries for the Opéra to hear Haydn's *Creation*. A wagon with a large barrel on it blocked a narrow slum alley, the Rue Saint-Nicaise, not far from the Tuileries. Bonaparte's escort pushed the wagon aside. Soon afterwards the wagon exploded, killing 22 onlookers and wounding another 56 people. Josephine, her daughter and Caroline Bonaparte† in the second carriage had a lucky escape, Hortense being slightly injured by flying glass. Bonaparte blamed the attack on Jacobin agitators and ordered action to be taken

The attempted assassination of Bonaparte in the Rue Saint Nicaise, Paris, 24 December 1800

against the former Jacobins arrested after the Aréna Conspiracy† in October. The assassination was planned by three royalists, two of whom (Carbon and Saint-Rejant) were arrested in January and guillotined on 21 April; the third, a Breton named Limoélan, was smuggled out of the country by supporters of Cadoudal† and eventually became a priest in the United States. Bonaparte ordered the damaged slum to be razed as part of a project to improve the approaches to the Tuileries.

RUMYANTSEV, Nicholas Petrovich
(1765–1826)

Russian Foreign Minister: born in St Petersburg, the son of a distinguished soldier, and entered the diplomatic service in 1779. Tsar Paul† made him a State Councillor and he was Alexander's Minister of Commerce in 1802. Rumyantsev was extremely wealthy, with some 30,000 serfs on his estates, and was a natural Anglophobe. He took effective charge of foreign affairs in September 1807 in succession to Budberg† but was not officially styled Foreign Minister until February, 1808. More than any other Russian statesman, Rumyantsev favoured collaboration with Napoleon. He welcomed the chance to acquire Finland†, accompanied Alexander to Erfurt†, asserting that the Continental System† stimulated Russian industry. Although he was created State Chancellor in 1809, by the following year the Tsar was looking elsewhere for advice on foreign policy. In May 1812 Rumyantsev suffered a stroke but he clung to office until August 1814, urging appeasement of France even during the first weeks of Napoleon's invasion of Russia in 1812. The Tsar took him to Åbo† for the discussions with the Swedes in late August 1812 but thereafter ignored him, depending increasingly on Nesselrode†.

RUSSIA

Emerged as a Great Power during the eighteenth century. Under the German-born Empress Catherine the Great (reigned 1762–96) a huge tract of territory was annexed from the Baltic to the Black Sea, establishing the empire's frontier westwards to the rivers Niemen† and Dnieper so as to give Russia a common border with the two other east-central European autocracies, Austria and Prussia. At the same time, the acquisition from Turkey of the Crimea, the coast of the Sea of Azov, Odessa† and much of the Caucasus opened new routes to the south, posing the 'Eastern Question'† to trouble diplomacy. Russia's new-found status in world affairs was shown in 1780 when Catherine took the initiative in establishing the first 'Armed Neutrality'† confederacy, to protect shipping rights. In her last years Catherine denounced the evils of the French Revolution but was too absorbed by the problems of Poland† to join the First Coalition†. Her successor, Paul 1†, went to war against France primarily over a question of little concern to Tsardom, the seizure by Bonaparte of the island of Malta†. The rapidity with which Paul reversed policy after Suvorov's brilliant campaigns in Switzerland and northern Italy and began to plan a march across central Asia on British India shows the extent to which Russian policy still appeared dependent on the whim of the autocrat in St Petersburg. Alexander 1†, too, could make astonishing changes in foreign alignment: amicable collaboration with the First Consul until the murder of Enghien†; vigorous participation in the War of the Second Coalition†; peace and alliance with Napoleon at Tilsit†; uncompromising defiance of France from 1811 to 1814. But Alexander was more responsive than Paul to the advice of his ministers: his friends in the 'Secret Committee'†, Speransky†, Rumyantsev†, and the sinister Arakcheev†. Gradually Russia acquired an apparatus of sound administration although the fundamental character of autocratic rule remained unchanged.

The Russia of Napoleon's day was an empire of slightly over 41 million people, of whom seven in every hundred lived in a town. 'The Tsar's realm is no more than an empire of villages', wrote a German traveller in 1795. Most people lived and worked on large self-contained estates, the economy resting on obligations of personal serfdom†. The prosperity of a noble was counted by the number of male serfs whom he owned and his class status was dependent on the degree of direct service which he rendered to the Tsar. On the eve of the Napoleonic invasion in 1812 some 58 per cent of the men in European Russia were constrained by direct obligations of serfdom. The greatest internal threat to Russia was a rising of the serfs; their loyalty to the Russian state in the crisis weeks of 1812 sprang partly from the hope that the Tsar was sufficiently enlightened to ease their burden but mainly from the influence of the most powerful institution in Russia, the Orthodox Church. The deep religious feeling of the Russian soldiery had nothing to do with the condemnation of Napoleon as Anti-Christ; the priests' encouragement of a mystical sense of inner contentment made external suffering acceptable. 'Holy Russia' was a community in which the Tsar was 'the little Father' but which accepted the egalitarian humility of all believers before relics of the Faith. This other-worldly lowliness of the person distinguished Orthodoxy from the social influence of the Church in western Europe and perplexed foreign observers, especially those who left written records of the 1812 campaign†.

The penetration of the Tsar's armies to Paris in 1814 was to contemporaries in the West the most startling legacy of Napoleon's primacy in Europe. The apparently limitless resources of Russian manpower, the extraordinary resilience of the Tsar's empire, and the unfamiliar ways of a society rooted in serfdom and Orthodoxy, speedily conjured up the 'Russian bogey' which was to obsess public opinion in the West for so many generations that people forgot how it had come into being.

SAINT-CLOUD

Was, in Napoleon's time, a small sub-urban town about nine miles west of central Paris on the left bank of the Seine. In 1658 Louis XIV purchased an existing château which was converted into a palace for his brother, the Duke of Orleans. Louis XVI presented the palace to Marie Antoinette in 1782. It was in the Oranger-ie of the palace on 10 Novemeber 1799 that the Council of Five Hundred† was dispersed by Bonaparte's troops in the Brumaire† *coup*; the two Councils of the Directory† had gathered at Saint-Cloud after warnings from Bonaparte of a pos-sible Jacobin rising in the capital itself. The First Consul ignored the existence of the palace until 1801 despite a petition from the townsfolk to make it an official residence. While at Malmaison† in November 1801 he told Berthier† that he wanted a more impressive suburban palace for state receptions, and his architects, Percier and Fontaine, refur-bished Saint-Cloud for three million francs in time for Bonaparte and Josephine to go into residence on 20 September 1802. As Consul and Emper-or, he spent more days at Saint-Cloud than at any other palace in Paris or its vicinity, staying there for the last time in the third week of November 1813. Elabo-rate ceremonial attended the ambassado-rial receptions and state occasions at Saint-Cloud although the proclamation of the Empire, in the presence of the Senate and Council of State on 18 May 1804, was a quiet affair. Marie-Louise† liked Saint-Cloud and remained there for most of the five months in which Napoleon was absent on his Russian campaign. Blücher† set up his headquarters there in July 1815. Fire destroyed the palace on 13 October 1870 during the Franco-Prussian War.

SAINT-CYR

A small town five miles from Versailles. A convent school for ladies of high birth and low means was founded by Madame de Maintenon in 1686, under Louis XIV's patronage. The school was closed in 1792, as a privileged preserve of the nobility; Elisa Bonaparte† was one of the last pupils there. On 1 May 1802 the First Consul established a military academy (*École spéciale militaire*), planned origi-nally for Fontainebleau† or Versailles, but opening in the former convent school in 1803; extensive new buildings were added five years later. Napoleon personally stu-died the detailed curriculum of the academy, which supplied him with 4,000 officers between 1805 and 1815. Some 700 Saint-Cyriens perished in the Napoleonic campaigns, the first three falling at Au-sterlitz†. After the Second World War the academy was moved to Coëtquidan, south-west of Rennes.

ST HELENA

Volcanic island in the South Atlantic, 1,200 miles west of southern Africa. It was a British colony, occasionally used as a port of call on the long voyages to and from India: Wellington† spent a month there while returning from service in India in 1805. The decision to exile Napoleon to St Helena was taken while he was aboard *Bellerophon*† in Torbay; he was told the news by Admiral Lord Keith on 31 July.

St Helena; Napoleon dictating to Las Cases

HMS *Northumberland*, with 'General Bonaparte' aboard, arrived off the island on 15 October 1815. He stayed for seven weeks at the home of the East India Company's agent, 'The Briars', before moving to Longwood where he spent the last five years and four months of his life. Petty restrictions imposed by the Governor, Sir Hudson Lowe†, in 1816 irked Napoleon and his small group of French attendants (see *Bertrand, Gourgaud, Las Cases, Montholon*). The Emperor was frequently unwell, his doctor – O'Meara† – diagnosing hepatitis; and his physical condition declined rapidly from mid-March 1821. He died on 5 May, a post-mortem finding evidence of stomach cancer; tests on hair preserved by descendants of his servants showed an unusually high level of arsenic (which may have been absorbed from the medicines of the day). His coffin was exhumed on 15 October 1840 and conveyed in the French frigate *Belle-Poule* to Cherbourg for interment in Paris.

ST VINCENT, Earl of (John Jervis, 1735–1823)
Admiral: born in Staffordshire, entering the Royal Navy at the age of fourteen and distinguishing himself in successive campaigns against the French between 1759 and 1782. He led the first naval expedition to the West Indies† (1793–4). As Admiral Sir John Jervis he was given command in the Mediterranean in 1795, with Nelson† as one of his captains. Jervis gained a resounding victory over France's Spanish ally off Cape St Vincent on 14 February 1797, commemorating the triumph in the title he assumed when created an earl later in the year. Addington† brought him into the cabinet in February 1801 as First Lord of the Admiralty; he reformed naval administration and also improved food and conditions at sea. So confident was he of the navy's ability to hold off an invasion in 1803 that he told the House of Lords, 'I do not say the French cannot come; I only say they cannot come by sea.' Pitt†, thinking him too cautious, did not retain

him as First Lord in 1804. Two years later St Vincent returned to sea as commander-in-chief in the Channel, taking a squadron to the Tagus in the autumn of 1806 so as to strengthen Portugal† against the incursions of the French. He retired in 1807. 'Old Jack' was a tough disciplinarian, respected by his men. After 1795 he tended to despise politicians because of a vote of censure moved by members of the Commons who found their West Indian profits falling by emergency defence contributions he had levied while serving in the Caribbean.

SALAMANCA

University city on the River Tormes, some 110 miles north-west of Madrid. It was occupied briefly by Sir John Moore† in late November 1808 and used as a base to threaten Napoleon's flank in the short campaign which ended at Corunna†. The Battle of Salamanca of 22 July 1812 gave Wellington† his decisive victory in the Peninsular War†. The city had already fallen to Wellington on 27 June after token resistance from three forts garrisoned by Marmont†. Three weeks later, with the war in a condition of stalemate, Wellington gave the impression that he was ordering a retreat to Ciudad Rodrigo†. Marmont duly moved his army across the Tormes to the south-east of the city hoping to cut Wellington's line around two groups of hills, the Greater Arpiles and the Lesser Arpiles. This manoeuvre, however, dangerously extended the French forces; they were caught in the heavy cannon fire, Marmont himself badly wounded. Sir Edward Pakenham's Third Division then led a cavalry charge which 'beat 40,000 men in 40 minutes'. The infantry completed the assault with muskets and bayonets. Only the failure of Spanish troops to occupy a vital bridge over the Tormes enabled the French to avoid total disaster. As it was, Salamanca destroyed the French hold on northern and central Spain.

SALONS

During the years 1750–85 high society in Paris reverted to a social practice of the days of Richelieu and Mazarin in convening informal assemblies in a private house regularly once or twice a week to discuss literature, art or politics. These *salons* normally met on the initiative of the lady of the house, the hostesses thereby acquiring considerable influence. Political salons revived as early as 1792·and at first Bonaparte encouraged the institution, partly as a means of reconciling old and new nobility. Mesdames Récamier† and de Staël† soon achieved a social eminence as intellectual hostesses; Laure Junot† had fleeting success while her husband was military governor in Paris. Under the Empire the salons became increasingly associated with the ex-émigré opposition and with the *Idéologues*†; there was a group of liberal salons in the Faubourg Saint-Germain, led by hostesses of aristocratic descent such as Mme de Laval-Montmorency and the Princesse de Salm-Dyck. Talleyrand† moved in this circle, while Chateaubriand† and Benjamin Constant† were fêted by Mme Récamier.

SALZBURG

City 155 miles south-west of Vienna, an archiepiscopal principality secularized by the Imperial Recess† of 1803 and transferred to Austrian rule by the Treaty of Pressburg† (1805) as compensation for Habsburg losses in Italy. Salzburg was surrendered to France's ally, Bavaria†, by the Peace of Schönbrunn† (1809) but became Austrian again five years later. Napoleon never visited Salzburg.

SAN SEBASTIAN

Port in north-western Spain, on the Bay of Biscay, besieged by the British 25 July to 8 September 1813. Wellington was unwilling to cross the Bidassoa† and invade France so long as San Sebastian was in enemy hands, threatening his communications. The town was taken, with heavy casualties on 31 August after the French had repulsed the first assault. The French commandant, General Rey (1768–1846), then continued resistance on the peninsula citadel of Monte Urgullo for another nine days. During this period there was an extraordinary outburst of looting and arson as the Peninsular Army sacked the town. Wellington, by contrast, allowed Rey to march out with full military honours on his surrender.

Santo Domingo (Saint-Domingue)

The name formerly given to Haiti†, but now, more precisely, the eastern half of the island. A revolt led by Juan Sánchez Ramírez in 1808 routed a French force at Palo Hincado and successfully besieged the city of Santo Domingo, securing freedom from French, Haitian and Spanish rule from 1809 until 1814 when the region passed nominally under Spanish sovereignty. Independence followed in 1821; and in 1844 the Dominican Republic was set up.

Saragossa

Spanish provincial city, former capital of mediaeval Aragon, stands on the River Ebro 160 miles west of Barcelona. Saragossa was twice besieged by the French in 1808–9: (i) 15 June to 17 August; improvised defences thrown up by Palafox† repulsed Bessières's† army in a 'war to the knife'; on 4 July there was a famous episode in which Augustina ('the Maid of Saragossa') manned and fired a deserted cannon at a critical moment as the French tried to break through the Portillo Gate; (ii) 20 December 1808 to 20 February 1809; five weeks of grim fighting, with Mortier† enveloping the city and Lannes† forcing his way in, street by street. More than 50,000 Spaniards perished in this second siege, the French losing 10,000 troops. Thereafter the French hold on Aragon remained secure until 1812–13.

Sardinia-Piedmont, Kingdom of

The Dukes of Savoy, rulers of Piedmont since the sixteenth century, increased their power astutely at the start of the eighteenth century, receiving the island of Sardinia in 1720. The sovereign of Piedmont was proclaimed King of Sardinia in Turin on 24 August 1720 and his successors bore that title until 1860, even though the richest and strategically most important part of their realm remained on the Italian mainland, between Nice and the River Ticino. By 1750 Sardinia-Piedmont had become the principal military state in northern Italy, the peninsula's Prussia; but the army could not resist the sustained power of the French Republic. Defeat by Bonaparte at Montenotte† in April 1796 was followed by the Armistice of Cherasco†, giving France control of all the Piedmontese fortresses. Victor Amadeus III, king since 1773, died six months after Cherasco and was succeeded by his son, Charles Emmanuel IV. The new king was devout but politically weak. Faced by liberal unrest in Turin, he fled to the island of Sardinia in October 1798, abdicating in favour of his brother, Victor Emmanuel I, in June 1802. From 1799 to 1814 Piedmont, on the mainland, was under French domination, becoming four départements within metropolitan France; Sardinia, however, remained in Allied hands, protected by the British fleet. Victor Emmanuel I returned to Turin in 1814; he eventually secured Genoa† as well as recovering Nice and Savoy, lost to France as early as 1792. Desultory fighting took place in June 1815 along the new Franco-Piedmontese frontier when Marshal Suchet† led his small Army of the Alps eastwards during the Waterloo campaign. Victor Emmanuel's folly in seeking to restore the old regime in its entirety in Piedmont aroused liberal resentment, for his subjects had benefited from the Napoleonic Codes and the growth of religious toleration. Liberal revolts forced Victor Emmanuel I to abdicate in March 1821 but it was another twenty-seven years before the kingdom was granted an enduring constitution.

SAVARY, Anne Jean Marie René
(1774–1833)

French general and Minister of Police: born at Marcq, in the Ardennes, his father being a cavalry major in the Sedan garrison. After service on the Rhine he became aide-de-camp to Desaix† from 1797 until his death at Marengo†. In 1803–4 he was assigned to counter intelligence work and, in this capacity, played a sinister role in the abduction and eventual execution of Enghien†. He was at Austerlitz†, undertaking two special missions from Napoleon to Alexander† on the eve of the battle which it was hoped might avoid an engagement. The two missions also enabled Savary to spy out the land. Early in 1807 Savary distinguished himself in temporary command of V Corps at Ostrolenka in Poland. By the end of July that year, however, he was in St Petersburg as Napoleon's first personal envoy to the Tsar, following Tilsit†. Napoleon created him Duke of Rovigo in May 1808 and entrusted him with special tasks in Spain. Savary was later blamed for 'trapping' Charles IV† and Ferdinand IV† into surrendering the Spanish crown at Bayonne†. In June 1810 he succeeded Fouché† as Minister of Police, holding the post until April 1814, acting vigorously when faced by discontent over the price of bread† and tightening press censorship† but showing laxity towards the opposition salons in Paris. The British refused to allow Savary to accompany Napoleon into exile aboard *Bellerophon*†, even though he had conducted some of the negotiations at Rochefort† for the Emperor's surrender. Savary, probably with justification, feared a death sentence for his part in the Enghien crime; he fled to Turkey but was eventually pardoned, living for several years at Rome. Briefly in 1831–2 he commanded Louis Philippe's army pacifying Algiers.

SAVONA

Small Italian city on the Ligurian coast, twenty-four miles west of Genoa. Bonaparte occupied the bishop's palace (10–12 April 1796) on the eve of the battle of Montenotte†. In July 1809 he recommended the palace as a suitable place of internment for Pope Pius VII†, who arrived there a month later. The Pope was removed to Fontainebleau† in June 1812, for fear that he might be rescued by a British warship. Briefly Pius VII stayed there again on his return to Italy in February 1814.

SAXONY

Historically the duchy of Saxony goes back to the ninth century but its geographical boundaries have been almost as amorphous as those of Poland. Duke Frederick the Valiant (1370–1428) was made the first Elector of Saxony in 1420. From 1697 until 1763 the Electors of Saxony were also the elected Kings of Poland; the most famous of these rulers was Augustus the Strong (Elector, 1694–1733), who had one legitimate son and 354 acknowledged bastards and who abandoned the Lutheranism of his Saxon subjects for the Catholicism of his Polish ones, all later Saxon rulers retaining the Catholic faith. By 1790 Saxony was an impoverished state, partly because of Augustus the Strong's extravagance in beautifying Dresden†, partly through the cost of the Polish connection, but even more through the ravages of successive wars. Elector Frederick Augustus† accordingly maintained neutrality until 1806, when the Prussians cajoled him into alliance. Saxony provided 20,000 men for the Jena campaign but, by the Treaty of Posen (11 December 1806), made peace and accepted proposals put forward earlier in the year by Napoleon: Frederick Augustus became King, Saxony joined the Rhine Confederation†. The Polish connection was renewed in 1807 when Frederick Augustus became Napoleon's

The exiled Pope Pius VII about to leave Savona for Fontainebleau, June 1812

puppet Grand Duke of Warsaw†, an act that brought down on Saxony in the post-war period the wrath of the principal partitioners of Poland, Russia and Prussia. Saxony was again devastated by the campaign of 1813, a Russian general administering the kingdom from November 1813 to November 1814 when he was succeeded by a Prussian general. In April 1815 the Vienna Congress† ceded two-fifths of Saxony to Prussia, allowing Frederick Augustus to retain the title of King and the cities of Dresden and Leipzig in what remained of his inheritance. Saxony was again defeated in 1866 when she fought alongside Austria against Bismarck's Prussia, but from 1871 to 1918 the kingdom survived as an integral part of the German Empire. Saxony is now divided into three administrative districts (*Bezirke*) of the German Democratic Republic.

SCHARNHORST, Gerhard Johann von (1755–1813)
Prussian soldier: born at Bordenau in Hanover, his father being a sergeant in George III's army. Scharnhorst fought as a junior officer under the Duke of York† in the Netherlands in 1792. His subsequent writings on military affairs aroused interest in Berlin; he was invited to become an instructor at the Prussian War Academy in 1801, receiving a patent of nobility at the same time. At Auerstädt† he was Brunswick's chief-of-staff and was taken prisoner, slightly wounded, but was later exchanged for a senior French officer. His valour at Eylau† won him promotion to major-general (1807) and he became Director of the War Department, reforming the Prussian army after its defeats. Between 1808 and 1810 he increased the number of trained soldiers by instituting a short service system he abo-

General von Scharnhorst, the Prussian army reformer

lished savage punishments, held out in-ducements of promotion from the ranks and improved field mobility and training in musketry. So alarmed was Napoleon by Scharnhorst's programme that he forced Frederick William III† to dismiss him in June 1810, but Scharnhorst maintained contacts with the court, and even with St Petersburg. He was reinstated on the outbreak of the War of Liberation. On 2 May 1813 he was gravely wounded at Lützen† and died two months later at Prague. His reforms were completed by Gneisenau†, his teachings developed by Clausewitz†.

SCHELLING, Friedrich Wilhelm Joseph von (1775–1854)

German philosopher: born at Leonberg in Württemberg, became a friend of Hegel† and from 1798 to 1803 was a professor at Jena† where he influenced the literary circle associated with the Schlegels†. His philosophy, expressed in works on trans-cendental idealism published during his Jena years, was intellectually confused and more mystical than that of most of his German contemporaries. Yet in elevating the importance of imaginative thought over any quest for a logical system he became the natural philosopher of Romanticism† in Germany. His later years were spent in Würzburg, Munich and Berlin.

SCHÉRER, Barthélemy Louis Joseph (1747–1804)

French general: born in Belgium, served the Austrians in the Seven Years War, Louis XVI in 1780 and the Dutch from 1785 to 1790. Two years later he helped orga-nize the French 'Army of the Rhine', was promoted general in 1794 and won a succession of victories along France's northern frontier. In the winter of 1795–6 he commanded in northern Italy, but was so often drunk that he quarrelled with the Directory† and was ordered to hand over his Army of Italy to the young Bonaparte in May 1796. After the fall of Carnot†, Schérer was Minister of War, and in February 1799 assumed command of French armies in Italy, hoping to check the invasion by Suvorov†. Schérer was defeated at Magnano by the Austrian General von Krajova on 5 April 1799 and handed over his command to Moreau†. Charges of peculation against Schérer were dropped on the First Consul's orders after Brumaire.

SCHILLER (Johann Christoph) Friedrich von (1759–1805)

German dramatist: born at Marbach in Württemberg, the son of an army surgeon. He was himself from 1780 to 1782 a medical officer at Stuttgart where he was reprimanded by the reigning Duke for writing *Die Räuber*, a passionate dra-ma rich in young and angry revolt. Schiller then left Württemberg, eventually settling in Weimar† in 1790, with a great verse tragedy *Don Carlos* (1787) to his credit. From 1794 until his death he was encouraged by the friendship, patronage and occasional critical collaboration of Goethe†. The greatest of Schiller's dramatic works were written and presented at Weimar virtually within the brief span of the French Consulate: the trilogy on *Wallenstein* (1798–9); *Maria Stuart* (1800); *Die Jungfrau von Orleans* (1801); *Wilhelm Tell* (1804). He died from tuberculosis at Weimar in May 1805, less than eighteen months before French troops overran the area.

SCHIMMELPENNINCK, Rutger Jan
(1761–1825)
Dutch political leader: born at Deventer in Overijssel province, studied law at Leiden and became an advocate in Amsterdam. As leader of the moderate bourgeois 'Patriot' party Schimmelpenninck organized the Batavian Republic in July 1798 in a political form which he assumed would be acceptable to France but in which he was determined to assert Dutch independence. He hoped in vain for French military evacuation of the Netherlands during the Peace of Amiens†. Thereafter he never trusted Napoleon, an instinct which was reciprocated: 'M. de Schimmelpenninck is too virtuous for the century in which we live', the Emperor sardonically remarked after meeting him in Paris. Nevertheless, Schimmelpenninck agreed to Napoleon's proposal that he should become virtual dictator of Holland† ('Grand Pensionary') on 22 March 1805 and for a year he was able to carry out a series of progressive reforms. In May 1806, however, Napoleon had become so suspicious of the Dutch that he presented Schimmelpenninck's executive council with a choice between accepting a Bonapartist kingdom or being absorbed into France. Schimmelpenninck thereupon retired with dignity, although Louis Bonaparte† assiduously tried to court his favour.

SCHLEGEL, August Wilhelm von
(1767–1845)
German poet and critic; born in Hanover, educated at Göttingen but joined the intellectual group associated with Jena† university in 1796, at first in collaboration with Schiller†. Together with his brother (*see below*) he shaped early German Romanticism†, especially in the periodical *Das Athenäum*, which the brothers produced from 1798 to 1800. In later years he became a literary adviser to Mme de Staël† and was much respected as translator and lecturer, particularly on dramatic art.

SCHLEGEL, (Carl Wilhelm) Friedrich von
(1772–1829)
German critic; born in Hanover, educated at Leipzig university and collaborated with his elder brother at Jena until 1802 when, after quarrels with Schiller, he moved to Paris. He settled in Austria in 1806, became a zealous convert to Catholicism and was an anti-Bonapartist writer for Metternich†.

SCHÖNBRUNN
Maria Theresa's rococo summer palace a few miles from the centre of Vienna†. Napoleon was in residence there on three occasions: 13–16 November 1805, after the capture of Vienna; 12–28 December 1805, after Austerlitz†; and, in the Wagram campaign†, intermittently between 10 May and 16 October 1809. His only son, the Duke of Reichstadt (see *Napoleon II*), died there from tuberculosis in 1832.

SCHÖNBRUNN, Treaty of (14 October 1809)
Followed Austria's defeat at Wagram†. Emperor Francis lost three and a half million subjects, ceding Croatia, Fiume and Trieste to France (see *Illyrian Provinces*) and transferring Salzburg† and

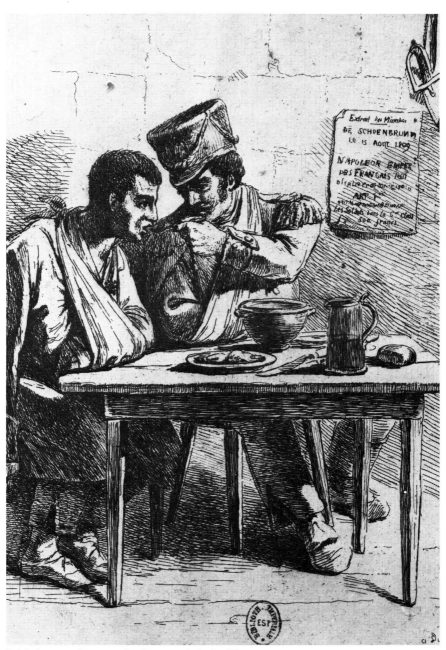

Schönbrunn, 1809: care for the wounded after Wagram

Berchtesgaden to Bavaria†, western Galicia† to the Duchy of Warsaw†, and Tarnopol to Napoleon's nominal ally, Russia. Austria also agreed to pay a considerable indemnity to the French, to join the Continental System†, and to accept limitation of the army to 150,000 men.

SCHWARZENBERG, Karl Philip, Prince von (1771–1820)

Austrian field marshal and diplomat: born in Vienna, commissioned in the cavalry in 1788, seeing action against the Turks as well as against the revolutionary armies in the Netherlands. By 1800 he was a general, ably extricating the Austrian right wing after Moreau's victory at Hohenlinden†. He rallied the survivors from Mack's† army at Ulm† in 1805, falling back to defend Prague. From 1806 to 1809 he was Austrian ambassador in St Petersburg, showing tact and determination. He became ambassador in Paris after the Treaty of Schönbrunn (*see above*) at a time when Metternich† was promoting the Habsburg-Bonaparte marriage. On 1 July 1810 Schwarzenberg invited 1,500 guests to a grand ball at his embassy in the Rue de Provence to celebrate the marriage. A decorative garland caught fire and the flames spread rapidly. Napoleon and Marie Louise† escaped through the gardens, the Emperor returning to direct the fire-fighters. Several guests perished, including Schwarzenberg's sister-in-law.

Napoleon's admiration for Schwarzenberg's bravery and intelligence led to the ambassador-soldier's appointment as commander of the Austrian auxiliary corps on the right flank of the *Grande Armée*† during the invasion of Russia in 1812. Schwarzenberg, however, shrewdly avoided protracted fighting and in January 1813 concluded an agreement with the Russians by which the Austrian corps withdrew from the war, thus enabling Russian troops to cross the Vistula and seize Warsaw. When seven months later Austria joined Russia and Prussia in the final coalition against France, Schwarzenberg was appointed supreme commander, with the rank of field marshal. He was defeated at Dresden† but his armies won Leipzig†. In January 1814 he led the 'Army of Bohemia' from the Langres Plateau up the River Aube towards Paris. In mid-February he was rebuffed at Troyes and tactically defeated at Arcis†, but sheer weight of numbers was sufficient to sustain the momentum of the Allied offensive. Schwarzenberg duly entered Paris on 31 March 1814. In June 1815 he set out from Vienna but his army had only reached Heidelberg when news came of the decisive Allied victory at Waterloo; his troops crossed the Rhine (23–6 June 1815) and had a sharp engagement with Rapp†, but Schwarzenberg's campaigning days were over. He was grossly overweight for a man of forty-four and in 1817 was paralysed by a stroke.

SCOTT Walter (1771–1832)

Scottish poet and novelist: born and educated in Edinburgh and became interested in the ballad as a form of literature largely from the German poetic tradition. *The Minstrelsy of the Scottish Border* (1802–3) and *The Lay of the Last Minstrel* (1805) made his reputation for verse romance. With the rise of Byron†, Scott looked for an alternative outlet for his literary skill and from 1814 to 1826 was, first and foremost, a novelist, although he did not acknowledge authorship of the *Waverley* novels until 1827. The last phase of his life produced more historical fiction, some plays and a quantity of hack work, including in 1827 one of the earliest biographies in English of Napoleon. The Prince Regent† greatly admired Scott's poetry and created him a baronet in 1820. When, as King George IV, he made the first visit of a ruling member of the House of Hanover to Scotland (August 1822), Sir Walter stage-managed the expedition with astonishing success. Scott's literary achievement was to create out of the stained-glass escapism of early Romanticism† a pseudo-historical realism which was to influence writers and readers in an increasingly nationalistic Europe.

SÉBASTIANI, Horace François (1772–1851) French soldier: born at La Porta in Corsica and was training for the priesthood when the Revolution cut short his studies. He served as an infantry officer in northern Italy and fought with distinction at Marengo†. In the autumn of 1802 he was sent on a special mission to Egypt and Syria with orders to contact local dissidents secretly. On 30 January 1803 the *Moniteur*† took the unusual step of publishing extracts from his official report, in which he claimed that 6,000 French soldiers could reconquer Egypt. Britain regarded the 'Sébastiani Mission' with deep suspicion, the report contributing to the tension which soon ended the Peace of Amiens†. When war resumed Sébastiani commanded a brigade; he led the cavalry into Vienna† in 1805 and was wounded at Austerlitz†. In 1806–7 he was ambassador in Constantinople, encouraging the Turks to resist British assaults on the Dardanelles (February-March 1807) and raising French influence on the Straits to a height unknown since the Revolution. He then participated in the conquest of Andalusia, serving without particular distinction in Spain until 1811. A year later he accompanied Murat† into Moscow. Although wounded at Leipzig†, he recovered to fight under Macdonald† in the final battles of the French campaign†. For several years he represented Corsica in the Chamber of Deputies of the Restoration. Under Louis Philippe he was Minister of Foreign Affairs 1830–2, briefly ambassador in Naples and then succeeded Talleyrand† as ambassador in London (1835–40). In 1840 he was created a Marshal of France.

SECRET COMMITTEE (*Neglasny Komitet*) An informal council of advisers established by Alexander I† in July 1801 to discuss reform at home and the guiding principles on which to base a foreign policy. The Committee comprised four close friends of the Tsar from his years as heir to the throne: Czartoryski†, Novosiltsov†, Stroganov† and Kochubey†. The Committee successfully initiated several reforms: the creation of eight new governmental ministries so as to improve administration; a pioneer project in public education; improved conditions for the sale of serfs†; and definition of the duties of Russia's Senators. But the Tsar rejected proposals for serf emancipation and for cabinet government. There were differences, too, over foreign policy, the Committee favouring continued isolation from the European struggle, while the Tsar was inclined to seek collaboration with Prussia. The Committee's regular meetings ended in June 1802 although the Tsar often consulted his four friends until the summer of 1806. His reluctance to fulfil the recommendations of the Secret Committee was the first of many frustrated hopes in his reign.

SEMAPHORE
Was developed as a signalling system through masts with movable arms by Claude Chappe† in 1791–3 and was encouraged first by Carnot† and later by Bonaparte. A Military Telegraph Service was attached to the *Grande Armée*; it manned visual semaphore stations linking Paris to the frontiers and then supplied flag relay posts to headquarters as the battle front advanced. The system proved remarkably effective in clear weather, conveying news and orders at 120 miles an hour; but couriers on fast horses outpaced the semaphore in the rain and cloud during the first week of the Wagram campaign† in April 1809. In England the Admiralty established a semaphore system along the London to Portsmouth

road. In Portugal Wellington had five semaphore stations operating along the twenty-two miles of defences at Torres Vedras†.

SENATE (French)

The *Sénat Conservateur* originated in the proposals of Sieyès† for what became, in December 1799, the Constitution† of the Year VIII. Sieyès wanted a body which would ensure stability of government, having some of the responsibilities of a Supreme Court of Constitutional Appeal rather than merely proposing or passing laws; and the Senate was therefore intended by Bonaparte's suspicious political allies in Brumaire† to curb the General's dictatorial pretensions. In 1799–1800 it compromised sixty distinguished men over the age of forty, who would hold office for life; twenty-nine were nominated by Sieyès and his political associates, and the remainder by the First Consul, who chose heavily from his companions, military and scientific, in Egypt†. The Senate had the task of choosing, from national lists submitted to it, the composition of the Tribunate† and the Legislative Assembly†; it also possessed, until 1802, certain rights of appointment: magistrates in the appeal Court of Cassation, government accountants, and even the consuls, should they need to be replaced. Bonaparte instituted in 1801 the device known as the *Sénatus-Consulte* (*see below*) which made the Senate little more than an affirmative body for government by decree. There was some reluctance to accord Bonaparte the life consulate after the Peace of Amiens† but thereafter the Senate acquiesced in a succession of measures which reduced its power and lifted its attraction as the most rewarding social institution of the Establishment. Membership was raised to 120 during the Life Consulship, and increased still further by the ex-officio inclusion of imperial dignitaries after 1804. By the end of 1812 the Senate had come to number 141 worthies

(who dutifully turned against the Emperor in April 1814). The Constitution of the Year X deprived the Senators of their rights of appointment; they were, however, compensated by the creation of *Sénatoreries*, certain senators being rewarded with a residential palace and estates so as to give them the dignity of a regional governor. Holders of *sénatoreries* had their senatorial emolument of 25,000 francs a year doubled and would be welcomed into residence on their estate with military honours, including the salute of ceremonial cannon. The Senate became an amenable body, trimming the constitution rather than preserving it as Sieyès had anticipated.

The First Consul also experimented with nominated Senates in the Helvetic Republic and in Italy. In Russia a Senate had been created by Peter the Great in 1711, primarily as a judicial body; in 1801 Alexander I set up a commission to extend the scope of the Senate's work, but little real change was made during his reign.

Sénatus-Consulte

A legislative decree, the *senatus consultum* of classical Rome modified for French needs. These decrees were issued from January 1801 onwards and enabled Napoleon, as Consul and Emperor, to impose laws without debate in the assemblies. The decree merely needed to be 'witnessed' by the Senate†. By this means Napoleon enjoyed an arbitrary power to change the constitution. A *sénatus-consulte* legalized the Constitution† of the Year X in August 1802; and another established the Empire in May 1804.

SENYAVIN'S SQUADRON

From 1798 until 1807 the Russians maintained a considerable naval presence in the Mediterranean. Admiral Ushakov sailed through the Bosphorus and Dardanelles in September 1798 and, in col-

253

laboration with Turkish ships under Admiral Cadirbey, occupied the Ionian Islands† in a series of operations over the following six months and bombarded French-controlled ports in southern Italy. On the eve of the War of the Third Coalition† in 1805 Tsar Alexander I used the Russian foothold on Corfu as the base for a squadron of five warships and several thousand troops, commanded by Admiral Dmitri Senyavin (1763–1831). Over the following two years Senyavin concentrated in the Adriatic. He attacked Franco-Italian vessels off Bari and Ancona and in January 1806 occupied Cattaro† (Kotor), in order to prevent the Austrians from handing over this fine naval anchorage to France. From Cattaro he was able to raid Ragusa (Dubrovnik) and other French outposts in what became known as the Illyrian Provinces†. He also encouraged the Montenegrins and Serbs to collaborate with Russia. His activities were halted by Russia's change of sides at Tilsit†. The squadron tried to sail back to the Baltic but was forced to take refuge in the Tagus estuary and surrendered to the British in 1808 on honourable terms.

SERBIAN REVOLTS

Serbia passed under Turkish rule at the end of the fourteenth century but the Serbian Orthodox Church survived and a sense of nationhood was retained by the many Serbs who lived outside the Ottoman Empire, in southern Hungary and Montenegro. The rapacious rule of local officials and the cruelty of the Janissaries† led the Serbian peasantry to rise in revolt in 1804 under the leadership of Karadjordje† Petrović. Belgrade was taken and an assembly, meeting there in April 1805, petitioned Constantinople for local autonomy. When this plea was rejected, fighting was resumed against the Turkish forces; by June 1807 the heart of mediaeval Serbia was in rebel hands. Factious quarrels and the withdrawal of Russian support in order to concentrate against Napo-

leon enabled Turkey to stamp out the Serbian Revolt by October 1813. A second rising, led by Miloš Obrenović, began in April 1815 and gained a series of military successes which, on this occasion, were backed by Russian diplomatic support, as the great European war was now over. Serbia was accepted as an autonomous principality within the Turkish Empire in 1817 with Miloš as hereditary prince. But the rivalry between the Serbian peasant leaders ran deep and the murder of Karadjordje in June 1817 left a feud between their families which lasted for almost a century.

SERFDOM

During the eighteenth century the line separating a nominally free peasantry from rural labourers constrained by serfdom moved steadily eastwards across Europe. There was no serfdom in Britain, Italy, Spain or Portugal, most of western Germany and France, the Netherlands or Switzerland by 1780. It was legally abolished in Denmark and Norway in 1788 and its remnants were swept away in France in August 1789. But east of the River Elbe and in Hungary† the conditions of the serfs had worsened and their numbers increased during the half-century preceding the French Revolution. Maria Theresa and Joseph II in the Habsburg lands and Frederick the Great in Prussia had attempted to impose legislation easing the burden of serfdom but in Austria and Hungary serfdom survived until 1848 and in Prussia it was ended only by the Emancipation Edict† of 1807; the eastern European autocrats were too dependent on the landed nobility to impose upon them the social revolution of freeing their serfs. There were more than twenty million serfs in Russia at the accession of Paul I†, some committed to household duties and some assigned to working in the new factories rather than in the fields. Conditions had been little better in Poland† before the partitions. The eastward advance of Napoleon's armies meant the ending of serfdom in any region which came within the French Empire or its dependencies. The Poles of the Grand Duchy of Warsaw† benefited most from the Napoleonic social revolution as no attempt was made to reimpose serfdom in the 'Congress' Kingdom of Poland established under the Tsar's auspices in 1815. Until serf emancipation came in Russia in 1861, there remained a constant fear on the part of the authorities that the serfs, quiescent in the Napoleonic invasion, would rise in a bloody revolt as they had in 1773 on the Volga under Pugachev.

SÉRURIER, Jean Mathieu Philibert (1742–1819)

Marshal of the Empire: born at Laon, fought with the infantry in the Seven Years' War, later serving in Portugal and Corsica. Although suspended briefly as a crypto-royalist in 1793, he was a general by 1795, having attached himself to the Barras† faction. He was with Bonaparte at Borghetto† and received the surrender of Mantua† in February 1797. Apart from an unhappy interlude when he failed to check Suvorov† in 1799, his later years were spent in administrative posts. He supported Bonaparte in Brumaire, became a senator, a marshal in May 1804 and a count in 1808. From 1804 to 1815 he was Governor of the *Invalides*, ordering the burning of 1,500 captured colours in March 1814 as Paris was about to fall.

SHELLEY, Percy Bysshe (1792–1822)

English poet: born near Horsham, educated at Eton and University College, Oxford. Almost all his poetry was written after his elopement with Mary Godwin to the Continent when the Napoleonic Wars ended in 1814. His most lyrical poems belong to the last two years of his life, when he had married Mary and settled in Pisa. His ethereal style is in contrast to the youthful rebelliousness of his personal life and to the earthy qualities of his friends Byron†, Keats† and Leigh Hunt†. Shelley was drowned in the Gulf of Spezia on 8 July 1822. Mary Shelley created the character Frankenstein, in a novel which she planned at Byron's villa on the Lake of Geneva in 1816.

SICILY

Island ruled by the Aragonese from the early fourteenth century and directly by Spain from 1504 to 1707. It was under the sovereignty of the Duke of Savoy from 1713 to 1718 when it was united to the Kingdom of Naples†, on the mainland. While Naples was twice overrun by French armies, Sicily defied both the Revolution and Napoleon. Under the protection of the British fleet Sicily gave sanctuary to Ferdinand IV† from 1798 to 1800 and again from 1806 to 1815. The British envoy in Palermo, Bentinck†, raised an Anglo-Sicilian Expeditionary Force in 1813, ostensibly to liberate the Italian peninsula from French rule, but it saw action only briefly in Spain. So anarchic were conditions in Sicily during Ferdinand's years of residence there that wealthy landowners hired gangs of toughs (*mafiosi*) to protect their property; the chief legacy of the Napoleonic Wars in Sicily was therefore the Mafia. In 1815 the island was given a new titular status when Ferdinand's realm was renamed 'Kingdom of the Two Sicilies', an entity which survived until 1860.

SIEYÈS, Emmanuel Joseph (1748–1836)

French revolutionary theorist: born in Fréjus, becoming a priest without a vocation who refused to hear confessions or preach a sermon. After serving as an episcopal secretary in Brittany, he settled in Paris in the winter of 1788–9 and wrote his famous 20,000 word manifesto, *Qu'est ce que le Tiers État?* 'What is the Third

Estate?' which demanded recognition of the right of the commonalty's representatives to prepare a constitution for France. It was Sieyès who, on 17 June 1789, proposed that the Third Estate should assume the title 'National Assembly', and he took the lead in proposing the new territorial division of France into départements rather than the historic provinces. He was elected to the Convention but took little part in its affairs. In 1795 he helped prepare the Constitution† of the Directory† but in 1799 he assisted Bonaparte overthrow it in Brumaire†. Sieyès drafted the Constitution of the Year VIII which established the Consulate, intending to create sufficient safeguards in the Senate† to check any dictatorial ambitions of Bonaparte. Briefly in 1799 Sieyès was Second Consul, handing over to Cambacérès† within a month because Bonaparte rejected so much of the constitution he had drawn up. Thereafter he sat in the Senate, having received a special annual endowment for 'services to the nation'. The 'Abbé Sieyès' went into exile in Belgium from 1815 to 1830 but spent his last years at his home in the Faubourg Saint-Honoré.

SLAVE TRADE

Was organized in the seventeenth century, London merchants and Bristol vessels taking the lead in carrying Africans from the Guinea coast to the Caribbean and Virginia. Most colonizing nations participated in the trade, the French building up Nantes as a slave merchants' port to rival Bristol and Liverpool in prosperity. In the late eighteenth century humanitarian sentiment turned against the slavers. An Anti-Slavery Committee was set up in London in 1787, with the approval of Pitt†. Wilberforce† began his parliamentary campaign to outlaw the slave trade in 1789; three years later the King of Denmark gave notice that none of his subjects were to participate in the slave trade after 31 December 1802. British

participation was formally prohibited by parliament in 1807, with effect from 23 May 1808. Americans were forbidden to trade in overseas slaves from 1 January 1809. Castlereagh† secured formal condemnation of the slave trade by the Vienna Congress† in February 1815 but the Spanish and Portuguese could not be persuaded to ban it until 1820. The French havered; but Napoleon, in a bid for liberal humanitarian support, announced abolition of the slave trade within three days of arriving back in Paris from Elba, and Louis XVIII confirmed the prohibition after his second restoration.

SLAVERY

The Law of 16 Pluviôse, Year II (4 February 1794), a decree of the French Convention, abolished slavery in France's colonies. Little notice was taken of the decree in Mauritius, while Martinique† was under British occupation. It was, however, implemented in Haiti† and Guadeloupe. The succession of black risings in the Antilles group of the West Indies† made the powerful planter pressure group in Paris urge Bonaparte to reimpose slavery so as to revive sugar production quickly. On 20 May 1802 the First Consul ordered slavery to be 'maintained' in France's colonies, an act which precipitated an abortive revolt in Guadeloupe and the successful second black rising in Haiti. Slavery survived on Martinique and Guadeloupe until the triumph of 'France's Wilberforce', Victor Schoelcher (1804–93), in the decree of abolition which he carried in the National Assembly of the Second Republic on 27 April 1848. Slavery was abolished in the British Empire in 1833. Emancipation of American slaves was proclaimed by Lincoln on 1 January 1863. Most of the former Spanish colonies in Latin America had ended slavery by 1860. In the former Portuguese empire of Brazil slavery was abolished in a series of emancipation decrees between 1870 and 1888.

SMITH, (William) Sidney (1764–1840)
British admiral: born in Westminster and
entered the Royal Navy at the age of
thirteen, gained rapid promotion and saw
service in the West Indies, for a time
serving with the Swedish fleet in the
Baltic. He participated in the attack on
Toulon†, was captured in a raid on shipping off Le Havre in 1796 and made a
remarkable escape from the Temple Prison in Paris. As a commodore he served in
the Mediterranean under Nelson but the
two seamen were of totally different char-
acters and did not collaborate. Smith was
sent to the Levant to work with the
Turkish vessels and he particularly distinguished himself at Acre† from March to
May 1799, his actions winning for him a
pension, a formal vote of thanks from
parliament and a fund of reminiscences
upon which he constantly drew for conversation. He assisted Abercromby† in
the landings in Egypt and his initiative at
Lisbon in 1807 enabled the royal family of
Portugal† to sail, under British naval
protection, to Brazil in the face of a
French invasion. Sir Sidney Smith, a vain
and garrulous man, was out of favour with
his sovereign and later with the Prince
Regent† because of his indiscreet
friendship with Princess Caroline† of
Brunswick. He attended the Congress of
Vienna†, claiming to represent the Swedish royal dynasty, and augmented the
entertainments by organizing a subscrip-
tion picnic which proved a social disaster.
By June 1815 he was in Brussels, witnes-
sing Waterloo and adding his energy and
authority to the orderly evacuation of the
wounded. Although he did not become a
vice-admiral until 1810 nor a full admiral
until 1821, people talked about Smith
more than about more distinguished seamen of lesser personality. When Napoleon dined aboard *Bellerophon†* on the
first evening out from Rochefort†, Smith
was his principal topic of conversation; he
had decided, at Acre, that the admiral was
crazy and held to this view.

SMOLENSK

City on the River Dnieper 230 miles west
of Moscow and 80 miles south-east of
Vitebsk. The Russian First Army, under
Barclay†, retreated to Smolensk on 31
July 1812 and was joined two days later by
Bagration† and his Second Army. Napoleon had planned an enveloping movement, encircling the city from the south; in
this manoeuvre he was thwarted by a
Russian infantry division, commanded by
General Nicholas Neverosky and supported by a small force of cavalry which
checked the invaders south of the river.
This rearguard action induced Napoleon
to change his plans; his army assaulted the
ramparts and fortified towers of Smolensk
on 16–17 August. The bombardment continued for thirteen hours and left
Smolensk in flames. First Bagration and
later Barclay withdrew from the city,
while bitter fighting lasted well into the
night at the foot of the walls. Napoleon
lost 10,000 men, the Russian defenders
about 12,500. French hopes that Russia
would sue for peace after the loss of
Smolensk were not realized. Napoleon
stayed there for only six days before
setting out in pursuit of the decisive battle
which had eluded him ever since his
crossing of the Niemen. Marshal Victor†
fitted out Smolensk as a base and staging-
post while the Emperor was in Moscow,
and Napoleon headed for the city when he
retreated from Maloyaroslavets†. The
main body of the *Grande Armée†* reached
Smolensk on 9 November 1812, with the
first heavy snow already impeding their
retreat. The double Russian threat from
Wittgenstein† to the north and Chicha-
gov† to the south-west forced Napoleon to
resume the retreat and head for the Bere-
zina† after only five nights of partial
recuperation. Ney† and the rearguard
remained until 17 November, exploding
mines beneath the ramparts as they pulled
out. Smolensk was speedily rebuilt after
1815, thanks mainly to the ruthless administrative bullying of General Arak-
cheev†.

SMORGON (now in Byelorussia)
A small town 48 miles south-east of Vilna†. At Smorgon on the night of 5–6 December 1812 Napoleon left the *Grande Armée*† in order to hurry back to Paris and restore morale after the rumours of disaster in Russia. He made the eleven hundred mile journey by a succession of carriages, and occasionally by sledge, in thirteen days. Caulaincourt† was his constant companion and has left a fine account of the journey in his Memoirs. They travelled by way of Warsaw, Dresden, Mainz and Verdun.

SOULT, Nicolas Jean de Dieu (1769–1851) Marshal of the Empire: born in Gascony, at Saint-Amans, south of Castres. He enlisted as an infantryman in 1785 and was

Marshal Soult before his long campaigns in Spain (1807–14)

a sergeant by 1791. Rapid promotion in the revolutionary armies gave him command of a brigade by October 1794 and of a division in April 1799. He was wounded and taken prisoner while assisting Masséna† in the defence of Genoa†. From 1800 onwards Soult was especially favoured by Bonaparte who admired his tactical gifts and his 'iron hand' as a disciplinarian. His cavalry led the attack on the Pratzen Heights at Austerlitz†, he fought with distinction at Jena† and Eylau†, and he captured Königsberg (Kaliningrad) in June 1807. Soult accompanied Napoleon to Spain in November 1807 and remained there until 1814, apart from a few months in the spring and early summer of 1813. He was responsible for the pursuit of Moore† to Corunna† and in 1809 he marched into Portugal as far south as Oporto† before being checked by Wellington†. Although Soult was successful in Andalusia in 1810, he had mixed fortunes at Badajoz† and was defeated at Albuera† in May 1811. A year later he restored the French hold on Madrid and at first repulsed Wellington. He tenaciously sought to delay the Allied advance through the Pyrenees in the autumn of 1813 and the following winter, but his strategic sense seemed to desert him and he was often outmanoeuvred by Wellington in the final phase of the Peninsular War†. Soult became Napoleon's chief-of-staff for the Waterloo campaign but was slower to perceive the significance of intelligence reports than Berthier† had been. He was in exile for four years, mainly in Düsseldorf, but he returned to public office in 1830 as Louis Philippe's Minister of War. From May 1832 to February 1836 and again from May 1839 to March 1840 Soult was Prime Minister of France; and he represented his King at Queen Victoria's coronation in June 1838. He was made Marshal-General of France in September 1847, an honour created for Turenne and held by only two other commanders, neither of whom had survived military defeat with such resilience as Soult.

SOUTHEY, Robert (1774–1843)

English Poet Laureate: born in Bristol, educated at Westminster School and Balliol College, Oxford, and at the age of twenty became a close friend of Coleridge†. From 1802 until his death he lived principally in Keswick, although in earlier years he had travelled extensively in the Iberian Peninsula. A passing early enthusiasm for the French Revolution gave way to a patriotic Toryism. By 1813 he was felt to be so politically sound that he was offered, and accepted, the office of Poet Laureate. Yet, though Southey was one of the 'Lake Poets'†, he is remembered less as an exemplar of Romanticism in England than as the author of biographies – Nelson, Wesley, Bunyan – and the first multi-volume Peninsular War history (soon surpassed by Napier's classic).

SPAIN

The decline of Spain, so rapid in the years 1665 to 1714, was checked by the four Bourbon kings of the eighteenth century and by a succession of reforming statesmen, who improved finance, industry, trade and communications. Nevertheless, Spain in 1793 was still a second-class Power, dependent on her colonies for revenue and hampered by almost sixty years of 'family pact' collaboration with France in foreign affairs. King Charles IV†, having failed to save the life of his kinsman Louis XVI, declared war on the French Republic in March 1793 but was faced by a French invasion of Catalonia in 1794–5. Under the influence of Godoy†, Spain and France concluded peace at Basle in June 1795 and in August 1796 began twelve years of political alliance. The Spanish fleet shared in the naval defeats off Cape St Vincent (February 1797) and, more sensationally, at Trafalgar† in 1805. Across the Atlantic, Trinidad was lost to Great Britain and the Royal Navy cut off Spanish America†. Limited success was gained by Spain in the 'War of Oranges' (1800–1) against Britain's ally, Portugal†, which was followed by a joint Franco-Spanish invasion in the autumn of 1807. At the end of that year Napoleon ordered the occupation of Spain by 100,000 French troops to defend the country from an English seaborne invasion. This action, together with resentment of Godoy's ambitions and policy by both nobility and commonalty, led on 17 March 1808 to an uprising at Aranjuez, twenty-seven miles south of Madrid. Charles IV abdicated, but his successor, Ferdinand VII†, found himself politically isolated. Contempt for Madrid court politics induced Napoleon to summon the Spanish royal family to Bayonne† (April 1808) where they were cajoled into surrendering the Spanish crown. The new king, Joseph Bonaparte†, was unacceptable to most Spaniards even though he brought with him the promise of a constitution, of educational reform and of laws based upon the Napoleonic Codes. A national insurrection spread throughout Spain in the summer of 1808, bolstered by the military victory of Castaños† at Baylen†. Joseph was forced to leave Madrid (1 August 1808) although the city was reoccupied four months later. The defiant mood of Saragossa† impressed Europe almost as much as Baylen. Resistance was co-ordinated by a Central Junta, thirty-five unrepresentative delegates who gathered at Aranjuez in December 1808 and claimed to be the 'Sovereign Majesty' of Spain. Military defeat in November 1809 discredited the Junta, whose members retired to Seville and Cadiz† and established a Regency; armed resistance was maintained primarily by guerrillas†. At Cadiz a liberal Cortes gave the Spaniards their first constitution, while Spanish regular troops collaborated with Wellington† in the Peninsular War†. Marmont's defeat at Salamanca† in July 1812 forced King Joseph to evacuate Madrid and Wellington's triumph at Vitoria† (21 June 1813) led to the total withdrawal of French troops. Ferdinand VII, after bargaining with the French at Valençay†,

Spanish Royalist propaganda depicting King Charles IV under strict guard in a French prison. In reality he enjoyed considerable liberty in the chateaux of Chambord and Compiègne.

re-entered Spain on 24 March 1814 but after his return to Madrid in May he disavowed both the Regency and the Cadiz constitution. Although Spain recovered her independence, the loss of her colonies in America accelerated national bankruptcy; the monarchy lacked the moral authority and political enterprise to prevent the country's drifting into incipient civil war.

SPANISH AMERICA

At the end of the eighteenth century comprised the Viceroyalty of New Spain (Mexico and much of the modern United States, including California and Texas), the Viceroyalty of New Granada (Central America, Colombia and Ecuador), the Captaincy-General of Venezuela, the Viceroyalty of Peru, the Captaincy-General of Chile, and the Viceroyalty of the Rio de la Plata (Bolivia, Paraguay, Uruguay and Argentina), together with islands in the West Indies, of which Cuba was the most important. Geographical isolation, the exclusion of native born Creoles from government posts, economic exploitation, the separation of Spain† from her colonies by the Bonapartist domination of the old historic provinces, and the intrusion of British naval power into the southern Atlantic all contributed to a movement for independence of the South American colonies, active from 1806 to 1815 but more successful in the period from 1816 to 1825. The outstanding liberators of Latin America were Miranda†, Bolivar† and (from 1814 onwards) General José de San Martin (1778–1850).

British attempts were made in 1806–7 to gain a foothold in either Buenos Aires or Montevideo. Plans were also made in June 1808 for sending an expeditionary force of 9,000 men, encamped at Cork in Ireland, to assist Miranda to spread rebellion against Spain (France's ally) in South America. News of the insurrection in Spain† induced the British government to change its plans: the expedition (under the future Duke of Wellington†) was sent to Mondego Bay in Portugal†; and thereafter the British were content to keep influence in Latin America short of intervention, thus finding there in the postwar world valuable opportunities for trade and investment.

SPERANSKY, Michael (1772–1839)

Russian reformer: born, the son of a village priest, near Vladimir. He was

Michael Speransky as Tsar Alexander's State Secretary, 1811

educated at the Alexander Nevsky seminary in St Petersburg, becoming principal secretary to one of Tsar Paul's chief advisers at the age of twenty-three. From 1802 onwards he enjoyed much influence at the Ministry of the Interior, drafting reforms of the social system, but it was only in August 1807 that Alexander I recognized his abilities. He was the Tsar's secretary at Erfurt†, where he impressed both Talleyrand and Napoleon. Until March 1812 Speransky was Alexander's chief political confidant, ranking as State Secretary from January 1810. He was responsible for Russia's Council of State†, for the first carefully prepared budgets in Russia's history and for defining the duties of the various government departments; he wished also to set up representative assemblies. These reforms aroused conservative opposition at court; Speransky was alleged to be, if not a French agent, at least a Francophile, more dangerous than the trimmer State Chancellor, Rumyantsev†. Speransky offended Grand Duchess Catherine Pavlovna† who bullied her brother, the Tsar, into dismissing him (29 March 1812). He was exiled to Nizhni-Novgorod (now Gorki) but was reinstated in the public service in 1816 as Governor of Penza, a town 300 miles east of Moscow. Three years later he became Governor-General of Siberia. His great task of codifying Russia's laws was not accomplished until 1832, in Nicholas I's reign.

STADION, (Johann) Philipp von, Count (1763–1824)

Austrian Foreign Minister: born at Warthausen, into a family with huge estates in Swabia between Ulm and Lake Constance. He entered the foreign service in 1787, and was successively in Stockholm, London (1790) and Berlin before going as ambassador to St Petersburg in 1803. In November 1804 he concluded a secret military convention with the Russians for joint action in a new war with France. He succeeded Cobenzl† as Foreign Minister at the beginning of 1806, eager for a war of revenge after the Peace of Pressburg†. More than any other Austrian statesman he possessed a personal hatred of Napoleon; and the War of 1809 was his doing, intended to be launched at a time when Napoleon was deeply immersed in Spanish affairs. Defeat at Wagram† led to Stadion's resignation early in October 1809; he refused to serve Austria so long as his successor, Metternich†, favoured a policy of appeasing France, but he became Austria's special envoy to Russo-Prussian headquarters in May 1813. Stadion was responsible for turning earlier verbal agreements between Metternich and Alexander I into the Convention of Reichenbach† of June 1813 which firmly associated Austria with the Allied cause. He presided over the Châtillon Conference†, signed the Treaty of Fontainebleau† on behalf of Austria, and served as Austria's Minister of Finance in 1814 and again from 1816 until shortly before his death. Remarkably he succeeded in balancing Austria's budgetary needs.

STAËL, Mme Germaine de (1766–1817)
French writer and intellectual: born in Paris, the only child of the famous Genevan financier Jacques Necker (1732–1804). In 1785 she married the Swedish ambassador to France, Baron de Staël-Holstein, who died in 1802. She wrote two novels, *Delphine* (1802) and *Corinne* (1807), strongly feminist in sympathies, and her great critical study on German literature and thought, *De l'Allemagne* (1810), as well as political-philosophical works. An autobiographical *Dix anneés d'exil* (1821) was written during the years of mounting Franco-Russian tension and war (1810–13) and contains some important analyses of Russian social life and of the Russian character. Mme de Staël was the greatest of all the presidents of a *salon*† – in Paris on the eve of the Revolution, again in 1795, from 1797 to 1803,

briefly under the Empire, and from 1814 until her death. The Necker family home at Coppet† also became, in effect, a residential salon and in 1804 she rekindled the intellectual fire of Weimar† during her remarkable tour of Europe's centres of culture. August von Schlegel† and Benjamin Constant† were influenced by her optimistic assumption that mankind advances through material progress to moral perfection. She had begun by flattering General Bonaparte in 1797 but by 1802 onwards regarded him as an enemy and the 'oppressor' of Europe. Napoleon, to her indignation, refused to take her as seriously as she took herself.

STEIN, (Heinrich Friedrich) Karl vom und zum, Baron (1757–1831)
Prussian statesman: born on the ancestral estate in the Rhineland, facing the town of Nassau across the River Lahn. He was educated at Göttingen, entered the Prussian civil service in 1780 and undertook administrative tasks concerned with the improvements of communications, becoming known as an advocate of widescale reforms. After Tilsit, he enjoyed a brief period of power in Prussia, introducing the Emancipation Edict† and preparing schemes for reorganizing the central government. Napoleon regarded him as an enemy and insisted that Frederick William III† dismiss him. In November 1808 Stein fled to Bohemia, travelling to St Petersburg in 1812, and was an adviser to Alexander I on German affairs throughout the 1813 campaign. In October 1813 he became president of the central administration of occupied territories in Germany, but the Prussians distrusted his nationalism and, although he attended the Vienna Congress†, his plans for an effective Germanic Confederation were countered by Metternich† and the Austrians. He held an administrative post in Westphalia from 1825 until his death, but the Prussian administration remained so afraid of his Germanic patriotism that he

was not honoured in Berlin until 1827, eighteen years after he had been forced to leave the city under French pressure.

STENDHAL: see *Beyle, Henri.*

STROGANOV, Paul (1772–1817)
Russian statesman: born near Moscow, a cousin of Novosiltsov†. Both men first met the future Alexander I at his father's coronation in Moscow (April 1797) and became prominent among the liberal advisers who later constituted the Secret Committee†. Stroganov was deputy to Kochubey at the Ministry of the Interior (1802–6), accompanied the Tsar in the Austerlitz campaign and then undertook a special mission to London. He never held office again after Tilsit, but remained an important member of the Russian Senate.

STYLE EMPIRE
The decorative style of the Napoleonic era in France favoured majestic magnificence so as to evoke, through neoclassicism, the power and grandeur of the regime. In architecture it may be seen in Paris in the Arc de Triomphe†, the façades of the Rue de Rivoli, the column in the Place Vendôme, and the neo-classical exterior of the Madeleine. The paintings of David† and Gérard†, the sculpture of Denis Chaudet (1763–1810) and of Joseph Chinard (1756–1813, notably his famous bust of Mme Récamier†, at Lyons), and the sumptuous table decorations and candelabra which the enterprising firm of Odiot

Le Style Empire; *Napoleon's library at Malmaison*

hired out for elegant Parisian dinner parties all sought the purity of classical line within a proudly imperial framework. Furniture carried carvings, gilt motifs of crowns and caryatids and griffins; couches were often shaped like gondolas; ornate 'camp beds' were covered by drapes shaped like a tent; and armchairs looked as solid as a throne. Women's fashion, too, followed classical lines although more discreetly than in the early days of the Consulate when semi-clad representations of the goddess Diana proliferated in high society. Under the Empire waists were high, dresses and tunics straight so as to outline physical form without emphasizing it, sleeves were short and puffed, the hair cut short and decorated with jewels and ribbons. Men's dress, too, was at times eccentric, never more so than in the robes designed for Napoleon and his brothers at the Champ de Mai† ceremony in 1815.

SUCHET, Louis-Gabriel (1770–1826)

Marshal of the Empire: born at Lyons, a silk merchant's son. He was commissioned in the National Guard in 1791, later fighting under Bonaparte at Toulon†, Lodi†, Arcole† and Rivoli and in all the major battles of 1805–6. From 1808 to 1814 he served in Spain, a country whose people he well understood. He was a good administrator with a natural shrewdness which allowed him to exploit the separatist loyalties of the Aragonese and the Catalans. A series of victories in 1811 which culminated in the capture of the port of Tarragona won him his marshal's baton (1 July 1811). The respect with which Suchet and his wife were held by the Catalans was in contrast to the general record of the French soldiery in the peninsula. 'Had I been served by two marshals like Suchet, I would have conquered Spain and kept it', Napoleon later remarked. In 1815 Suchet led the 'Army of the Alps' (20,000 men, mostly inexperienced) successfully into Piedmont until

forced to conclude an armistice on 28 June. Louis XVIII pardoned him and reinstated him in 1819.

SUVOROV, Alexander (1729–1800)

Russian field marshal: born in Moscow, fought in the Seven Years' War and was a brigadier by the age of thirty-four. Service in Poland and against the Turks won him a reputation for ruthlessness, notably at Jassy in 1788, Ismail in 1790 and Warsaw in 1795. Catherine the Great heaped honours on him: Governor of the Crimea, field marshal, count. Tsar Paul compulsorily retired him on his accession, believing Suvorov had slighted him by refusing his services in the field against the Turks. But in 1799 Suvorov was recalled, leading the Russo-Austrian army which, between April and August 1799, undid the gains of Bonaparte's first Italian campaign†. Suvorov drove the French from Milan and Turin and pursued them across the St Gotthard into Switzerland. Masséna's successes against Suvorov's subordinate commanders around Zurich† forced the Russians to pull back across the Alps into Austria. Paul, who had earlier created Suvorov 'Prince of Italy', used this rebuff to discredit the Marshal, whose triumphs he envied. In late October 1799 Suvorov returned to St Petersburg, broken in health and out of favour. Within a few weeks he was dead, a hero admired by all his officers. His use of bayonet charges to storm prepared positions – assaults causing heavy casualties – was copied by many Russian commanders in the later Napoleonic campaigns.

SWEDEN

Under Gustavus III (1771–92) Sweden benefited from the reforms of an enlightened despot, until the French Revolution imposed caution on the monarch in the last three years of his reign. Gustavus was assassinated in March 1792 by a member of the Swedish nobility, and during the following eighteen years the influence of the military aristocracy increased at the cost of royal authority. Sweden participated in the War of the Third Coalition†, losing what remained of Pomerania† (briefly recovered in 1810). Russia, encouraged by Napoleon at Tilsit†, attacked Sweden in 1808, occupied the Åland Islands (thus threatening Stockholm) and annexed Finland. These disasters, together with an unresolved conflict with Denmark, led to a palace revolution on 13 March 1809 when the thirty-year-old king, Gustavus IV Adolf, was arrested by two leading generals. He abdicated at the end of the month in favour of his uncle, Charles XIII†, who had no heir. The *Riksdag* (Diet) reasserted rights lost in Gustavus III's reign and in August 1810 proposed that Marshal Bernadotte† should be elected Prince Royal. At that time Franco-Swedish relations were close, the Swedes having joined the Continental System†, but by the beginning of 1811 it was clear that Napoleon had no intention of supporting Swedish ambitions in the Baltic. Bernadotte recommended a change in Swedish policy, personally achieving a reconciliation with Tsar Alexander at Åbo† in August 1812. The Swedes entered the Fourth Coalition†, sending an expeditionary force to campaign in Germany under Bernadotte's leadership from July 1813 onwards. By the Vienna Settlement† of 1814–15 Sweden gained Norway from Denmark in return for giving up all claim to Pomerania. A Swedish army under Bernadotte occupied southern Norway and, on 4 November 1814, the Norwegian parliament (*Storting*) at Christiania (Oslo) declared the country an independent kingdom united to the crown of Sweden. Bernadotte's policies shaped Sweden's development for the remainder of the century; Sweden has not been at war since the Vienna Settlement.

SWITZERLAND

Developed as a loosely-knit league of communities hostile to Habsburg rule following collaboration between the three 'forest cantons' of Uri, Schwyz and Unterwalden in 1291. Effective Habsburg rule ended in 1386 although the Swiss League's independence was recognized only in 1648. Differences between the democratic forest cantons and the more bourgeois cantons (Berne, Lucerne, Basle, Zurich) led to unrest in 1798. The French thereupon occupied Switzerland, establishing a Helvetic Republic which was transformed, under Bonaparte's guidance, into the Helvetic Confederation† of 1803. In 1813 Schwarzenberg's troops violated Swiss neutrality at Basle†, the Austrians subsequently supporting those cantons who opposed the 'democrats'. Each of the nineteen cantons sent a delegation to the Vienna Congress† which, on 29 March 1815, established a Swiss Confederation of twenty-two cantons. The Confederation, pledged to permanent international neutrality, was recognized by the major European Powers in a joint declaration eight months later.

SYRIA

At the end of the eighteenth century comprised five Pashaliks within the Ottoman Empire†. But the effective ruler of all Syria since the 1770s was the formidable Ahmed Djezzar, governor of Beirut and Pasha of Acre. 'The Butcher', a sadist of Bosnian origin, hated all European traders, expecially the French. He was capable of raising an army of 100,000 men to oppose Bonaparte in Egypt†. In order to meet this challenge and secure the Levant, Bonaparte marched into Syria (23 February 1799). The French brushed aside opposition at Gaza and stormed Jaffa (6 March) where 4,400 Turks were massacred, ostensibly because they had broken earlier pledges of parole. From 19 March to 20 May Bonaparte unsuccessfully besieged Acre†, the resistance of Djez-zar being supported by a British naval flotilla under Sidney Smith†. On 16 April intervention by the Pasha of Damascus was routed by Bonaparte and Kléber† at Mount Tabor, east of Nazareth. But, despite this victory, the failure of successive assaults on Acre and the spread of bubonic plague led Bonaparte to call off his invasion of Syria and return to Egypt (21 May to 1 June). Of 13,000 men whom he had led into Syria, 1,000 perished in battle or from desert exhaustion, another 1,000 died from the plague and some 2,500 were wounded or broken in health. The enterprise had proved a costly failure, a disaster long concealed from the French public by astute propaganda.

T

Town on the north bank of the Tagus, seventy miles south-west of Madrid. A plain extends three miles north of the town to the foothills of the Sierra de Guadarrama, the scene of a battle on 27–8 June 1809. Wellington†, having penetrated into Spain from Portugal† to make contact with Spanish resistance troops in Castile and guerrillas, encountered the French, under Jourdan† and Joseph Bonaparte†, in defensive lines between the foothills and the town. Bitter fighting was made even more horrible by a fire which spread rapidly through parched scrub and caught hundreds of wounded in its path. As the French withdrew towards Toledo, Talavera was reckoned a joint British and Spanish victory. Wellington did not, however, exploit his success; he considered his line of communications overstretched and he complained that the Spanish troops possessed a disturbing tendency to withdraw rapidly from the fighting line so as to reassemble elsewhere; he therefore ordered a deep retreat down the Tagus and into Portugal. For two and a half years after Talavera he treated the Peninsular campaign† as a war of attrition.

TALLEYRAND, Charles-Maurice de Talleyrand-Périgord, (1754–1838)

French Foreign Minister: born at Paris into a distinguished aristocratic family. He was crippled at the age of four, educated at the seminary of Saint-Sulpice, attended the coronation of Louis XVI in 1775 and became a priest in 1779. Ten years later he was consecrated Bishop of Autun†. He attached himself to the 'national' revolutionary cause in 1789–90 and in July 1792 was sent on a diplomatic mission to London, largely because some years earlier he had made the acquaintance of Pitt†. In his absence the Convention condemned him as a traitor and he spent the years 1793 to 1795 quietly in America, mainly in Philadelphia. On 19 September 1796 he arrived back in Paris and, in the following July, was appointed Foreign Minister under the Directory†, largely through the patronage of Barras†. Five months later he first met Bonaparte (6 December 1797), soon afterwards proposing that he should strike at British overseas power by an expedition to Egypt†. The formation of a hostile Second Coalition – a threat against which Talleyrand had warned the Directory – made him resign in late July 1798. But he strongly backed Bonaparte on the eve of Brumaire† and was rewarded with a return to the Foreign Ministry on 22 November 1799. Over the next years he helped secure the Concordat†, the Peace of Amiens† and the establishment of the Rhine Confederation†. When the Empire was created he became Grand Chamberlain of the Court and was made Prince of Benevento on 5 June 1806. By 1807 he was alarmed by Napoleon's boundless ambition and by the Emperor's disregard of his advice. A month after Tilsit† he left the Foreign Ministry (9 August 1807), but he retained some influence as Vice Grand Elector and accompanied Napoleon to Erfurt†. He strongly disapproved of Napoleon's Spanish policy, particularly the dynastic upheaval settled at Bayonne†, and he established secret contact with St Petersburg and

Talleyrand, Prince of Benevento, former Bishop of Autun

Vienna. Suspicion of Talleyrand's treachery led Napoleon to lose his temper on 28 January 1809 when he deprived him of his post at court in a famous stormy scene. Talleyrand was still consulted, as Vice Grand Elector, and Napoleon does not seem to have appreciated that in 1814 he was in close touch with the advancing Allied commanders. When Paris fell, Talleyrand housed Tsar Alexander at his home on the corner of the Rue Saint-Florentin, where Caulaincourt† and Marshals Ney†, Macdonald† and Mortier† came to discuss the abdication† of Napoleon. Talleyrand headed the provisional government, negotiating a settlement with Louis XVIII† and becoming both 'Prince de Talleyrand' and Foreign Minister again on 13 May 1814. As Louis's representative at the Vienna Congress Talleyrand secured Allied recognition of France as a Great Power and succeeded in exploiting differences between the British and Austrians on one side and the Russians and Prussians on the other. After the

Hundred Days, Talleyrand served as French Prime Minister (July to September 1815) before retiring to his estate at Valençay† to write highly contentious memoirs which, much edited, were not published until 1891–2. Talleyrand was back in Paris in 1830 to help bring Louis Philippe to the throne in succession to Charles X; and he was ambassador in London from September 1830 to August 1834.

TALLIEN, Mme Thérèse (1773–1835)
French society hostess: born Thérésa Cabarrus at Carabanchel Alto, near Madrid, the daughter of a banker. She married, when young, the Marquis de Fontenay, who divorced her. She then married the radical journalist, Jean-Lambert Tallien (1767–1820) whom she is said to have encouraged to lead the anti-Robespierre movement at Thermidor, 1794. Later she became a mistress of Barras† and of the banker, Ouvrard†. She met and befriended Josephine† Bonaparte. Mesdames Tallien, Bonaparte and Récamier† were the queens of society in the salons† of the Directory, Thérèse Tallien setting a fashion for neo-Greek costume, frequently diaphanous. Napoleon unsuccessfully warned Josephine off Mme Tallien's company. She remained loyal to the fallen Empress, continuing to visit her at Malmaison† after Napoleon's marriage to Marie Louise. Mme Tallien divorced her second husband and, in 1805, married the Comte de Caraman who later became Prince de Chimay.

TALMA, François Joseph (1763–1826)
French tragic actor: born in Paris, spent some of his early years in England, making his debut at the Comédie Française† in November 1787. Two years later he caused a sensation by declaiming the revolutionary speeches of Chénier's *Charles IX* with great fervour. At the Théâtre de la République, under both the

Convention and the Directory, he played the great classical roles. Napoleon much admired his talent, Chateaubriand† later asserting that Talma had shown Napoleon how to act an emperor. Talma encouraged reforms in acting and production: less artificial declamation of speeches; the scenery and costumes to represent the period of the drama, not the present. Napoleon invited Talma to Erfurt† where, on 4 October 1808, he appeared in Voltaire's *Œdipe* before the rulers of France, Russia, Bavaria, Saxony, Weimar, Westphalia and Württemberg. On 21 April 1815 Napoleon went to a theatre for the last time and was deeply moved by Talma's performance in *Hector*. Talma played at the Theatre Royal, Covent Garden, in 1817 (with Mlle George†); he retired from the stage in June 1826, only four months before his death.

Talma in the role of Brittanicus

TAUROGGEN, Convention of (30 December 1812)

Marked the beginning of Prussia's change of policy, away from reluctant collaboration with Napoleon into a war of liberation. In the last week of 1812 Prussian contingents serving under General Yorck† on the northern flank of the *Grande Armée* were cut off on the lower Niemen by a Russian force under General Diebitsch, a Prussian in the Tsar's service. The German émigrés contacted Yorck at Tauroggen (now Taurage, in Lithuania) and it was agreed that Yorck's men would remain non-belligerent. They were allowed to return home. Although Frederick William III† condemned Yorck's conduct, great pressure was put on the King by his officer corps to conclude a Russo-Prussian alliance, a task achieved by the Treaty of Kalisch† two months later.

TEPLITZ

Bohemian spa, now known as Teplice, in northern Czechoslovakia. After their defeat at Dresden† in August 1813 the Allied sovereigns (Alexander†, Francis†, Frederick William III†) retreated through the Erzgebirge Mountains to Teplitz, only twenty-five miles south of Dresden. The spa remained Allied headquarters for a month while Schwarzenberg†, as allied generalissimo, built up his forces to advance on Leipzig†. Negotiations between Metternich†, Hardenberg† and Nesselrode† led, on 9 September 1813, to three bilateral pacts which bound Austria, Prussia and Russia in a joint alliance against Napoleon. Publicly these Teplitz Treaties defined the Allied war aim – 'the re-establishment of a just equilibrium between the Powers'. Secretly the treaties agreed to abolish the Grand Duchy of Warsaw† and the Rhine Confederation† so as to allow the German states 'entire and absolute independence' and enable Austria and Prussia to recover 'as closely as possible' their 1805 frontiers. The Polish Question would be 'settled amicably' by the three Powers at a later date. More issues were shirked than resolved at Teplitz, but the treaties had the effect of binding Austria closer to her Allies. A Grand Alliance, linking Britain with the three autocracies, was not concluded for another six months, at Chaumont†.

TEXEL

Dutch island off the approaches to the Zuider Zee, its southern channel providing a traditional anchorage for the Dutch fleet. Texel was captured by the French in late January 1795, the Dutch warships being icebound at the time. Thereafter for nineteen years Texel served French needs and was blockaded by the Royal Navy. Napoleon visited Texel on 16 October 1811, giving orders for the establishment of a new naval base at the nearest point on the mainland, Den Helder.

THIBAUDEAU, Antoine (1765–1854)

French bureaucrat: born at Poitiers, where he practised law. He was a deputy to the States-General in 1789, became a Jacobin and sat in successive political assemblies, including the Convention and the Council of Five Hundred†. The First Consul appointed him to the Council of State† and his legal knowledge was of value in drawing up the Civil Code†. In the last years of the Empire he was at Marseilles as Prefect of the Bouches-du-Rhône. During a brief spell of exile he wrote some of the fairest and most interesting memoirs of the period. Later he returned to his estate near Tours.

THUGUT, Baron Franz von (1739–1818)

Austrian Foreign Minister: born at Linz, becoming an old-style aristocratic diplomat. He was much praised by Colloredo†, who secured his appointment as director-general of Emperor Francis's† chancery in March 1793. Twelve months later he became Foreign Minister. He was more interested in central Europe, especially Poland, than in containing France in the west and he was criticized in Vienna for ignoring the threat to Austria's Italian possessions. It was largely on Thugut's initiative that Austria made peace with General Bonaparte and accepted the humiliating Treaty of Campo Formio† in 1797. Privately Thugut defended his policy on the grounds that (as he told Emperor Francis) he had made peace so as to secure a respite in which to approach Britain and build up a more powerful coalition. The defeats of the War of the Second Coalition†, however, finally destroyed Thugut's standing in Vienna and he was curtly dismissed by Francis on New Year's Day, 1801, Cobenzl† succeeding him. There was talk of recalling him to office in 1809 but Francis preferred Metternich†.

TILSIT

Town on the lower River Niemen†, now known as Sovetsk, but in 1807 on the Prussian side of the frontier with Russia. Napoleon, reaching Tilsit on 19 June 1807 after his victory at Friedland†, received a Russian peace envoy, an armistice being signed two days later. On 25 June, in response to suggestions from Tsar Alexander I†, the two sovereigns met on a specially constructed raft moored in midstream. At a second meeting next day Frederick William III† of Prussia (Russia's ally) was present. For a fortnight Napoleon and Alexander exchanged visits, holding discussions over the affairs of Europe and Asia. Two treaties were signed on 7 July and ratified within forty-eight hours: a public treaty concluded peace between France and Russia (and Prussia); there was to be a French-dominated Grand Duchy of Warsaw†, recognition of a Kingdom of Westphalia† in western Germany, and the reduction of Prussia to half its size. A secret treaty stipulated that if Britain rejected Russian

Tilsit, 1807: the first meeting of Napoleon and Alexander I on a specially constructed barge on the River Niemen

mediation for a general peace, the Tsar would join the Continental System†. Similarly, if Turkey refused French mediation, Napoleon would join Alexander in partitioning Turkey-in-Europe (apart from Constantinople and its hinterland). Russia was given a free hand in the Baltic, with French encouragement to detach Finland† from Sweden. Alexander also agreed to withdraw the Senyavin† naval squadron from the Adriatic and evacuate the Ionian Islands†. Tilsit thus marked a major reversal of alliances. Despite strained relations over Turkey and Poland and only limited agreement when the two emperors met again at Erfurt†, France and Russia collaborated until 31 December 1810. On that date Alexander gave

271

way to pressure from Russia's merchants and took his empire out of the Continental System, opening Russian ports to neutral shipping and imposing tariffs on French goods.

TORIES

The word 'Tory', originally applied to Catholic outlaws in seventeenth-century Ireland and entering English politics about 1680 to describe upholders of the royal prerogative, had come by the 1790s to imply support for restrictive measures against the concern of the Whigs† for 'the rights of man'. Pitt† – and all his close supporters apart from Canning† – denied being a Tory and there was never an organized Tory Party. It is, however, generally accepted that the governments of Perceval† and Liverpool† were predominantly Tory. Every administration from December 1783 to February 1806 and from March 1807 to November 1830 was Tory in the sense that it united factions which, if not entirely in agreement over such issues as Catholic Emancipation† or colonial slavery†, were collectively determined to exclude the Whigs. The more positive term 'Conservative' was used by Canning in 1824 but really dates from Peel and the Tamworth Manifesto ten years later.

TORRES VEDRAS

A small town, the centre of a Portuguese wine-growing region, commanding a crossing of the River Sizandro, forty miles north of Lisbon. The town gave its name to the Lines of Torres Vedras, a defensive position created by Wellington† to save Lisbon from a second French occupation in 1810. Wellington ordered construction of the Lines to begin in October 1809. Eighteen Royal Engineer officers supervised the construction by 10,000 Portuguese labourers of 108 forts, planned in three lines to a depth of from six to nine miles through hilly country, much of it

wooded. The forts were linked by a semaphore† system. The lines extended from the mouth of the Sizandro, on the Atlantic, to Alhandra on the River Tagus, thirty miles to the south-east. Wellington's army, outnumbered by Masséna's force, fell back on the Lines early in October 1810 and held them for five months. Masséna, finding the defences impregnable, was halted; winter conditions threatened his army with starvation. The Anglo-Portuguese defenders could rely on steady supplies from Lisbon and harbours along the coast and the lower Tagus. Almost inevitably Masséna lost this campaign of attrition, calling off his invasion of Portugal† and retreating northwards on 5 March 1811. The Anglo-Portuguese army emerged to blockade Almeida† and defeat Masséna at Fuentes de Oñoro†.

TOULON

The chief French naval base in the Mediterranean, some thirty miles east of Marseilles. It is a good natural harbour, with an inner and outer roadstead. Arsenal and docks date from the early seventeenth century, most of the forts being Vauban's work, eighty years later. Contempt for the political chaos in Paris induced the townspeople of Toulon to accept occupation by an Anglo-Spanish naval force in August 1793. The French besieged the port early in September. Captain Bonaparte was given command of the artillery and developed a plan to recover Toulon by seizing the key position, Fort Éguillette, which dominated the peninsula separating the two roadsteads. Carnot†, in Paris, approved the plan, promoting Bonaparte lieutenant-colonel, and between 14 and 18 December 1793 a successful attack was made on the Fort, forcing the British and Spanish to withdraw. Death sentences were imposed on those who had collaborated with the enemy. Bonaparte's skill won him promotion in February 1794 to the rank of brigadier-general. Among his brother officers were Masséna†, Marmont† and Junot†.

Bonaparte returned to Toulon in May 1798 at a time when Nelson† was blockading the port. A storm, which forced Nelson back to Sardinia, allowed Bonaparte to get his expedition for Egypt† out to sea during the Royal Navy's absence. A close blockade was again attempted by the Royal Navy during the critical months of 1804–5 but could not prevent Villeneuve† from slipping out of Toulon on 30 March 1805 with the squadron intended to lure Nelson to the West Indies.

TOULOUSE, Battle of (10 April 1814)

The final engagement of the Peninsular War†, fought before either Wellington† or Soult† had heard of Napoleon's abdication†. Soult made good use of the natural barriers formed by the rivers Garonne and Hers and the heights commanding the approaches from the east. Beresford's Sixth Division and the Spanish contingents suffered heavily in storming the outer defences. Soult withdrew northwards on the night of 11–12 April, the news of Napoleon's fall reaching both armies on the following evening.

TOUSSAINT L'OUVERTURE, Pierre Dominique (1743–1803)

Haitian leader: the grandson of an African brought to Santo Domingo as a slave. Toussaint, a natural leader who hated anarchy and destruction, helped check the spread of a black rising on the island of Haiti† in 1791. Two years later, with the French promising slave emancipation, he helped the Frenchman, General Laveaux, to beat off attacks by the Spaniards and British. Laveaux is reputed to have commended Toussaint's tactical initiative with the phrase, 'Cet homme fait ouvertures partout' (This man makes openings everywhere), thus giving Toussaint his distinctive name. By 1795 Toussaint was recog-

Pierre Dominique Toussaint l'Ouverture, the Haitian leader

nized by the French as a major-general (*général de division*) and virtual governor of the island. But, while continuing to harass the British and Spanish, Toussaint expelled the French Commissioners from Haiti and set up a black republic, briefly unifying the island. When General Leclerc arrived with 40,000 French troops in February 1802, Toussaint resisted the initial landing but he then went to French headquarters to negotiate an armistice and was seized by General Brunet. Toussaint and his family were shipped to France. He was held captive in the fortress of Joux in the Jura Mountains where he died from cold and privation in March 1803.

TRAFALGAR, naval battle (21 October 1805)

The culmination of a long campaign in which Nelson† and Collingwood† sought to bring the French commander, Villeneuve†, to a decisive engagement (see

273

Naval Warfare). Villeneuve, with a fleet of 40 vessels (18 French ships-of-the-line, 15 Spanish, 7 frigates), sailed from Cadiz on 19 October for the Mediterranean. A preliminary encounter with four blockading British frigates gave Nelson (with 27 ships-of-the-line) an opportunity to intercept Villeneuve off Cape Trafalgar, some thirty miles south of Cadiz and at the approach to the Strait of Gibraltar. Nelson, leading the windward column in HMS *Victory*, and Collingwood, with the leeward column in *Royal Sovereign*, attacked the centre of the Franco-Spanish line from the port quarter at a time when Villeneuve had turned about and was heading northwards, back to Cadiz. The line was pierced in the centre, the British then turning so as to engage the enemy closely. Eighteen Franco-Spanish ships-of-the-line were sunk or captured, including Villeneuve's flagship, *Bucentaure;* and 14,000 Franco-Spanish seamen perished. No British vessels were lost but some 1,500 officers and men were killed in action, among them Nelson, shot on his quarterdeck by a sharpshooter aboard *Redoutable*. Trafalgar confirmed Britain's naval supremacy; Napoleon had, however, already abandoned his plans for a cross-Channel invasion, the *Grande Armée* leaving Boulogne† for the Danube more than a month before. London had news of Trafalgar on 6 November, Napoleon not until 17 November. By then he was at Guntersdorf in Lower Austria, marching northwards from Vienna in the Austerlitz campaign†.

TRIANON

On 13 March 1805 Napoleon, in residence at Malmaison†, visited Versailles. He thought the palace too dilapidated for his use, but he gave orders that the two villas in the parkland, the Grand and Petit Trianon, should be renovated. He lunched at the Grand Trianon on 1 September 1808 but did not reside there until the day after his divorce from Josephine, in December 1809. During August 1810 he spent four days there with Marie Louise, issuing the Trianon Decree (5 August 1810) regulating the sale of licences for exports within the Continental System† and imposing a high tariff on colonial goods. In 1811 he considered rebuilding both Trianons and Versailles but the project made little headway. Marie Louise and Napoleon stayed for a final fortnight at the Trianon in March 1813.

TRIBUNATE

The French legislative chamber established by the Constitution† of the Year VIII (15 December 1799). It was intended as a House of 100 members, all aged over twenty-five; they might discuss draft laws sent down to them by the Council of State†, recommending their acceptance or rejection. Several liberal intellectuals were appointed to the original Tribunate. Among them were Pierre Daunou†, Benjamin Constant†, and Marie-Joseph Chénier (1764–1811), the poet and dramatist who had written the *Chant du départ*. This group organized an opposition, the 'Committee of the Enlightened', which irritated the First Consul by detailed criticism of proposed measures as early as January 1800. When, at the beginning of 1802, one-fifth of the Tribunate came up for renewal, Bonaparte removed twenty trouble-makers and replaced them by his brother Lucien Bonaparte†, by Daru† and other pliant nominees. Even so the Tribunate opposed the Concordat†, the first plans for a Legion of Honour† and the re-establishment of colonial slavery†. The Constitution† of the Year X (4 August 1802) accordingly halved the number of tribunes and divided the fifty survivors into sections, each responsible for considering particular aspects of policy. Thereafter the Tribunate became a mere collection of specialist committees, incapable of organizing any real opposition to the autocratic plans of Napoleon.

TUGENDBUND ('League of Virtue')

A patriotic society founded in Königsberg in April 1808 by a group of Prussian army officers and university teachers and intended to regenerate noble feelings and combat self-centredness. It was originally called 'The Moral and Scientific Union' (*Sittlich-Wissenschaftlicher Verein*) in order to conceal its character as a vehicle of anti-French propaganda. In this form it received a licence from Frederick William III† and soon had branches throughout Prussia. When, in 1809, Napoleon complained to Frederick William of the League's subversive character and asked for its suppression, it continued to function underground. The League deeply influenced the growth of German national feeling after the Convention of Taurog-gen†. More than any other association it trained the minds of young Germans for the 'War of Liberation' in 1813–14. The *Tugendbund* was dissolved in 1815, giving way to more radical student bodies such as the equally virtuous *Burschenschaften* at Jena University.

TUILERIES

Palace of the French kings in central Paris, dating from 1564 but serving only rarely as a royal residence between 1661 and 1789. Louis XVI and his family were constrained to remain at the Tuileries from 5 October 1789 until the mob attacked the palace on 10 August 1792 – an event witnessed by Captain Napoleon Bonaparte. From May 1793 until October 1795 the Convention met in the north wing of the Tuileries, the Council of Ancients† succeeding them. On 19 February 1800 the First Consul took up residence, Bonaparte holding a succession of receptions and parades there. By 1801, however, he was keeping the Tuileries for official occasions, staying at Malmaison†, and from autumn 1802 transacting as much work as possible at Saint-Cloud†. Increasingly rigid etiquette controlled the balls and receptions at the Tuileries. Napoleon recognized that the

palace was the sovereign's chief residence, as did Louis XVIII after him, and it was there that he returned in triumph from Elba on the evening of 20 March 1815. He moved out, however, to live in the smaller Élysée† Palace on 17 April. The Tuileries was fired by Communard incendiarists on 23 May 1871 and never rebuilt.

TURNER, Joseph Mallord William (1775–1851)

English artist; born in the Covent Garden district of London, sold drawings before he was ten and exhibited water-colours at sixteen. He was elected RA in 1802, the year in which he took advantage of the Peace of Amiens to hurry to Paris and inspect the French Poussins and the looted art treasures†. His *Calais Pier*, exhibited in 1803, is a precursor of Romanticism† but was unpopular with the critics of the day. By the summer of 1807 the London public was viewing his *Trafalgar*, contrasting it with patriotic canvases that gave a more traditional visual interpretation of recent history. Turner's first visits to Italy in 1819 and 1829 broadened his sense of landscape, encouraging him to experiment more freely with mist and sunlight. His greatest period of artistic composition did not begin until he was in his late fifties.

TUSCANY

Became a Grand Duchy, with its capital at Florence, in 1569 and was ruled by the Medici family until 1737, when it passed to the House of Habsburg†. Grand Duke Ferdinand, a brother of Emperor Francis†, entertained General Bonaparte in Florence on 1 July 1796 but was driven from his throne in 1801. The Peace of Lunéville† made Tuscany the core of the 'Kingdom of Etruria', the dispossessed Duke of Parma† entering Florence as king by the grace of the First Consul on 10 August 1801. Etruria was annexed to the French Empire in October 1807, Tuscany itself becoming three départements,

Napoleon's throne in the Tuileries Palace

administered from Paris. In May 1808 Elisa Bonaparte† was appointed Governor-General of Tuscany and was created Grand Duchess by her brother in the following March. Her presence in Florence improved local administration; she refurbished the palaces in some grandeur. The old order was restored in May 1814, Tuscany joining the new Italian kingdom in March 1860.

TYROLEAN RISINGS (1809, 1813)

The Austrian province of the Tyrol was ceded to Bavaria† by the Treaty of Pressburg† in December 1805 as recognition for the Bavarian contribution to the defeat of Austria. Secret talks were held in Vienna in January 1809 between Archduke John†, Stadion†, and a Tyrolean soldier, Captain Hofer†. In the following May Hofer led a successful revolt against Bavarian rule in Innsbruck. Only French intervention suppressed the revolt at the end of the year. In February 1813 Archduke John made contact with survivors of Hofer's insurrection and planned a second rising, which would force Austria to follow the example of Prussia and turn against Napoleon. Metternich's agents discovered this conspiracy. Metternich† complained to Emperor Francis† that the revolt would destroy his chances of bargaining independently with Napoleon and the Archduke was put under house arrest. The Tyrol therefore did not erupt in 1813. Austria recovered the province a year later.

ULM

Cathedral city in Bavaria, on the upper Danube, forty-six miles south-east of Stuttgart. The advance of the *Grande Armée* in October 1805 cut off the principal Austrian army (commanded by General Mack† and the Archduke Ferdinand†) in Ulm after some 200,000 men had crossed the Danube at various points and converged on the city. When Mack's attempts to break out failed, there was dissension in the Austrian high command, the Archduke setting out independently for Bohemia with a cavalry force. Napoleon set up his headquarters at Elchingen Abbey, north-east of Ulm on 15 October and Mack began surrender negotiations two days later. The Austrians capitulated on 20 October. This was probably Napoleon's greatest triumph of strategic planning; his enveloping movement around Ulm had eliminated more than 50,000 crack Austrian troops from further participation in the war. On 21 October, while Napoleon at Elchingen planned his march on Vienna, his seamen were losing Trafalgar†.

UNIVERSITÉ: see *Educational Reforms*.

VALENÇAY

A magnificent château, south-east of Tours, purchased by Talleyrand† in 1805. From 1808 to 1814 Valençay housed the interned King of Spain, Ferdinand VII†, together with his uncle and younger brother. On 11 December 1813 Ferdinand signed the Treaty of Valençay: Napoleon would restore Ferdinand to his throne, provided he pardoned the supporters of Joseph Bonaparte†, concluded a favourable trade agreement, and forced the British to evacuate the Iberian Peninsula. This was a totally impracticable agreement and was at once repudiated by the Spaniards, but the French released Ferdinand nevertheless, in the hope that he would cause dissension between his subjects and their British ally. By the last week of March 1814, when Ferdinand returned to Spain, his presence was too late to influence military events.

VANDAMME, Dominique Joseph René (1770–1830)

French general: born, of Flemish origin, near Dunkirk. He fought as an infantry officer in Belgium in 1793–4 but was suspended for looting in June 1795. By 1799, however, he was a divisional commander on the Rhine, later returning to the Netherlands. He was in trouble with the First Consul in 1800 for embezzlement, talking his way out of the accusations. His career thereafter follows a strange pattern: enterprising leadership of IV Corps at Austerlitz† and service in all Napoleon's campaigns; interludes of garrison command near his birthplace; and frequent accusations of looting and bri-gandage from, among others, Ney†, Soult†, Jerome Bonaparte†, and Tsar Alexander I†. Vandamme was probably the worst disciplined of France's senior generals, restrained only by Napoleon himself and the awesome Davout†. He was defeated and captured at Kulm in August 1813 but was again a corps commander in the Waterloo campaign, distinguishing himself by courage and initiative at Ligny† and Wavre†. From 1816 to 1819 he was in the United States, spending his last years in retirement in northern France.

VAUCHAMPS, Battle of (14 February 1814)

Was fought some three miles east of Montmirail† where Napoleon had defeated Blücher† three days previously. On 14 February Marmont† tempted Blücher's Prusso-Russian army to lay itself open to surprise in a careless pursuit towards Montmirail, thus enabling Grouchy's cavalry to strike on its right wing from the north-west. When Blücher recognized the Imperial Guard uniform among the earliest attackers, he thought Napoleon himself was present with an overwhelming force. Blücher therefore retreated towards Champaubert† and would almost certainly have been captured had not the heavy mud slowed the pursuit. Vauchamps, primarily a victory of morale, increased Napoleon's reluctance to compromise on peace terms at Châtillon†.

VENDÉE

Was technically a département created in 1789–90 covering the area of Poitou south from the Bay of Bourgneuf to the mouth of the Vendée River at L'Aiguillon-sur-Mer. La Vendée was the heart of a royalist resistance movement from 1793 to 1796 which spread northwards into Brittany. After a landing of émigré troops on the Quiberon Peninsula in July 1795, order was restored ruthlessly by General Hoche (1768–97). A new wave of resistance spread through western France during the crisis months of the Directory in the summer of 1799. So embarrassed were the authorities in Paris that General Hédouville was instructed to arrange a truce with the rebels, concluded on 9 December, almost a month after Brumaire†. In his eagerness to pacify the West the First Consul gave assurances of religious liberty and the restoration of civic rights; on 28 December the *Moniteur*† published a general amnesty for all rebels who surrendered within ten days. General Brune then undertook the pacification of the Vendée, with orders to make drastic examples of any captured insurgents who had failed to submit. Seven leaders, including the Comte de Frotté, were shot at Alençon in February 1800. Thereafter the West remained quiet. The principal town in La Vendée, La Roche-sur-Yon, had been destroyed by republican troops in 1794. A week after becoming emperor, Napoleon ordered that La Roche should be rebuilt, with meticulous town-planning, and that the new town should be called Napoléon-Vendée, as a gesture of reconciliation between the dynasty and a troublesome region of France. On 8 August 1808 Napoleon made a six-hour visit to the town but was extremely displeased with the slow progress made in its construction. Napoléon-Vendée dutifully changed its name to Bourbon-Vendée at the Restoration, reverted under the Second Empire, and finally settled for La Roche again in 1871. It is, however, one of the few towns in France to retain a Place Napoléon as the centre on which five roads converge; and an equestrian statue of the Emperor has survived the political vicissitudes.

VENDÉMIAIRE 1795

An abortive rising in Paris by royalist sympathizers opposed to the new Directory† and the Constitution† of Year III. The rising took place on 5 October 1795, 13 Vendémiaire by the revolutionary calendar†. Barras†, as director responsible for the Interior, called on several generals, including Bonaparte, to safeguard Paris against the mob. Bonaparte posted guns so as to rake any demonstration marching down the Rue Saint-Honoré on the Tuileries, where the politicians were in session. Further cannon, under the command of Murat†, were on Bonaparte's orders commanding the exits from the road. Withering fire (the legendary 'whiff of grapeshot') dispersed the mob as it turned from the Rue Saint-Honoré towards the Tuileries. Other senior officers restored order next morning; thus it was the relatively unknown General Vachot who seized rebels holding out in the church of Saint-Roch. But credit for suppressing the rising was given in the *Moniteur*† to 'Citizen Buonaparte'. Some 300 people were killed or wounded. The military success made Napoleon's national reputation.

VENICE

The Venetian Republic, a prosperous mercantile community from the tenth to the seventeenth centuries, decayed rapidly in the eighteenth century. The city of Venice itself became Europe's favourite elegant playground. The Republic remained at peace until in April 1797 a French frigate illegally entered the lagoon and was fired upon and boarded. Bonaparte declared war on the Republic on 1 May and a fortnight later sent some 3,000 men to occupy the city, where they met with only token resistance. The Venetians lavished compliments on General Bonaparte, entertaining Josephine† sumptuously on what was virtually a state visit in September. Bonaparte, however, handed over the Venetian territories in

Italy and Dalmatia to Austria in the Treaty of Campo Formio† (17 October 1797), retaining the Ionian Islands† as a French possession. But Austria was forced to surrender all her Venetian gains to France by the Treaty of Pressburg† of December 1805. Venice formed part of the 'Kingdom of Italy'† from 1806 to 1814 when it became an Austrian possession, retained until 1866. Napoleon only visited the city of Venice once; he made a spectacular state entry up the Grand Canal on 29 November 1807 and stayed for nine days.

VICTOR, Claude-Victor Perrin, known as (1764–1841),
Marshal of the Empire: born at Lamarche, in the Vosges, the son of a farmer. Although he was briefly a bandsman in one of Louis XVI's artillery regiments, his military career began in earnest in 1791 and he became a major in the crisis weeks of invasion in 1792. He served at Toulon†, along the Pyrenees and in Italy. He fought at Rivoli, became a divisional commander in March 1797, distinguished himself at Marengo† and commanded the army in Holland from 1801 to 1805. Briefly he was a prisoner of the Prussians in January 1807, but later in the year he led I Corps at Friedland† so effectively that he was awarded his marshal's baton as soon as the campaign was over. From 1808 until February 1812 he was in Spain, sustaining a defeat at Talavera†. He kept the rearguard together after the crossing of the Berezina† in 1812, fought at Dresden and Leipzig, but was rebuked by Napoleon for tardiness in the 1814 campaign in France, and he remained loyal to the Bourbons in 1815. Napoleon created him Duc de Bellune in 1808; Louis XVIII made him a Peer of France and he was Minister of War in 1821.

VIENNA
A capital city since the thirteenth century, having twice withstood sieges by the Turks, and by the late eighteenth century, the recognized musical centre of Europe (see *Beethoven, Haydn*). French troops under Murat† entered Vienna on 13 November 1805. Napoleon inspected the city next day but remained at Schönbrunn†. Similarly although Vienna capitulated in 1809 after three days' resistance (10–13 May) he again preferred to remain in suburban Schönbrunn, only once riding through the old city. Upon his downfall in 1814 Vienna served for six months as the social and political centre of Europe. The heads of five reigning dynasties and of 216 princely families flocked to the city 'like peasants to a country fair', as Blücher† said, and the Vienna Congress (*see below*) became a succession of entertainments as well as the greatest international conference for many centuries.

VIENNA, Congress of
Met in the Austrian capital from the end of September 1814 until the conclusion of the 'Final Act' (generally known as the Treaty of Vienna) on 19 June 1815. The Congress settled the boundaries of Europe after the Napoleonic upheaval and also settled questions of diplomatic precedence so as to facilitate the conduct of diplomacy over the following century. The main decisions of the Congress were taken by the Allied Great Powers (Austria, Britain, Russia, Prussia) but Talleyrand†, as the representative of Louis XVIII, exploited differences between Britain and Austria, on the one hand, and Russia and Prussia on the other. There were long disputes over Saxony† and Poland†; many differences were only resolved with the news that Napoleon had landed in France after escaping from Elba. The principal territorial changes of the 'Final Act' were: recognition of a United Kingdom of the Netherlands (Holland, Belgium, Luxembourg); the establishment of a German Confederation of 39 states; the creation of a Kingdom of Lombardy-Venetia, ruled by the Emperor

281

The Congress of Vienna; a sketch by Isabey for the official canvas which he painted later in 1815, in which the composition of the group is considerably changed. Here, Wellington is seated on the far right, Metternich is standing (left), Castlereagh is sitting with his legs crossed and Hardenburg is seated on the left. Talleyrand, seated on the right with his arm resting on the table, is unrecognizable here even though Isabey was under his patronage in Vienna

of Austria; the creation of 'Congress Poland', a kingdom ruled by the Tsar of Russia; the extension of Prussian lands in Westphalia, Saxony and Pomerania†; the setting up of a free city of Cracow†; the unification of Sweden† and Norway; the retention by Britain of Malta†, Ceylon, Mauritius, the Cape of Good Hope, Tobago and St Lucia; the establishment of a British protectorate over the Ionian Islands†; and the cession to Austria of Dalmatia. The Swiss Confederation was recognized, with a special neutral status. The legitimate dynasties were restored in Spain, Sardinia†, Naples†, Tuscany† and Modena. The Congress recommended an extension of the rights accorded in Europe to the Jewish communities, condemned the slave trade†, and established the principle of free navigation on the Rhine and the Meuse. The settlement with France was embodied in the two Treaties of Paris†.

VILLENEUVE, Pierre de (1763–1806)
French admiral: born at Valensole in Provence and saw service in Louis XVI's navy from 1778 until the Revolution, mainly in the Caribbean. As a rear-admiral he commanded the outer division of the French fleet at the Battle of the Nile† and was able to escape, with four other vessels, to Malta. At Christmas 1804 he took command of the Toulon squadron, sailing for Cadiz, where he was soon

Admiral Villeneuve

joined by the Spanish fleet. Throughout April 1805 he sought to lure the Royal Navy away from the Channel and the western approaches in order to win temporary command of the narrow seas for Napoleon, thus making possible an invasion of England. This ruse failed: Villeneuve was pursued across the Atlantic and back by Nelson†, fought an indecisive action with Admiral Calder off Finisterre and then again sought shelter in Cadiz. Villeneuve, knowing that Napoleon thought him a coward and intended to supersede him, wished to give battle while sailing back, on the Emperor's orders, into the Mediterranean. He engaged the British blockading frigates off Cadiz but sought to return to port at the approach of Nelson's main fleet. Nelson intercepted him off Cape Trafalgar†. Villeneuve's flagship was captured during the ensuing battle and the admiral held prisoner for six months before being freed on parole. He returned to Brittany but committed suicide at Rennes rather than face Napoleon's anger.

VILNA (also known as Vilnius and Wilno) Now the capital of the Lithuanian Soviet Socialist Republic. Tsar Alexander† made Vilna his advanced headquarters for the two months preceding the French invasion of 1812; it was some seventy-five miles from the point at which the *Grande Armée*† crossed the Niemen† on 24 June. The Russians evacuated the city five days later and Napoleon established his headquarters there. He remained in Vilna for eighteen days hoping that his advancing troops would bring the Russians to battle or that Alexander would sue for peace. The French Foreign Minister (Maret†) and the diplomatic envoys of six governments (including the United States) came to Vilna, which became the temporary administrative capital of Napoleon's Europe; Maret stayed there for three months. A Dutch general, Dirk van Hogendorp, was given responsibility for amassing supplies in the citadel when the *Grande Armée*† began to retreat. Napoleon, however, did not stop there on his hurried journey from Smorgon†. When Murat† arrived with the main army on 8 December there was chaos and he decided he could not hold the city. Ammunition in the citadel was blown up by Éblé†. Kutuzov† recaptured Vilna on 13 December; ten days later he welcomed Tsar Alexander back there.

VIMEIRO
Portuguese village ninety-seven miles north of Lisbon by road. On 21 August 1808 Junot† attacked Anglo-Portuguese positions there, defended by Sir Arthur Wellesley (later Duke of Wellington†, but then newly promoted to lieutenant-general). Successive attacks by Junot's columns were repulsed and the French fell back with over 2,000 casualties. Wellesley's superior, General Burrard, watching the action from a warship offshore, landed in the afternoon and forbade Wellesley to pursue Junot with his unseasoned troops. The French sought an armistice; the much criticized Convention of Cintra† was concluded next day.

VINCENNES

A fortified château to the east of Paris, a royal hunting lodge converted into a prison and military command post. The Duke of Enghien† was brought there in March 1804 after being kidnapped in Baden. A court martial condemned him to death for treason and he was shot in the moat of the château.

VITEBSK

Town in Byelorussia on the River Dvina, eighty miles north-west of Smolensk†. The *Grande Armée* entered Vitebsk on 28 July 1812, Napoleon being disappointed that Barclay† had evacuated the town overnight rather than give battle. At first Napoleon planned to make Vitebsk his headquarters and not resume the Russian campaign† until the following spring. He remained, however, only until 13 August, becoming impatient at his isolation and accepting Murat's† argument that he could not halt the campaign until he had won a decisive victory. The base which he left at Vitebsk was taken from Marshal Victor† by Wittgenstein's First Corps, advancing from the north, on 7 November 1812. The loss of Vitebsk was a serious blow to Napoleon as he had planned to retreat through the town and on to Vilna; and he was forced to take the dangerous and more exposed southerly route to Borisov† and the Berezina†.

VITORIA

Spanish provincial capital, thirty-two miles south-east of Bilbao and north of the River Ebro. The Battle of Vitoria was fought on an eight-mile front west of the town on 21 June 1813. Wellington's Anglo-Portuguese army (63,000 men), supported by 7,000 Spanish regulars, engaged 50,000 French troops under Jourdan† and Joseph Bonaparte†. In a series of converging assaults Wellington† threw the French on to the congested centre of Vitoria. He then cut the historic 'Royal Road', north-eastwards to the French frontier and Bayonne, thus forcing the French to scatter eastwards. Heavy rain, and the temptation of loot, hampered pursuit of Jourdan's broken army. Wellington's victory was celebrated in the Allied capitals as marking the effective end of Napoleon's power in Spain.

VORONTSOV, Alexander Romanovich (1741–1805)

Russian Foreign Minister: born in St Petersburg into one of the greater Russian families and became Russian Minister (ambassador) in London as early as 1762. After twenty years as an important senator under Catherine the Great he retired from public life in 1791 but returned to government service ten years later with the accession of Alexander I†, as he was a natural liberal of the Enlightenment. In September 1802 he became Foreign Minister and State Chancellor, carrying out administrative reforms in the cumbersome government ministries at St Petersburg. He favoured collaboration with Britain although he was not so devotedly Anglophile as his brother, Simon Vorontsov (1744–1832), ambassador in London throughout the premiership of his friend, the younger Pitt†. Ill health forced Alexander Vorontsov to go on permanent leave in February 1804 but he trained Czartoryski† to fulfil his policies. Vorontsov's prestige and experience helped to create the Third Coalition†.

WAGRAM, Battle of (5–6 July 1809)
Fought in the Marchfeld, the low-lying countryside north-east of Vienna†, beyond the Danube. Archduke Charles† had concentrated his forces here after the fall of Vienna on 13 May and successfully repelled Napoleon's first assaults at Aspern† and Essling on 21–22 May. A six-week lull enabled Napoleon to bring up reinforcements and gave Berthier† the opportunity to plan a new crossing of the Danube in meticulous detail. A pontoon bridge, erected from Lobau Island on the night of 4–5 July, helped the French to take the Austrians by surprise and establish themselves during the day along a fifteen-mile front from the site of the previous battle at Aspern to the village of Deutsch-Wagram. On the second morning Archduke Charles, hoping for reinforcements from his brother John†, launched an unexpected attack which overwhelmed the Saxon Corps serving under Bernadotte†. Davout†, however, began a major enveloping movement from the north of the Austrian position, while Masséna† checked a sustained attack on the French centre. Macdonald† struck against Prince Liechtenstein's corps to the south of the central Austrian defences and broke through, after hard fighting. At this point (mid-afternoon) Charles began to withdraw; his brother John's army arrived from Hungary three hours too late to alter the outcome of the battle. Casualties were heavy, about 40,000 Austrians and 32,000 French, nearly a quarter of the troops engaged in the battle. The Austrians could not sustain a protracted campaign in Moravia and Hungary. An armistice was signed six days later, followed by the Peace of Schönbrunn† on 14 October. Napoleon honoured Berthier with the title Prince of Wagram, to acknowledge his brilliant staff-planning, and awarded Macdonald his marshal's baton; Bernadotte, in disgrace, never again fought for France.

WAIRY, Louis Constant (1778–1845)
Napoleon's valet, generally known as Constant; was the son of a Belgian innkeeper. He became Bonaparte's valet in 1800 and remained with him until the first abdication†, in 1814. Constant then retired to Breteuil in Picardy where he was persuaded to allow ghost writers to build up notes he had taken so that they filled up the ten volumes of *Mémoires de Constant, premier valet de chambre de l'empereur*, published in Paris in 1830. Much of what they say is clearly fabricated, but as a record of daily life ('the Emperor without his clothes') they have an air of authenticity and make vivid reading.

WALCHEREN EXPEDITION (1809)
A landing was made on the Dutch island of Walcheren, commanding the Scheldt estuary, on 11 August 1809. The expedition was commanded by the second Earl of Chatham (elder brother of the late Prime Minister, Pitt†). Some 40,000 men sailed in transports which were escorted by no less than 58 warships. Chatham lacked the experience to open up a Second Front. The port of Flushing (Vlissingen) was seized but no attempt was made to penetrate the Scheldt and take Antwerp. Hopes of a general rising against the French throughout the Netherlands and

Germany proved illusory. The British contracted a form of malaria which, literally, decimated them. After seven weeks in Flushing, Chatham's force was evacuated, having suffered the loss of 106 men killed in action and 4,000 dead from fever. Apart from pinning down French forces in garrison duty against further incursions, the Walcheren Expedition achieved nothing. Chatham was disgraced and Castlereagh† was heavily criticized at Westminster as the War Minister allegedly responsible for mounting the operation.

WALEWSKA, Marie (1786–1817)
Polish countess: born in Warsaw, Marie Laczinska, marrying at seventeen the seventy-year-old Count Walewski. On 1 January 1807, while Napoleon's coachmen were changing horses at Bronie (south of Pultusk†) she was presented to the Emperor by Duroc†, having asked to meet her country's liberator. She later captivated Napoleon at a ball in Warsaw but yielded to his advances only when urged to do so as a national duty by some leading Polish patriots. In the spring of 1807 she was with Napoleon at Finkenstein† and she visited him in Paris in 1808 and at Schönbrunn† in July and August 1809. A son, Alexandre Walewski (1810–68), was born at Walewice in Poland the following May and was acknowledged by Napoleon as his child. Mme Walewska lived in Paris, 1810–13, was accorded special privileges by Napoleon, and received with her son by Josephine at Malmaison† in November 1812. Mother and son visited Napoleon on Elba on 1–2 September 1814; she was with him at the Élysée† before Waterloo and at Malmaison on 26 June 1815. Count Walewski died in 1814 and in 1816 his widow married Napoleon's distant cousin, General d'Ornano, in exile at Liège; but her health gave way and she died, at her home in Paris, on 15 December 1817. Her son became Napoleon III's Foreign Minister from 1850 to 1855 and presided over the Congress of Paris at the end of the Crimean War; he vividly remembered saying farewell to his father at Malmaison in June 1815.

WAR OF 1812 (Anglo-American)
A separate conflict from the Napoleonic struggle. It was caused by American resentment at the impressment by the Royal Navy of US seamen, by the blockade of American ports so as to prevent trade with France, by the interception of American vessels seeking to reach harbours in Europe controlled by Napoleon and by alleged backing given by the British authorities in Canada to Indian raids on American settlements. The declaration of war was made by the US Congress on 18 June 1812 at the request of President Madison†, but with a narrow margin of votes, and surprised the British, who had not allowed for the depth of US feeling against the Orders in Council†. American attempts to penetrate into Canada at three points were repulsed in 1812 but in April 1813 an American force raided and fired Toronto. Four thousand veterans were brought over from Europe a year later, landing in Chesapeake Bay and occupying and setting fire to Washington on 24–5 August 1814; the British, however, failed to take Baltimore a fortnight later. Off Boston in June 1813 a 'duel' between USS *Chesapeake* and HMS *Shannon* resulted in the American vessel's capture. A peace treaty, signed at Ghent in Belgium on 24 December 1814, restored relations between Britain and the USA without seeking to settle the issues which had led to the war. Fifteen days after the treaty was signed General Andrew Jackson defeated a British attempt to seize New Orleans by an expedition which sailed up the Mississippi from the Gulf of Mexico. News of the signing of the peace treaty did not reach America until 11 February 1815.

WAR OF LIBERATION (*Befreiungskrieg*)
The German name for the campaign† of 1813–14, beginning with the Treaty of

Kalisch† (28 February 1813) and Frederick William III† of Prussia's Breslau proclamation *An mein Volk* (17 March 1813) summoning his subjects to rise against French tyranny.

WARFARE

Land warfare in the years of Bonaparte's primacy (1796–1815) was based on attempts to adapt the disciplined columns which had won Frederick the Great's victories to the needs of the massive formations of conscript armies. Casualties mattered less to the French when conscription† promised up to 80,000 recruits a year. Independent army corps, following separate routes to a battlefield, replaced the march of a single column. Cavalry and artillery could be concentrated in specialist formations. Massed guns were used to break through the enemy positions. These developments called for brilliant staff work and a sense of grand strategy, not merely of battle tactics. Yet until the formation of the *Grande Armée*† and the concentration of overall planning in the Emperor's *Maison*†, the shortage of veteran regimental officers and the need to rush enthusiastic volunteers into battle with little training made successive commanders of the French revolutionary armies improvise their own methods of winning victories. Bonaparte's successes in Italy led to the elaboration of a standard battle plan which envisaged: (i) initial searching out of the enemy by cavalry patrols; (ii) concentration of his main corps in a series of frontal attacks so as to engage the enemy along a specific front of Bonaparte's choosing; (iii) envelopment of the enemy's position by troops held in reserve, ideally moving behind the cover of a wood, a ridge or other geographical feature so as to bring surprise to the final assault; (iv) concentrated artillery fire to break through the weakened enemy sector; (v) pursuit by light cavalry, seeking to turn defeat into a rout. The Napoleonic enveloping movement was seen at its best at Lodi†, Ulm†, and Friedland†, and with greater strategic sophistication at Austerlitz† and Wagram†. Shortage of cavalry horses after the losses in 1812 ruined the final pursuit at Lützen† and other setpiece battles of the 1813 campaign. To some extent, Waterloo† saw the British and Prussians adapt a Napoleonic-style battle plan to defeat the Emperor: the timing and the site of the battle were chosen by Wellington; and Blücher's Prussians provided the outflanking force which, behind the cover of a wooded ridge, enveloped the main French position. In general, by the end of the Napoleonic Wars, Prussia and Austria had profited most from their experience of Napoleon's tactics and strategy. The Russians remained schooled in the Suvorov† tradition, favouring ruthless and costly frontal assaults; the British perfected a restrained defensive discipline by which the infantry, in well-chosen positions, held their fire until the enemy was near enough to be caught with concentrated volleys at close quarters (see *Campaigns; Naval Warfare; Peninsular War;* and under individual battles).

WARSAW

Was the capital of the elective kingdom of Poland† from 1550 to 1795 when it passed to Prussia. After Tilsit† in 1807 Napoleon organized the Grand Duchy of Warsaw, an embryonic Polish state which comprised all the lands taken by Prussia from Poland since 1772, together with Danzig (Gdansk). The Grand Duchy received the benefits of the Napoleonic Code, but the Polish landowners complained that membership of the Continental System† led to a fall in grain prices. Frederick Augustus† of Saxony was nominal Grand Duke of Warsaw, his territories being enlarged in 1809 by the incorporation of western Galicia† and Cracow†. Serfdom† and all other feudal obligations were abolished by a decree in December 1807. An attempt was made to give the Poles a constitution on the French model, with equal civil rights to Jews† and non-Jews, but in 1809 Jewish civil rights were suspended for ten years, with certain exceptions granted under licence by the aristocratic and clericalist Senate in Warsaw. The city was occupied by the Russians on 8 February 1813, subsequently becoming the capital of the 'Congress Kingdom' of Poland, established in 1815. The Napoleonic Codes were retained and no attempt was made to reimpose serfdom.

WATERLOO, Battle of (18 June 1815)
Waterloo was a village ten miles south of Brussels on the road to Charleroi. Wellington†, in command of an army of 68,000 men (one-third British), established his headquarters at Waterloo on 17 June, having selected the defensive ridge

of Mont-Saint-Jean, a mile south of the village, as the best means of preventing Napoleon's 72,000 men from advancing on the Belgian capital. During the course of the day Blücher†, with 72,000 Prussians, was to advance westwards so as to take the tired French troops on their right flank, from behind the cover of woods east of the hamlet of Plancenoit. The battlefield was a plateau, four miles from east to west and two and a half miles from north to south, a smaller area for manoeuvre than in any of Napoleon's major battles since Marengo†. Napoleon made the initial mistake of delaying his attack on 18 June until the sun had begun to dry out ground sodden by heavy overnight rain. The principal frontal assault on Wellington's position around the farmhouse of Hougoumont did not come until about midday; it was beaten off with heavy

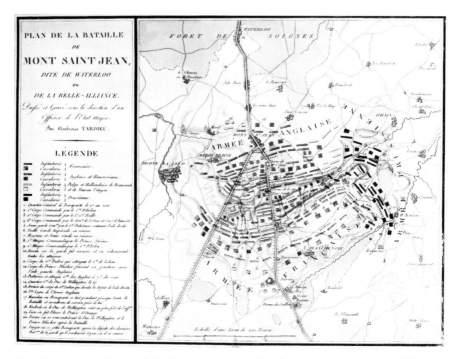

Waterloo; a map of the battlefield printed in Paris after the Bourbon Restoration. The French preferred the name 'Mont Saint Jean' to 'Waterloo'; Napoleon is called 'Bonaparte' but his brother is 'Prince Jerome'.

losses on both sides. A furious cavalry attack was made by Ney† about 3.30 in the afternoon when it became clear that the Prussians were approaching, but was met by infantry in defensive squares and by devastating artillery fire concentrated on a narrow sector. Two hours later Kellermann† had to save what was left of Ney's cavalry while the main reserves, the Imperial Guard†, were unleashed against the Prussians in Plancenoit. Shortage of ammunition led Wellington's central position at La Haye Sainte to come close to collapse when Ney committed his remaining horsemen together with guns and infantry. About 7 p.m. the Old Guard faced Wellington's British Guardsmen to the west of his central position, where the French found themselves trapped by the British and by Prussian troops advancing from Plancenoit. The union of the two

Allied armies sealed Napoleon's fate. He had lost 41,000 men; Allied casualties were about 22,000. Within four days of his defeat Napoleon had signed his second abdication†.

WAVRE, Battle of (18 June 1815)

A parallel engagement to Waterloo (*see above*), fought beside the River Dyle on the Brussels-Namur road, nine miles to the east of the main battle. To some extent Wavre was a resumption of the fighting at Ligny† two days previously, Grouchy† seeking to prevent the Prussians from joining forces with Wellington† against Napoleon. Grouchy successfully delayed the movement of Blücher's troops to the west and the French cavalry under Exelmans† constantly threatened to turn the Prussian position, but Wavre remained

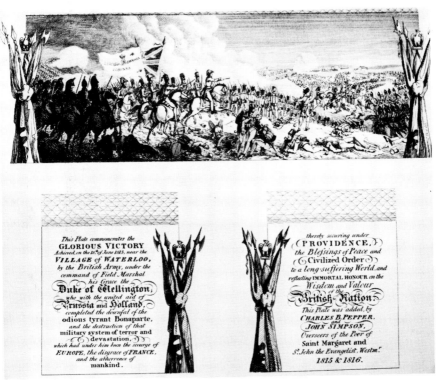

A British celebration of 'the glorious victory of Waterloo'

.tactically an indecisive engagement, both sides losing some 2,500 men. Grouchy did not succeed in detaining the Prussians long enough to allow Napoleon to dispose of Wellington's army.

WEIMAR

Town on the River Ilm, fifty-two miles south-west of Leipzig† and now in the German Democratic Republic. It was the capital of the Duchy of Saxe-Weimar-Eisenach which, from 1758 to 1828, was ruled by Duke Karl August, a great patron of literature and the arts. Weimar was the home of Goethe†, Schiller† and other writers closely associated with the cultural movement at Jena University, only twelve miles away. Napoleon first stayed at the ducal palace of Weimar on 15–16 October 1806 after his victory at Jena†. A year later Duke Karl August joined the Confederation of the Rhine†; as an ally of France he entertained Napoleon, Alexander I† and the Kings of Bavaria, Württemberg, Saxony and Westphalia at Weimar during the Congress of Erfurt†, on 6 October 1808. It was on this occasion that Napoleon talked at length to Goethe. In 1815 the Treaty of Vienna† awarded Karl August some 600 square miles of additional territory at the expense of Saxony†; and in the same year he became a Grand Duke. Weimar joined the North German Confederation in 1867 and the German Empire in 1871. The dynasty ceased to reign on 9 November 1918.

WELLINGTON, Duke of (Arthur Wellesley, 1769–1852)

British field marshal and prime minister: born in Dublin, the third surviving son of the first Lord Mornington. He was educated at Eton and, for ten months in 1786, at the French Military School of Equitation at Angers. In 1787 he was commissioned in the 73rd Foot Regiment and was a major when the war with republican France began in 1793. After serving in Flanders in 1794–5, he was sent to India† where his brother was Governor-General. Arthur Wellesley took part in the storming of Seringapatam in May 1799 and the battle of Assaye in 1803. He was knighted a year later, returned to England in 1805 and was elected Tory MP for Rye, Sussex, in the spring of 1806. From April 1807 to April 1809, while still continuing his military career, he was Chief Secretary for Ireland in Portland's government. He took part in the Copenhagen† expedition of 1807, was sent to Portugal† in July 1808, winning the Battle of Vimeiro† but later having to defend himself in England when court-martialled for concluding the armistice preceding the Convention of Cintra†. From the spring of 1809 until 1814 he commanded British forces in the Peninsular War†, becoming Marshal-General of the Portuguese Army in July 1809 and generalissimo of the armies of Spain† in September 1812. He developed a patient long-term strategy, securing his Portuguese base by the Lines of Torres Vedras† and waiting his time to gain a remarkable series of victories, of which the greatest were Salamanca† and Vitoria†. In February 1812 he was created Earl of Wellington, becoming a Marquess six months later and a Duke in May 1814, to celebrate the downfall of Napoleon. In August 1814 he took up the post of ambassador in Paris, succeeding Castlereagh† as Britain's plenipotentiary at the Vienna Congress† in February 1815. His presence in Vienna when news of Napoleon's escape from Elba reached the Congress on 7 March ensured that he was appointed to command the Allied troops which gathered in Belgium after Napoleon's return to Paris. Wellington left the Vienna Congress on 28 March and established his headquarters in Brussels only seven days later. His troops were in action at Quatre-Bras† on 16 June and he gained his greatest victory at Waterloo† two days later. From October 1815 until November 1818 he was commander-in-chief of the

Allied army of occupation in France. He entered Lord Liverpool's cabinet as Master-General of Ordnance in the closing week of 1818, and headed important diplomatic missions to the Verona Congress and to St Petersburg until he resigned from Canning's government in April 1827. He was Prime Minister from January 1828 to November 1829, finally carrying into law Catholic Emancipation†. Although unpopular in 1832 because of his hostility to parliamentary reform, he became the idol of Victorian England, the 'Iron Duke'.

WEST INDIES

At the end of the seventeenth century the British, French and Dutch challenged the original Spanish hold on the islands of the Caribbean and imposed a colonial economy based on sugar, rum, coffee and plantation slavery†. So rewarding were the profits from West Indian trade that the capture of more and more islands became a basic objective of British naval policy in the successive wars with France during the eighteenth century. Admiral Lord Rodney (1719–92) made his reputation as commander-in-chief in the Leeward Islands from 1761 to 1763 and fought a second successful naval campaign there, 1780–2. Nelson†, commanding in the Leeward Islands in 1784, created a splendid protected dockyard on Antigua as a guarantee that Rodney's gains would be maintained. On the outbreak of war with France in 1793 the West Indian political faction at Westminster encouraged Pitt to resume Britain's traditional policy in the West Indies. Jervis (see St Vincent) sailed for the Caribbean in November 1793 with 7,000 men; the expedition captured Martinique† and St Lucia, was able to hold Guadeloupe only from April to June in 1794, and established a foothold in Santo Domingo (Haiti†), where the colonial authority of France, Britain and Spain was challenged by Toussaint L'Ouverture† and his successors. When Godoy† col-

laborated with France, the British turned their attention to the remaining Spanish possessions and seized Trinidad in 1797. These military ventures in the West Indies were costly in lives; the ravages of yellow fever caused more British soldiers to perish in the West Indies between 1794 and 1797 than were lost by Wellington, in battle or from sickness, in the Peninsular War. By the Peace of Amiens† the French recovered Tobago and Martinique but Britain retained Trinidad. The British gave tacit approval to the expedition which the French sent to Haiti in 1802 in an abortive attempt to restore the old order on the island. When war was resumed in Europe, Napoleon ordered naval support for his garrison on Martinique, hoping to draw away British vessels from the western approaches and so secure momentary French naval command of the Channel. Admiral Missiessy sailed from Rochefort† for the Caribbean on 11 January 1805 and, although his squadron was absent from European waters for less than ten weeks, his raids on the sugar plantations and on the capital of Dominica caused more panic in the City of London than the threat of a cross-Channel invasion. Villeneuve† arrived at Martinique in mid-May 1805, posing a further threat in the Caribbean until he sailed again for Cadiz on 9 June, having heard that Nelson in pursuit had reached Barbados five days before. In 1809 the British determined to mop up the remaining French West Indian islands, largely because City interests complained that the lucrative Caribbean trade was suffering from attacks by privateers, harboured by the French. Martinique was taken by an expedition from Barbados, and by the end of 1810 the whole of the West Indies was controlled by the British, apart from Haiti and islands loyal to the anti-Bonapartist Regency in Spain†. After the restoration of peace in 1815 Britain retained Tobago and St Lucia as well as Trinidad; Guadeloupe and Martinique remain overseas départements of modern France.

WESTPHALIA

An improvised kingdom created by Napoleon after the treaties of Tilsit†. Westphalia comprised the area along the Rhine which had belonged to the Archbishops of Cologne from the late twelfth century until 1803 and had been known as the Duchy of Westphalia, together with Hesse-Darmstadt, Hanover†, Brunswick and Prussian lands west of the Elbe. Jerome Bonaparte† was made King of Westphalia on 8 July 1807, ruling until October 1813 when his realm disintegrated. From 1 January 1808 the Code Napoléon† became the legal system of Westphalia, local government following the French pattern of départements, with Prefects and other officials nominated in Paris. Conscription was introduced, some 600,000 men serving Napoleon during the six years of the kingdom's existence. Reforms improved educational opportunities, removed civil disabilities, clarified the rights to hold property and curbed the power of the Catholic Church. But the burden of military service, together with the extravagance of Jerome's court at Wilhelmshöhe, made the kingdom unpopular as an institution. A serious rising in 1809 was suppressed by Jerome's troops. The 1813 campaign proved that there was no sense of cohesion within so artificial a kingdom.

WEYROTHER, Franz von (1755–1806)

Austrian general: born in Vienna, saw service against the Turks (1788–90) and at Mainz (1794), but first attracted attention as an Austrian staff colonel in September 1799 when he mapped out an Alpine route for his Russian ally, Suvorov†, over the St Gotthard to Schwyz; it was found to end in a precipitous wall of mountain. As a full general in 1804 he conducted manoeuvres in Moravia, a province where he claimed to know every stream and hillock. Weyrother was chief-of-staff to Emperor Francis† in 1805 and impressed Tsar Alexander†, who ordered his commanders to accept Weyrother's battle plans even

though two senior Russian commanders – Bagration† and Miloradovich† – had no confidence in them, having suffered from the Austrian's map error six years before. On the eve of Austerlitz† Weyrother expounded his plan for three hours: it envisaged a massive enveloping movement against the French but was so rigid in detail that it could not be modified when Napoleon forestalled the Russo-Austrian allies by an assault on the weakest point in their line. 'The wretched Weyrother wandered from place to place bravely risking his life to redeem the disaster of which he was a chief cause', wrote Czartoryski†, an eye-witness of the battle. Defeat broke Weyrother's health; he died ten weeks later.

WHIGS

Traditionally the name used in English politics from the 1680s to describe the upholders of popular rights against the royal prerogative. It became associated with John Locke (1632–1704) and his theories of 'civil government' and with the 'Glorious Revolution' of 1688 which made Britain a parliamentary monarchy. Most governments between 1714 and 1783 were technically Whig, although the 'Whig connection' split into so many factions that by 1790 the term was almost meaningless. However, in the 1790s Charles James Fox† revived the Whig tradition, grafting a radical demand for parliamentary reform on to older concepts which upheld the rights of the individual against the state. The Fox-Grenville coalition of 1806–7 ('Ministry of All the Talents'†) was the only administration between 1783 and 1830 to include genuine Whigs in government office.

WILBERFORCE, William (1759–1833)

British philanthropist: born in Hull, educated at St John's College, Cambridge, and was elected MP for his birthplace in 1780; he was member for Yorkshire 1784–

1812 and for Bramber in Sussex 1812–25. Politically Wilberforce was a friend of Pitt†; in religion he was a determined Evangelical. For nineteen years he led a parliamentary campaign to abolish the slave trade†; his first Bill against the trade was introduced in 1791, but the West Indies† political lobby prevented the reform from passing through the Commons until 1804, and even then it was twice rejected by the Lords before becoming law in 1807. Wilberforce then championed the abolition of slavery† throughout the British Empire, a measure accepted in parliament only a few weeks before his death.

WILSON, Robert (1777–1849)

British soldier: born in London. As a junior officer in the Dragoons he helped save Francis II† from capture at Villers-en-Couché in April 1794. He served in Egypt in 1799 and then as a colonel at the Cape of Good Hope. Although he had a brief experience of the Peninsular War in Portugal, he became in effect an itinerant military observer on the Continent, with the Prussians and Russians in 1807, at Constantinople in 1811 and from July 1812 to September 1813 with the Russians. At Leipzig† he was attached to the Austrian staff, under Schwarzenberg†. Politically he was a Whig and maintained a lively correspondence with the Opposition in Westminster. In 1816 he helped a Napoleonic officer to escape from prison and was himself condemned to three months' imprisonment in France. On his return to England he became something of a sensationalist, an early writer on the Russian bogey. He entered the Commons in 1818, incurring the Prince Regent's displeasure for his support of Caroline† of Brunswick. His demand for an inquiry into action taken against the mob as Caroline's coffin was being conveyed to Harwich led to his dismissal from the army in 1821, but he was reinstated nine years later, ending his public career as a lieute-

nant-general and Governor of Gibraltar (1842–8). His earliest book on the *Character and Composition of the Russian Army*, published in London in 1810 and based on his observations in 1806–7, was in Napoleon's personal library and was used by his staff in planning the 1812 campaign, narrated by Wilson with some egocentricity in three later volumes.

WINDHAM, William (1750–1810)

British politician: born in London and educated at Eton. As a young man he was a literary dilettante, a friend of Dr Johnson and politically a follower of Portland†. In 1784 he entered the Commons as MP for Norwich, and was appointed Secretary at War by Pitt in 1794, holding the office until 1801. Windham was the chief champion in Pitt's cabinet of the émigrés and was opposed to any compromise peace. He regarded the Treaty of Amiens† as a disaster and thought Addington† pitiably weak, but he then turned against Pitt's conduct of the war from 1804 to 1806; when the young Prime Minister died, Windham opposed the erection of a monument to him in Westminster Abbey. Grenville† appointed Windham Secretary for War and Colonies in 1806–7. Here Windham showed administrative originality: he devised a new scheme for army recruitment, but failed to see that his proposals were carried out in detail and his sound intentions merely caused chaos. His strategic ideas were muddled: he liked profitable sideshows, especially those bringing about the capture of French colonies. Portland and Perceval† thought him too brilliantly erratic to be entrusted with office.

WITTGENSTEIN, Ludwig Adolf Peter (1769–1843)

Russian soldier: born in St Petersburg, his father having come from the Rhineland to serve in the Russian army. The son helped suppress the Poles (1794–5), fought

293

against the Turks and participated in the Austerlitz† campaign and the invasion of Finland†. From July to November 1812 he commanded I Corps, threatening the northern flank of Napoleon's army and protecting the approach to the Russian capital. Wittgenstein was successful at Polotsk† and recaptured Vitebsk† while advancing south-westwards to the Berezina†. In 1813 he collaborated with the Prussians in crossing the Elbe at Rosslau on 2 April; stiff resistance and heavy casualties forced him back over the Elbe five weeks later. After being defeated at Lützen† and Bautzen† he accepted a subordinate command in the Leipzig campaign and the advance into France. Alexander I created him field marshal in 1825; he commanded the Russian troops fighting the Turks in the Balkans in 1828 but lack of success induced him to resign because of poor health. As a soldier he was courageous and stubborn; as a commander he had no panache and no strategic originality.

William Wordsworth; a Regency silhouette

WORDSWORTH, William (1770–1850)
English poet: born at Cockermouth, Cumbria, but spent his early life at Hawkshead in the Lake District, going up to St John's College, Cambridge, in 1787. He travelled in France in 1790, lived for over a year at Blois (1791–2), but found his early enthusiasm for the Revolution give way to disillusionment. From 1795 onwards he devoted his time to poetry, at first in Dorset and Somerset and in collaboration with Coleridge†. *Lyrical Ballads* first appeared in 1798; they included *Tintern Abbey*. In 1798 he travelled in Germany, with his sister Dorothy and with Coleridge. A year later he settled in Grasmere. The second edition of *Lyrical Ballads* in 1800 contained a Preface which defined the principles of the new Romanticism†, which Coleridge and Wordsworth were introducing into English poetry. A short visit to Calais during the Peace of Amiens was followed by the most intense-

ly patriotic phase of Wordsworth's writing, with a series of sonnets fiercely hostile to Bonapartism (and published originally in the *Morning Post*). He joined the Westmoreland Volunteers in 1803, ready to defend the Lake District from a French invasion. At the same time he began a friendship with Walter Scott†, whom he twice visited in Scotland. Wordsworth's autobiographical poem, *The Prelude* was completed in the year of Trafalgar but not published until 1850. A denunciatory pamphlet in 1809, 'Concerning the Relations of Great Britain, Spain and Portugal . . . as affected by the Convention of Cintra†' was followed by a sonnet ('Britannia sickens, Cintra, at thy name'). *The Excursion*, a philosophical poem in nine books, was published in 1814, when Wordsworth was coming under greater classical influence. *Ecclesiastical Poems* followed in 1822, further poems in 1835.

From 1843 to 1850 he was Poet Laureate, but it was the first decade of the century which had seen his poetic imagination in full flood.

WREDE, Karl Philipp, Prince of
(1767–1833)
Bavarian soldier: born near Regensburg, entered the Bavarian army and was a colonel before he was twenty-eight. In 1799–1800 he prevented the disintegration of the Allied force after defeat at Hohenlinden†. As France's ally, Wrede twice led Bavarian armies against Austria, penetrating the Salzkammergut and the Tyrol, in 1805 and 1809. By 1812 he was in command of the Bavarians serving under Gouvion Saint-Cyr† at Polotsk†. In 1813 he held the line of the River Inn for Napoleon until the reversal of alliances which brought Bavaria on to the side of the Allies in the autumn. Wrede then made an unsuccessful attempt to trap Napoleon on 30 October 1813 as he pulled back towards the River Main after his defeat at Leipzig†. Wrede's troops accompanied Blücher† in the advance on Paris. He was appointed field marshal by King Maximilian Joseph† and continued as chief military adviser in Munich until 1835.

WURMSER, Dagobert Sigismund
(1724–97)
Austrian soldier: born in Strasbourg and served briefly in the French army before entering Austrian service in 1750 and fighting with distinction against Prussia in the Seven Years' War. He commanded the Austrian Army of the Upper Rhine in 1795 but is best remembered as Bonaparte's antagonist in northern Italy in 1796–7. Wurmser succeeded in relieving Mantua† early in August 1796 but was defeated at Castiglione† a few days later and then suffered disastrously at Bassa-

no†. He then fell back on Mantua, rallied the besieged garrison and defied the French until February 1797. Soon afterwards he died, a bold and inspiring commander but by 1796 too old for tactical improvisation.

WÜRTTEMBERG, Kingdom of
A mountainous region in south-west Germany with Stuttgart as its capital since 1482. In 1799 Württemberg was ruled by Duke Frederick II (sovereign 1797–1816). He took the Duchy into the War of the Second Coalition† but accepted peace after the French victory at Hohenlinden† and benefited considerably from the reorganization of Germany following the Imperial Recess† in 1803. Württemberg assisted Napoleon against Austria in 1805, received further territorial rewards and was proclaimed a kingdom on 1 January 1806. Seven months later Württemberg joined the Confederation of the Rhine†, forming part of Napoleon's European system until the Confederation broke up in 1813. Frederick, however, introduced fewer Napoleonic reforms than did Maximilian of Bavaria†; the legal system was unified, but with no adoption of the Civil Code†; Jews† were allowed to trade and to own land; there was a higher degree of religious toleration; but the sovereign retained absolute right to decide on sentences in the law courts and to control all local municipalities. His eldest daughter, Catherine, married Jerome Bonaparte† and became Queen of Westphalia. Württembergers fought under Ney† and Junot† in Russia, but Frederick maintained contact with the Tsar and throughout the summer of 1813 secretly negotiated with Metternich†. The Treaty of Fulda (2 November 1813) allied Württemberg with Austria, safeguarding the independence and status of the kingdom – which survived until the fall of the German Empire in 1918.

YORCK, Hans David Ludwig von
(1759–1830)
Prussian soldier: born in Potsdam, of English descent. He commanded an infantry brigade at Jena† and, as a major-general, led the Prussian corps which helped Macdonald† hold the northern flank of the *Grande Armée* in Russia. In the last days of the year 1812 Yorck's Prussian patriotism induced him to negotiate the Convention of Tauroggen†, by which Prussian troops withdrew from the campaign. As a full general he fought against Napoleon at Bautzen†, Leipzig† and Montmirail†. His Tauroggen initiative was, by 1814, accepted as the signal for the War of Liberation†. To the Prussians he became a national hero, created Count of Wartenburg in 1814 and promoted field marshal in 1821.

YORK, Frederick, Duke of (1763–1827)
Second son of George III: born at Buckingham House, London and in 1791 married Princess Frederica of Prussia, the half-sister of Frederick William III†. The Duke of York was appointed commander-in-chief in the Netherlands in February 1793 and, over the following two years, his campaigning won him lasting fame in a nursery rhyme, but no victories. From 1801 to 1809 the Duke was commander-in-chief of the British army, with the rank of field marshal. His administrative determination improved conditions of service for the troops, gave them pride in their uniforms and created, almost from scratch, the organization of an army for continental war. He founded the Royal Military College at Woolwich and a military academy at High Wycombe (later Sandhurst). Scandals over the purchase of commissions (through the influence of his mistress, Mary Anne Clarke) forced him to resign in February 1809 but he was reinstated as commander-in-chief in 1811 and unanimously thanked for his services by parliament in 1815.

YOUNG GUARD: *see Imperial Guard.*

ZURICH

The largest city in Switzerland, was the site of two battles in the War of the Second Coalition†. The city was defended by Masséna† against the Austrians in early June 1799, the French eventually falling back to high ground in the north-west. On 26 September Masséna emerged from the hills and launched a surprise attack on the advance guard of Suvorov's army at Zurich. The Russian commander, General Rimsky-Korsakov (1753–1840), was defeated and Suvorov† began to pull back towards Austria.

Bibliographical Note

The fullest readily available bibliography of the Napoleonic Period in English may be found in the translation of G. Lefebvre's classic *Napoleon* (two volumes, London, 1969); it includes books and articles in the major languages of western Europe but does not list works published later than 1966 and, inevitably, has omissions. To it may be added two English biographies of Napoleon (F. Markham, *Napoleon*, London, 1963; V. Cronin, *Napoleon*, London, 1971) and the refreshingly critical C. Barnett, *Bonaparte* (London, 1978). David Chandler's monumental *The Campaigns of Napoleon* (London, 1966) may be supplemented for the Peninsular War by his *Dictionary of the Napoleonic Wars* (New York and London, 1979); these two books amplify V. Esposito and J. Elting, *A Military History and Atlas of the Napoleonic Wars* (New York and London, 1964), a work warmly sympathetic to Napoleon personally. The most stimulating and comprehensive general history of Europe in this period is Franklin L. Ford, *Europe 1780–1830* (London, 1970), with useful bibliographies to each chapter. In English the best source for current work on Napoleonic France is the periodical, *French Historical Studies*, published by the University of North Carolina.

There have been many relevant biographies, in English, published over the last twenty years. Among them are:

M. Glover, *A Very Slippery Fellow . . . Robert Wilson* (London, 1977)

C. Hibbert, *George IV* (Two volumes, London, 1972 and 1975)

M. Jenkins, *Arakcheev, Grand-Vizier of the Russian Empire* (London, 1969)

E.J. Knapton, *Empress Josephine* (Cambridge, Mass., 1963; London, 1964)

E. Longford, *Wellington, The Years of the Sword* (London, 1969)

G. Martineau, *Madame Mère* (London, 1977)

Carola Oman, *Napoleon's Viceroy, Eugène de Beauharnais* (London, 1966)

J. Orieux, *Talleyrand, The Art of Survival* (London, 1974)

A. Palmer, *Metternich* (London, 1972); *Alexander I* (London, 1974)

R. Parkinson, *Moore of Corunna* (London, 1975); *The Hussar General, Blücher* (London, 1976)

M. Raeff, *Michael Speransky* (The Hague, 1961)

C. Wright, *Louise, Queen of Prussia* (London, 1970)

Other comparatively recent books include:

L. L. Bergeron, *France under Napoleon* (Princeton, N.J., 1981)

A. Brett-James, *The Hundred Days* (London, 1965); *1812, Napoleon's Defeat in Russia* (London, 1966); *1813, Europe against Napoleon* (London, 1970).

R. Carr, *Spain 1808–1939* (Oxford, 1966)

R. Cobb, *The Police and the People, French Popular Protest 1789–1820* (Oxford, 1970)

C. J. Duffy, *Borodino* (London, 1972); *Austerlitz* (London, 1977)

K.W. Epstein, *The Genesis of German Conservatism* (Princeton, N.J., 1966)

J. C. Herold, *The Age of Napoleon* (London 1964, published as *The Horizon Book of the Age of Napoleon* in New York, 1963)

E. H. Kossmann, *The Low Countries, 1780–1940* (Oxford, 1978)

E.E. Kraehe, *Metternich's German Policy, 1799–1814* (Princeton, N.J., 1963)

E. Tangye Lean, *The Napoleonists* (Oxford, 1970)

C. A. Macartney, *The Habsburg Empire 1780–1918* (London, 1968)

A. Palmer, *Napoleon in Russia* (London, 1968)

R. C. Raack, *The Fall of Stein* (Cambridge, Mass., 1965)

S. Sadie (ed.) *The New Grove Dictionary of Music and Musicians* (London, 1980)

H. Seton-Watson, *The Russian Empire 1801–1917* (Oxford, 1967)

P. Young, *Napoleon's Marshals* (London, 1974)

Important books on the Napoleonic period in all languages are listed in the occasional *Bulletins Historiques* of the *Revue Historique* (Paris), first published as a supplement to Volume 187 in 1939. From 1954 onwards the *Revue de l'Institut Napoléon* has contained lists of current work on Napoleon; the lists appeared in the *Bulletin de l'Institut Napoléon* from 1940 to 1954. The massive *Dictionnaire de Biographie Française* (edited by M. Prevost and others) began publication in Paris in 1929 and, by the summer of 1983, had reached surnames beginning 'Gir-' (Volume XVI, first section); it is an authoritative source of great value, more reliable than the *Dictionary of National Biography* (London, 1882–1909). L.P. Garros, *Quel Roman que ma Vie!* (Paris, 1947) remains the best itinerary for the whole of Napoleon's life.